THE WAY THE WORLD WORKS

REVISED AND UPDATED EDITION

JUDE WANNISKI

A TOUCHSTONE BOOK
Published by Simon and Schuster
NEW YORK

TOUCHSTONE and colophon are trademarks of Simon & Schuster, Inc.
Manufactured in the United States of America

10 9 8 7 6 5 4 3 2 1 Pbk.

Library of Congress Cataloging in Publication Data
Wanniski, Jude, date.
  The way the world works.

  (A Touchstone book)
  Bibliography: p.
  Includes index.
  1. Economics.   2 Taxation. 3 Supply-side economics.
I. Title.
HB171.W22   1983   330   83-548
ISBN 0-671-43862-X Pbk.

TO

John Rusinskas, my grandfather

and

Michael Wanniski, my father

who

planted

the

seeds

that

grew

into

this

book

CONTENTS

INTRODUCTION
TO THE REVISED AND UPDATED EDITION

In the almost five years since completion of the first edition, the ideas presented in *The Way the World Works* have taken hold with astonishing swiftness. The "Laffer Curve" and its implications have been furiously debated around the world. The Republican Party has been reborn as a party of economic growth, with Ronald Reagan winning the Presidency by a landslide on ideas best identified with this model of the political economy. The "Reagan Revolution" began with enactment in 1981 of the most daring tax reform of our time. And the concept of reconstructing an international monetary system around a modern gold standard—an idea considered not worth mentioning a few years ago—now seems almost inevitable. In 1978, the handful of people who had associated themselves with Representative Jack Kemp of New York and his political exposition of these ideas began referring to themselves as "Supply Siders," a term I coined after we were referred to scornfully as "Supply-side fiscalists" by a former economic adviser to President Nixon, Herbert Stein. Supply-side economics has been subjected to various interpretations, but the broad idea of production incentives has spread worldwide. The efficient Japanese, who have been operating in a production-oriented framework for decades, casually refer to the ideas in shorthand fashion as "S.S.E." In Peking, we get reports of an Institute for the Study of Supply-Side Economics listed in the telephone directory. "S.S.E.," after all, is nothing more than classical economics in modern garb—nothing really new, but of profound importance nevertheless. Robert Bartley, editor of *The Wall Street Journal*, simply suggested that I had "discovered a lost continent of economics." And as in the discovery of any new territory, the process of exploration and settlement is a story that is, in itself, worth telling.

It is in the nature of revolution, the overturning of an existing order, that at its inception a very small number of people are involved. The process, in fact, begins with one person and an idea, an idea that persuades a second, then a third and a fourth, and gathers force until the idea is successfully contradicted, absorbed into conventional wisdom, or actually turns the world upside down. A revolution requires not only ammunition, but also weapons and men willing to use them and willing to be slain in the battle. In an intellectual revolution, there must be ideas and advocates willing to challenge an entire profession, the establishment itself, willing to spend their reputations and careers in spreading the idea through deeds as well as words. In the preface to my first edition, I made it clear that the ideas originated with Robert Mundell, the Canadian economist, whose insights began in the 1950s, when he was in his twenties. The economic mechanisms were developed further by his American protégé, Arthur Laffer, who began communicating them to me in 1971.

The first political activist to fully grasp the importance of these ideas was Jeffrey Bell, who in 1975 was employed by the former governor of California, Ronald Reagan, as a general political factotum. In the spring of 1975, my essay "The Mundell-Laffer Hypothesis—A New View of the World Economy" appeared in Irving Kristol's quarterly, *The Public Interest*. Bell, then thirty, read it and was converted on the spot. When later that year Reagan declared his candidacy, challenging President Ford, Bell worked assiduously to integrate the ideas into the campaign. But without knowing me or Mundell or Laffer, he translated the ideas into a Reagan policy pronouncement that seemed eccentric, a proposed $90-billion reduction in federal spending and taxes. At the outset of the campaign, in New Hampshire, Reagan found himself unable to defend the hybrid proposal. He dropped it abruptly, and Bell, discredited in the process, was demoted, and Martin Anderson was installed as economist.

In the interim, though, I met Bell and introduced him to Laffer, who in turn was introduced to Reagan. Because of Bell's persistence, our ideas percolated through the campaign staff, albeit with only vague comprehension. But the foundation was laid for 1980.

Jack Kemp, like Bell, was also ripe for conversion when I met him early in 1976. Indeed, Kemp had read a 1974 article that I had written about Mundell in *The Wall Street Journal*, "It's Time to Cut Taxes," and also like Bell, on his own, translated the ideas into a cumbersome policy prescription, a "Jobs Creation Bill," largely devoted to cutting business taxes. I persuaded him to scrap his proposal and focus on an across-the-board personal-income-tax cut, a suggestion out of which emerged the Kemp-Roth bill and the centerpiece of the 1978 Congressional races and the 1980 Presidential race. During Reagan's 1976 campaign, efforts were made to have him embrace the new Kemp tax legislation, but Martin Anderson vetoed the idea on traditional "fiscal responsibility" grounds.

Bell, leaving the GOP convention in Kansas City in 1976 after Reagan's defeat, was determined to advance the ideas himself. While hounding me relentlessly to write a definitive book on the model, so that the ideas could be rapidly broadcast, he moved to New Jersey, where he had lived as a boy, and began planning a run for the United States Senate in 1978. His plan was to use the supply-side ideas as a basis for challenging Senator Clifford Case, a five-term Republican who was thought to be unbeatable by Republican or Democrat. Absolutely unknown in the state and with savings of a few thousand dollars, Bell had spent all of 1977 girding for the battle quietly by studying the state, cultivating the press corps, and learning how to shake a hand and make a speech.

At the same time, across the nation, a revolutionary figure forty years Bell's senior was loudly planning a frontal assault on the California establishment. Howard Jarvis, a salty, outspoken curmudgeon who had spent most of his life fighting the encroachment of government on private freedom, utilized the most democratic instrument available to an American (although not all Americans) to bring down tax rates. California provides for an initiative by the citizens themselves, and Citizen Jarvis collected a million signatures that forced a public question on the June 6, 1978, ballot. Proposition 13, as it was called, would slash state property taxes by half and provide constraints against raising taxes in other ways.

I looked upon Proposition 13 as a dramatic test of both the political model I present in this book and the proposition expressed in Chapter 3 that "the electorate understands economics." Only Laffer and the late Neil Jacoby of UCLA among California economists supported Jarvis with the argument that the tax cut would have positive revenue effects through economic growth. Most of the profession predicted "chaos," the word Professor Walter Heller used in radio commercials to urge a vote against Proposition 13. The array of elite opposition to 13 was almost total. Democratic Governor Jerry Brown, Democrats and Republicans of the state legislature, mayors, county executives, labor unions, the Business Roundtable, and the news media, "liberal" and "conservative," all opposed Proposition 13, many with doomsday predictions of fiscal collapse. The previous year, unaware of Jarvis and his movement, I had written, in Chapter 9, of Henry Brougham, a middle-class agitator who in 1815, against the dire predictions of fiscal experts, led a tax revolt in England. Jarvis was his reincarnation, I thought, and I told him so in late June of 1978, on his triumphant tour of Washington and New York. By a margin of 3 to 2, Californians voted with Jarvis, against the advice of the elites. In the following eighteen months, California's real economic growth led the nation, and aggregate tax revenues never missed a beat in their continued climb.

June 6, 1978, Proposition 13 day, was also the day of the Republican primary in New Jersey. At the stroke of 8 P.M., as the polls closed, Senator Case left his hotel for campaign headquarters, where he expected to make his statement of victory over young Jeff Bell as soon as the first returns rolled in. At 8:15 P.M., the Senator's car turned back to the hotel as the first returns showed Bell in the lead. At 11 P.M. it was clear that Bell had won a stunning victory, although public-opinion polls a week earlier had insisted that he would lose badly. The news media proclaimed a "tax revolt" from coast to coast, and the Republican Party planned to clean up as tax-cutters in the November elections.

As it turned out, the GOP scored only minor gains in November (although liberal Democrats in the Senate suffered their worst losses in a generation) and Jeff Bell lost the general election to Democrat Bill Bradley, a popular former basketball player and Rhodes scholar.

The elections were a setback to the supply-siders. The political establishment, Republican and Democratic, was quick to blame us for preventing greater GOP gains, which would have come about on a Republican platform of austerity and spending cuts—or so it was said. The "tax revolt" was over and done with, a flash in the pan.

The by-now growing cadre of supply-siders was frustrated but hardly discouraged. The only thing the elections proved to us was that the issue would have to be decided in a Presidential race, with a single leader carrying the revolutionary banner. In the Congressional races, only a handful of candidates looked at economic growth through tax reform and incentives, the great majority dropping the idea before the campaign began in earnest in late September. As in 1976, it was difficult to defend against Democratic charges of "economic snake oil," a phrase coined by MIT's incorrigible Keynesian, Robert Solow. The Republican National Committee spent no money at all on a national media campaign, and the Republican Congressional Campaign Committee in fact devoted its $600,000 media fund in the closing weeks to budget-balancing themes. Establishment figures, including the always hostile economists associated with the Nixon-Ford Administrations, had successfully directed the campaign away from revolutionary ideas and then blamed those very ideas for the poor showing.

In New Jersey, Bell's defeat by Bradley was taken as proof positive that the issue was dead at the hands of the voters. But Bradley had simply outmaneuvered Bell. He had won the Democratic nomination as a straightforward liberal, expecting to run against the liberal Senator Case in the fall. But in the general election, Bradley wisely adjusted, countering Bell's tax-cut proposal with his own, echoing Bell's antiregulation themes, and thumping for a stronger military. Bell's postelection polling showed 3-to-1 support for his tax position among all New Jersey voters, but this was not enough to overcome Bradley's popularity.

The conventional view of the 1978 elections was critical in setting the stage for Reagan's victory in 1980. The other leading GOP contenders misread the elections and uniformly wrote off the supply-siders. But Reagan's camp did not. John Sears, who was Reagan's campaign manager in 1976 and at the opening of the 1980 campaign, had watched the development of the tax issue in general and the Bell campaign in particular, and he came away impressed with the strength of the new ideas. He had been on friendly terms with Bell and had even come to view Bell as a protégé in the art of politics. While unschooled in economics, he accepted the political power of the ideas, not only in Bell's win over Senator Case, but in Jack Kemp's ability to run up 80- and 90-percent pluralities in his Buffalo Congressional district.

As soon as the 1978 elections were over, Bell and I began a campaign among the supply-siders and Kemp's political friends, to persuade him to seek the GOP Presidential nomination. The chief argument was that no other candidate would or could carry the supply-side banner and that in a crowded New Hampshire primary, Kemp would be the only growth candidate and the only candidate able to win over the traditional austerity Republicans, including Reagan. Bell, distrustful of the Reagan aides who had demoted him in 1976 after the "$90 billion" fiasco, argued that Reagan would not break new ground unless he were forced to do so by competition. Sears, aware of Kemp's growing interest in the race by the spring of 1979 and reckoning that he would be a genuine threat to Reagan, began meeting and telephoning Kemp regularly. He presented arguments against a Kemp candidacy and also suggested that Reagan believed in Kemp's issues and would embrace them in the campaign. We argued that Reagan would forget the ideas as soon as Kemp was in his pocket, but suddenly there was Reagan—at Sears's instigation—making speech after speech lavishing praise on Kemp and the tax-and-growth agenda, and telephoning Kemp at home and at the office, neutralizing our arguments.

The final turning point came in early summer of 1979, when Laffer gave a dinner party at his home in Southern California for the Reagans, with the Kemps, in town visiting his brother's family, also invited. Sears arranged to have Reagan invite the Kemps to a private lunch that same day, and for more than three hours Kemp quizzed Reagan on economic issues, testing the depth of his understanding and commitment. That evening, after dinner, Kemp and Reagan strolled around Laffer's cactus garden, and Kemp pledged allegiance to Reagan. On his return to Washington, Kemp informed us that he had done so, that Reagan is "eighty-five percent with us on the issues, which doesn't give me enough reason to go against him."

Our skepticism was profound, deepening in subsequent weeks as Reagan's speeches clearly moved back to his traditional themes. In early September I flew to Los Angeles and met with Martin Anderson at Reagan headquarters. Three years had made a big difference in his outlook. He not only had read *The Way the World Works* soon after publication in May 1978, but he also (I learned subsequently) had encouraged the Smith-Richardson Foundation to give me financial support during its writing. His enthusiasm seemed genuine and his young staff of assistants, Kevin Hopkins, Doug Bandow and Jim Pinkerton, turned out to be the most energetic and persistent supply-siders in the Reagan entourage. Only on the question of the gold standard was there a suggestion of troubles that would come later. Anderson agreed with us on gold, he said, but did not think it should surface in the campaign, that it was too controversial. The remark troubled me, but in all I came away less skeptical about our new supply-side leader, Ronald Reagan.

In January 1980 these doubts about Reagan's commitment were almost entirely removed. From January 3 to 5, the basic Reagan team of about twenty-five people were brought to Los Angeles for three days of discussions and briefings on issues. The event was instigated by Sears, who worried that Anderson had not been adequately preparing Reagan. I attended with Kemp and so did Laffer. In a room that resembled a classroom, with Reagan at the teacher's desk, we spent more than twenty solid hours discussing foreign and defense policy, intelligence gathering, Iran, Afghanistan, the Middle East, tax policy, supply-side economics, energy and money. The third day was given over entirely to economics, and all four presentations were given by our group. Kemp led with a discussion of tax policy in a political environment, I followed with a thumbnail lecture on supply-side economics and its history, beginning with detail in the 1920s. Laffer's briefing was on money and the imperative of a gold standard. And I came back with a supply-side presentation on energy, much of which has been incorporated into an additional energy chapter in this second edition.

The upshot was a giddy celebration that night by the supply-siders, including Dave Smick and John Mueller of Kemp's staff. Reagan was so thoroughly in tune with the day's discussion that the thought struck me with full force that he had the basic model before we arrived, indeed before any of the Kemp group was born. He had studied economics from 1928 to 1932 at Eureka College, Illinois, when classical, supply-side theory was all there was in the curriculum. We were especially thrilled to see that we would not have to break down his resistance to gold at the center of a monetary reform. He was ready to issue a statement to the press stating his support for a return to a gold-convertible dollar. Again, the fear that the gold position would embarrass Reagan gripped his California aides, and as the supply-siders departed, Milton Friedman was hastily invited to Los Angeles, where he "debriefed" the candidate. No progold statement was issued by Reagan. The news was only mildly disappointing, though, because we had seen Reagan's predilections.

Then, too, there were offsetting gains. We wanted not only domestic economic policy, but a "supply-side foreign policy" as well—United States leadership in promoting Third World economic growth through supply-side institutional reforms in the countries themselves. Reagan's longtime speechwriter Peter Hannaford had become an early convert to our ideas in 1976 and was familiar with the foreign-policy aspects. Before the Los Angeles meetings, I had talked to Hannaford about using the "experiment in Puerto Rico" (which he had read about in Chapter 12 of this book) as a showcase for a Caribbean initiative. I suggested a Reagan essay more or less along these lines for the op-ed page of *The Wall Street Journal* (which I had long since left), and Reagan approved the project, with only minor changes of my original draft. The essay, "Puerto Rico and Statehood," ran under Reagan's byline on February 11, 1980.

A third reason for the Kemp group's being thrilled with the motion and direction of the campaign was Sears's decision, that same January, to turn the media campaign over to Jeff Bell. The expensive television commercials that had been prepared for use in the primaries, Sears had decided, were conventional, stale, downbeat. In a few weeks and with a few thousand dollars, Bell and the Philadelphia producer he had used in his Senate campaign, Elliot Curson, turned out a series of Reagan "talking head" spots, with Reagan simply talking at the camera, enunciating the themes we had developed for Kemp and Bell. The most controversial of the spots, which we referred to as the "Good Shepherd" spot, was an upbeat, growth-incentive, tax-cutting spot that concluded with a line that I had written for Bell's 1978 TV spots: "If we put incentives back into society, everyone will gain. We have to move ahead. But we can't leave anyone behind." Reagan also cut a gold-standard spot, but it was withheld. The other spots were decisive in winning the nomination, however.

The campaign experience confirmed for me the validity of my political model. Reagan began the campaign well ahead of the other candidates in the public-opinion polls, although he had almost no support from the Republican elitists. Reagan came on as a Western populist, with talk of radical change, and the Eastern establishment of businessmen and bankers lined up with George Bush or John Connally. "Let George have the Fortune 500," Reagan had said casually during the January meetings. "I've got to be the candidate of the farmer, the small businessman, the independent, the entrepreneur."

The first event of the season was the GOP precinct caucuses in Iowa, on January 21. Sears, I thought, had wisely decided to keep Reagan out of the first event, which would be dominated by the party elite, country-club Republicans, while Reagan's strength was with the grass roots. Bush had been shaking hands with Iowans for a year in preparation for the caucuses, and there was little chance of Reagan's overtaking him with a last-minute effort. Nor were the new TV spots ready, and Bell had long since persuaded me that the primary source of information that the electorate gets from the candidates is on 30- and 60-second television spots in prime time. The rest is relatively trivial.

Bush was the winner in the Iowa caucuses, but because the Reagans had expected to win even without a campaign, Sears was the loser. He had made many enemies in the Reagan entourage, especially among the old hands who had been with Reagan in his years as California governor. In a series of "either-he-goes-or-I-go" showdowns over policy in late 1979, he had Lyn Nofsiger and Mike Deaver removed from the campaign, and he was posing a similar threat to Edwin Meese III, perhaps Reagan's most trusted counselor. The Iowa defeat gave the Californians the weapon they needed to defeat Sears, and they persuaded Reagan to dismiss Sears the day *after* the New Hampshire primary, on the assumption that Reagan would at best win unconvincingly in New Hampshire. After Iowa, Bush had become the betting favorite, while Reagan's chances were being quoted in London at 7 to 1.

The Bell-Curson spots began running in the second week of February, and Bush's lead in the polls began a steady decline. On February 22, in a televised debate, Reagan and Bush took opposite sides on Kemp-Roth (which Bush later called "voodoo economics"). Reagan pulled ahead of Bush in the spot polls being taken by Richard Wirthlin, Reagan's pollster. On primary day, February 26, a morning survey of voters at the polls indicated that Reagan could win by 10 percent. The Californians, realizing that it would be hard to explain the firing of Sears the next day with such a decisive victory, persuaded Reagan to fire Sears and his lieutenants Charlie Black and Jim Lake that afternoon, before the polls closed. That night, Reagan seemed stunned, almost speechless, trying to explain how he had come to defeat Bush by twenty-seven percentage points.

The firing of Sears was a disaster for the Kemp group. Effective power in the campaign concentrated among the Californians, who naturally viewed us as Sears's partisans who properly belonged outside looking in. Immediately, the Bell television spots were ordered scrapped for the coming primaries. But William P. Casey, the Wall Street lawyer appointed campaign director, fortunately was known to Bell, who persuaded him to restore them. Casey, an elderly gentleman relatively uninterested in electronic political communication, never understood how Reagan's landslide primary triumphs were built on those commercials. Where they did not run, in Pennsylvania and Michigan, voters were not alerted to the new Reagan message and balloted on their preconceptions. Bush won both states.

The Republican National Convention, held in Detroit in July, was a supply-side festival. It was the first happy and buoyant GOP convention, as opposed to "angry and anti," in memory. Instead of being against things, the GOP was now for something, and the economic agenda was the foundation of it all. Kemp chaired the foreign-policy subcommittee of the Platform Committee, Senator Roth the monetary and fiscal subcommittee, and Representative David Stockman of Michigan—Kemp's best friend in the House and an early supply-sider—chaired the energy subcommittee. At Jeff Bell's instigation, I wrote a monetary plank that put the GOP on the path to a gold standard. After Stockman adjusted the final wording, it was whisked through Senator Roth's subcommittee by a 25-to-0 vote. The Californians were informed after the vote. The plank read in full:

> Ultimately, inflation is a decline in the value of the dollar, the monetary standard, in terms of the goods it can buy. Until the decade of the 1970s, monetary policy was automatically linked to the overriding objective of maintaining a stable dollar value. The severing of the dollar's link with real commodities in the 1960s and 1970s, in order to pursue economic goals other than dollar stability, has unleashed hyper-inflationary forces at home and monetary disorder abroad, without bringing any of the desired economic benefits. One of the most urgent tasks in the period ahead will be the restoration of a dependable monetary standard—that is, an end to inflation.

Reagan's selection of Bush as his running mate was a disappointment to those of us who hoped it would be Kemp. But by this time the political apparatus had been overtaken by the forces of timidity. Richard Wirthlin, Reagan's pollster, was put in charge of strategy. At best, polls are static tools, certainly not the raw material for strategic planning. They are comfortable, though, permitting the Californians to blame Wirthlin if something went wrong, and Wirthlin in turn could blame the numbers. Wirthlin, for example, took a national poll to pick the running mate and found Bush the favorite. The result was predictable, though, if only because Bush's challenge made him known to the electorate, while Kemp's loyalty kept him submerged at the national level.

At the same time, there was bad news regarding the fall media campaign. Casey, also going the low-risk route, decided to go with a big-name political advertising firm in Los Angeles instead of small-fry Elliot Curson in Philadelphia. This was a waste of several million dollars as the new glossy spots turned out to be almost empty of relevant information. The conservative elites could watch them with satisfaction, but the grass roots were given little reason to expect the kind of change that would warrant expelling Jimmy Carter. When Carter and Vice-President Walter Mondale, at the Democratic convention in August, attacked the Reagan economic program, Wirthlin's polls, of course, showed support for the program declining and he counseled retreat. There was no public counterattack. All this added up to a steady erosion of Reagan's enormous lead of early August over Carter. On the stump, Reagan was as irrepressibly upbeat as ever, hitting the economic-growth themes at every stop. But this was reaching relatively tiny audiences. The vast national audience was seeing only the bland commercials and the network-news accounts, which focus not on the message but on the mistakes.

The gold issue was shelved again in early September, again because of arguments that it would prove embarrassing to Reagan. At Wexford, Virginia, where the Reagans were staying during the campaign, the five "key" economic advisers met to resolve differences on how the economic themes could be played out during the homestretch. Kemp, one of the five, was asked by George Shultz, on behalf of the high command, to shelve the gold issue for the duration. Shultz was the Nixon Treasury Secretary who decided in early 1973 to permanently "float" the dollar, ending its gold link; a labor economist with little knowledge of money and banking, he had been Milton Friedman's tennis partner at the University of Chicago. Another of the five was Walter Wriston, Chairman of Citibank, who joined Friedman in urging Shultz to float the dollar. Another present was Charles Walker, Undersecretary of the Treasury in 1971, when John Connally, then Treasury Secretary, closed the gold window. The fifth was Alan Greenspan, chairman of the Nixon Council of Economic Advisers in 1974.

Kemp agreed, and monetary policy was no longer an issue in the campaign. As John Sears had warned months earlier, the high command had decided to "sit on the lead" and coast to election. In the process, Reagan seemed to be transforming himself from revolutionary to a neuter who did not have a grasp of the facts on any particular issue. His slide in the polls continued, stopping just a hair above Carter, who taunted Reagan both on the economic program, still undefended, and on his refusal to debate him man to man. Again, it was pollster-strategist Wirthlin who argued that the election was won, surely on electoral votes, and that Reagan should do nothing to risk defeat. The supply-siders, knowing that the voters wanted a vigorous pledge of economic growth and tax cuts and would not get it on Reagan's paid advertising, pleaded with the high command to permit the debate. Bell personally urged the candidate and Mrs. Reagan, on one of their swings through New Jersey, to debate. When the decision to debate Carter was made, we anticipated victory, knowing that Reagan's message would reach the electorate.

Reagan's landslide victory in electoral votes and the GOP's stunning gains in Congress were cause for great celebration, of course, but it was clear that the struggle for supply-side objectives was barely beginning. Even before Election Day, our opponents inside the Republican Party were jockeying for the key economic posts that would enable them to block the revolutionary approaches that would be required. The Eastern Establishment that had fought Reagan's candidacy showed its strength in September by getting Reagan to agree to Robert McNamara's replacement as president of the World Bank several months before his term was up. The multinational commercial banks feared that Reagan would appoint someone out of their control if he had time to focus on it. They hurriedly arranged, through George Shultz and Lloyd Cutler of President Carter's staff, to present the name of A. W. Clausen, chairman of the Bank of America, to Reagan, on the artificial pretext that unless he was appointed immediately, the Europeans would somehow fill the chair. Reagan, on the campaign trail, fell for the argument and agreed.

At the same time, the entourage that had done so much to undermine the Reagan campaign by trying to replay the Old Guard themes of the Nixon-Ford years was congratulating itself on victory and awarding each other the spoils. Shultz would be Secretary of State, William Simon would get the Pentagon, Walter Wriston would be Treasury Secretary, and so forth. The Reagan Administration would go backward with these "retreads," as they came to be called, and bitter behind-the-scenes campaigns were waged to keep them out.

Our aim was to get supply-side partisans into several key posts, particularly at Treasury, either the top job itself or the two second positions, Undersecretary for Monetary Affairs and Undersecretary for Tax Policy. Lewis Lehrman of New York, an enormously successful young businessman and intellectual and an ardent advocate of a modern international gold standard, was our candidate for Treasury or the Treasury monetary post. Here, we were the losers in a long bitter struggle with the Old Guard and the influence of Milton Friedman. Lehrman was blocked for every position because of his advocacy of gold, with Martin Anderson, Simon and Greenspan helping to undermine the appointment.

When the smoke cleared, we had won very little. Norman Ture and Paul Craig Roberts got the top Treasury jobs in tax policy, and while

Roberts particularly would prove decisive in winning the 1981 battles over tax legislation, neither he nor Ture had much interest in monetary policy. "Supply-side fiscalists," we called them. The same was true of David Stockman, the young Michigan Congressman who was the only supply-sider named to the Cabinet. Although Stockman was involved in writing the "monetary standard" plank in the GOP platform, he had not schooled himself in the arguments. As director of the Office of Management and Budget, a purely fiscal bureau, he was rapidly drawn by Alan Greenspan to the Old Guard's fiscal theory of inflation—namely, that high interest rates and inflation are caused by budget deficits. Even before he was sworn in, Stockman had been driven by this idea away from the supply-side agenda. When the President-elect came to Washington in January, he learned that Stockman proposed to give budget-cutting priority on the legislative schedule and put the tax legislation second. The upshot was that Stockman also proposed deferring the effective date of the first 10-percent cut to July 1, which would mean a 5-percent cut for the calendar year. Later in the year Stockman urged a second delay to October 1, with a reduction of only 5 percent, which meant that the first-year tax cut would amount to only 1¼ percent on personal-income-tax liabilities, across the board.

We warned Stockman and his assistant Lawrence Kudlow that their efforts would prove to be futile. Interest rates would not come down without recession, unless there was a monetary reform, that it was not a fiscal problem, and deferring the tax cuts would only invite recession and expand the deficits. Stockman, determined to do it his way, became a major liability to the supply side and finally revealed himself as an opponent, unsuccessfully trying to persuade the President to raise taxes.

As poorly as we had done in the Cabinet-selection process, there were some other appointments we took as hopeful signs. Donald Regan, chairman of the leading Wall Street brokerage firm of Merrill Lynch, was named Treasury Secretary. This was encouraging if only because Regan was not a banker, or directly controlled by the bankers, who could always be counted on to resist major change. We had urged the appointment of Donald Rumsfeld, who had been President Ford's chief of staff and Defense Secretary, to the State Department—to insure a "supply-side foreign policy." But Reagan appointed Alexander Haig, and we were pleased at least because the four-star general had no entrenched views on foreign-economic policy. We couldn't land even one of the three spots on the President's Council of Economic Advisers, but took solace in that Murray Weidenbaum, appointed chairman, was professionally neutral on the monetary issues. The most interesting and promising Reagan appointment, though, was James Baker III as chief of staff instead of Edwin Meese III. Baker had been Vice-President George Bush's campaign manager. But the importance of the move was that Baker by temperament is a "doer," while Meese is a procrastinator, always worried that something might go wrong. The supply-side idea would surely have wilted in Meese's hands as it had done during the campaign. Instead, Meese was given an assignment appropriate to his attributes, Counselor to the President, where he could caution without killing. It was Jeff Bell who pointed out the great significance of Reagan's Baker appointment to the supply-side revolution. Months later, it was Baker who took charge at the White House of shepherding the tax legislation through Congress.

When the Economic Recovery Act of 1981 was signed into law by President Reagan in August, newspaper reporters asked us frequently if we were surprised at how quickly the supply-side idea had borne fruit. I could only think to myself that where the reporters saw whirlwind success from the first time they encountered the idea, a year or two previously, it had been more than ten years since I had met Laffer, and twelve years since Mundell had forecast the breakdown of the international monetary system and the turmoil of the following decade. It takes a great deal of time and effort for one idea to replace another, and clear victories are always elusive. Within days after the tax bill was signed by Reagan, for example, there were columnists, commentators and politicians of both parties issuing pronouncements that the "supply-side idea had failed" because interest rates had not come down and the stock market had. And Stockman's people at the budget office were immediately grinding out memorandums on the need to raise taxes quickly— "revenue enhancement" as they put it. In January 1982, there was a day or two when Jack Kemp was the only official of the government, executive or legislative branches, who was clearly identified in opposition to the planned excise-tax increases that Stockman had plugged into the new budget. Even the President had momentarily caved in, agreeing to the increases, when a delegation from the U.S. Chamber of Commerce—including their supply-side chief economist Richard Rahn— tipped him back emphatically to Kemp's side. Ironically, in the final stages of the debate, Jim Baker sided with Stockman and Ed Meese supported the supply-siders.

Baker, Stockman and the "Old Time Religionists"—as we came to call them—finally, in the summer of 1982, persuaded the President that the steep recession into which the United States had fallen was caused by the federal budget deficits. Art Laffer and I had warned Dave Stockman in January 1980 that without monetary reform he would find the economy stagnating and would risk massive budget deficits. But having helped to bring on the recession by supporting a deflationary monetary policy and deferral of tax cuts in 1981, Stockman could now only insist that interest rates were kept high by the deficits, and if spending cuts and tax increases were employed, the lessening of federal borrowing needs would "crowd out" fewer private borrowers and interest rates would fall. Herbert Stein, Alan Greenspan, George Shultz, William Simon and other "Old Time Religionists" backed Stockman in his Hooveresque argument. Senate Finance Chairman Bob Dole and Senate Budget Director Pete Domenici embraced these arguments on Capitol Hill. The pressure became too much for Reagan to withstand. Even as the United States was sliding into the deepest recession in half a century, Reagan helped push through Congress a $98-billion tax increase that cut against all the theoretical arguments of 1981. "Supply-side economics" was at a nadir, somehow blamed for the economic mess.

But, as it turned out, monetary reform and prosperity were just around the corner. On October 6, 1979, Federal Reserve Board Chairman Paul Volcker had embarked on his monetarist experiment, strictly fixing the quantity of money within specified ranges and letting the price of money fluctuate. Three years later, to the day, Volcker and the Fed announced abandonment of the experiment, and the financial markets soared in celebration. The experiment had been characterized by the wildest swings in the price of gold in United States history, in reaction to the Fed's attempts to fine-tune the quantity of money without regard for the fluctuating demand for money. Gold went from $350 to $850 to $500 to $675 during the summer of 1980, to $625 at Reagan's election, to $312 in mid-March of 1982 and between $300 and $500 in the months that followed. The Reagan Administration's first two years had been dominated by the monetary deflation that saw gold's slide from $625 to $300, the steepest since the post-Civil War period when the United States was in its earlier experiment with "greenbacks."

The experience Volcker had in observing the destructiveness that can be caused by controlling the supply of money instead of its value finally caused him to draw away from the experiment in June 1982. The monetary deflation, causing collapse in the dollar price of gold and other commodities, had snowballed the bankruptcy rates at home and abroad, and throughout the world fears spread of an international banking collapse and another Great Depression. The movement now at the threshold of 1983 is toward a money that will hold its value in terms of real goods combining with the tax reforms still in place to produce the dramatic economic growth I anticipated when this book was first written. On December 6, 1982, Treasury Secretary Donald Regan even issued a call for a new Bretton Woods international monetary conference to restore economic stability. But it was Paul Volcker's scrapping of monetarism that was critical and pivotal.

At such times, when it appeared that the fate of the supply-side revolution hung on a single decision by one man, it seemed fragile indeed. "Is this the end of supply-side economics?" reporters did ask in those few moments when President Reagan appeared to be calling it quits. The question would be asked mockingly, by those who had years ago underestimated the political power of our ideas, without ever understanding the ideas themselves; I learned that there are countless such people who become barriers to change in order to avoid admitting an initial error in judgment. But there also were those who would ask the question poignantly, people who had an equal ignorance of the ideas, but who rooted for us because we seemed to be expressing the politics of hope when all others were practicing despair.

Of course, the "supply-side model" is here to stay, as it always has been, along with "demand-side" economics. At bottom, there are only these two kinds of economics, focused on one side or the other of the law of supply and demand. I made the distinction clearly, I thought, in the first edition of this book. For this edition, I have added a further clarifying section to Chapter 6. The supply-side revolution will be complete when it cannot occur to a reporter to ask, "Is this the end of supply-side economics?" The ideas can fall into eclipse, as they did for half a century. But they are now as inevitable as rain after a long drought. Had Ronald Reagan abandoned policies dictated by the supply-side model's evaluation of the economics problem, it would only mean that we would have to return to the people for renewal. In the fall of 1981, I ran into Peter Hannaford in Washington and asked Reagan's former speechwriter and confidante, "Pete, are we going to have to go through another Presidential election to get a gold standard?" Hannaford, who expressed the hope that we would not have to, knew the full thrust of my meaning. The world is divided not into Communists and Capitalists, or Republicans and Democrats, or liberals and conservatives. It is divided into Populists and Elites, the ruled and the rulers. Hannaford, like Ronald Reagan, is a Populist, who believes in the overarching wisdom of the electorate and is willing, even eager, to reform our institutions in ways that would give greater expression to that wisdom. Californians, more than most, appreciate the particular fineness of democracy, owing to their initiative system that can bring a Howard Jarvis to political power. Hannaford and I have both been part of a separate movement to bring about a federal initiative that could put crucial questions on the national ballot as is done in Switzerland. If such a system were in place now, we would quickly have a gold standard. As any opinion poll will indicate, the grass-roots support for sound money is formidable, as formidable as the electorate's support for nonconfiscatory taxation.

The economic validity of the supply-side model is overwhelmingly documented in the historical record, and as Mao Tse-tung put it, "The masses are the creators of history." The people know, en masse, as Ronald Reagan does individually, that "No great nation has ever left the gold standard and remained a great nation." He also knows, as the masses know, that oppressive taxation yields little revenue. The elites care nothing for historical records as evidence of rightness or wrongness. Even less do they care about reason and logic. They have their own axes to grind, even if the general welfare must be submerged to their own personal calculations. We should not expect different behavior. David Stockman, for example, can be a supply-side "revolutionary" to the moment when he puts on his budget-director's hat. But thereafter, dominated by his job description and assigned goal of "balancing the budget," he has no time for talk of tax or monetary reform. In fact, he sees that his neck is on the line, and if his old supply-side allies are wrong, he will be blamed. The appeal of convention is powerful: If you are wrong, you are at least in the company of people who are in a position to find suitable scapegoats.

If we can in this fashion rationalize Stockman's behavior, how can we expect greater fidelity to our ideas from the business and financial community, from opinion leaders, or across the breadth of government? Stockman was part of the small band of revolutionaries, and he went over. Why should we expect to succeed in converting those of lesser faith when all they see is that we propose to *displace the idea they have been a part of*?

The answer is that elites are not converted by faith or logic or evidence, but by political power, the power to change the tide of fortunes and careers. The human species, after all, has learned over the millennia that losing an economic argument doesn't seem to matter very much, but that it is not healthy to be on the wrong side of a political struggle. We really got nowhere in the early 1970s with our supply-side evidence and arguments and Laffer Curves, until we captivated two men: Jack Kemp, who was willing to stake his political career on the unconventional; and Jeff Bell, who was willing to demonstrate the power of the idea in a go-for-broke run for the Senate.

The electorate is the source of strength for a revolutionary idea, because the people, en masse, will support an idea that makes sense, although, unconventional, while the elites will support it only when they see they have no choice.

In the spring of 1980, at dinner one evening with William F. Buckley, Jr., he took issue with my political model as outlined in Chapter 1, in which I argue that the electorate is wiser than its components, and that elections always are won by the right candidate, given the information available to the voters. So that he would have a clearer understanding of my meaning, I asked him to imagine that we could take his brain out for examination, and have his brain cells laid end to end so that it would stretch for miles. If we examined each of his brain cells, we would discover that each one of them was "dumb." But that when arranged in one integrated circuit, the brain itself is brilliant. In the same way, I suggested that if he left the restaurant and on the sidewalk outside questioned pedestrians for several weeks, he would find each inferior to himself in their powers of reason, logic and knowledge, but if they were all brought together in Yankee Stadium and linked together somehow to confer and express their wisdom collectively, Buckley could not hope to defeat them on any test. And wasn't it Buckley, I asked him, who several years ago said he would rather be ruled by the first fifty people in the Boston telephone directory than by the entire faculty at Harvard?

By the same token, I had been criticized, even by close friends, for having written in Chapter 4 about the Soviet Union, "it is by no means clear that its political economy is inferior to that of the United States." It is, of course, clear to me that the Soviet political economy is inferior, but as one individual, I may be wrong. History may still yield a Soviet Empire amid a twenty-first-century decline of the West, but I don't think so. The electorate decides such things, and in my model the electorate will always tend toward systems that are superior in gathering and expressing the wisdom of the masses, the human integrated circuit in Buckley's Yankee Stadium.

Still, I have sympathy for the Russians in any case, in somewhat the way in which I can sympathize with my "demand-side" adversaries in the United States: I'm confident that they know they are losing and are genuinely afraid of that prospect. In December 1981, martial law was declared in Poland to contain the civil unrest that had grown out of the collapse of the Polish economy, which in turn reflected the recessions in the West into which the Polish economy had become integrated. Many of my friends, who view the Russian leaders as "evil" people, urged economic warfare on Poland as a way of getting at the Soviet Union. They argued that the crisis in Poland was an opportunity for us to deal a blow to the Socialist system. I argued that we were already doing so, unwittingly, but that weakening our adversaries by causing a crisis in our own economy was not my idea of a competition that would produce a superior political economy. I expressed sympathy for all the actors in the Polish crisis, on our side and theirs, "including the Russians," on the grounds that nobody knew what he was doing. When one friend protested my sympathy for the Russians, I had to explain again that I view them as adversaries, doomed to defeat because they are contesting with a superior system. I wrote the friend: "What worries me in the current period is that our political leadership is trying to demonstrate that our system is inferior, by causing an economic crisis among our own people and in the world at large." This had happened before and it only encourages xenophobia in the East. I explained that my grandfather sympathized with the Russians all his adult life, and through him I came to see how they view the world in a kind of desperate way.

"From their vantage point," I wrote my friend, "they have lost tens of millions of Russians in two wars in this century because of the greed and power and stupidity of the capitalists in London, Wall Street, Paris, Berlin, et cetera, with their constant tariff wars and their monetary manipulations and their power plays that always went to benefit some elite. When I put myself in their shoes, I see their vision with horror and realize it is as correct as the view I have of them when I step back into my shoes, and see the Gulag, the secret police, the SS-18s, terrorism, all designed to keep *their elites* in power."

In the epilogue to the first edition, I expressed great optimism about the future of the world political systems, an optimism based largely on my sense that the world was rediscovering a lost continent of economics and it was only a matter of time before the exploration process was complete. I observed about as early as anyone that China in 1977 was rapidly moving toward classical economic forms, upon the death of Mao, and that China's electorate itself could transform the political economy into one resembling that of Taiwan, rather than the other way around.

Now, five years later, Mikhail Suslov, Mao's counterpart in the Soviet Union, has died. For forty years the party's theoretician, Suslov was the last true believer in the Communist idea that a political economy could be designed to produce equality of result. He had vetoed almost all attempts to invigorate the Soviet economy through incentive systems, and stagnation and malaise have compounded. With Suslov gone, it becomes possible to contemplate a general global economic advance that includes a Soviet Union willing to experiment with economic and political freedoms. Leonid Brezhnev, who was a Suslov protégé, in death recently gave way to a potential Soviet-style "supply-sider," Yuri Andropov, who is not an ideologue. There are no more *Communists* anymore, only military regimes of different colorations, protecting one intellectually hapless elite or another.

The tide, then, is with us as we publish this second edition of *The Way the World Works*. The ideas have dug in and even helped to elect a President. So, while I've added a section on gold and a new chapter on energy, there has been no revision of the model. Nor has there been an abridgment of its optimism.

Morristown, N.J.
December 1982

PREFACE

There is no way of knowing how the world works, beyond a rough approximation; absolute knowledge of the mechanisms of civilization will always escape the mind of man. But individuals have been groping forever toward such an understanding—why economies fail and why they succeed, why empires and golden ages appear and recede, why war interrupts peace. If you could know how something works, there would be at least a chance of repairing it when it malfunctions. The history of the world, down to the present day, testifies to the crudity of our knowledge of the world mechanism. Malfunctions occur, and more often than not the modern political leader is baffled as his attempts at repair result in even worse disorders. This book sets forth a new view of the global political economy, a view that provides, I think, a more satisfactory explanation of the disorders of the past and present. I offer it in the belief that the world's political leaders will find it of compelling usefulness in diagnosing and treating the maladies of the global polity.

In 1972 the world economy was already sliding toward the worst depression in forty years and the worst inflation of the century. Yet on the very eve of collapse there seemed to be a general euphoria among economists and political leaders, if not the people in general, that the tremors of 1971 had passed. The monetary crises of 1971, viewed in world capitals as an international "attack on the U.S. dollar," seemed to have subsided with President Nixon's shock treatment of August 15, 1971. He had frozen wages and prices in the United States to arrest the nagging inflation. He had announced a series of steps to stimulate the economy and reduce the growing unemployment. And he had ordered a 10 percent surtax on all imports as a means of forcing U.S. trading partners to negotiate new monetary arrangements and halt the attacks on the dollar. It all seemed to work. At the end of the year the wisest finance ministers of the Western world had signed the Smithsonian Agreement in Washington, establishing new currency exchange rates as Nixon lifted the surtax. Nixon had proclaimed this the most important monetary agreement in history. In the same period U.S. relations with China had been opened and an arms-limiting agreement with the Soviet Union signed. The foundations had been laid for global peace and prosperity for at least the rest of the decade and perhaps the century, or so it was said. The world's economists, almost without exception, failed to anticipate the convulsions brewing just beyond the horizon. As 1973 opened, commodity prices soared around the world, a general worldwide inflation ensued as people fled paper currencies for gold and other commodities, and before spring began the Smithsonian Agreement collapsed altogether.

When the convulsions came, it struck me that if an economist could not foresee that a major economic event would follow a specific set of economic policies, he couldn't be much use to a policymaker. His view of the world must be seriously flawed if he consistently recommended that if X were done, Y would follow, yet when X was done, Z followed. It also seemed that such an economist would have a difficult time explaining why things went wrong. If he had not changed his basic theory, his hindsight would surely be as flawed as his foresight.

There were, though, two international economists known to me during this period who anticipated the economic events with such clarity that I was drawn into learning their theories. They are young now, and were younger still when they first began warning that if policymakers did X, Z would follow. Arthur B. Laffer, thirty-six, is a professor of business and finance at the University of Southern California; Robert A. Mundell, forty-five, is a Canadian who teaches international economics at Columbia University. In the weeks after the Smithsonian Agreement was signed, Mundell forecast its doom and predicted a dramatic increase in the price of oil and thence all other commodities. They both foretold the rapid price inflation of 1973 and the climb in the price of gold to $200 an ounce. They also warned in early 1974 of the recession that began late that year and deepened in 1975.

They do not claim originality. Their modern ideas largely reflect theories of the nineteenth-century French classical economists Jean-Baptiste Say and Leon Walras. Roughly speaking, Laffer is a modern Say, arguing that the supply of goods creates a demand for goods and that the supply of goods can be increased by removing government impediments to production and commerce. The idea seems novel only when set against the alternative idea that has dominated Western economic thought for forty years, the notion that the demand for goods creates its own supply and that the demand for goods can be increased by increasing the purchasing power of individuals through deficit finance or money creation.

Mundell, roughly speaking, is the modern Walras, a general equilibrium economist in a world dominated by partial equilibrium economists. In a "general equilibrium," X not only causes Y, but Y has an impact on the rest of the world that ripples back on the country of origin causing a near-final result of Z. It is this deeper appreciation of the interconnection of the world economy that put Mundell and Laffer in a position to apply these old ideas to present events. They saw the breaking down of the international monetary system having detrimental secondary effects far in excess of the primary beneficial effects alleged by the Nixon economists: for the first time in the history of civilization, a global inflation would be experienced during an era of almost universal progressivity in national tax structures. Economic contraction would occur in accordance with Say's proposition because rates of taxation would automatically increase in the inflation, increasing government impediments to production and commerce. A detailed exposition of these ideas and events will be found in chapter 10.

But this book ranges well beyond economic insights into the recent past. The full force of the ideas of Mundell and Laffer struck me in May, 1974, when I first met Mundell at a Washington, D.C. conference on global inflation. It occurred to me that their framework might offer useful hindsights to earlier periods of history. I began laying down their economic model against the boom of the 1920s and the Great Depression of the 1930s, two economic periods that had always puzzled me, and I discovered more satisfying explanations of the flow of history than those I had been taught in school or read about before. I discovered a rationale for the cause of the boom and for the Crash of 1929 far more compelling than any in the current literature. A new perspective on all of economic history emerged in this process, and I chased backward further and further into history to find a timeless coherence to this global mechanism. At the same time, ideas that I had been taught about the political flow of civilization—concepts that had never fit together snugly in my mind—now meshed easily as a result of this fresh, oblique view of economic man. History was not an unbroken advance of ideas in accordance with a Hegelian or Marxian dialectic, but rather a trial and error search by mankind for systems superior in the production of political leadership. The limiting factor, I sensed, had never been the ignorance of the masses—the electorate— but the inability of individual political leaders to draw upon the wisdom of the masses. From this vantage point, religion became not the opiate of the masses, but a force elaborated by the electorate to nurture and humanize individual political leadership. From this different angle there came a parade of historic figures—Alexander, the Caesars, Napoleon, Jackson, Peel, Bismarck, Mussolini, Coolidge, Hoover, Roosevelt, Hitler, Stalin, Mao, Kennedy, and more.

I came to see these political figures pushing against what I have come to call the Laffer Curve, an exceedingly simple but powerful analytical tool for almost any form of human social or political interaction. From the dawn of civilization, the tension in any political economic unit and in the global economy as a whole lies between income growth and income distribution. The Laffer Curve merely posits that in any political economy, there are always two tax rates that will produce the same revenues. Political leaders must forever strive to find that rate which maximizes income growth while permitting a distribution of income consistent with welfare. When political leadership has had this insight, empires and golden ages have been built on one end of the Curve; when political leadership fails, it crushes empires and produces the friction of war against the other end of the Curve.

The result, then, is this general theory, which is also very much a personal perspective on the way the world works; the way it works now and has always worked. The plan of the book is first to present a basic political model—why people behave the way they do in political settings, and why this behavior is the same between individuals or aggregates of individuals. In chapter 2, I apply this simple model up through history. The aggregate of all individuals is shown always to aim rationally at ultimate concord and unity—implying world government, but discord has at the same time been the driving force. Chapter 3 outlines the importance of economics to this political drive of mankind. As astonishing as it may seem, I argue and demonstrate that individuals learn the most important basic economic concepts from infancy through early childhood. Chapters 4 and 5 lay out the basic economic model of the general theory: why individuals or nations work, produce, and transact with each other, and why they do not. Chapter 6 introduces the Laffer Curve. The remaining six chapters then examine historical examples in empirical support of my general theory.

Much, but not all, of this theory of the way the world works is shared by Mundell and Laffer. But because it is colored by my personal experiences, it reflects my eccentricities, and I offer it here in that spirit. It is meant as a framework for thinking about the world, not as a picture of the world in hard and fast colors and images. Should the reader find it useful as such a framework, I would expect there to be lines and images reflecting the reader's own eccentricities and experiences. What cannot be abridged, though, is the soaring faith in mankind that this framework evokes, the idea that from the beginning of civilization the community of man has moved rationally, purposefully toward a unity, and that it can be delayed but not deterred.

Following on this assumption, the epilogue to the book projects a flow of history into the future that is essentially optimistic.

It was in February, 1972 that I came to *the Wall Street Journal's* editorial page, as oblivious as almost everyone else in the world to the economic events that loomed over the horizon. It was the only place in the world, I now believe with hindsight, that could have been the intellectual "hothouse" for the theory of this book.

Vantage point is crucial when you sit in an ivory tower, a passive observer watching active man struggle with an epidemic, using trial and error to experiment with advertised remedies. The vantage point had to be in the United States, the key currency country in the international monetary system; the rest of the Western world was (and is) in this sense suburban. And the vantage point had to be in New York City, the financial center of a financial storm. The view from Washington, too, is parochial, conducive only to hysteria in a crisis; the political capital imports ideas created elsewhere.

The vantage point had to be at a newspaper, one without a political commitment to economic dogma, and the one with an international, not regional, bias. It could only be *the Wall Street Journal* and it could only be the editorial page of the *Journal*, an enclave of generalists surrounded by the finest specialists in economic and financial writing that the journalistic profession can assemble. Fortunately, I came to the editorial page in 1972 ignorant of all economic dogma, with none to defend. At the right time, my comparative advantage was that I was in the right place, with probably the best seat in the house for making critical observations. It was in this sense, when I completed this book in September, 1977, that I had the awkward feeling I had not written it at all. It had arranged to write itself.

My special thanks to the following, who helped arrange the writing of this book, knowingly and unknowingly, in order of participation: William Russin, Henry L. Wood, Martin Wolfson, Sidney Gold, Robert Ernst Cosgrove, Peter Wallinsky, Robert Rutland, Michael Creedman, Robert L. Brown, Harry W. Polk, William Giles, Lionel Linder, Arthur B. Laffer, Robert A. Bartley, Robert Mundell, Irving Kristol, R. David Ranson, Alan Reynolds, Wendell W. Gunn, Jeffrey Bell, Warren Phillips, Randy Richardson, Marianne Burge, Jack F. Kemp, William J. Baroody, Sr., Midge Decter, . . . and Christine, my wife, and my children, Matthew, Jennifer, and Andrew.

ACKNOWLEDGMENTS

Permission to reprint material from the following sources is gratefully acknowledged:

Victor S. Clark and associates, *Porto Rico and Its Problems*, copyright © 1930 by the Brookings Institution; Hugh Patrick and Henry Rosovsky, eds., *Asia's New Giant: How the Japanese Economy Works*, copyright © 1976 by the Brookings Institution; Joseph A. Pechman, *Federal Tax Policy*, copyright © 1977 by the Brookings Institution. Reprinted by permission of the Brookings Institution.

John Maynard Keynes, *The General Theory of Employment, Interest, and Money*. Reprinted by permission of Harcourt Brace Jovanovich, Inc.

Material from the following issues of *The New York Times*: 24 March 1929, 26 March 1929, 5 January 1962. Copyright © 1929/62 by The New York Times Company. Reprinted by permission.

Material from the following volumes of *The Story of Civilization: Our Oriental Heritage*, copyright © 1935, 1963 by Will Durant; *The Life of Greece*, copyright © 1939, 1966 by Will Durant; *Caesar and Christ*, copyright © 1944, 1971 by Will Durant; *The Age of Napoleon*, copyright © 1975 by Ariel Durant and Will Durant. Reprinted by permission of Simon & Schuster, a Division of Gulf & Western Corporation.

K. B. Smellie, *Great Britain Since 1688*. Reprinted by permission of University of Michigan Press.

Material from the following issues of *The Wall Street Journal*: 8 January 1975, 24 January 1975, 5 February 1976, 10 May 1976, 24 August 1977, 1 September 1977. Reprinted by permission of *The Wall Street Journal*. Copyright © 1975, 1976, 1977 by Dow Jones & Company, Inc. All rights reserved.

The Way the World Works

CHAPTER 1

The Political Model

The political model holds that the electorate is wiser than any of its component parts. Civilization progresses in a political dimension through the ability of politicians to read the desires of the electorate. Neither the press corps nor other "opinion leaders" influence the electorate, except in the sense of broadcasting the political menu. Their influence instead bears on the politicians, who look to opinion leaders for help in ascertaining the wishes of the electorate. The decline of a nation state or political unit is a sign of repeated failure of the political class to read the wishes of the electorate. Emigration is a sure sign of relative political failure. At the extreme, the electorate resorts to revolution, thereby adjusting the political framework and raising to power a new political class better able to read the desires of the electorate. Modern nation states have built into their political frameworks various safety valves that can bring about urgent corrections in the avoidance of violent revolution or war.

It is probably safe to say that most voters believe they are smarter than the average voter. Certainly most politicians, most educators, most academics, most artists, most journalists, most businessmen, most labor leaders, etc., believe they are smarter than the average American voter. Liberals believe the country would be better served if there were fewer conservatives, and vice versa. Republicans often argue that the republic will not survive as long as voters remain short-sighted and self-indulgent instead of being fiscally responsible.

Liberal Democrats assert with equal vehemence that the nation is burdened with racists, jingoists, and economic reactionaries. Dixiecrats declaim against Northern elitists who think they are superior because they can do the *Times* crossword puzzle, but who can't park a bicycle straight, always want to cut the defense budget and cozy up to the Russians, and who are ever ready to bus other people's children and spend other people's money.

Put another way, there are few Americans who believe they are less competent in making political choices than Americans in general. Those who make such an admission to themselves will, in acting out of self-interest, not vote, willingly giving up the franchise of political responsibility to the superior general electorate.

The point is almost axiomatic and true of most human experience. When four people sit down to dine, for example, each will choose the entree that suits his or her taste. But when the four have to "vote" on the selection of the wine they are confronted with a political problem.

Those who believe their judgment of wines is inferior to the others will give way, and, with a minimum of communication back and forth across the table, it is usually the person with the most knowledge of wines who is chosen to make the selection. But if price as well as quality is a consideration, even the least expert may cast a ballot for the *vin ordinaire* in order to protect his pocketbook.

Many voters act this way explicitly and consciously when they cast ballots in some contests and on some questions and leave others unmarked. The voter who skips a line on the ballot, though, does not admit to lesser intelligence, only to lesser knowledge, based on insufficient preparation. To the contrary, the fact that so many lines on the average ballot are left unmarked is evidence of the electorate's wisdom. Voters perceive that their interests, however slight in, say, the alderman's race, would not be served by casting a ballot at random, thus diluting the efforts of those who went to the trouble of preparing to vote in that contest. A housewife who trusts her husband's judgment, and who has not had the time or the inclination to study candidates and issues, will accept his selections. And if he evinces no preference in certain contests or referenda, she will leave those ballots unmarked too. But it will take only the word of a friend or neighbor, whose judgment she trusts, or an insight gleaned at a PTA meeting or from a news broadcast, for her to make a choice in one of these contests while her husband abstains or accepts her lead.

Americans who are eligible to vote but do not exercise that privilege are in a different category. Given the choices presented to them, and their general level of satisfaction or dissatisfaction with the world around them, they do not perceive that their interests are sufficiently at stake to warrant the inconvenience of a trip to the polls. They are prepared to be satisfied or dissatisfied to a minor degree however the election turns out.

There are those who do *not* vote and are seriously troubled by the outcome of elections. This need only mean that during the hours of balloting their short-term interests superceded their long-run political calculations. An unemployed worker may be called out of town for a job interview and thus cannot vote for the candidate who is promising the public works program that may provide him future work. The political zealot may be incapacitated on election day by illness. At an extreme, an old man may struggle from his death bed to vote if he perceives that his legacy is sufficiently endangered by the outcome of a political contest, his long-run political calculations outweighing what remains of his short-run.

Having made themselves eligible to vote through registration, individuals have clearly prepared themselves to go through the inconvenience of a trip to the polls should their interests become magnified in the ensuing campaign. But citizens who abstain from voting after having prepared themselves to vote are also serving the democratic process, implicitly acknowledging that because they have only trivial preferences among the candidates and issues, their votes—by being given equal weight with those who have stronger feelings—are bearing too heavily on the final outcome. After the 1965 Voting Rights Act passed, federal officers registered hundreds of thousands of Southern blacks who had previously failed to meet state voting requirements. Many, quite elderly, went to great inconvenience to register, traveling many miles from their rural homes to central registration points and having to acknowledge their illiteracy to registrars. Their fearful pride in becoming eligible voters was evident on the spot. Yet the civil rights activists, usually young Northern whites, were stunned by the exceedingly low voter turnouts of these newly registered blacks in the elections that immediately followed. The conventional explanation was that the blacks were intimidated by having to go to polling places run by Southern whites. This may have been true to a degree. But a more likely explanation, supported by personal interviews with the non-voting eligibles, was that many were afraid to make the wrong choices at the ballot box. To them, the act of voting without sufficient preparation ran counter to their interests. Others, perhaps prepared to choose on the basis of recommendations of someone they trusted— their minister, for example—nevertheless felt timid about the new experience of voting and awaited reports from the braver among them that the process was not a painful one. In subsequent years, as local organization and leadership emerged and as word spread from those who had tested the water, politicians competed in a way that sharpened the perceptions of these new eligibles and voter turnout increased.

Those people who do not prepare themselves to vote by registration are generally those who have systematically failed to perceive their interests at stake in the choices offered. They may have become repeatedly disillusioned by politicians who say one thing and do another. Many in this category will even boast of never voting, cynically asserting that those who do are dupes in a shell game. Some feel they have much more efficient ways of participating in the political process, either contributing financially to candidates or causes prior to elections, or "buying" politicians after they have won elections. But even these people may be drawn back into the voting process if they sense their interests will genuinely be advanced or retarded by an election's outcome, perhaps, for example, the cynic whose son is a candidate for office. Even a heroin addict, whose only abiding interest is his supply of heroin, would engage himself in the process if he saw his heroin supply somehow hinging on the outcome of an election. More typically throughout history, though, suppliers of illegal goods and services—drugs and prostitution—have relied on the purchase of political protection.

Insofar as every voter thinks he or she is smarter than the average voter—the average voter being the purest expression of the political consensus—then any single voter would be able to make political selections consistently superior to the consensus. This of course can't be true; everyone cannot be superior to everyone else, except in the sense that each voter is superior to the consensus in making choices that suit his or her own perceived interests.

But this is an extremely important exception, the very essence of democracy, and in a broad sense the mainspring of all political systems—from the family unit to the foursome having to choose a dinner wine to the nation state. When stated another way, it reveals the inescapable efficiency of this political model: no individual can possibly be as wise as the electorate, the consensus, in discerning the preferred tastes of all the individuals who compose the electorate. Can it be agreed that every individual who casts a ballot or abstains from voting does so after weighing his or her perceived interests against the available choices and the issues at stake? If so, then it is plain that the results of an election represent the best judgment of the body politic in accommodating the interests of its individual parts. Insofar as elections are honestly conducted, *they always turn out right*. No individual, no philosopher king, could possibly be a superior judge of the interests of the electorate than the electorate itself. To put it even more emphatically, barring fraud, the winners of every election are superior to those who lose. Every referendum, every bond issue that goes to the voters turns out correctly. And in every national or local election, each and every citizen who is elected to the Presidency, the Congress, or City Hall is the optimum reflection of the national or local interest, given the choices available to the electorate.

But for the last qualifying phrase, "the choices available," the efficient political model would be a Panglossian extreme. It would force us to conclude that this was the best of all possible worlds because it is precisely what the citizenry desires. Without the qualifying phrase, it forces those who believe in the democratic system and who trust in the wisdom of a self-interested electorate to come to one of two possible conclusions: either the planet itself imposes limits to a better world, or some individuals are inherently inferior to others—racially or culturally—and are dragging down the rest. But *with* the qualifying phrase, "the choices available," it is possible to construct a satisfying political model that allows the possibility of limitless planetary resources and an electorate that has no inferior parts.

In the current period of history, politicians all along the political spectrum are questioning the system in these terms. American liberals, and their relevant counterparts in Europe, have dominated the system for a generation or more with their theories of political economics and government. And they thus believe the electorate is on the whole smarter than it was when it was electing conservatives to dominate the system. The obvious fact that imperfections exist in the society must, to liberals, have less to do with the wisdom of the electorate than with the limits of the planet. The only alternative explanation for why the nation and world are in such imperfect condition relative to other periods of history is that liberal theories of government were never as correct as liberals have assumed. Liberals naturally find this alternative the least likely, having over the years persuaded themselves that their theories have been reliable. To acknowledge error would suggest that over those years the voters have been imperfect in making political selections.

If the planet is the limiting factor, if the Club of Rome is correct and we have now reached a point in the history of civilization where economic growth as we've known it is no longer possible, then the policies that governments should follow become obvious. Individual freedom to grow at the expense of the planet must be restrained, and because growth by the poor and the weak strains the planet as surely as does growth by the strong and the rich, limitations on freedom carry with them the burden of promoting equality through a redistribution of power and wealth. That is, if the poor can no longer have the freedom to attempt greater wealth by exploiting the planet's resources, the political order requires a more equitable distribution of income and wealth, both among individuals and among nation states.

Conservatives, though, hold the other view—that the electorate is at fault, being imperfect in making political selections. Because they are persuaded that their theories of government are the more correct ones and that the planet has not yet imposed limitations that cannot be overcome by human initiative, conservatives argue that the political system itself must be imperfect. Otherwise, why are so many liberals elected? Conservatives usually argue two main types of imperfections in the system. One, which has a racial and cultural texture that moderate conservatives try to avoid, is that the electorate is too heavily weighted with short-sighted voters who have discovered how easy it is to vote themselves the resources of the public treasury. Voters who are "present oriented" will elect political demagogues to distribute the seed corn. The work ethic is being destroyed by liberal welfare programs. The goose that lays the golden eggs, i.e., capitalism, is being slaughtered by the votes of the unwashed masses. We are becoming more and more a nation of grasshoppers and less and less a nation of ants.

An adjunct to this theory of imperfection, one that is given more emphasis by moderate conservatives, is that the electorate would be wiser in selecting political leaders (more conservative ones) if they possessed the correct body of information on which to base decisions. Conservatives of this persuasion have a higher regard for the efficiency of the voters than do those who hold strictly to the grasshopper/ant theory, and thus tend to have more optimism about the perfectability of the system. In the United States, they are the traditional Republicans and Democrats who style themselves "Jeffersonian." Indeed, Jefferson neatly described their political model in a sentence: "I know of no safe depository of the ultimate powers of society but the people themselves; and if we think them not enlightened enough to exercise their control with a wholesome discretion, the remedy is not to take it from them, but to inform their discretion."

That's it, say the conservatives. The voters are being indiscreet in electing so many profligate, budget-busting liberals to positions of political power because they don't know any better. The problem lies not in conservative ideas, but in their communication. If only conservatives could "get their story out"; the fundamental problem lies not in the conservative politician or the electorate but in their medium of exchange. In this view, the problem is the news media, which is seen to constantly disseminate biased or erroneous information to the electorate. Just as liberals declaim against the inordinate influence of Tory publishers during those periods when conservatives are winning elections, Tories are outraged by the excesses of Whig scribblers when liberals are doing the winning. The most ardent exponents of this view yearn for some sort of controls on the press, which is not a Jeffersonian approach. The more benign solution is to somehow make strenuous efforts to "educate" the news media, with carrot, stick, or a combination of both. These more benign conservatives, who do not wish to tamper with the First Amendment and freedom of the press, have in recent times suggested that errant, liberally biased communicators be publicly criticized and shamed whenever possible. Forums and peer-group tribunals have been established to receive and judge criticisms of the press corps. At the same time, businessmen who have felt themselves damaged by anti-business bias in the news media have been encouraged by conservatives to "fight back" through paid advertisements. And conservative academics and foundations have established programs, seminars, and publications that explicitly seek to instruct well-meaning but ignorant newsmen on, for example, the law of supply and demand and the merits of the capitalist system. This view of modern America imputes vast powers of leverage and influence to journalists, holding out the hope that society could improve rapidly if only journalists had a greater appreciation of ants and less concern with grasshoppers. The assumption is that the map to a better society is a known commodity, but that it cannot work so long as the society's opinion molders do not sell it to the electorate.

In the political model described here, however, the news media have only a trivial influence on the electorate and have none of the leverage attributed to them. Political pundits or television commentators who are thought to condition and propagandize the masses have a difficult time even influencing the votes of their wives and children and frequently spend decades in fruitless attempts to change the voting habits of their parents. As long as the news media are free to broadcast the political menu, their own biases have no bearing on the tastes of the electorate, which cannot be persuaded to "try the fish" when it has come to the table craving meat.* The news media, and other so-called opinion leaders, influence the outcome of elections not by bearing directly on the electorate, but on the candidates.

The chief problem in the political process is not the communication of the candidates' views and personalities to the electorate, but the communication of the electorate's interests to the candidates. The electorate knows its best interests and cannot be persuaded by a biased press of the left or the right to vote against that self interest. But the politician who seeks to impose his tastes on the electorate and allows himself to be blinded by

---

*The only possible exceptions are last-minute erroneous or fraudulent reports that either alter the electorate's perception of its interests or its perception of the candidates. Because balloting can only occur within a limited number of hours on one day of the year, erroneous information coming to the electorate in the period immediately preceding can cause temporary confusion sufficient to affect the outcome of an otherwise close race. For this reason, voters heavily discount new information received on election eve, and in this period candidates as well as communicators traditionally halt electioneering. The outcome of an election could still be altered by, say, an erroneous radio report that heavy rains have closed a road or washed out a bridge, discouraging a segment of the electorate from going to the polls. When contests are so close that they can be affected by such minutiae, however, it stands to reason that there was probably less than a dime's worth of difference between the competing candidates.

a friendly, biased press that shares his tastes can only win if his opponent's platform or personality is even further from the electorate's desires. The flow of information from the candidate or the political leader to the electorate is relatively much less important than the flow of information from the electorate to the candidate or politician. This is true in any political system. Citizens have no way of escaping the results of political decisions, either Washington's, Moscow's, or Nairobi's. They learn about them directly even if there is no news report at all. As a perhaps extreme example, suppose the radio and television networks and newspapers secretly decide not to tell the public that the Vietnam war has escalated. How do they keep from the public the news that their sons are being conscripted, killed, and wounded at an accelerated rate, that their work is shifting faster out of consumer goods to munitions, and that their wealth is being conscripted through taxation and bond issuance at a greater clip? The political reaction to this first-hand news will be no different just because the public cannot read in the newspapers what is happening to it in reality. Congress passes laws, bureaucrats alter regulations, the Federal Reserve expands or contracts the money supply. And whether or not the evening news reports these events, or does so with a bias, cannot change the effects of such actions when they impinge directly on the electorate. So too, the voters who wish to learn where Candidate Jones stands in relation to Candidate Smith can develop alternate sources of information, and always seem to do so, when the mass media is either biased, controlled, or silent on the issues the voters think pertinent.

Myriad alternatives to the mass media already exist. Political parties themselves provide networks of communication in the form of organization, which carries news from the precincts to the politicians in City Hall, statehouses, Congress, and the White House. The successful big-city Democratic "machines" of the past century were not instruments of plunder or oppression, but rather networks of communication that permitted "bosses" to ameliorate tensions in their earliest stages. They eventually broke down both because "bosses" became less efficient in reading messages on the grapevine and dealing with them, and because more efficient channels of communication developed. A more educated citizenry can transmit grievances directly, or through specialized "lobbies," rather than through the precinct captain. And the mass media itself has become more efficient in "covering" a city and thus bringing news of the precinct to the politician.

The communication networks of the political parties also interlock with the sophisticated grapevines of the trade unions, businesses, and financial interests. Political communications developed in the world of commerce far surpass the broadcasts of the mass media in volume, detail, and accuracy. The business and financial community, through its interlocking directorships or corporations and banks, connect sources of pertinent commercial and political information. These communication networks literally have terminal collection points not only in most hamlets in the nation but almost everywhere on earth. The financial press, say, The *Wall Street Journal*, rarely provides a bit of "news" that is unknown to this grapevine, but rather taps into it for the most important news it is already carrying in order to speed dissemination of it.

Early in 1977, a bureaucrat in the Internal Revenue Service proposed a change in the tax codes affecting the housing industry. A bureaucrat in Treasury approved the proposal and a few lines announcing the proposed change were printed in the Federal Register. Within hours of the Register's publication, union business agents and contractor associations and bankers throughout the nation were calling their congressmen in Washington to complain of the proposal. The first the mass media learned of the entire episode was through a curt announcement at Treasury that the Secretary had withdrawn the proposal. The announcement also made it plain that the Secretary had not been aware the proposal had been made.

When a political action is clearly a "wrong" one in that it cuts against the interests of almost everyone, as in this example, communication between the electorate and the politician is sharp and clear, and even the poorest of politicians will "get the message" and act accordingly. But political contests almost always involve the competition of legitimate interests and it is more difficult for a candidate to get feedback from the electorate or for a political leader to learn the results of a political action. For while an idea or action is gauged precisely by a member of the electorate against his perceived self-interest, and he knows whether he approves or disapproves with an exact degree of intensity (or neutrality), the results that flow back to the candidate or political leader are aggregated in the confusing voice of the multitude. If a politician lets himself be persuaded by a biased or controlled press that what he has said or done was approved or was correct, and in fact the opposite was true, the electorate is forced to develop alternate sources of expression to communicate with the politician. They will write letters to him or letters to the editor, contribute to his opposition, demonstrate against him, vote against him, attempt to remove him from office through recall, impeachment, or assassination. And if his successors prove as maladroit in "getting the message," the electorate will arrange a revolution to alter the framework of the system with the aim of improving the process by which politicians are selected for rule. "Rule," says José Ortega y Gasset, "is the normal exercise of authority, and is always based on public opinion, today as a thousand years ago, amongst the English as amongst the bushmen. Never has anyone ruled on this earth by basing his rule essentially on any other thing than public opinion."[1]

Roughly twenty-five hundred years before this observation was penned, Confucius offered it as a precept and it was woven into the Chinese philosophy of government:

Tsze-kung asked about government. The Master said, "(The requisites of government) are three: that there should be sufficiency of food, sufficiency of military equipment, and the confidence of the people in their ruler." Tsze-kung said, "If it cannot be helped, and one of these must be dispensed with, which of the three should be foregone first?" "The military equipment," said the Master. Tsze-kung asked again, "If it cannot be helped, and one of the remaining two must be dispensed with, which of them should be foregone?" The Master answered, "Part with the food. From of old, death has been the lot of all men; but if the people have no faith (in their rulers) there is no standing (for the state)."[2]

The surest sign that public opinion is dissatisfied with political rule is emigration. A child does not run away from home unless he is unhappy with his parents' rule. And when children come of age and leave, it is to establish their own political units. A nation state can appear to be politically peaceful, modern Britain being an example. It remains so by exporting its malcontents, who choose emigration over bomb-throwing. The southern states of the United States exported their malcontents to the North in a great wave of black migration in the 1950s, and having no place else to migrate and still unhappy with political rule, the black malcontents in fact erupted violently until their message got through. Surely the campus violence associated with the Vietnam war would have been magnified had those citizens most violently opposed to the war—those being conscripted perhaps to die in it—not been able to migrate to Canada and Sweden.

Businessmen unhappy with the economic policies of New York migrate to South Carolina. Puerto Ricans unhappy with the political rule of their government migrate to New York. Cubans unhappy with the political rule of Fidel Castro migrate to Puerto Rico. And Chilean communists unhappy with the military-political rule in Santiago migrate to Havana. In popular parlance all this movement is known as "voting with your feet," and the United States was almost wholly formed by this process, importing the malcontents of the rest of the world for three centuries.*

Our political model, then, is only slightly different from Jefferson's, who believed that the people themselves are the most honest and safe depository of the public interests, although not necessarily the most wise. The electorate itself, in our model, is wiser than any of its component parts. Which is not to say, of course, that some individual members of the electorate are not wiser than others in their ability to gauge the interests of the whole. But we reject the notion that the electorate learns its self-interest from the lectures of politicians. Great political ideas are not those which can be *sold* to the people, but are those ideas which the electorate craves even prior to their conception by philosophers or politicians.

The most successful and enduring political revolution in the history of civilization, the development of Christianity, could not have happened if a carpenter's son had to market his idea by educating the electorate to its attractions. Rather, the multitudes had awaited expression of the Christian idea and embraced it eagerly. Nor did the idea spread through the propagandizing of a biased press, blaring the gospel incessantly until the electorate was properly conditioned. The structure of the church grew almost entirely out of the handful of St. Paul's epistles that circulated throughout the Roman Empire.

The welfare of nation states is, then, not limited by the degree of political education of the populace. It is limited by the capacity of its politicians and philosophers to understand the wisdom of people.

ii

The electorate, being wiser than any individual in the society, is society's most precious resource. It is the job of the politician to try to divine what it is the electorate wants. Politicians have the most

---

*In Durant's *Story of Civilization*, he recounts a tale from the life of Confucius that marvelously equates voting and migration:

Returning to Lu, Confucius found his native province so disordered with civil strife that he removed to the neighboring state of T'si, accompanied by several of his pupils. Passing through rugged and deserted mountains on their way, they were surprised to find an old woman weeping beside a grave. Confucius sent Tsze-loo to inquire the cause of her grief. "My husband's father," she answered, "was killed here by a tiger, and my husband also; and now my son has met the same fate." When Confucius asked why she persisted in living in so dangerous a place, she replied; "There is no oppressive government here." "My children," said Confucius to his students, "remember this. Oppressive government is fiercer than a tiger."

important and difficult task in all the society, for they are the only channel through which the electorate can realize its self-interest and in so doing preserve itself and progress. If politicians repeatedly fail to discern the interests of the electorate, winning office only because their political competitors have even less discernment, the society will ultimately resort to either war or revolution to bring about a correction.

As an example of this political model in its simplest terms, consider the following caricature. Assume that the purest expression of the electorate's self-interest is a chicken. It attempts to communicate this desire to the politicians through a multitude of voices in a great variety of ways. Only a very few of the individual voices will come close to expressing this desire precisely, most of the voices expressing negative tastes for everything that is not a chicken. If there are two keen politicians contesting, on election day one might have refined his platform to express a duck. The other thinks the voters want a parrot. And because a duck is more like a chicken, the electorate will choose the candidate who expresses duck. Personality is as important as substance, however. If the duck candidate has shown sufficient signs of being untrustworthy, so weak and vacillating that in post-election he might easily become a hawk, the electorate would choose the more trustworthy parrot.

If the two contesting candidates were not keen, but insensitive to the expressions of the multitudes, on election day one might express a vulture, the other a worm. The vulture might win if in addition he showed signs during the campaign of moving in the direction of a more peaceful bird, and perhaps thereby being educable in office. Otherwise, the voters would likely choose the less threatening worm and wait for the next election, hoping for the best. The fact that the vulture candidate had at least expressed a bird might not be sufficient to persuade the voters that their interests were being given first consideration; the vulture candidate might have confronted the electorate as being an obstacle to be surmounted, his expression of a bird of prey being a purely personal taste rather than a reflection of the electorate's tastes.* In any case, with such a poor showing by the political alternatives, voters would be inclined not even to make a trip to the polls.

The only difference in reality from this simple chicken-duck-parrot

---

*In our earlier example of four diners who must choose one among them to select the wine, we noted that the most expert in wines may not be chosen if there are other considerations. If the expert is known to his associates as a snob, for example, who will impose his own expensive tastes and a share of the bill on the whole group, the penultimate expert will be chosen. If the expert announces that he will pay for the wine, though, the group will always give him the political honor of making the selection.

model is in the number of variables that compose the consensus of the electorate's desires. The electorate may desire in addition to a domestic policy of chicken a foreign policy of eagle, and the task of the contending politicians becomes geometrically more difficult. A candidate may be near perfect in discerning the domestic desires of the electorate, but if he is widely off the mark on foreign policy he could easily lose to an opponent who is less correct on domestic policy, but less incorrect on foreign policy. No single candidate could possibly satisfy all the electors, however. In the modern nation state, individual electors have self-interests that are diametrically opposed to the interests of other electors. There are individuals whose well-being is served by economic growth and there are those who benefit by economic contraction or stagnation. So too, there are individuals whose welfare requires peace and those who benefit from tension. Each such interest is, in its own way, a legitimate one that the politician must in some sense take into account, for as long as peace and prosperity are not always society's condition, it has need of those who can deal with the alternatives. Pediatricians benefit directly from life; undertakers from death.

But while a politician can not satisfy electors who are diametrically opposed, neither can he ignore one class of elector or another, perhaps with the idea that because he can not possibly satisfy both, he will throw in his lot entirely with the one. Even when an issue can be settled by numerical voting, ninety-nine-to-one, the politician must attempt in some way to accomodate the one. At the extreme, if the issue settled ninety-nine-to-one is perceived by the one as in some way threatening his very survival or directly inviting his extinction, the one may resort to extralegal balloting to defend himself, perhaps even attempting assassination. In determining the consensus of the electorate, then, the successful politican does not view the electorate as a collection of numerical units, but as a bundle of individual interests each with a different set of intensities. To determine, for example, that the electorate desires a domestic chicken and a foreign eagle, the politician can not rely on public-opinion surveys, which merely measure numerical preferences.* In 1975-76, as contenders for the presidential nominations began to assemble their political platforms, several of the Democratic hopefuls included a plank that called for the breaking up of the big U.S. petroleum companies. They relied chiefly

---

*If, of four diners who must choose one bottle of wine, three announce that their first preference is the French burgundy, but the fourth indicates he would drink anything but the French burgundy, which he detests, there is small chance that the person selecting the wine will choose the burgundy.

on public-opinion polls that showed a majority of Americans favored such action. They did not seem to consider the possibility that the 55 percent who said they would approve such action felt far less intensely about their position than the 45 percent who disapproved and that the minority would more likely base their selection of a candidate on this issue than would the majority. The contender who took the mildest position relative to the oil companies was Jimmy Carter.

Indeed, on a range of domestic issues, Governor Carter's opponents were far more explicit and aggressive in their advocacy of ideas. But they frequently recommended policies that implied benefits to shifting majorities *at the expense of* minorities, i.e., take from the rich to give to the unrich, break up the big companies to benefit the little companies. While Carter seemed less sure of himself and was frequently criticized by his opponents for failure to advance clear specifics, he consistently seemed less threatening to the shifting minorities. A relative unknown, Carter was successful in winning the Democratic nomination by being less eager than his opponents to impose his political tastes on the electorate and at the same time openly conceding that his method was to attempt to gauge the desires of the electorate. His opponents at times criticized this admission as a lack of "leadership" on his part.

On the Republican side, Ronald Reagan almost won the nomination from the incumbent, Gerald Ford, by honing his positions to the reactions of his audiences. Reagan scored heavily on foreign policy, especially after critically raising the issue of the Panama Canal negotiations and arguing against the Ford administration's proposed "giveaway" of the Canal. Critics of Reagan accused him of "stirring up" the emotions of the voters in demagogic fashion. Reagan explained that he did not develop the issue for the voters, but was drawn into it by his audiences, who continued to encourage him to expand upon the theme after his first, almost accidental, mention of the issue in the earliest stages of the campaign.

Throughout his political career, Governor Reagan was frequently scorned as a mere "movie actor," but the one ingredient of his earlier career that he successfully carried over into politics was this sensitivity to audiences. The successful actor, comedian, and vaudevillian constantly strives to find what it is that audiences want and then attempts to give it to them. Stage plays are frantically reworked after testing in Philadelphia and Boston, when preconceptions of what will play are measured against theater electorates. Comedians throw out gags and routines that do not bring forth laughter, although they may have gone to great trouble and expense to have them written, yet are frequently astonished at the hilarity evoked by an "ad lib" which of course immediately becomes part of the routine. After President Ford lost a series of primaries to Reagan in the spring of 1976, his White House advisers grumbled that Ford was having a hard time "getting his act together." He did so just in time, at least sufficiently to win the GOP nomination, not by continuing to resist the message Reagan was obviously getting from the electorate (shall we say a foreign-policy "eagle"), but by incorporating much of it into his own routine. At the same time, though, Jimmy Carter was observing Reagan's success in reading this element of the electorate's wishes and weaving it into his own campaign. In the general election, Carter and Ford were almost indistinguishable in their offering of a foreign-policy eagle to the electorate, and the election appeared to turn on domestic issues, with Carter looking more like chicken than President Ford.

iii

The political model thus far described is one of obvious optimism. Progress and general welfare are not limited by external forces, such as planetary resources. Nor will the electorate itself limit its own well-being by systematically making unenlightened choices. Decadence occurs in a political society only when the politicians themselves lose their way, which occurs most readily when they come to believe that a set of ideas exists which must be forced on an unwilling electorate for its own good. The basic optimism of the model rests not on any prospect that politicians may now be on the brink of new enlightenment, although they may well be, but on the assumption that the emergence of keener politicians can happen overnight. This is at least a more promising assumption than the prerequisite of the alternative model, which is that the darker impulses of "mobocracy" have to be checked through the careful education of the masses. The model thus has neither a "liberal" nor a "conservative" bias as we currently understand those labels. It holds, rather, that both general impulses are legitimate, but that the electorate itself does not choose one bundle of ideas assembled by one group of politicians or philosophers over another bundle of ideas assembled by a competing group. Because it is forced to choose from a narrow menu of political alternatives, the electorate does its best to assemble its own bundle in a liberal/conservative consensus that always falls short of the ideal.

Massachusetts, for example, proclaims itself to be the most consistently "liberal" of states. It has in recent years uniformly sent representatives to Washington who style themselves in the fashion of liberals. It was the only state to vote for George McGovern over Richard Nixon in 1972. And in 1976 it voted heavily for Carter over Ford and again sent a contingent of liberals to Congress. But on each selection the voters had to choose one bundle of ideas over another, each candidate espousing not one single issue but many. Consistent with our political model is the notion that each of the more conservative candidates who lost may have had within their campaigns a single flaw which, if corrected, could have resulted in their wholesale elections over the liberals. Indeed, on the 1976 ballot, nine single-issue referendum questions were put to the voters of Massachusetts, and in each case the side identified with the "conservative" position won a majority of the votes. By a two-to-one margin, the voters supported the principal of a refinery and deepwater port for Massachusetts. They opposed a ban on handguns. They opposed a state power authority. They rejected a constitutional amendment that would have permitted a graduated state income tax. They rejected a system of uniform electric rates. And they narrowly defeated the environmentalists on a measure to require returnable bottles for beer and soft drinks. Are we to assume the voters of Massachusetts are at heart conservative, as evidenced by these referendum votes, but mistakenly vote for liberal Democrats out of habit or confusion? Or are they truly liberal at heart, but bamboozled by conservative demagoguery into reactionary votes on the issues?

The usefulness of the political model is that it enables us to consider that the Massachusetts electorate was in no way confused by either candidates or issues. It knew exactly what it was doing.* Assuming the elections were all honestly conducted, they all turned out right. It could be inferred that insofar as conservative candidates were in harmony with the voters on the referenda, they gathered more votes than they would have otherwise. Similarly, the winning liberals would have won bigger if they were closer to the voters on the specific referendum issues. But it isn't possible to say why the conservatives lost, only that for some reason they deserved to lose.

The model does permit us to hold that Massachusetts voters were not only correct in voting for Jimmy Carter, but would have been correct even if he had lost in the national balloting. The extension of this idea is that the U.S. electorate was correct in choosing Jimmy Carter, and it will be no less correct if Jimmy Carter is "outvoted" by the global electorate.

*In a conversation with the author in the autumn of 1975, former Texas Governor John Connally suggested that the American voters in 1968 and 1972 elected a Republican President and a Democratic Congress because they did not agree with the program and platform of either party, and so purposely arranged a political stalemate in order to minimize the damage either party could do.

CHAPTER 2

The Global Electorate

The world is a closed political economy. It is the only political unit that totally contains the effects of political and economic events within itself. All humans are members of the global electorate. In the absence of a world government, toward which it moves, the global electorate "votes" among competing political systems. Civilization advances and retreats in a trial and error process, groping toward systems capable of producing more capable politicians. Political, economic, and military spheres intertwine and the global electorate engages in political, economic, and military "forms of voting" in striving toward an ideal—though unattainable—global system. Superior systems maximize welfare by minimizing legitimate tensions between economic growth and wealth distribution and between freedom and equality. All competing systems are, broadly speaking, different forms of capitalism and democracy.

"The world is a closed economy," said Canadian economist Robert Mundell in 1971, almost in exasperation. Mundell offered his observation and continues to offer it in answer to those of his colleagues who profess economic theories that assume closed systems smaller than the world. Economists do this when they say: "Holding the rest of the world constant, if the U.S. government does such and such, employment will rise." In doing so, they ask the policymakers they advise to assume that the U.S. economy is, for all practical purposes, the only economy. For all practical purposes, Mundell is saying, the world is the only closed economy. Economists cannot ask U.S. policymakers to hold the world constant, for if the U.S. government does such and such, the impact of those actions on other nations might well feed back on the U.S. economy, causing unemployment. The world is not fragmented, but integrated, which means that every economic event that takes place someplace in the world is felt virtually everywhere in the world. And theories that treat the U.S. economy as if it were closed when in fact it is in constant interaction with the rest of the world are likely to be deficient or worse.

Among non-economists, physicists seem to be able to grasp this concept quickly, for they are comfortable with the idea that the world is a bundle of atoms, and the movement of one against another causes a chain reaction that is felt throughout the planet. Jump up and down and the whole earth shakes a bit.

Transpose this idea into the economic realm and the same kind of chain reaction becomes apparent. Imagine, for instance, that someone buys a bottle of Coca-Cola in a shop in New Delhi. The transaction not only adds to the revenue of the shopkeeper, but to the revenues of Coca-Cola at its Atlanta headquarters. There is also an infinitesimal impact on the world sugar market, as well as the markets for all the other ingredients of Coca-Cola. Coca-Cola's shareholders and Jamaican sugar farmers trade their receipts from the sale of that one bottle in further transactions that ripple again and again through the world until every human being but the most remote hermit has been touched in some microscopic way.

In the same way, the world is also a closed political economy, and any general political theory that treats smaller units as being closed is likely to be deficient. To the degree the world is economically integrated it is also politically integrated, because there can be no divorcement of economic and political events. Somewhere, the perspective of a politician was microscopically altered by the economic chain flowing from the New Delhi Coca-Cola transaction, governments and marketplaces being linked in many ways, especially through taxes and money.

If the whole world, then, is the only closed political economy, it is the family which is the smallest political system that is open. Of all the trillions of political decisions made on this earth each hour, the vast majority involve family "votes" aimed at reaching a family consensus. When four people go out to dine, the wine selection requires a political decision because four tastes must be satisfied with one bottle. The choice of entrees in no way requires a political decision because individual taste can be satisified without consensus. The family unit is constantly involved in political decision-making; endlessly forced to face the problem of selecting one wine for four persons—one entree, one toothpaste, one hometown, one home, one vacation spot, one church. The division of the family income is, in its way, as complex as the legislative process in Congress. For example, Mom, who appears to have dictatorial powers in filling out her supermarket order, is in fact the chief executive of family legislation. She reaches for the creamy peanut butter instead of the chunky variety, although the latter may be on sale, because the children have voted against chunky style by expressing distaste for it and bringing home half their sandwiches in their lunch boxes. But if the family budget is desperately tight, and chunky is consistently cheaper than creamy, she may attempt to push through a change in taste. The voters as a group may grumble, but they usually must defer to the arguments of the finance committee.

The success of the family as a political unit depends upon the political skills of each of its members, particularly, of course, the political skills of the parents. The system is democratic even though formal voting does not take place, and in those instances where families do playfully go through an exercise of formal voting the results appear confused and are subtly scrapped. "Where shall we go?" Dad asks, having announced that the family will be treated to dinner out. The three children announce an eager preference for the MacDonald hamburger restaurant. Mom says nothing, and Dad, knowing she detests MacDonald's, observes that "We went there last week" and steers the conversation to alternate restaurants until a consensus is reached, accommodating the intensity of his wife's dislike for the place the numerical majority has chosen. If the three children, though, are obviously disappointed, Mom will speak up and cast her ballot for MacDonald's, demonstrating her skill as a politician.

"Should we go to the mountains or the shore?" Dad asks in planning the family vacation. His wife and two of the children vote for the shore, which he himself prefers, and junior says nothing, feeling he has been outvoted so why bother. Mom observes his quiet disappointment and realizes the problem. You can swim at both places, but junior has become passionately involved in baseball, and all his baseball buddies are going to the mountains. She takes the intensity of his preference into account, weighs the mixed preferences on the other children, and with a word or two to Dad swings the voting toward the mountains, winning an advance commitment from junior that next year it will be the shore. The political success of mother, father, or the children, rests on their ability to size up the preferences of the family electorate and then act in a way that maximizes welfare. In the above example, the electorate is trying to communicate "mountains" although superficially it seems to be saying "shore." In terms of the "chicken-duck-parrot" model described in chapter 1, the mother is an exceptionally skilled politician. If she had less discernment, the family would have chosen the shore and family welfare would have been diminished. A succession of individual political failures within the family system in the extreme causes a breakdown of the family.

This smallest political unit, the family, is "open" because it is difficult, if not literally impossible, to conceive of a political choice by that family that does not impinge even slightly on another family, ad infinitum, until the frontiers of the world political economy are reached. Does the family choose to move to Savannah from Memphis? Does it choose Pepsi over Coke? Does it go to the mountains instead of the shore? The political and economic marketplaces of Savannah and Memphis reverberate. Pepsi's shareholders exult and Coke's despair and perhaps the one switch makes the marginal difference—the "straw that break's the camel's back"—and Coke's advertising agency loses its account. The mountain vacation resort becomes marginally more prosperous relative to the shore resorts, but also slightly more crowded, and another family that had slightly preferred mountains to shore hears of the relative crowd at the mountains and elbow-room at the shore and alters its political choice.

Each family's political decisions not only reverberate through the world political economy, but also are made within the context of the world political economy. If the United States was at war, a family deciding whether or not to move to Savannah from Memphis would take that fact into account. And in a negative, but still real, sense the fact that the United States is at peace would also bear on such a decision. Which isn't to say that because of war the family would not make the move. War might actually require the family's presence in Savannah, or at least positively influence such a move. We only say the fact of war will somehow be weighed.

It's more difficult to see, but no less true, that a family choosing between Memphis and Savannah or Pepsi and Coke will take into account the presence or absence of war in Indonesia or Bolivia, or whether or not a family in Australia will vacation at the shore. They need know nothing explicit about either Indonesia or Australia, and most probably do not. They learn of distant political-economic events, even the most trivial, in the same way they learn first hand the decisions in Washington, through all kinds of price changes: consumer prices, interest rates, share prices, and through changes in production patterns, changes in wealth, minute shifts in ideas. The effect most often is as trivial as the physical effect on the planet when one person jumps up and down. But it is inescapably true that unless you are totally cut off from the world, in one way or another you are forced to weigh into every calculation of a political or economic nature the effects of every other such transaction.

Stated less explicitly, the notion of a fully integrated world political economy may seem less extreme. The environmentalist image that we are all passengers on the spaceship Earth, for example, expresses the sense of a closed political economy. It's a small world. Everyone on earth belongs to the same family unit, the family of man. Each has his or her own bundle of tastes and preferences which is "voted" through political and economic choices in arriving at a global consensus. And just as a family's welfare *as a family* is limited by the political skills of its leaders in determining the consensus of its members, global welfare is limited by the deficiencies of world political leaders in interpreting a global consensus.

From this perspective, we see the path of civilization as being one of advance toward one system of government, an ideal world government, whose perfection lies in its ability to consistently produce political leaders capable of interpreting the global consensus. At the same time, the ideal system is unattainable, for by definition it would have to produce politicians capable of interpreting the global consensus to absolute perfection. This does not mean that in some distant future world government is not possible, but that when and if world government becomes reality, the trial and error process of improving the system of world government cannot end until that system always produces politicians who are as wise as the electorate, a condition that is inconceivable. But the world electorate is, and always has been, moving in that direction.

We can imagine that at some long-ago starting point in the history of civilization the global electorate consisted of, say, one family, which by definition constituted a closed political economy and composed a world government.* The system of world government at that point could not have been ideal or, by definition, it would remain to this day. We can hypothesize that as the population multiplied, a second family unit emerged as offspring of the first and found the system of day-to-day politics within one unit unwieldy, the divergency of tastes overtaking the skills of the political leader. It is likely, in this hypothesis, that the rupture occurred over the division of family income. It is always easier politically to match reward and effort when the electorate is smaller than larger.**

As families multiply, the same problem occurs at a higher level. Say the global electorate has multiplied to one hundred families. Say they all go naked and live in caves, which are in surplus, so that for illustrative purposes the only "income" is food, and they only eat fish. If one fisherman is incapacitated, the survival of his family unit is threatened. It will be extinguished unless a method of income redistribution exists within the political economy. The consensus of the global electorate undoubtedly desires some form of redistribution to prevent the elimination of the fisherman and his family. Individual members of the electorate feel this desire for positive or negative reasons. Some may be next of kin or cave neighbors. Those more

---

*For a more elaborate and elegant theory of history, beyond these meager hypotheticals, the reader will be rewarded by William H. McNeill's *The Rise of the West* (Chicago: University of Chicago Press, 1963).

**Two roommates part when one concludes that the other is not holding up his end, in terms of finances, cleanliness, or courtesies. Three roommates create an even more unstable relationship. Communes always break down unless they are strictly organized to reward effort and punish non-effort.

distant kin or neighbors may simply understand the concept of risk pooling, insurance. Others may simply calculate that the fisherman's friends and neighbors feel so strongly about his survival that they will attempt to expropriate their hoard of fish, and that it would be less costly in the long run to hand over a few.

But by what process does the distribution take place? Of the ninety-nine healthy fishermen, many are barely able to keep their families alive with their daily catch and others are so agile and experienced that they actually have stockpiles of fish. Does each fisherman contribute one percent of his catch? Or do the few draw from their hoards? Probably neither process will approximate the consensus of the electorate, which we suspect involves some intricate combination of the two methods. Some of the marginal fishermen could contribute a share and work more diligently to make up the difference, while others may already be stretched to the limits of their capabilities, and even a small share would threaten the survival of their families.

The wealthy fishermen, those with hoards, have varying attitudes about the idea of being the sole contributors. Those who are next of kin or neighbors are not entirely opposed, but calculate that if only they contributed, the hoards would soon be depleted and they could not work hard enough thereafter to maintain the two households. Those more distant are flatly opposed to being the sole contributors, and some resist the idea of any contribution at all, arguing that the incapacitated fisherman should have been more careful.

Then there is the matter of repayment. Is the fisherman, once he has regained his health, merely expected to contribute to a pool when the next of his fellows becomes incapacitated? Or will he be asked to repay the fish over time? That is, will the system of income distribution be based on taxation or on bond finance? Perhaps some of the daily catch of the able fishermen will be taxed away from them. The recipient fisherman will not have to repay, except insofar as he returns to the insurance pool. Another portion is financed with bonds, so that the wealthy fishermen more willingly give up fish from their hoards on the promise that the taxation of all the fishermen will continue after the recipient has regained his health, until their hoards are replenished. The system of bond finance enables those who feel especially friendly to the fisherman to give up more fish in exchange for more bonds. And even the distant wealthy see an advantage in holding their hoards in promises (bonds) which cannot be easily stolen or spoiled, and are perhaps happy to participate in this arrangement. All it takes to work this out is a politician with consummate skill.

One can imagine that such consummate political skill does not exist, and the tensions resulting from the inability of political leadership to resolve the problem confronting the community cause a fracturing of the community. World government ends and the closed political economy thereafter consists of two or more open political economies. Each of these two or more political economies represents a distinctive system designed to deal with the kind of problem that caused the single community to fragment. There will then be, say, three competing experiments in political economy, each attempting to maximize welfare in a world where individual members are subject to incapacitation because of accident or illness, and the community as a whole is subject to the whims of a variable planet. Not only must the community face the problem of redistributing income when one of its members falls sick, but it also must deal with natural disaster. Flood or fire wipe out a third of their fishing boats, or the fishing grounds become depleted and one of the three tribes must move on in search of new fishing grounds or fragment into yet another tribe, which migrates. In addition to each of the three tribes experimenting in domestic policy, once they are three, instead of one "world government," each must also evolve a foreign policy. The leadership of tribe A has perhaps determined that a major component of its *domestic* policy will be to make up shortages in its income by war and plunder of tribe B. The political leadership of tribe B may have evolved a sophisticated system of financing income shortages, but unless it is prepared to survive the potential attacks of tribe A it will be extinguished. It may disagree with the domestic policy of tribe C but centers its foreign policy on a mutual security arrangement with tribe C in the event of an attack upon either by tribe A. The point here is not precisely to guess what forms the earliest political economies took, but to suggest the likelihood that the variables of policy were basically as complex then as now. It is of course possible to imagine the first "world government" fragmenting for reasons other than economics, as we have hypothesized, i.e., a struggle for accession, a dispute over women, etc. Over the millennia societies have struck upon ways to resolve these kinds of tensions, ways that are more or less acceptable to the global electorate. The fundamental problem of resolving tensions between income growth and income redistribution is, however, the one that remains to this day as the principle cause of political experimentation.

We are forced to assume, in other words, that if at some point in past history one of the experimenting "tribes" struck upon a system that resolved the economic issue it would be with us today. Superior systems cannot be replaced by inferior systems. A truly superior system would, over time, be adopted by nations having inferior ones, either willingly or through conquest. The obvious fact that there are widely diverse political systems tells us that while each is superior to that which it replaced, it is not possible to conclude that one is superior to another, for only history itself draws such conclusions. We can say with certainty—because within the terms of our political model it is axiomatic—that the systems which can more consistently produce better politicians will outlast the others.

This is true for all political units. The business enterprise or corporation outlasts its competitors when it consistently casts up managers who are superior to those of its competitors. The successful father and son enterprise remains competitive only insofar as the sons retain the qualities of their fathers. Here too, in conformance with the simple political model, the qualities are those which enable father or son to discern the desires of their constituents, their business electorate. They must sense as precisely as they can the goods and services which consumers desire to buy, at what price, and at the same time they must come as close as they can to discerning the consensus of their workers, and manage to fit one to the other.

In the modern corporate environment, in which management science has evolved methods of manufacturing managers of roughly homogenous consistency, the father and son tradition competes less successfully over time. In a subtle sense, the modern corporate manager spends much of his working time choosing his successors, "bringing them along," although the actual selection is done by the board of directors. When those several "brought along" do not appear adequate to the task in the eyes of the board, it can of course reach outside the corporation for the person it wants. The chances of finding superior managers in this broad pool of talent are greater than a father's chances in choosing among his sons and daughters. While the quality of sons and daughters may hold up for two or three generations in exceeding the quality of managers manufactured in the corporate system, eventually it is bound to break down.

In the same sense, nation states that have competed over the centuries have discarded the method by which heredity is a major factor in choosing political leadership. In earliest civilization, when succession to the throne was among the most traumatic political events, electorates encouraged heredity as the general rule for succession as a way of avoiding genocidal transitions. Bloody warfare as the method of finding the most superior political leaders is no doubt the most expensive system. Heredity at least offers the rough probability that successful political instincts can be transmitted, genetically and through careful education, and what the electorate may lose by occasionally turning up a lemon it more than gains in the avoidance of violence.*

The experimentation with hereditary rule occupied most of civilized history, with communities groping toward systems that at times seemed to approximate the current state of the art of managerial science. Through the middle and near east, polygamy enabled the "talent pool" to be broadened, with Chinese emperors and Arab sheiks—working with their counselors and cabinets—bringing along many sons of many wives or concubines so that one could be selected for succession. The Chinese developed an elaborate civil service system that supported their method of succession, for it brought the ablest men to the ear of the emperor during the selection process; men steeped in the wisdom of Confucius on the art of government. And while the Chinese emperors ruled by divine right—the "Mandate of Heaven"—the teachings of Confucius and Mencius provided a necessary loophole, i.e., the ruler who arouses the enmity of the people has obviously lost the Mandate of Heaven and can be overthrown in favor of a new dynasty. The system worked wonderfully for 2,000 years although it ultimately broke down because the wisdom of Confucius was flawed, in that he believed that China could be treated as a closed political economy. The ideal political rulers, he wrote, "would avoid foreign relations as much as possible, and seek to make their state so independent of outside supplies that it would never be tempted to war for them." In essence, China followed the path of our hypothetical "tribe B," developing the most successful and sophisticated domestic policy of all civilization, but leaving itself open to the predators of tribe A. The Great Wall discouraged the barbarian hordes for a time, and minor successful invaders were either bought off with gifts or, as in the case of the Mongols, assimilated. But when major invasions came from the West during the last century, the system could not keep up with the demands for tribute. The resulting economic convulsions led to revolutions in the way political leadership is produced, first in 1911 and then in 1949. The current experiment, still evolving, treats China as an open political economy that allies itself with tribe C (for the moment the United States) against a potential threat from tribe A (for the moment the Soviet Union). Prior to 1949, when Mao Tse-tung

---

*The violent solution produces a leader more capable of discerning the consensus of the electorate, but only through the process of eliminating divergent tastes. If four members of a family mildly prefer vacationing at the shore and one feels strongly about going to the mountains, the consensus of the four can easily be satisfied regarding resort preferences if the fifth is, say, killed by a truck, but the consensus of the group obviously would not prefer that "solution."

introduced a domestic policy of socialism, China also allied with the United States. But its domestic economic policies were too deficient to retain the support of the electorate, and there was no method by which a less deficient ruler than Chiang Kai-shek could succeed him other than by revolution. Like the Soviet Union and other socialist governments, the People's Republic of China currently selects its political leaders in "corporate" style, in much the same way as a modern American multi-national corporation chooses its chief executive officers.

Japan's emperors were also polygamous, as in China, explicitly to ensure dynastic continuity. As in China, too, the succession could go to a selected son, not necessarily the oldest. A Japanese proverb, though, observes that "the great man has no seed," and a discouraging succession of weak emperors forced the nation to experiment along another path in finding a system that would produce superior politicians. Unlike China, the Japanese clung to the divinity of the emperor without a Confucian-Mencian "loophole." Emperors remained as figureheads after the tenth century, with real political power passing to regents who were also polygamous and could choose a successor from many sons. At this second level, which held de facto political power, heredity as the means of succession was a practicality, but because heaven was not involved, deficient regents could be replaced. As a further variation on the experiment, adoption of sons became permissible as a way of broadening the pool of potential succession. In modern Japan, the idea has carried over into private enterprise, with corporate leaders officially adopting talented university students as sons, thus grafting the positive benefits of a father-son symbiosis to up-to-date managerial science.

Japan's system was for most of its history not as successful as China's in terms of domestic policy. But the Confucian flaw that caught up with China did not after the nineteenth century hamstring Japan. As the industrial revolution unfolded in the West, Japan lost little time in the mid-nineteenth century in scrapping its attempts at insularity and adopting a conscious policy of openness as a political economy in order to absorb Western ideas. This involved a period of humiliation, the conscious acceptance of the notion that some foreign ideas may be superior, but Japan's political leadership a century ago was skilled enough to see that its competitiveness as a nation state required the importing of ideas. The industrial revolution came to Japan, and so too did representative government (in 1889) as a method of discovering political leadership. The franchise, however, was tightly held to the upper classes in distrust of the electorate's wisdom. It was not broadened until Japan's defeat in World War II, when the American occupying forces imposed universal suffrage on Japan.

In the West, representative government flourished sufficiently in Greece to produce a golden age. But the Greek experiment with "democracy" was seriously flawed in that it was not designed to produce superior political leadership through competition, but rather to give every man a turn at the political helm. This method failed to appreciate the openness of the political economy, and the experiment ended by conquest, in the same way that General Motors today would inevitably lose its pre-eminence to competitiors if it began rotating management by a democratic lottery.

Rome selected out of the Greek model a variation of representative government. It aimed at producing superior leaders by competition but weighted different classes of voters. During the centuries of the Republic, this weighting led to inevitable frictions during periods of economic distress. The consensus was bound to be distorted on the crucial issue of the basic economic issue of growth versus redistribution. The Roman system, though, was capable of producing superior leadership, and Julius Caesar emerged to minimize the economic problem. Through economic and social reforms, Caesar produced economic growth. His approach, which we will recount in some detail later in this book, was so attractive that he could extend it to neighboring tribes by conquest and retain the support of public opinion in those conquered regions, which became the Roman Empire. Caesar's political deficiency lay in his failure to somehow accommodate the perceived interests of the aristocracy as he welded his political coalition of the commercial and working classes of Rome. And it was the aristocracy, of course, that assassinated him.

Augustus, Caesar's adopted son, through good fortune and great skill, extended and consolidated the Empire. The political consensus he arranged was so successful that the emperorship was thrust upon him, ending the experiment in representative government. Augustus, though, merely demonstrated the obvious—that monarchy is superior to democracy when the monarch is superior to the elected democrat. It remained for history to demonstrate that democracy *as a system* can, more often than monarchy, produce superior political leadership. It was by fortune rather than by "system" that the Empire entered its golden age in A.D. 98 with the accession of Trajan. For the following eighty-two years, the Empire enjoyed an unbroken reign of peace and prosperity under four emperors, coming closer than any other system before or since to making a legitimate claim to world government. The decline and fall followed, though, because Rome had not even come close to systematizing the political selection process; circumstance and chance had done all the work.

Augustus had left a strong, prospering Empire, but poor to middling heirs, who weakened the Empire even while extending it by conquest. The hereditary chain snapped in A.D. 96, with the assassination of the inept Domitian. Domitian's fatal error was one common to early autocrats whose dictates met popular resistance. He proclaimed himself and his family divine, demanding worship and persecuting resistance. The resultant grumblings from the populace included rumors of conspiracy against him, and Domitian, slightly mad, ordered the execution of one of his household servants because of a vague suspicion. The rest of the servants, fearing for their lives, joined in a pact and murdered him. Not always can assassinations be so clearly seen as instruments of the general electorate, a method of voting.

The Roman Senate, which had been docile for more than a century, asserted itself by naming Domitian's successor rather than permitting power to remain in his family. It chose sixty-six-year-old Marcus Cocceius Nerva from its own ranks because of his mildness and age, and Nerva reigned only sixteen months. Before his death, Nerva, who had no son, adopted one as Julius Caesar had done. He chose forty-two-year-old Marcus Ulpius Traianus (Trajan) on merit, after determining his acceptability to the Senate. Similarly during this golden age, Trajan adopted Hadrian who adopted Antoninun Pius who adopted Marcus Aurelius. In each case, the careful selection was made out of the broadest talent pool, the available populace, and approximated the corporate method employed by modern socialist nations. Gibbon marks the decline of the Roman Empire as beginning with Commodus, the son of Aurelius, who acceded in A.D. 180. Gibbon also observes that during the eighty golden years the emperors "must often have recollected the instability of a happiness which depended on the character of a single man. The fatal moment was perhaps approaching when some licentious youth, or some jealous tyrant, would abuse, to the destruction, that absolute power which they had exerted for the highest benefit of their people."[1]

The economic depression of the 1930s is sometimes referred to as the Great Contraction. In the sense that the world economy underwent a sharp, violent contraction in a very few years, the period deserves the appellation. But the economic contraction that began with the accession of Commodus extended to the French Revolution. It was of precisely the same nature, a gradual unwinding of the economic efficiencies achieved in the Roman experiment. In other words, the contraction occurred not because of plague, flood or crop failure, but as a result of the splintering of the political economy.

This is also what occurred in our hypothetical fishing community at the dawn of civilization, when the "world" economy broke into three parts. One central marketplace fractured into three smaller markets over failure of the political leaders to solve the central economic issue—growth versus redistribution. In the process, the world loses the efficiency of a one market system. Imagine the United States one political economy—one marketplace, broken into fifty separate nations. Each would be responsible for its own currency. Each would have to provide for its own national defense. Trade across borders would be subject to a welter of tariffs and excises. Fifty separate populations would all have to work much harder to accomplish the same tasks, in the sense that segments of each population would have to be diverted into these new activities. Unemployment would not necessarily rise, but everyone would be poorer. If the hundred fishermen in our hypothetical world economy split into three tribes, they would all still have jobs. But ten of them could no longer fish, now being forced to do jobs formerly unnecessary—national defense, for example, and the management of three marketplaces instead of one.

The Caesars did the opposite. By their political genius they made the Roman currency so attractive, the military efficiency of the legions so attractive, the mildness of Roman taxation so attractive, the standardization and justice of Roman law so attractive, the openness to unorthodox ideas and religions so attractive, that the one marketplace spread by the force of demand. Under the Caesars, the Empire expanded not by conquest but by liberation. And when it collapsed, the legions were helpless against the barbarians who offered less oppressive government. Durant cites a report that in the fourth century, "thousands of citizens fled over the border to seek refuge among the barbarians."[2] (As a modern parallel, we could observe the citizens of Manhattan fleeing to the hinterlands of New Jersey to escape what to them seems an oppressive burden of taxation.)

Gibbon's conclusion was that Christianity was the chief cause of Rome's fall, that it eroded the old faith and institutions and turned men's thoughts away from the tasks of the present world to preparation for a hereafter. This theory is wholly incorrect. In our hypothesis, Christianity and other religions were embraced by such a large part of the global electorate as a means of communicating to the political leaders. In this way, the embracing of Confucianism in China worked as a message from the people upward to their political leaders as a guide to the conduct of policy. In our hypothetical fishing community, the central ideas common to both religions—love, brotherhood, the golden rule—would have assisted the political leader in grappling with those questions that ultimately fragmented the community when he could not discern the consensus of the electorate. How will the community deal with the incapacitated fisherman? What are the rules of behavior between families within the community and what should be the punishment when the rules are broken? And how is the leader to be selected? By might or by some peaceful selection process?

If the fishing community were Christian or Confucian, or any of the other great religions, the leader himself would be a believer. Depending on the strength of his conviction weighed amongst all his other calculations, he undoubtedly would provide answers to these questions tending closer to the consensus of the electorate than if he had no such credo. At least the fragmentation of the political economy would have been delayed. But by the same token, if he were the ideal political leader, and thus could precisely determine the consensus of his constituents, he would have no need for the intellectual assistance that a religious credo would offer.

What we are saying, then, is that Christianity developed as a private, extralegal form of influencing deficient political rulers, at least pushing them in the general direction of the consensus. This is directly opposed to Voltaire's view that the political class uses religion as a means of pacifying the mob. Nor is religion Marx's "opiate of the masses," but rather one of the chief means throughout history by which the masses have voted. Religion, though, is not a theoretical necessity to the management of a political economy in this model, as long as there are sufficient other media of exchange between the electorate and the politicians.

Christianity has been the most vigorous and enduring of the religions *as a political force* because it is not only open to anyone, but evangelical, and as a credo scrupulously absent of specifics on matters of public policy, rendering unto Caesar that which is Caesar's, and to God that which is God's. Mohammedanism, which constituted a serious threat to the Christian world during the extension of the Ottoman Empire, was also open and fiercely evangelical. But like Judaism, Islam was and is rigidly anti-separationist on the specifics of church and state.

The economic impulse of the Christian credo may appear to be biased toward egalitarianism and socialist forms, leaning away from income growth toward income redistribution through its counsel of brotherhood and charity. Income growth, obviously, is maximized for those who have when they never need share with those who have not. Freedom is maximized and equality minimized when those who still have fish are free to keep them all and those who have none are free to starve. But there is nothing in Christianity's doctrine that would specify to the leader of the fishing community what that balance should be and under what variable conditions it should shift. Over the centuries, the church as an institution has shifted along this spectrum, supporting growth and freedom in good times and supporting redistribution and equality during contractions.

During the long contraction of the Middle Ages, the church slipped from the role of private counselor of brotherhood and charity into a frequently corrupt instrument of inept rulers. It became specific in legislating church law against the taking of interest on money and against "profit." These strictly egalitarian measures would have brought about sure economic collapse and, probably, the collapse of the church itself had not the Jews been on hand to lend money and take profits in trade under no fear of damnation.

Judaism, like Confucianism, treated itself as a closed system. But unlike Confucianism, which merely counseled against foreign involvement and urged self-sufficiency, Judaic law emphatically prohibited racial mixing ("race" used here in the sense of common lineage or tribal stock). The prohibition was specifically drawn out of fear that the elaborate rigidities of the Mosaic code could not be sustained if alien ideas breached the system. It is as if one of the tribes of our earliest fragmented political economy designed a way of solving the economic and social issues within the tribe, but feared the method would fail if a broader consensus had to be reached. Evangelism was shunned; the requirement of circumcision was the equivalent of China's wall, for it explicitly aimed at insuring racial loyalty by making race, in Durant's words, ultimately unconcealable.

Judaism's powerful and benevolent religious impulse has sustained it for twenty-six hundred years. But its economic impulse contains this subtle bias against redistribution with its neighbors, and it is this bias which has invited persecution through the ages. In periods of general economic expansion, persecution of the Jews has receded—notably during the nineteenth century—while persecution has intensified during sharp contractions, the worst period being in Germany following World War I. Jews, after all, were always in the position of being creditors during periods of contraction, driven to sustain themselves in commerce and finance not because of any "natural" ability as traders and moneylenders, but because of the pressures of Christian laws. Because Jews were prohibited from owning Christian slaves, they could not economically compete as farmers, and Jews became farmers only where they lived under Islamic law.

Jews not only monopolized money-lending prior to the fourteenth century, when Christian prohibitions against usury broke down. The dispersion of Jews throughout the known world, east and west, also gave them international advantages in global trade and finance because family and tribal linkages were maintained on an international scale. The earliest terrible pogroms against the Jews occurred in northern Europe after the year 1000, the year of the "millenium," when Christians (but not Jews) believed the world would come to an end with the second coming of Christ. As the year approached, more and more Christians tended to become debtors and Jews creditors, Christians naturally believing they would not have to pay off loans after 1000. Additionally, Christians tended to give their wealth to the church, hoping to secure favorable positions in the afterlife, while Jews continued to pass their wealth on to their children. When the world did not end in 1000 A.D., economic tensions were inevitable, and for the following three centuries Jews were slaughtered throughout Europe in Crusades and pogroms.

The fact that the Jews throughout the ages have been a mighty force behind the expansiveness of the global economy has in no small way contributed to their survival. In no less a way has this Jewish instinct for survival through promotion of general economic growth contributed to the survival of Christianity, as in the Middle Ages. For while Christianity is not intrinsically biased on the economic issue, neither does it provide a counterforce. In other words, during contraction the Christian impulse is wholly redistributive, which does nothing to arrest the contraction and turn the economy once again toward expansion.

For this reason, Christianity cannot endure long periods of contraction; its bias toward charitable redistribution eventually feeds the contraction. In our hypothetical fishing village, for example, the Christian impulse would merely require the more able fishermen time and again to give up greater shares of their catch. They would eventually become less industrious and the general catch would decline, requiring even more Christian redistribution, and so on. Christianity needs and welcomes periods of economic growth to revive itself, but there is nothing in Christian doctrine or tradition that points a way toward growth.

Christianity thus weakened gradually as a faith in the closing centuries of the Middle Ages, sinking deeper and deeper into political support of egalitarianism that poisoned the initiative of the able, into persecution of the Jews, infidels, and scientists who were providing the only forces of real and potential economic expansion, and into preventing an advance in experimentation with political succession.

The church not only prohibited polygamy as a means by which the monarchs of Europe could broaden the talent pool of political leadership, but it prohibited divorce, and supported monarchs in their divine right to the throne. Given these constraints, the only avenues open to experimentation on the succession problem were relatively trivial. The supposedly eugenic notion that monarchs could not marry commoners was both a genetic limitation to a broadening of the talent pool and a barrier to the medium of exchange between the electorate and the political class.

On the other hand, the same limitation pushed monarchs into forging political alliances with each other—arranging royal marriages across national boundaries. This permitted some cross-fertilization of political perspectives, and kept open economic markets of a broader nature than might otherwise have been the case.

This was, however, only a tiny benefit against the negative forces that pushed toward explosion of the system. The blowup occurred with the Reformation. In England, Henry VIII, unable to produce a male heir with Catherine of Aragon, applied for permission to annul his marriage to her and was refused by the Vatican. In breaking this impasse by declaring himself head of the Church of England, Henry both opened the avenue of divorce to the succession problem and ended this western heavenly mandate. This opened the way to political revolution and representative government. At the same time, England was freed of the heavy taxes exacted by Rome. Henry squandered this cushion during his reign. But in broadening the talent pool through his marriage to Anne Boleyn, he gave England Elizabeth, who through determined frugalities used this cushion to nurse her nation back to a measure of prosperity. This gave England its head start over the rest of the western world in overcoming the long contraction.

In Germany, Martin Luther broke with the Roman church, over the church's selling of indulgences. Thus, a *proximate* cause of the Reformation here was economic. Contraction and war (which often results during a splintering of a political economy in contraction) had so shriveled national incomes that the percentage tithing of the church was no longer sufficient to sustain it and it had resorted to the taxing of gambling and prostitution and the promise of afterlife. In its break, though, Germany did not enjoy the same advantages as England because warfare increased as a result; Catholic and Protestant princes fought each other for thirty years (1618-1648) to resolve the issue.

In the century that followed, there occurred the first stirrings of economic advance in the world economy, fed by Elizabethan England, the commercial freedoms permitted by Protestantism, and the opening to the New World. The expenses of warfare eased throughout Europe as the New World provided an escape hatch for the most volatile political tensions; the malcontents of Europe voted with their feet by migrating to the colonies. This breath of expansion was just what the Catholic Church needed, and it not only revived through counter-reformation, but strengthened under the influence of the Jesuits. Only in France, with economic contraction continuing to the French revolution, did the Catholic Church reach its nadir both as an institution and as a faith.

Conventional perspectives view the French revolution as a mighty blow struck for equality and redistribution. But it was exactly the opposite. With the coincidence of the American revolution, it ended the long contraction in the West that had begun with the accession of Commodus in 180 A.D. On the eve of the revolution in France, the economy was strangled by taxation and government regulation that had evolved under the redistributive pressures of contraction. The revolution itself was a blind, angry rebellion against the strangulation caused by this system—voting by guillotine only after the imperious class of French political leaders steadfastly refused to hear the electorate's other attempts at communicating malaise, corruption, and despair. The French electorate could have no idea what would emerge in place of their oppressors, only that it had to be better. This is why a violent revolution is so rare; it is the least efficient means by which the electorate votes—even the assassin, in "voting," has a rough sense of who will follow as successor. A revolution reaches critical mass when the electorate knows what will follow cannot be worse.

At the moment of revolution in France, it is almost impossible to see how the system of income redistribution could have been worse. According to Hippolyte Taine, a French historian of the nineteenth century:

Before 1789, the peasant proprietor paid, on 100 francs income, 14 to the seignior, 14 to the clergy, 53 to the state, and kept only 18 or 19 to himself; after 1800 he pays nothing of his 100 francs of income to the seignior or the clergy; he pays little to the state, only 25 francs to the commune and *departement*, and keeps 70 for his pocket.[3]

Even replacement by a system that would leave the electorate with 30 percent of its production instead of a mere 18 or 19 percent would have permitted the populace to sink back into sullen despair. The electorate could not have foreseen the emergence of Napoleon Bonaparte, whose political and financial wizardry reproduced the prescriptions of the Caesars in putting the global political economy back on the rails it had jumped under Commodus.

Napoleon refused to talk to the economists of the day, who had been largely responsible for the economic schemes that had brought on the revolution. He brushed aside the income-redistribution ideas of Charles Fourier on the communal production of goods with an insight that one would not expect to find inside a crowned head. On Christmas day, 1799, he wrote his brother Lucien:

> Whilst an individual owner, with a personal interest in his property, is always wide awake, and brings his plans to fruition, communal interest is inherently sleepy and unproductive, because individual enterprise is a matter of instinct, and communal enterprise is a matter of public spirit, which is rare.[4]

It was because of Napoleon's insistence that the individual entrepreneur, who pre-revolution could keep only 18 or 19 percent of his production, could post-revolution keep 70 percent of it. The grateful electorate, as it had with Augustus, thrust the emperorship upon Napoleon as if to cement him and his progeny in place. But this left France no closer than Rome had been to a solution to the succession problem. Napoleon's progeny, after all, could immediately yield another Commodus and where would the electorate be? The difference fifteen hundred years made, though, was that the global electorate had pushed forward on the succession problem while awaiting Napoleon's economic and political insights. The problem for the electorate in 1800 was to merge a superior system of succession with Napoleon's superior economics (which we will detail later in this book). In 1800, the most advanced system of succession was probably the British combination of parliament and crown; the infant experiment in American democracy was just getting under way.

In 1793 Britain invited war with France upon hearing of the beheading of Louis XVI, and France complied. The war, then, was fought explicitly over the historic succession problem, and amid the democratic chaos of France under pressure of war, Napoleon was cast up to take charge.

By 1805, Napoleon had cut so relentless a swath through the crowned heads of Europe allied with George III that only Britain, Sweden, and Russia had not recognized the Emperor of France. Like Julius Caesar, Napoleon had extended the French Empire by a conquest that was also a liberating force to the degree his economic and political ideas knit together a larger marketplace. Like Augustus, Napoleon knew when he had gone far enough in extending his polyglot domain. In 1805 he pleaded with George III for peace. The plea was rejected and

Napoleon, unwilling to wage war defensively, embarked on a plan to starve England into submission through blockade.

His plan, we can now say with hindsight, was doomed from the start because of a flaw in Napoleon's understanding of international economics. He did not realize until it was too late that the only closed political economy is the world economy. Britain could not be starved into submission by blockade unless she were totally cut off from the world. As long as Britain could trade with any nation outside France, it was thus trading indirectly with France. And the more successful Napoleon was in pushing British trade away from France and the Empire, the more he weakened France.

As the war proceeded, the port cities of France decayed and merchants withered in support of the blockade. By 1810-11, Napoleon was forced to sell licenses for certain types of trade with Britain even as war continued, chipping away at his own plan in order to relieve political tensions at his back. When he could no longer finance his campaigns by exacting taxes solely from conquered lands, and added French taxes on top of the continual drain of French sons for slaughter in war, Napoleon had essentially lost the support of the electorate. He thereby lost the struggle over the succession question to Edmund Burke, William Pitt, and the British parliament.

The global electorate had come out far ahead as a result of these struggles. The French revolution had weakened monarchy and advanced democracy. Napoleon's victories had spread the modern Napoleonic Code through Europe, breaking down the remnants of the feudal system by freeing peasants from the land. In 1815, victory over Napoleon having ended twenty-two years of war, the British people clamored so loudly for an abrupt end to the crushing war taxes they had borne that their parliament gave in, ignoring the warnings of the economists that financial chaos would ensue. As Napoleon had demonstrated, it is prosperity that ensues when oppressive taxes are lifted. For sixty years, the British economy boomed as Britain built its own empire, lifting the entire world in one degree or another to a higher level of prosperity.

Blessed with such a long stretch of economic growth, the Catholic Church sprang back to robust life in Europe and, with the Protestant faiths, enjoyed a dazzling renaissance in the United States, which had gotten onto a balanced track of growth and distribution, freedom and equality, surpassing anything the world had ever seen. In 1875, the prime minister of the most powerful nation in the world was a Jew, Benjamin Disraeli.

The global electorate had come a long way, but there would be a long way still to go. The monarchs of Europe would insist on one last fratricidal war that would remove monarchy as a serious contender on the succession question. Great Britain would unlearn the economic wisdom that had brought it an empire, and would thus lose an empire. The twentieth century would bring a multitude of revolutions and political experiments, and a second world war necessitated by stupendous economic errors made by a handful of political leaders in the young democracies.

CHAPTER 3

The Electorate
Understands Economics

If the electorate as a whole is wiser than any individual member in understanding its interests, it is wiser than any economist or group of economists. Economics is merely the study of why and how people produce, distribute, and consume goods. The electorate does not have to be taught economics as a prerequisite to making wise political selections. Individuals learn the laws of economics from the cradle, within a political framework, and by early childhood have a fully developed sense of them. Every member of the electorate has the same basic understanding— whether they are taught it in New Hampshire or Outer Mongolia. And while they have different ideas on what they want to produce, distribute, and consume, they all follow the same laws of economics in the process by which they do so.

In the basic political model we have drawn, the global electorate is seen pushing, at every opportunity, in the direction of systems capable of producing superior politicians. This *political* process has as its ultimate aim a solution to the basic *economic* problem that for all time has confronted the global electorate, which is the tension between income growth and income distribution. Before we fit the history of the last century to this model and surmise implications for the present and future of the global electorate, development of the economic model is necessary. It is necessary in order to support our theorem that the electorate as a whole be wiser than its component parts in understanding its interests. It must, then, be wiser than any economist or group of economists in its understanding of economics, for unlike a physical scientist—who can know something his fellow human beings do not know (the existence of a previously unknown element, for example), an economist is a social scientist whose sole task is to study why people produce, distribute, and consume. The only way an economist can know something his fellow human beings do not know about this process is if people themselves do not know why they produce, distribute, and consume. And if this can be true, if an economist can have a wisdom superior to the people, our political model breaks down and forces us back into the Jeffersonian mode of educating people to their indiscretions. Our assertion, then, is that the electorate does understand economics, individually and *per force* collectively.

The very concept of economics, first of all, could not exist if there were only one individual. One individual would know precisely why and how he produced and consumed and thus would have no need of an economist. It takes at least two people before the concept of economics becomes possible, both because each does not know precisely why the other produces and consumes and because the notion of trade emerges.

In this hypothetical world of two people, one does not teach the other economics. They teach one another. That is, they communicate, one to the other, why it is they are producing, what they wish to consume, and under what conditions they are willing to trade. The process begins at birth, and by the time an individual has reached early childhood he has learned the basic laws of economics and has usually developed a sophistication in employing them. When we speak of economic "laws," of course, we do not have in mind any that are as inviolable as the laws of physics. Where human behavior is concerned, it is generally possible to imagine anecdotes that are exceptions to the common "law."

The economic law that most nearly approximates the nature of a physical law in its universality and inviolability is the law of supply and demand. But this is only because the law of supply and demand—that supply always equals demand—is less a law than a definition giving economists a starting point as they set out to study why people produce, distribute, and consume. In a sense, supply is defined as being demand and thus the "law" becomes as axiomatic as "a rose is a rose."

Consider an economy that consists of only two people, Jones, who fishes, and Smith, who picks coconuts. For there to be an economic event in this economy, each person has to be both a producer (supplier) and a consumer (demander). Jones has to want some of Smith's coconuts and Smith has to want some of Jones' fish, or there can be no economic event. Similarly, Jones has to be willing to give up some of his fish and Smith some of his coconuts. And finally, for the event to take place Jones and Smith must be able to agree on the *terms of trade*, i.e., be able to "come to terms." If Jones is willing to supply one fish for two coconuts and Smith agrees, the terms of trade are that one fish equals two coconuts or one coconut equals half a fish.

Yet even if Jones and Smith cannot agree on terms and do not trade, supply still equals demand, in the sense that Jones demands *his own* fish and Smith demands *his own* coconuts in preference to an exchange. The total or aggregate supply of goods in this two-person economy consists of one fish and two coconuts and the total or aggregate demand for goods consists of one fish and two coconuts. The purpose of this elaboration is to make clear that trade is not required for supply to equal demand. If Smith picks another coconut and Jones still refuses the terms, aggregate supply is one fish and three coconuts and aggregate demand is also one fish and three coconuts.

It is important to bear this in mind because, as we will show in later chapters, modern economic theories often falter by simply assuming that an increase in aggregate demand or an increase in aggregate supply is accompanied by an increase in transactions. Modern theories also tend to treat the law of supply and demand as if it only operated in one direction, as if, in a two-person economy, one is the supplier and the other the demander, and that supply equals demand at a single "price." But as we see, in every transaction there are two equations and two prices: Jones' demand equals Smith's supply; Smith's demand equals Jones' supply; the price of one fish is two coconuts; the price of one coconut is one-half fish. When transactions occur in a complex world economy this does not change. Price is not a single number, but a ratio.

This two-equation law of supply and demand is learned in infancy. The infant demands a clean diaper and is willing to supply peace and quiet in exchange. Mother demands peace and quiet and is willing to supply a clean diaper in exchange. The terms of trade are arranged. Baby whimpers and mother hears, but tarries on the telephone. Baby screams and mother hangs up and changes the diaper. One scream equals one diaper. The price of one diaper is one scream.

In this same example, the infant learns another of the important concepts of economics. All economic activity occurs "on the margin." One, two, three whimpers elicit no economic event. Nor does a muffled cry. Baby and mother come to terms at one scream. The infant increases its bid in what amounts to an auction market, bidding against Mom's interest in telephone conversation. The terms that bring about economic activity are not arranged until bidding hits a scream, which can be cashed in for a unit of peace and quiet. The point of activity is called the margin.

The concept of marginality is crucial to an understanding of economic behavior. Everyone knows about "the straw that broke the camel's back." It is always that "last straw" that causes a change in the situation, the marginal straw, even though it weighs exactly the same as each of the other 10,000. But it is one thing to see that change occurs on the margin and quite another to understand that each straw is equally to blame for the breaking of the camel's back. Very few people *think* on the margin, but everyone *acts* on the margin, which is why it is so hard to see that the electorate, as a whole, understands economics.

To get our meaning, consider the camel again. He does not blame the last straw for breaking his back, but all 10,001. If straws could think, though, each of the first 10,000 would not blame themselves for doing in the camel, but would blame the last. The last straw, seeing clearly that his addition caused the camel to break down, would be the only one of the 10,001 to both act and think on the margin. If the straws were replaced by an equivalent weight contained in one log, which had a single mind, that log would both break the camel's back and *understand* that it had caused the event.

It is in this sense that we argue that while individual members of the electorate do not seem to understand economics, in the aggregate they not only behave economically but understand the process. Individuals always behave as if they understood economics and the concept of marginality, but very few intellectualize their behavior.

The child wants to get his father's attention and says, "Daddy!" Father continues talking to mother about the office crisis. The child says "Daddy, daddy, I want to say something." Father remains oblivious. The child comes close and pulls his sleeve and asks again to be heard, and finally father breaks his discussion with mother and turns to the child. If you could ask the child what it was that got his father's attention, chances are he would think that it was the yanking of his father's sleeve. If he could think as well as act on the margin, though, he would see that it was a steady verbal prodding marginally capped with the physical contact.

Individuals who can think on the margin always have an advantage over those who cannot. In suffering less illusion, they have greater control over their lives. Parents more often think on the margin than do their children. Successful parents think on the margin more than unsuccessful parents. Mother sees father, for what appears to be little reason, yelling at the children. If she does think on the margin, she will probe to find out what is bothering him, thereby removing from his back not the 10,001st straw, but several down in the rest of the bundle. A woman may suffer in silence a steady accumulation of grievances against her husband, only to "boil over" as a result of some slight her husband considers trivial, and he will bark back at her for her seemingly irrational behavior. But if he can think on the margin, he will be able to replay in his mind the grievances she has accumulated against him and let her "blow off steam."

The same is true of managers, politicians, economists. The most successful are not necessarily those with the greatest raw intelligence, but those with the widest life experience feeding an ability to think on the margin. A character in Anthony Powell's *Dance to the Music of Time* observes that, "The smallest alteration in a poem, or a novel, can change its whole emphasis, whole meaning. The same is true of any given situation in life too, though few are aware of that."

A successful businessman knows he cannot simply put his son through Harvard Business School and then hand him the keys to the vice-president's office. The youth will be at a disadvantage unless he spends time working his way up, from the mail room to the shipping room through the shop floor, etc., if only for a few weeks each. The experience gives the youth a feel and sense of the whole enterprise that allows him a crucial, marginal advantage over competitors who do not have that simple, accumulated picture in their minds.

So too with politicians. Political genius lies in reacting to tension in the body politic not by direct surgery, but by removal or neutralization of some seemingly unrelated straw. Here is how Sir Isaiah Berlin puts it in "The Hedgehog and the Fox":

> Aquinas is praised by Maistre not for being a better mathematician than d'Alembert or Monge; Kutuzov's virtue does not, according to Tolstoy, consist in his being a better, more scientific theorist of war than Pfuel or Paulucci. These great men are wiser, not more knowledgeable; it is not their deductive or inductive reasoning that makes them masters; their vision is "profounder," they see something the others fail to see; they see the way the world goes, what goes with what and what never will be brought together; they see what can be and what cannot; how men live and to what ends, what they do and suffer, and how and why they act, and should act, thus and not otherwise. This "seeing" purveys, in a sense, no fresh information about the universe; it is an awareness of the interplay of the imponderable with the ponderable, of the "shape" of things in general or of a specific situation, or of a particular character . . .[1]

If there is an outbreak of crime in the community, there are always some politicians who immediately call for a violent crackdown, suspension of civil liberties, and a return to the death penalty. The electorate, which *must have* a marginal straw removed—any of the 10,001—will embrace such harsh measures only if other politicians do not offer indirect reliefs, perhaps measures to make employment marginally more attractive than crime.*

---

*Explicitly on this point, T'ai Tsung, one of China's greatest emperors (A.D. 627-50), could "think on the margin": "If I diminish expenses, lighten the taxes, employ only honest officials, so that people have clothing enough, this will do more to abolish robbery than the employment of the severest punishments."[2] Durant also relates a story in Plutarch that exemplifies thinking on the margin: ". . . an epidemic of suicide among the women of Miletus was suddenly and completely ended by an ordinance decreeing that self-slain women should be carried naked through the marketplace to their burial."[3]

It is difficult to realize that the electorate understands economics unless you think on the margin. The electorate must be seen as a faceless aggregate of individuals that moves rationally and glacially on the margin, even though the individuals who compose the electorate seem to be acting irrationally and abruptly. How often do we hear the news report that "17 million shares were traded on the New York Stock Exchange today. Prices were unchanged"? Imagine the volatility, the din of 17 million shares being traded, fortunes made and lost, people buying or selling on the spur of the moment, on a hunch, or after months of careful deliberation. Yet on the margin, prices were unchanged. How often does the family debate all Saturday afternoon over which movie it will go to that night, deciding after all to stay home? On the margin, prices were unchanged.

While the man in the street behaves in a way that contributes to the margin, it is plain that he does not often think on the margin. The smaller the marketplace, the easier it is for him to do both. In the family unit, he can comprehend the elements that went into the decision not to go to the movies on Saturday night. But few people directly relate their economic behavior to the activity in the world marketplace. When you buy a pound of coffee, the merchant is not right there at your elbow putting up the price and you thus are not reminded that the purchase has a microscopic impact on the world coffee price.

Even the infant learns to both act and think on the margin when small changes in behavior result in identifiable "price changes." The infant learns, for example, something that politicians and economists frequently forget, which is that there are always two rates of taxation that produce the same revenue. When the infant lies silently and motionless in his crib upon awakening, mother remains in some other room. The "tax rate" on mother is zero, yielding zero attentiveness. On the other hand, when baby screams all the time demanding attention, even when fed and dry, he discovers that mother also remains in the other room and perhaps even closes the nursery door. The tax rate is 100 percent, also yielding zero attentiveness. The infant gradually learns that by making some sound instead of remaining motionless he gets a measure of attentiveness and, at the other end of the scale, also gets a measure of attentiveness if he makes less sound. What a complex, perplexing problem confronting the infant. A steady increase in the rate of taxation seems to elicit a steady increase in the amount of revenue, or attentiveness, until a point is reached at which a further increase in the rate of taxation is followed by a decline in revenue. As if this problem were not difficult enough, the critical point at which an increase in tax causes a fall in revenue always seems to be shifting. At times, it only seems to require a happy little gurgling to bring a bottle, a diaper or a cuddling. At other times it takes a steady scream. The infant has to sort all this out. It seems to require no tax at all to get fed most of the time, because there is a schedule. There seems a definite range of taxes to get a diaper change. There is a wide range of taxes when baby just wants to cuddle and play, a range that seems to vary between daytime and nighttime. And when baby feels bad, feverish, any level of complaining seems to bring attentiveness, even if mother and father must take turns all night walking the floor.

By the time the infant is crawling, he has made rough assessments of which tax schedules should be used under different circumstances, and each day becomes more sophisticated in understanding the variables in this economy. It is always harder to get mother to play when mother is on the telephone than when mother is not. When mother is fixing dinner, it is very difficult to get her to play, but this means father will be home soon and it is usually easy to get him to play. The infant begins to perceive that there are other forces levying taxes on mother.

At this same stage of development, the infant usually is faced with a "tax schedule" for the first time. A mobile infant will explore indiscriminately. For the baby's safety and for the protection of items that mother does not want broken during these explorations, baby must be disciplined. Baby reaches for a porcelain figure and mother says "No, no!" Baby reacts to the sharpness in mother's voice with a glance, but touches the figure anyway. Mother slaps the infant's hand lightly and again admonishes, "No, no!" The baby will cry, but usually will try again, to make sure the relationships are what they seemed to be. It does not take more than two or three attempts before the infant understands the tax schedule. But if baby proceeds on explorations and everything within his reach becomes a no-no, the tax rate mother is attempting to apply approaches 100 percent and some form of rebellion will follow. The wise mother will place a few harmless, glittery items in locations within the infant's reach so that explorations from one part of the room to another are rewarded rather than punished. The parent who does not understand that there are two tax rates that yield the same revenue is a poor political leader in the family unit, and should not be surprised if the prohibitively taxed infant rebels in one way or another—becoming an incorrigible terror (revolutionary) or withdrawing into himself (the only form of emigration open to a child).*

*The wise ruler will never surround his adversaries with "no-nos." James I's prohibitions against the practice of Catholicism in an England two-thirds Catholic left no avenue but the attempted assassination by Guy Fawkes and his fellows in 1604. The prohibitive taxes imposed by the Allies on Germany at Versailles produced Hitler and

By the time children are three or four years old, they have acquired such a body of information by studying tax schedules and their variables within the family that they can consciously "think on the margin." One day a child will, say, spill his milk and mother will serenely mop it up. Another time, mother will fly into a rage, but after composing herself will signal in other ways that she is sorry for losing her temper. The child comes to understand that mother has tax burdens being levied by other forces. It is not unusual to see a well-adjusted child emerge from a violent household, where political leadership of the parents has broken down. The child is simply superior in thinking on the margin than are his parents, sensing that when they are screaming at him he is merely serving as a medium of communication for them.*

A child's principle trading partners are his parents, and perhaps brothers and sisters. When the child is six or seven years old, he has to be formally taught money values, and the idea of a currency being a medium of exchange. By that time he has learned most of what he is going to learn in his lifetime about general trade and money concepts. Even before a child can communicate verbally, it is clear he has learned the precision that trade involves. That is, the child wants something from mother and knows something must be traded in return, and that those two somethings will be of roughly equal value. The child is happy when the terms of trade are struck and mother seems happier too. The message that both sides benefit from trade is one repeated thousands of times in early childhood.

"If you eat your dinner, I will give you an ice cream," says mother to the toddler, who has thus far shown no interest in eating. A variety of economic concepts are directly involved in this offer of trade.

---

war with Germany in 1939. Roosevelt's oil embargo against Japan left no avenue but that which led to Pearl Harbor. Truman's atomic bombing of Nagasaki, and perhaps Hiroshima, would have been unnecessary if he had mitigated his demand for unconditional surrender by a marginal amount, permitting Japan to retain the Emperorship. President Kennedy wisely left Nikita Khrushchev an avenue out during the Cuban Missile Crisis (1962) by responding to the more conciliatory of two cablegrams received during the "eyeball-to-eyeball" escalation. Kennedy's determination to box in Cuba, which included plans to assassinate Fidel Castro, left Castro no avenue but the assassination of Kennedy, which followed by a month (November, 1963) the assassination of South Vietnamese President Diem. Diem's removal had the implicit support of the Kennedy administration.

*A politician rises to statesmanship when he can not only absorb personal attacks with equanimity, but also senses that the attacks are communiques from the electorate. Something else must be gnawing at the electorate which must be composed. One of the most striking personal characteristics of Henry IV, who ended the religious wars of France in the seventeenth century, was his toleration of personal criticism. Franklin Roosevelt and Dwight Eisenhower, renowned as "father figures" among American Presidents, remained placid in the face of personal attacks. President Richard Nixon was politically destroyed largely because he took personal abuse personally instead of perceiving its importance as communication from the electorate.

Up until now, mother and child have been bartering. Mother comes through with a diaper and baby stops crying. Goods and services are directly swapped in the marketplace. Now mother is offering to trade an ice cream for a "good" that must first be manufactured by the child, i.e., dinner must first be eaten. The child must invest in production on mother's promise to pay ice cream. Thus, the concept of "money" is introduced, in this case money being mother's *credit*, the medium of exchange in the transaction. Credit is nothing more than the promise to pay specified goods or an equivalent in currency upon receipt of goods. Money is a credit instrument just as, in the example, mother's verbal promise is a credit instrument.

The child ponders the offer. If he does not eat the dinner not only will there not be any ice cream, but mother will be irritated and unpleasant. Besides, the dinner isn't too bad anyway, there's just too much. The child silently undertakes the contract, finally leaving a little of the meat, a little of the potato and a little of the vegetable, and announces "finished." Mother, who did not expect the child to eat *that* much, accepts as if the contract were completed in full. The child, using the credit instrument as if it were money, asks for pudding instead, and mother, accepting the equivalency of pudding to ice cream, produces it. After they have gone through this exercise a few times, mother and child know precisely the equivalencies of the credit instrument offered by mother and the exact amount of dinner that can be left uneaten with the contract still considered filled. How frequently is there a final squabble, with mother insisting that the child eat one last bit of meat or two or three kernels of corn! In microcosm, we are seeing the United States trade Iran one Boeing 747 for 2,111,212 barrels of oil!

Observe, too, how rapidly the child demonstrates sophistication in understanding inflation, i.e., the decline in the monetary standard—in this case mother's promise. Say the child only eats a few portions of the dinner, asks for the ice cream, and gets it! The monetary standard has declined, and henceforth mother's promise cannot secure the same contract. In a subsequent event, the child may even assume that if he merely rearranges the food on his plate ice cream will be forthcoming. If mother now insists on strict compliance with the offer, the child will in some way resist, following the same path as if no offer of trade had ever been made. If, for example, the child is serious about not eating and mother announces that he will sit at the table until he finishes (in effect boxing the child in with a 100 percent tax rate and no escape), the child may impose an even higher tax rate on the parent by gagging on a mouthful of food, which almost invariably breaks the parent's will. Mother realizes that the price of the "good" she desires has become so exorbitant that she must drop out of the bidding altogether.

Another avenue open to the child if he is boxed in by mother is to make a speculative capital investment, sitting at the table and awaiting daddy's arrival from work. A capital investment is simply the giving up of current consumption in the hope of being able to consume in the future. A child who is given the option of eating dinner or not eating dinner and does not want to eat will leave the table and play (thereby consuming a pleasurable leisure activity). A child who is given no option and refuses to eat must sit at the table, giving up that current consumption of pleasurable leisure activity. He wants, more than to play, not to eat. If he believes there is a chance his father will have a more lenient attitude toward eating than mother, he will make this speculative investment, giving up leisure for a considerable time in the hope of father coming home and talking mother out of the rigidity of her position.

In mother and father, after all, the child has a diversified portfolio. From infancy, individuals learn the economic importance of portfolio diversification—that you should not put all your eggs in one basket. The importance lies in the oddity that you can reduce the riskiness of your investment by adding an even riskier investment to your holdings. Mother may seem like a sufficient investment for a long while, a solid AT&T yielding a steady 6 percent return day after day, But one day the bottom drops out of AT&T; mother is in ill humor. And Dad, who had been dragging along with almost no yield, suddenly spurts ten points on the market. No matter how stern a disciplinarian father may be, there are days when he has keener insights into what is bothering a child than does mother, especially if mother's sudden irritability toward the child has an external cause. The child cultivates the differing perspectives of his parents, who will marvel at the ability of a two-year-old to "play one off against the other," which is an unnecessarily negative way of describing the process. If the child feels a slight, an injustice, an inconsistency on mother's part, and is unable to communicate the grievance to mother, perhaps father will understand and somehow compose the differences with mother. The child, who has little but his affection to trade within this political economy, learns to use it skillfully. At times, it seems the child acts blatantly, crudely, as when he runs to father seeking consolation after a scolding by mother, or vice versa. Under extreme duress, he explodes at mother, "I don't love you any more." But see how difficult it is, when the child is at peace and thoughtful, to get him or her to tell you who is preferred, mother or father. It is neither politic nor economic to answer such questions, which would diminish the child's stock in trade.

The wise political leader and the successful businessman diversify their portfolios, always making room in their entourages of aides and advisers for diverse views, and in a positive way play their counselors against each other. The task of the political leader, after all, is to discern the wishes of the electorate. If he has in his cabinet of advisers representatives of only selected segments of the electorate, even if they are all Rhodes scholars (perhaps especially if they are all Rhodes scholars), the views of those unrepresented will have to come to him by different, less efficient ways, perhaps in the form of a crisis that could have been avoided had he a broader counsel. As a political class, American Democrats have understood the economics of portfolio diversification far more than modern-day Republicans have. That is, given the idea that the politician's aim is to determine the consensus of his constituents, a "ticket" balanced ethnically, racially, and religiously is marginally superior to a ticket of Rhodes scholars. A Republican businessman who would not think of putting his entire fortune into AT&T shares, and who spends fortunes out of the corporate treasury in market analysis trying to find out what people want to buy, runs for political office and surrounds himself with advisers who think exactly as he does, and then grumbles about "anti-business sentiment" when he loses badly at the polls.

Similarly, Republicans are publicly appalled (and Democrats privately appalled) at the pressure of black organizations and feminist groups for quota systems at the executive level of government and business. The notion *seems* uneconomic, a practice that should weaken both government and business because it seems to bear no relationship to intellectual merit. But a fixed quota is a crude way of expressing the essence of an idea that is sound and economic. If the top ten officials of the U.S. Treasury are white males with Phi Beta Kappa keys, the riskiness of this portfolio would be reduced by firing two, and appointing a black and a woman with lesser scholarly credentials, but with the ability the white male scholars lack to "think black" and "think female." These abilities have a "marginal utility," to use economic jargon, that outweighs their lesser credentials. "Thinking black" and "thinking female" are something that cannot be acquired by white males, but are valuable assets in government. Pressures for quotas fall off rapidly with the first such appointments made because, in every policy-making group, the electorate understands that marginal utility diminishes rapidly. (Replacing a second scholar with a black or woman of lesser credentials probably weakens the group.)

The same analysis applies in the reverse. Blacks and women enjoy a marginal advantage because of their blackness and femaleness as first additions to a policy group. But because the one cannot think white and the other cannot think male they have a marginal disadvantage in rising to the top of the group, and thus have to be superior in other ways to compensate. Of course, when the policy group itself is black or female—a political group or business enterprise—it is just as difficult for a white male to lead.

In earliest childhood, we discover these concepts, broadening our portfolios to embrace the marginal utility of grandparents, uncles, aunts, and playmates. At the same time we are discovering our own marginal utility in the portfolios of others. We do something cute and there is general laughter and approval, do it again and receive diminished attention from mother and father, do it a third time and get blank stares. The cycle, though, is repeated with grandparents, and so on, until the cuteness has worn thin generally, and a new routine must be developed.

Every individual within the electorate learns these concepts. It is not illogical to assume the electorate understands them too. When a political leader diversifies his portfolio of advisers, adding perspectives that cut against his own tastes and those of his party—devil's advocates—individual members of the electorate may express discomfort. They are apprehensive that the political leader may be influenced to change his views, as when a conservative Republican President admits a liberal to his inner circle. But the electorate as a whole will invariably approve of the opening of channels of communication to the political leader.

What is it that the electorate is not thought to understand about economics? As noted in the opening chapter, the most common complaint on the left is that voters do not sufficiently appreciate the "fact" that we are running out of planetary resources, that there are "limits to growth." On the right, the complaint is that voters do not understand any longer that free enterprise is superior to government manipulation of the economy, and that they are too willing to support political leaders who are fiscally irresponsible, i.e., borrow against the future to live it up in the present.

The small child, though, sees through the arguments of the Malthusians and the Club of Rome. Yes, there are physical limitations in the child's world, but they can be relentlessly overwhelmed by intellectual growth.

Indeed, to a child, life must at times seem to consist almost entirely of physical bounds and intellectual boundlessness. As he learns to crawl, to stand, to eat with a spoon, to climb stairs, to tie a shoe or to fit together a jigsaw puzzle, he learns again and again that seemingly insurmountable physical boundaries can be leaped by intellectual effort. Malthusians of any age are victims of their own despair, as if, having failed to put the puzzle together on the third attempt, they fling the pieces to the ground in frustration. The electorate itself, though, pays little heed to the despairing, except when they attempt to prove their case by imposing political limitations on intellectual growth. The global electorate has been so relentless and efficient over the centuries in punishing those who punish intellectual heresy that when men of science or learning today complain of political persecution, what they usually mean is that the taxpayers are refusing to subsidize them in lavish style.*

The politician who argues that the amount of land on earth is finite, or that there is just so much petroleum and natural gas under the earth's crust, will get no argument from the electorate. But the politician who acts as if these truisms mean the electorate must accommodate to policies of dearth—as if we are now up against planetary limits to growth—does not command a broad following. The electorate knew a dozen years ago that land is finite and the supply of petroleum is not inexhaustible. Why was the world, especially the United States, so bouyantly optimistic about the planetary cornucopia a dozen years ago? In fact, at that time the price of land and petroleum *in terms of other goods* was falling. What has happened in a dozen years to turn exhilaration about the earth's resources to despair, with no end in sight to a steady rise in the price of land and petroleum in terms of other goods? It cannot be an unexpected surge in population growth. In fact, birth rates have fallen worldwide from the anticipated paths of the early 1960s. Nor has demand for land and petroleum risen above the projected paths of a dozen years ago.

What has happened, simply, is that in 1966 the global economy entered a period of contraction. The global electorate has been aware of this contraction even though their politicians have not, for the global

*American conservatives viewed the 1970 congressional decision to kill the U.S. supersonic transport as a victory for the neo-Malthusians, representing a new anti-technology mood among the populace. They would have felt better, as conservatives, had they seen the decision as representing taxpayer disenchantment with a multi-billion-dollar subsidy of an uneconomic aircraft.

electorate *is* the global economy and knows precisely when expansion turns to contraction. During contraction, it is not the planet that breaks down, suddenly deciding to yield fewer of its resources. Contractions occur because of intellectual failure by political leaders, and in this case the failure was both of the left and of the right. The planet is as bountiful now as it was a dozen years ago, and that will once again be apparent when the world political economy resumes its growth curve.

The despair among conservatives, who basically reject the limits-to-growth notion, follows their failure to understand the contraction process. When their erroneous prescriptions and theories are rejected by the electorate, conservatives are left with the inevitable prognosis that both democracy and free enterprise are doomed.

The basic failure of this general school lies in refusing to acknowledge that "free enterprise" as an economic style requires economic growth as a precondition, and that government intervention requires economic contraction as a precondition. In any imperfect political economy, which is to say all of them, there are simultaneously elements of growth and contraction—as in the hypothetical fishing community described in chapter 2. Free enterprise is obviously superior to government intervention in that limiting case where there is no element of contraction at all. The premiere interventionist among political theorists, Karl Marx, concedes the point magnanimously in forecasting "a withering away of the state" at the point of the ideal. If the world economy in general and the U.S. economy in particular has been moving away from growth since 1966, *on the margin*, it should be no surprise that the global electorate in general and the U.S electorate in particular have been moving away from free-enterprise fashions toward policies of regulation and redistribution. Conservatives, though, frequently see regulatory and redistributive policies as *causing* contraction, which of course leads to bemoaning the economic ignorance of the electorate. But if the electorate is faced with contraction as a continuing condition, and no political leaders present a satisfactory alternative, the electorate can only pick and choose among varying redistributive options. The options chosen may superficially appear to add to the contraction process, but they are merely the electorate's way of buying time until superior political leadership appears with a genuinely satisfactory growth alternative.

Imagine that in our hypothetical fishing community, for example, the political economy is dealt a blow by, say, the weather; several fishermen and their families are put on the brink between survival and extinction. In the community hall, a conclave of fishermen hears proposals from the political factions. The conservatives propose a free-enterprise solution (every man for himself), plus a balanced budget that will "wring inflation out of the economy." The liberals propose a regulatory and redistributive policy that requires unbalanced budgets and inflation. The conservatives will deplore the liberal program as being fiscally irresponsible and will mutter about the economic ignorance of the voters when the conclave rejects their program and endorses the liberal alternative. The conservatives are lucky, however, for if there had been no liberal alternative, the desperate fishermen would have had no recourse but civil war. By these lights, the policies that conservatives view as being fiscally irresponsible should be considered "growth" policies in a relative sense, inasmuch as they are the least contractionary of all those being offered by the political class.

Conservative failure to understand the contraction process does not mean that conservatives fully understand growth. For if they did, we would have fewer contractions. As we will detail later in this book, some of the worst economic errors of our time have been made by conservative theorists in the name of growth. At the same time, we will also see that liberals have made astonishing errors in the name of charity, i.e., redistribution. If it was not true that the electorate itself has an exquisite understanding of economics, and has picked its way whenever possible along correct paths, the world could never have survived the errors of professional economists. Before we examine the economic models that have been a burden to mankind, and explain their deficiencies, it is necessary that the economic component of our general theory be described and understood.

CHAPTER 4

The Economic Model: Capital

The highest priority of the electorate is its self-preservation. To survive, the electorate must save, or portions of the electorate and ultimately all of it will be eliminated by the vagaries of the planet. Politics is the mechanism by which the electorate, and all its component parts, attempts to maximize savings. Savings are defined as "capital." Military/police power a form of capital made necessary by the fragmentation of the world political economy. All economic systems are, in this sense, capitalistic, mixtures of private and state capitalism. Individuals are part of an economy's capital stock. The differences in existing systems reflect the inconclusiveness of experimentation by the global electorate in striving toward a system that maximizes capital and welfare.

The global electorate is, and always has been, striving toward an ideal system of political economics that can maximize welfare for all its component parts. More specifically, the driving force of civilization is a quest for a system that will maximize capital, for only when capital is maximized can welfare be maximized.

Capital is the wealth available to the global electorate for the production of goods and services. Capital exists in two forms, physical and intellectual. Physical capital includes all of the planet's natural resources, animal, vegetable and mineral, including the bone and sinew of mankind. This form of capital is fixed, broadly speaking, in the sense that matter cannot be created or destroyed. The utility of this physical stock of capital can be increased through the skillful application of intellectual capital, which is not only not fixed, but is for all practical purposes of limitless potential. Intellectual capital *arranges* the fixed capital stock in a way that produces net benefits to the global electorate. Not all "intelligence" is part of the intellectual capital stock, in the sense that misdirected intelligence can either destroy intellectual capital or arrange the fixed physical stock of capital in a way that subtracts from welfare.

In our two-person economy, Jones produces fish and Smith harvests coconuts, each employing their intellectual capital to increase the utility of the fixed physical stock of capital. Suppose Jones will not eat coconuts, and after acquiring sufficient fish to satisfy current needs and future contingencies, spends his idle time in leisure. Smith craves fish, but either does not have the skill to catch them or is barred by

Jones from using the available fishing grounds. Smith has several options. He can threaten Jones with death unless he is provided with fish. Jones, after weighing his chances in a struggle with Smith, decides to give up some fish, which requires him to fish longer hours to maintain his own desired stockpile of fish. Smith, to take this option, has also had to weigh his chances in a struggle with Jones, and also consider that even if Jones gives up fish peacefully, he will subsequently find a way to defend himself against future expropriations, even if it means sneaking up at night and killing the stronger Smith in his sleep. If either Jones or Smith is killed over the fish, there is a net subtraction from the capital of this two-person electorate.

If neither is killed, there is still a net subtraction from capital. Smith is willing to trade his willingness to be subject to silent attack by Jones for the desired fish, there being no subtraction from capital on that account. Jones, on the other hand, must give up leisure for work in order to maintain the same consumption and stockpile, thereby reducing the utility of the fixed physical capital stock.

Smith's other alternatives, though, will add to the total capital stock. Whereas he used his "intelligence" in the first negative option to subtract from capital, he now employs intellectual capital. He approaches Jones in friendly fashion, amuses him with conversation, listens to his troubles, flatters him and his skills as a fisherman. Jones "gives" him fish. Jones still must give up leisure in order to replace these fish, which he has essentially traded away for psychic rewards, but the rewards strike him as being of greater marginal value than the leisure given up.

Smith could also offer to make Jones his fishing spears, and Jones will net the same amount of leisure although he must increase the amount of time he spends fishing. Or Smith might fashion an ornament out of a coconut shell. While Jones does not like coconuts, he simply must have the ornament, and is willing to give up leisure (and fish) in order to obtain it. Through any of these options, Smith has applied his intellectual capital in a way that has increased the utility of the fixed capital stock, increasing welfare to the economy as a whole.*

This broad definition of capital is not the conventional definition, which roughly holds that capital consists of those goods that produce

---

*If we apply modern measurements of economic activity to these varying options, we find the greatest increase in Gross National Product (GNP) occurs in the first of Smith's options. Jones increases the production of fish, and both Jones and Smith increase their production of national defense. Where Smith is now making Jones' spears, there is no GNP increase on that account, only an increase in fish production. The same is true of an exchange of fish for flattery, which can't be measured in the GNP accounts. The trade of a fish for an ornament, though, will show an economy almost as statistically healthy as the first.

other goods, in the sense of a factory or a machine tool or, in this two-person economy, a fishing spear. But the broad definition is the one the global electorate is interested in. Global capital includes conventional capital goods, of course. But in the broad sense, all "wealth" capable of producing goods and services is counted as capital in the ledgers of the global electorate. As long as people get pleasure from gazing on the Mona Lisa, it is capital. Clean air and clean water are capital. A Beethoven symphony or a rock tune is capital. Parks, statues, buildings, houses, sewer lines, waterworks; all are capital. Capital is anything that is not used up in consumption, but continues to produce satisfaction to some component of the global electorate. Seed corn that produces corn is capital. Seed corn that is consumed is capital destroyed. Leonardo da Vinci is, to the global electorate, intellectual capital. When he died, that intellectual capital was destroyed. While he lived, he *arranged* the fixed physical capital stock—pigments and canvas, paper and ink—in a way that left enduring capital, which can be consumed again and again, without destruction. In the same way, singer Frank Sinatra has in our lifetimes been almost pure intellectual capital through the way he has arranged the fixed capital stock. When he dies, or permanently retires, the intellectual stock of capital will be diminished. But thereafter, the recordings and motion pictures of Sinatra will remain a part of global wealth until such time as no member of the global electorate values them as goods or services.

Education is capital, to the degree it produces goods and services. After much effort and frustration, the child learns to hold a spoon and feed himself. Thereafter, until he dies, that initial investment will yield satisfaction and service again and again. The child learns to read and write, to add and subtract, adding to his intellectual capital and the capital stock available to the global electorate. The skills he learns as a farmer, a carpenter, a surgeon, etc., add to his, and the world's, capital stock. The skills he learns as an actor, a poet, a banker, a journalist, etc., add to his, and the world's capital stock. Soldiers, policemen, gamblers, and prostitutes are part of this capital stock. Politicians, chairmen of the board, commissars, and bureaucrats are part of it. So are children and their parents.

The inclusiveness of this catalog follows from the definition, that any wealth *available* for the production of goods and services is part of the capital stock. But we are not merely adding up people. Human capital does not consist of the 4 billion people who inhabit the planet, but the intellectual resources that *move* those 4 billion people in their physical production of goods and services. There is no way of measuring this pool of capital, however. No number can even roughly approximate the breadth and depth of the world's potential supply of intellectual resources. If a child's ability to read a primer is part of his, and the world's capital stock, how many units of capital is it? What is the capital value, in units, of Jones' ability to spear fish? What is the capital value of Smith's ability to entertain Jones so that Jones spears more fish to share with Smith?

Even though this concept of capital cannot be measured, it is important to begin an understanding of the economic model by bearing it in mind. Unless the idea is grasped, conventional measurements of capital—which attempt to put numbers to *segments* of capital stock—are misleading in attempts to understand the mechanics of the world economy.

The usual method of measuring capital stock begins with an assumption on the part of the economists who are doing the measuring that capital consists entirely of non-human objects that have been created by humans, or of animals or land owned by humans, capable of producing goods and services *in a way that can be counted by government.* This extremely narrow definition is necessary to the conventional measurers of capital only because it is not within the ability of man to measure anything else.

To begin with, the unit of measurement can only be government money. Economists are intellectually powerless to measure capital in any other terms. A nation's capital stock can only be expressed in terms of what it would cost to replace it in dollars, francs, rubles, etc. And the only portion of a nation's capital stock that can be measured in its currency is the part that is visible to an official of the government, an official whose job it is to estimate the value, in money, of capital. Only the government has the resources to collect such information, which is toted up by economists who have no other source of such information.

By this definition, an individual's home is counted as part of the nation's capital stock. After all, it yields goods and services as long as it is habitable. A local tax assessor ascribes a dollar value to it, based roughly on its replacement value, and this number finds its way into the national accounts kept in Washington, D.C. Any home or cabin that is not on the tax rolls, either because of remoteness or tax exemption (government housing, parish rectories, etc.) is not counted as part of the nation's capital stock, only because of the difficulty of including it in the count.

It is also the responsibility of the tax assessor to estimate the value of business capital, usually for the purpose of avoiding taxes on capital of this sort. Federal tax gatherers who are empowered to levy a tax on the income of a business must sort out the capital that produces the goods and services that yield an income from the income itself. If you build a factory and fill it with machines to manufacture widgets, the capital formed is not subject to tax. If you manufacture widgets and accumulate an inventory of them, additional capital is formed that is not subject to tax. But after the widgets are sold, and the enterprise subtracts its costs of production, whatever income remains is profit, and profit is taxable. The tax agent must separate out several elements. He must determine the cost of putting up the plant and buying the machines. Because the plant and machines are wearing out as they are being used, a portion of their original cost must be counted along with the cost of wages, utilities, materials, advertising, shipping, etc., which are the more easily determined costs of production. If this is not done, the portion of capital used up will not be subtracted from income, and the tax on "profit" will fall on both profit and capital. The tax agent must also be careful to ascertain the size of the widget inventory in order to avoid taxing it as capital. If there is anything that politicians and economists around the world, including "communists," agree upon, it is that the kind of fixed capital represented in a widget factory should not be taxed.

In the process of making these various calculations, the government and its economists can offer a single number that represents their version of what the nation's fixed stock of capital amounts to.

There is nothing at all wrong with such a calculation, and insofar as it accurately measures what it purports to measure it provides useful information about a segment of the political economy. But we cannot say for sure that the electorate's welfare increases or decreases when the measurable capital stock increases or decreases. We must also try to find out what is concurrently happening to the non-measurable capital stock of the economy, for an increase in the former may be accompanied by a decrease in the latter.

The government, for example, does not count personal property—except for housing stock—as capital. But most of what we consider personal property is not destroyed in consumption, except gradually. By the broad definition, this too is capital, for there is a yield of future goods and services after an initial investment. An automobile, for example, provides service for years after its purchase, but unless it is owned by a business rather than by an individual it is not counted as capital. A company executive drives back and forth to work in a company auto and flies thither and yon in the company jet, and these are counted by the government as capital. But if he buys an auto and an airplane out of personal income, he is considered to be holding consumer goods, not capital.

In countries that scrupulously avoid taxing business capital, but heavily tax personal income, we invariably find a relative shift to business and government ownership of autos and airplanes as individual ownership of autos and airplanes declines. The net effect may be an actual decline in the total number of vehicles available to serve the population. Certainly the population has less freedom to use business and government vehicles. Yet *statistically* the government is able to record steady advances in the nation's capital stock as a result of this process. In Great Britain, which levies no tax on the physical capital of business and extremely high tax rates on personal income, 60 percent of automobiles are owned by business or government. As the government continues to discourage private ownership of autos, thus pushing them into the collective ownership that constitutes measured capital, it can pretend that capital is being formed even as it is undergoing a net decline. Of course, when business and government own all the autos, there can thereafter be no statistical improvement in "capital stock" as a result of this sort of mirage.

The electorate, though, cannot be fooled by statistical reports of progress during a decline. It knows precisely how many automobiles there are available for service as well as the precise degree of freedom attached to that availability. Individuals can be fooled by such statistics, but the electorate cannot.

On the other hand, the electorate is also not discouraged when the government's statistical measures of capital run in the other direction. This is because there is so much capital that is not measured that what the government considers a sharp decline in measured capital may only be felt as a trivial decline by the electorate. Indeed, non-measured capital may be rising faster than measured capital is falling. In the above example, should Great Britain reduce tax rates on personal incomes the government would find itself measuring a reversal of the process. Individual ownership of autos and airplanes would increase and collective ownership would fall. The statistical capital stock would decline, but total capital—measured and non-measured—would rise as the availability of the vehicles increased with the freedom to use them.

Some economists and politicians are especially mesmerized by official statistics in wartime, when both measured capital stock and measured production of goods and services from that capital stock climb rapidly. When war is concluded and war contracts terminated, Gross National Product declines, but Gross National Satisfaction leaps for-

ward. Peace brings an end to the destruction of non-measured intellectual and human capital. Nor is the electorate fooled into thinking that
preparation for war or war itself brings a measure of economic prosperity. The electorate can go from depression and high unemployment to
war and no unemployment. But in wartime the electorate is working
harder to consume less than it did during depression, the difference
being the production and extinguishment of war materials. At the same
time, non-measured capital stock that is valued in peacetime is rapidly
liquidated for national survival. National defense is itself a non-
measured part of the electorate's capital stock, an investment that is
meant to yield future services, and which is consumed in war.

The capital the electorate values most highly is that which embraces
investments in family and friendships, and a system that attempts to
expand statistical capital at the expense of this immeasurable form of
investment and savings cannot endure for longer than it takes for
alternatives to emerge. Other things being equal, a political system that
must persistently expend citizens in war or civil strife will be outlasted
by one that economizes on human capital by finding ways to remain at
peace. In the same vein, a system that restrains communication between families and friends and thus limits this form of non-measured
capital will be outlasted by one that does not. Human rights are a
precious form of non-measured capital, one that the electorate will
most willingly defend through the expenditure of other forms.

An electorate will also maintain its patience with political leaders
who are otherwise inefficient in assessing the desires of the electorate
as long as this form of capital is not tampered with. The people of India
endured almost thirty years of economic mismanagement by their
political leaders, apparently satisfied that the political system was
sound and could not be overthrown without risking something worse.
If a political system is judged sound, it requires only patience for it to
produce keen politicians. Only when Prime Minister Indira Gandhi
and her son Sanjay embarked on a plan of economic development that
included government regulation of family size did the electorate stir
itself, bringing the country to the point of revolution. Mrs. Gandhi's
response, in the summer of 1975, was to suspend the political system.
During the "emergency" period that followed, she dictated economic
reforms superior to any she had ever proposed within the system and
the economy revived. Although she then restored the democratic
system and apologized for her earlier "errors," the electorate could not
afford to give the appearance of sanctifying her vacation from democratic rule. In March, 1977, the voters expelled her and her party from

power, defeating all the cabinet ministers associated with the suspension of the system, but retaining the minister who had designed the economic reforms.*

The other forms of capital that the electorate counts as important, although they are not measured statistically by government, are those associated with the intellect and the environment. Of these, education is probably the most valued form, and one that is largely curtailed during wartime.

The farmer can spend all of his time farming, maximizing output so that, in addition to satisfying his current needs, he can leave wealth in the form of fixed capital (the farm) and financial assets (cash savings and bonds). The farmer can, as an alternative, spend most of his time farming with these aims in mind, but also give some of his time and energies teaching his sons to farm. If he spends all of his time farming and none of his time teaching, government economists would show a sharp rise in statistical prosperity. But when he died, output would plummet. There is still the farm, the implements, the livestock, all fixed physical capital. But there is no intellectual capital to arrange it in a way that produces goods and services. The measured capital stock thus falls. Because the farmer's education of his sons cannot be measured, it distorts the government's picture of the economy. Almost everyone in the world thinks of education as an investment, as capital, but because there is no way to ascribe a financial value to it, no way to tax it, government economists can only treat purchases of education as consumption. And how often do we hear economists arguing that the trouble with the economy is that there is too much consumption and too little investment?

This is not to say that all education has the same capital value, as far as the electorate is concerned. If there were a way to measure education as capital, we would find the number fluctuating in the same way the stock market fluctuates, the stock market being the most precise measure of fixed business capital stock.

If, for example, the farmer took time to teach his son, but instead of teaching him to farm, taught him only how to swear, drink beer, dance and shoot rabbits, the stock market would tend to rise as a result of the son's education in these pursuits, because they will bring him future satisfactions, but the market would still tend to fall every day that the

*A poor Indian farmer, quoted in the *New York Times* of March 22, 1977, sums it up: "Just because a man is poor and maybe cannot read does not mean that he cares nothing for his human rights. The Congress Government has tried to shut my mouth, and therefore the Congress loses my vote."

farmer got closer to infirmity or death and the son got no closer to learning farming skills. The drop in the market would not be sharp, but very shallow and persistent, there always being a chance that the farmer would suddenly and unaccountably decide to give his son a crash course in farming. If that should happen, the market would rise abruptly, but not as far as the level it would have reached had the farmer been teaching his son all along. After all, there remains the possibility that the farmer would just as abruptly decide to call off the lessons, or that the son by this time couldn't be dragged away from the dance hall.

If we could put numbers on this stock market curve, showing the steady fall and then the abrupt rise, what would those numbers represent? At the bottom of the market, the number would represent the market's best guess about the total amount of goods and services the son's education would yield during his lifetime. The number at the top of the market is another best guess, given new information. The goods and services this market is estimating are not bushels of wheat or gallons of milk. The stock market of physical capital measures those. Our hypothetical market measures the capital value of education in providing satisfaction to the farmer's son over his lifetime, plus satisfaction to all other members of the electorate; satisfaction that includes the son's ability to teach his son farming skills.

If at the same time that the farmer was teaching his son farming he also decided to teach him to despise other members of the electorate, a class, a race, or a creed, the stock market would resume its fall, given the likelihood that this education would subtract from the satisfaction sometime in the future. If the son thereafter got contrary information from others in his family, or friends or church or school, the market would tend to rise, but again would not return to the level it would have reached had he not accepted his father's prejudices in the first place.

If we now broaden this market to include more of the electorate, we see that it is not necessary for the farmer to teach his son farming skills. Some other farmer may have two sons that are learning farming, one of whom will be intellectually equipped to take over our farmer's fixed capital. Our farmer could, instead, teach his son to read, infuse him with a hunger for learning, and use the surplus earnings from his extra farm work not to buy financial assets, but to purchase higher education for his son. The hypothetical stock market would also tend to rise, more or less. More, if the direction of his education seemed to promise a high yield in goods and services to the electorate. Less, if his education seemed to promise a lower yield. The market would fall, though, if the direction of his learning promised subtraction from the electorate's aggregate capital.

This market of intellectual capital stock will rise or fall most sharply because of the actions of government, because beneficial or perverse actions of government affect all individuals within the electorate at once. When Frank Sinatra or Bob Hope or John Wayne retire, the market will drop hardly at all, because the market has for years anticipated that sooner or later these entertainers will retire, and has thus been making small, daily downward adjustments from a point that could be considered the zenith of their careers. In a war, although future Sinatras, Hopes, and Waynes are undoubtedly being cut down in battle, the individual stock of these three entertainers rises, the electorate putting a premium on entertainment and the entertainers getting heightened satisfaction from performing, even without financial compensation.

In peacetime, the hypothetical stock market that measures intellectual capital is most likely to fall because of government tax and tax enforcement policies. The intellectual capital of entertainers is most clearly squandered as their talents and energies are distracted by tax gatherers and tax courts. This is because entertainment involves an extraordinarily high mixture of intellectual capital relative to fixed capital, compared to widget manufacturing, which requires a high level of fixed capital relative to intellectual capital. The extractive industries, those which make highest use of planetary resources, farming, mining, oil drilling, require the highest levels of fixed capital to intellectual resources. Because governments can measure fixed capital, they can avoid taxing all but the "profits" that flow from it. But intellectual capital cannot be measured, and there is thus no significant statistical decline readily apparent when high income tax rates destroy intellectual capital. The amount of revenue lost to the Treasury was so microscopic relative to the whole when the American motion picture industry was destroyed by tax rates and enforcement policies that Treasury scarcely noticed the loss. The global electorate still has the fixed capital represented by the film library accumulated during Hollywood's golden era, in the same genuine sense that it still has the Mona Lisa of the Italian Renaissance, but lost for all time is the capital stock of films that were not produced because of government policies during the last generation. The government, which cannot measure such capital values, makes no statistical distinction between *Gone With the Wind* and *Deep Throat*. The government can only tell us that the average worker had to work 1½ hours to take his family to see *Gone With the*

Wind in 1936, and now it only takes him 1¼ hours of work to take his family to see *Deep Throat*, which suggests to the government that real incomes have risen relative to movies. This government bias against taxation of fixed physical capital in favor of taxation of non-measurable intellectual capital has profoundly distorted the face of the American political economy, and to the degree the idea has been exported globally, there have been similar effects. The global electorate is entertained less and at the same time gobbles up more and more of the earth's resources. The global environmental movement has been an unwitting reaction to the tax policies of governments.

Entertainers are singled out as representative of intellectual capital, although all intellectual capital is affected similarly, but in lesser and lesser degree as it bears upon the fixed physical stock of capital. Professional sports, boxing and baseball in particular, have been ravaged by government economic policies. The nominal price of health care and housing, which require high degrees of craftsmanship, have been steadily climbing while the quality of health care and housing has been steadily declining. One day the civil engineer is engineering, fulfilling his potential in terms of intellectual capital; the next day he is driving a taxi. One day the carpenter is building a house; the next he is unemployed. The farmer is working industriously to be able to teach his sons and daughters any of these varied occupations, forming intellectual capital, and the government then destroys it by a mechanism which will be explained in the following chapter.

To round out this catalog of capital first, it is important to point out that governments do not put a value on capital that produces free goods or services, but to the electorate, as the song goes, very often the best things in life are free. Even when the government is misusing the fixed capital stock, and under-utilizing the nation's intellectual capital, the electorate will be patient with the system of government and await superior politicians because of "free goods." Public investments in parks, roads, museums, beaches, libraries, etc., are not counted as capital, but they clearly meet the broad definition of capital. Freedom of worship, freedom of assembly, of speech, of the press, are all counted as capital by the electorate; investments made by our forefathers to hopefully yield goods and services to the electorate for all time. The electorate seems prepared to willingly trade human capital in exchange for these freedoms even in times of gross economic mismanagement by the available political leaders.

Clean air and clean water are valuable capital assets to the electorate. So are landscapes and seascapes, flora and fauna. The electorate will accept dimunition of these forms of capital if human capital is at stake, or a sound political system is at stake, or even, at times, in exchange for fixed capital. Almost everyone in the United States would agree that the beauty of the Pacific coastline has a capital value that exceeds any conceivable string of widget factories that might be constructed along it. But if a country has a surplus of coastline relative to industrial plants, its electorate might make a different set of calculations about the values of these forms of capital and set aside an industrial zone on a section of coastline.

When environmental "zealots" argue that we have reached the planetary limits to growth, they are not arguing that the limits to capital expansion have been reached, in the sense that capital has here been defined. What they do sense, without explicitly understanding how and why it has happened, is that the government bias against intellectual capital has been making inordinate demands upon non-measurable fixed capital. If that bias could be altered, pressure on planetary resources would be relieved. The intellectual capital that should have been entertaining us closer to its potential over the past generation—particularly the last dozen years—should also have been utilized on behalf of the environment, through scientific research. In addition, the electorate understands the concept of marginal utility, and employs this concept when it makes judgments on environmental issues. Hardly anyone but the environmental zealots themselves understand why a dam or a power plant should be delayed to preserve from extinction a flower or a snail that only a handful of people are aware of. But the electorate, which aggregates these individual views, seems to support the environmentalists. After all, once the snail or flower becomes extinct, it is no longer capital. It provides no goods or services. The electorate may thus consider that the capitalized value of those little bits of pleasure scientists or hobbyists will get from the snail or flower through the end of time adds up to a value exceeding the loss of goods and services caused by delaying the dam or power plant. Is there any human being who does not feel even a slight twinge of regret upon learning, for the first time, of the burning of the library at Alexandria two thousand years ago? Consider the tomb of King Tut, three thousand years old, drawing millions of tourists wherever it is exhibited around the world, still producing goods and services.

In this broad sense, the driving force of civilization has been and remains a search for a way to maximize capital. If we had a chart to measure the ups and downs of this quest, calling the number plotted something like Gross National Satisfaction, we would first have to pull together all the forms of capital outlined in this chapter, and assign each a weight. While there is no conceivable way to produce such a measure, the concept is useful in itself, if only because it helps us think more clearly about the world.

Although it did not have the economic model described in these pages in mind, the Economic Development Council of Washington, D.C. in 1977 moved in the direction of the concept of Gross National Satisfaction. It developed an alternative to Gross National Product as a measure of a nation's health and wealth. It is called the Physical Quality of Life Index (PQLI). It measures each country's rates of infant mortality, life expectancy, and literacy, assigning each equal weight, and ranking them on a scale of 1-to-100. The index is admittedly crude, but in a vague sort of way it might be argued that most forms of physical and intellectual capital are felt in these indices of life quality. There are no weights for personal freedoms, though. But then, the GNP has no such weighting either, but simply measures the "money" economies of those nations using this standard. That is, the GNP measures the commercial transactions visible to tax collectors, which gives it even less usefulness than the PQLI in measuring life quality. Most commercial transactions in the United States are visible to tax collectors and most transactions in, say, India, are not. The $8,000 per capita GNP income of the United States is derived by dividing the $1.8 trillion in money transactions by the U.S. population of 220 million. India's per capita income of $152 is derived in the same way, except that the population of 600 million has to be divided into a tiny number of money transactions that scarcely represent the genuine level of business activity in India.

On the PQLI Index, Sweden scores 100, Switzerland 99, the United States 97, the USSR 94, Taiwan 88, the People's Republic of China 59, and India 41. On the GNP measure, the United States is almost 35 times "better off" than India, while on this PQLI measure, it is about two and a half times "better off" than India. While neither number is especially persuasive as a measure of relative life quality, the PQLI has fewer statistical distortions (because literacy, mortality, and life expectancy are more easily measured than business transactions). But because the GNP does not pretend to measure quality of life, only money transactions, the PQLI's failure to measure personal freedoms while pretending to standardize life quality is a serious flaw. Because "quality" of life is a matter of subjective judgment, the only conceptually satisfying way to measure it is to have individuals do it themselves. Imagine that every country in the world had a policy of free movement across its borders, free immigration and free emigration. Every individual on earth would be free to migrate to any other country, restrained only by the cost of transportation. In effect, each member of the global electorate would be free to vote with his feet on the relative life quality of his native country and all others. The net migration patterns would provide us with the only imaginable true picture of relative life qualities. Each prospective migrant would, in trying to decide whether and where to move, consider all the elements weighed into the GNP, plus the PQLI, plus personal freedoms, plus the ties of family, friends and native soil.

If such a policy of free global migration were announced today, there would immediately follow a great wave of migration, releasing streams of malcontents that are now blockaded by immigration laws. It is easy to imagine that this tidal wave would flow to the United States and Western Europe out of the Communist countries and the impoverished "Third World." But insofar as individuals perceived that this new policy would be permanent, not temporary, there would probably be much less migration than we would now imagine. After all, the most important form of capital available to individuals is in family, friends and homeland. Economic opportunity, i.e., the opportunity to maximize intellectual capital, has to be sufficiently greater in an alien land to offset the pull of these attractions.*

Most of the citizens of the Soviet Union or the People's Republic of China would not even consider leaving their homeland for this reason. And if the prohibition against emigration was lifted as an announced policy of permanency, there would be even less emigration. One of the reasons people desire to migrate is the prohibition against migration. That is, they do not desire to emigrate *now*, but may wish to migrate in the future. This is true of all personal freedoms. Freedom to communicate with other citizens—through speech, the press, assembly, worship, migration—is capital even though such freedoms are not exercised for political purposes. The "hotline" between Moscow and Washington is capital in this sense. At some moment, ability to communicate may prevent disaster.

People communicate through migration when less desperate forms of political expression are not heard. The United States for the most part was peopled by migrants who were frustrated by governments at

---

*This is as true of migration within countries as it is of international migration. In the 1950s, when the decline of the bituminous coal industry left Appalachia impoverished, emigration was much less than economists could explain given the expansion of opportunities elsewhere in the United States. The majority of Appalachian citizens, especially those middle-aged and older, preferred to accept a lower standard of living in GNP terms rather than abandon lifelong ties to the network of family, friends and community. Additionally, while staying in place, they exerted political pressure on Washington to provide transitional relief. As part of his Great Society program, Lyndon Johnson established the Appalachian Regional Commission to transfer national resources into Appalachia.

home. The relative peacefulness of Europe between 1815 and 1914 was in part due to the open frontier in America, which permitted a safety valve for European political frustrations. As long as there remained a frontier in the United States, its governments could not engage in the kind of oppressive tax policies that drove so many migrants here from Europe. In the 1840s, for example, Ohio defaulted on its canal bonds, explaining to British bondholders that it had no other choice. If it raised taxes to pay off the bonds, so many citizens would simply move West that revenues wouldn't increase anyway.

Another reason mitigating against a major emigration from the Soviet Union, given our hypothetical policy of freedom, is that it is by no means clear that its political economy is inferior to that of the United States. Its political model, while still in the formative stage, has in the last twenty-five years adequately handled the succession problem. And while there are no free elections à la the Western democracies, the Soviets seem able to draw upon the broadest pool of talent in selecting political leadership. There are no apparent restrictions that would prevent anyone born in the Soviet Union from growing up to be head of state. Personal freedoms to communicate are still severely restricted, but marginal improvements have been made over a quarter century; in the last several years, the Soviets reacted to Western pressures by permitting the emigration of thirty-five thousand Jews to Israel, and several thousand returned. In addition, it is important to note that since 1945 more than one hundred thousand Americans have died in warfare and only a fraction of that number have died on behalf of the Soviet system. The crime rate and the divorce rate are apparently much lower in the Soviet Union than in the United States; crime and divorce are both signs of tension in the political economy that subtracts from intellectual capital. There have been violent outbursts among Soviet satellites, Hungary in 1956, Czechoslovakia in 1964, Poland in 1970. Each of the outbursts was followed by sufficient economic reform to relieve political tensions to below boiling points. These are all signs of political durability and vigor.

The Soviets also show a deftness in international politics and, whether one likes it or not, are in much better standing with most countries of the world than they were in 1952. They have a foothold in the Western hemisphere, in Castro's Cuba, which seems to be gaining in relative strength to much of the free Caribbean nations. Militarily, the Soviets have at least strategic parity with the West and to many people seem to be opening a lead.

With all its economic inefficiencies, especially its troubles in the farm sector, the Soviet system also seems capable of sustaining real growth, which of course makes its political and diplomatic advances possible.

All of which reflects the inconclusiveness of experimentation by the global electorate in striving toward a system that maximizes capital and welfare. We can now look deeper into the economic model to understand why this has been happening.

CHAPTER 5

The Economic Model: Production

A nation's economic output is maximized when its people have the maximum incentive to produce. How are incentives maximized? Why do people work? People work when work is more attractive than non-work. The more a worker is rewarded for non-work and penalized for work, the less he will work. The wedge model. Comparative advantage and division of labor. Work disincentives and leisure. The modern barter economy and tax avoidance. Communes and private plots. Productivity, trade, and marginal tax rates. Incomes policies, the minimum wage, and the economics of crime and prostitution. The relationship between individual and nation-state economic motivations: If a government prohibits imports, will it export? If a worker is prohibited from consuming, will he work?

In any economic unit—the family, the community, the nation-state, the world—people work for one reason and one reason only: to maximize their welfare. Each individual has a unique personal assessment of what constitutes welfare. Most people have to work simply for physical survival. But after providing minimum necessities for survival—food, clothing, shelter, etc.—the individual is free to choose between work and leisure. Under a given set of conditions, an individual's personal assessment of what constitutes welfare will lead him to work *up to a point* and then not work. This *point* shifts from moment to moment during an individual's lifetime, because conditions constantly shift, requiring new welfare calculations. For brief periods an individual can work to the limits of his or her physical/intellectual capacity, but must then rest.

During the course of a workday, an individual operates within a broad spectrum of leisure and work. Superficially, the worker seems to be at leisure when he is motionless and working when he is in motion. It seems clear that when the worker is on a coffee break or drinking at the water cooler he is on the leisure end of the spectrum, and when he is moving vigorously at his work space he is near the limiting end of the work zone of the spectrum.

But appearances can be deceptive. At the water cooler, Jones is indeed thinking about his girlfriend while he kills a minute between work efforts. But Smith's mind is still churning over the project on his desk even as he appears to be idling at the cooler. On the assembly line, Peters and Johnson appear to be doing identical work, fitting widgets to widget sleeves. Each is fitting one widget per minute, precisely. Peters, though, is thinking about his girlfriend today, his mind idling as his hands and eyes run through the familiar mechanical process of widget assembly. Johnson, who is bent on becoming fore- man, is going over shop politics in his mind, observing weaknesses in assembly patterns, calculating possible efficiencies, and keeping a fraction more of his attention on his own widget assembly. Every hour Johnson produces one less defective widget than does Peters.

These examples do not tell us whether Smith is good or Jones is bad, or whether Johnson or Peters is the better worker. We still do not have enough information. Perhaps Jones, after giving his girlfriend a mo- ment's thought, returns to his work with complete concentration and completes his project sooner than Smith. Peters may be working his way through engineering school at night, and normally he is a better widget assembler than Johnson—who never will get to be foreman— but because he has just fallen in love he temporarily can't keep his mind on his work.

The important point of this discussion is that work, a combination of physical and intellectual effort, is something more complex than the common understanding of it. For shorthand purposes, we speak of people working a forty-hour week and think of leisure in terms of the time spent away from the forty-hour work week. We speak of "equal pay for equal work," and mean that if two people perform the same task during the forty-hour work week they should receive the same wages. In reality, the individual moves through varying degrees of work and leisure throughout his waking hours, forming capital when he or she is working, consuming capital during leisure periods. The housewife works vigorously for an hour cleaning the kitchen and the thought crosses her mind that she deserves a break and a cup of tea so she sits down pleased with her work and the cleanliness of her kitchen. The banker keeps "bankers' hours," takes long lunches, and plays golf one or two afternoons a week. He appears to be a man of leisure, but talk to his wife, friends, and business associates and when they report that he thinks, eats, and sleeps banking, it is easier to understand why his bank and the community it serves are thriving. Consider Leonardo da Vinci, who seemed to spend all his hours in idleness, strolling the streets of Milan, but whose friends observed that periodically he would leave them abruptly, walk to his studio, put one brush stroke to the Last Supper and then return to their company.

Work is the *process* of forming capital, i.e., goods and services for future consumption. People work not only when they make widgets, but also when they learn how to make widgets. Education is capital, and as people are learning they are working, in the sense that learning is part of the process of forming capital. A clean kitchen, to the housewife, is capital; its cleanliness rewards her into the future, and she consumes this capital bit by bit as the kitchen gets dirtier by degrees and she decides it needs another cleaning. At the same time that she is taking her break and sipping tea, moving on the work-leisure scale toward more leisure, she still has part of her mind occupied with the process of forming capital, thinking about what she will do next, and arranging work priorities. Every moment in an individual's waking life is a mixture of work and leisure, leisure being maximized in sleep and work maximized at the individual's physical/ intellectual limits.

We do not normally think of work in this light because the government and its economists have no way of converting these gradations into statistics, no way of measuring the moment-to-moment trade off between work and leisure. A man, for example, marries his housekeeper and the government statistics record a decline in national income. When she was housekeeper, she was paid a wage taxable by the government, thereby making it measurable. As housewife, she does the same work and more. The two are still living on his money income, as before, but her work is no longer visible to the tax collector. Similarly, the government will take no notice when the following occurs.

Jones, a plumber, needs carpentry work. Smith, a carpenter, needs plumbing work. Jones could put his plumbing skills on the market and Smith could offer his carpentry services; each would work for the other. Instead, Jones spends Saturday doing his own carpentry work, while Smith does his own plumbing. In the latter case the needed work gets done although each man, being less skilled at the other's trade, takes much longer to do the work. The government records no increase in Gross National Product, although it would have done so in the former case. However, if Jones cuts his finger on the unfamiliar chisel and Smith skins his knuckles on the unfamiliar pipewrench, they each must purchase Band-Aids and iodine, which the government notes as an increase in consumer demand.

By extending this example we see that there are two "economies" in which people can work. They can work in the barter economy or they can work in the money economy. If Jones and Smith are neighbors, relatives, or friends they will negotiate with each other in friendly fashion and do each other's work. If they trust each other sufficiently, Smith will even do Jones' carpentry work although at the moment he does not need plumbing work in return. If the bonds of friendship, neighborliness, or family are strong enough, the "negotiations" will be wordless, there being a silent understanding that when Smith needs plumbing work he need only mention it to Jones or communicate through their wives, and Jones will cheerfully offer to complete the transaction.

If there is a lesser degree of trust, if only because Smith and Jones are not next-door neighbors but live several houses apart, the transaction may be completed in a different form. After Smith completes Jones' carpentry work, Jones may present Smith with a bottle of whisky, or do him a string of small favors in the period immediately following the carpentry work. Jones' wife, also aware of the debt to Smith, may chip in with small favors to Smith's wife (picking up her groceries, watching her children), and Smith's wife will communicate this news to her husband at the same time Jones' wife communicates it to him. Myriad transactions may flow from the first exchange, as the Smiths and Joneses add page after page to the ledgers in their heads, over time balancing accounts with almost absolute precision. The relationship breaks down when, over time, the accounts do not balance.

When accounts become so unbalanced that there is almost no way for Jones' debt to Smith to be repaid, Jones will initiate the break, for it is he who feels the burden of debt. For example, Jones' son gets Smith's daughter pregnant and runs off, without her, to parts south. Smith feels enormous hostility to Jones' son, not Jones, but beneath the surface Smith knows that Jones, the political leader of his political/ economic unit, is responsible for his son, and Jones knows he is too. Jones will not be able to face Smith. The trading relationship breaks down, and the families merely smile and wave to each other when they pass each other's houses.

Debts can be forgiven, even to the satisfaction of the debtor, when the passage of time diminishes them. This is because individuals keep accounts in their heads *vis-a-vis* all mankind. Jones cannot repay his debt to Smith, but in his relationship with Peters it is Peters who is in Jones' debt. And if Smith and Peters have a trading relationship in which Smith is in Peters' debt, all accounts in the system are in balance. Your debt to someone seems less onerous when someone is in debt to you; in the money economy, if Jones owes Smith $1,000 and

Peters owes Jones $1,000, there is less tension between Jones and Smith than between Jones and Peters.

When relationships between neighbors or friends break down, they generally tend to be irreparable. Balancing accounts indirectly takes time (which heals all wounds), and neighbors and friends usually drift apart geographically before sufficient time has elapsed to permit new experiences. The bonds of family or clan are stronger in the sense that time is given a chance to heal, and the linkages of family or clan will eventually draw back together once-hostile relatives. Brothers who have not seen or spoken to each other for twenty years out of hatred developed over an imbalanced account, when pulled together even across a continent for a wedding or funeral, often bury the hatchet, the debt being forgiven (although never forgotten).

Clans are efficient political/economic units because the existence of these bonds, which can survive time and distance, permit accounts to be balanced indirectly over a wide number of individuals. A member of a clan does not think, when he extends himself for Uncle Harry, that Uncle Harry must reciprocate directly. Uncle Harry will extend himself for Cousin Sue, who extends herself for Grandmother, who extends herself for the initiator of the chain. Individuals within the clan who do not keep their own personal accounts balanced over time with all other members of the clan will be punished by the clan as the final method of keeping the accounts of the entire system in equilibrium. Most such adjustment mechanisms are relatively pacific: Uncle Harry gets the silent treatment, is lectured and embarrassed by Grandfather, or is greeted without enthusiasm by the children. At the other extreme, Cain slays Abel, not to punish his brother, but his parents.

Clans are *private* economies, in that work is exchanged between members without government interference. The government does not regulate transactions between members of the clan, nor can it tax transactions between members of a clan, not necessarily because it wouldn't like to, but because it cannot measure or observe what it is that members of a clan do for each other.

Only so much of an individual's needs and wants can be satisfied within the clan, which brings us back to Jones the plumber and Smith the carpenter. We have seen how they have managed to barter their skills, through the neighborhood, family, or friendship. But suppose none of these connections apply because Smith lives on one side of the city and Jones on the other, each unknown to the other.

Smith mentions to his brother-in-law that he needs some plumbing work, and his brother-in-law says he knows of a good plumber, Jones, who charges reasonable prices. Smith calls Jones and makes an appointment for an estimate. Jones figures it will take him two days, which is sixteen hours at $10 an hour, or $160 plus material. Smith pays cash and Jones pockets it with no intention of reporting it for tax purposes. A year later, Jones needs woodwork and, in the same fashion, contacts Smith, who also estimates the work at sixteen hours at $10 an hour. Jones pays cash, which Smith pockets without paying taxes.

This is still the barter economy although government money—currency—is being used as the medium of exchange in the transaction. The same work is completed as in the earlier examples, when Smith and Jones were friends, neighbors, or family, and the medium of exchange involved only verbal or non-verbal commitments to balance accounts over time through an exchange of work. In our example, Smith has given Jones $160 and Jones has given Smith $160, which is the same as if no money had changed hands at all. The value of money is that it substitutes for trust. When there is sufficient trust between transacting individuals, the money substitute is less efficient as a medium of exchange and is not used. A husband does not pay his wife a wage in currency. She takes care of the household and is repaid with shelter, food, caring in times of illness, etc. Accounts are balanced in their heads.

Until this point, Smith and Jones are entirely operating within private economies. Every village, town, city, and nation has always had such private economies. Of all the "work" transactions between people in the course of a day, now or thousands of years ago, under any form of government, *almost all of them* occur in this private or barter dimension of economic activity.

The relatively small number of transactions that occur outside of this private dimension are in the public or "money" economy. The single feature that distinguishes the public economy is the visibility of transactions within it to the government. Once a transaction is visible to the government, it becomes subject to the possibility of government intervention for one reason or another. We loosely describe governments as being "capitalistic," "socialistic," or "communistic" depending on their relative degrees of intervention in public transactions, but they all intervene to one degree or another. The primary need of government, after all, is to raise money with which to sustain itself. A government can do nothing without money, so inevitably it must tax transactions in order to obtain money. That is, those citizens wishing to participate in the public economy must be willing to give a share of their work to the government.

Why should Smith and Jones wish to participate in the public economy? The answer, simply, is that they will shift from the private to the public economy when it is easier to trade their work for somebody else's in the public economy.

Suppose Smith and Jones live on opposite ends of town and have no mutual acquaintances that will permit them to trade plumbing for woodworking. Each sits at home, idle, only because they are unknown to each other.

Jones decides to break this impasse by offering his skills to the public at large, on the chance that this effort will increase his trading opportunities. The moment he becomes visible to the general public he is visible to the government. Before he can even broadcast his services, in fact, he must obtain a license from the government for which he pays a fee. He may spend a day, a week, or a month in government offices filling out papers, and perhaps must hire special assistance to do it for him—a lawyer. He may have to prove his plumbing skills to a government board of plumbing experts. In addition, he then becomes visible to the tax collectors, not only those of local government, but also those representing state or provincial governments and the national government. As soon as he receives a license to do business, the event is broadcast through the communication channels of government and Jones is thereby alerted that of every transaction he completes in this public economy, various portions of his receipts are owed to the governments.

Jones can now offer his skills in the general marketplace by competing with other plumbers among those most likely to need his skills in the public economy—general contractors—or simply aim at the repair market by opening a shop and hanging out a sign or advertising through the information media. This might consist of anything from knocking on doors himself to running an advertisement in the yellow pages.

At the same time, Smith has been going through the same process in setting up a one-man woodworking enterprise. As a result, Jones calls Smith and Smith calls Jones. Just as before, their estimates each come out at sixteen hours at $10 an hour and they give each other $160. But while they each had $160 after the work was done in the barter economy, they must now each give up a portion to the government, say $20. They might each consider adding $20 to the estimates, but they are both marginal workers in the sense that they are the latest entrants to the public market with plumbing and carpentry skills. They both know that there are plumbers and carpenters spotted all over town in the private economy, willing to do the work for $160 if they are only lucky enough to make connections. They both know there is a competitor who would charge $180 for the same work and a competitor that would charge $200 for the same work. But the $180 outfits have been around long enough that the public is aware of their reliability and will pay the extra $20 for peace of mind. The $200 outfits have both a reputation for reliability and superior workmanship, and cater to the carriage trade that can afford the highest quality and is willing to pay for reputation. In the basic sense, the price of the work at the margin is $160, and what people are paying for when they agree to $180 or $200 is work over and above the work that is merely specified.

So Jones is left with $140 and so is Smith, but they are both pleased. Instead of sitting around, or trying to do each other's work, they have now used their intellectual capital by getting out into a broader market. They have each had to give up two hours of their work to the government for this privilege, and each has had to incur one-time entrance costs, paying fees and going through red tape. They feel that it has all been worth it because now that they are in the broader public marketplace, they are more efficient. They can do the same amount of work with less effort, and now have time and energy left either to enjoy more leisure or to work more in exchange for the work of others. It is important for us to bear in mind that before Smith and Jones entered this public marketplace, they were each demanding goods and supplying labor, but because they were not visible to each other the exchange could not be made and they were unemployed.

Having achieved this gain in efficiency, Smith and Jones will now offer more labor to the market as long as there are goods in the market that they wish to trade for at manageable terms of trade. Jones wants to trade for groceries, housing, clothing, insurance, and entertainment. He wants to trade his labor for the labor of those who manufacture automobiles, for those who manufacture and operate airplanes, and run vacation resorts. He wants to trade for the education of his children and he wants to accumulate claims on goods and services (bonds or other financial assets or pension rights) to provide for himself and his family in his old age when he is no longer able to trade his labor. Above that, he perhaps would like to accumulate such claims that will permit him to enjoy an early retirement in style. We may as well say that the individual's appetite for consumption of goods and services is essentially unlimited. The only way Jones' demand for goods and services can rise or fall is if goods or services are added to or subtracted from the marketplace through invention or prohibition.

Given the nature of human beings, economists need give scant attention to the "demand" side of their law of supply and demand. To Jones,
as to all workers, the limits to his ability to demand rest entirely on the
supply side of the equation. Jones goes into the marketplace and
always finds that after he has traded all the work he wishes to trade,
there are still vast quantities of goods and services he wishes he could
afford, but he wants none of them so much that he is willing to give up
more leisure.

The only way to consume more of the goods and services he
demands is to become more efficient in his supply of labor. Otherwise,
he must wait for those whose goods he desires but can't afford to
become more efficient in the supply of their labor. Say, for example,
that Smith has come upon a device or method that doubles his
efficiency as a carpenter. He still charges $10 an hour, but takes only
one day to do the work, his bill coming to $80 instead of $160. Jones
now has $80 (less tax) to buy more of the goods he desires but
previously could not afford.

If Smith was the inventor of the new efficiency, he will benefit most
during the time it takes his competitors to learn and employ it. If, as
with Jones, he lowers his price, he takes business away from them on
that basis, some individuals accepting the risk of lower reliability or
lesser quality because of the lower price. To compete, they will have to
begin lowering their prices, meanwhile inquiring as to his methods. If
Smith decides to compete directly on reliability and quality, leaving
the price the same, at $160, he will also force them to lower their price
to keep from losing business. Whatever he does will work to bring
down the price of woodworking until two hours of plumbing equal
one hour of woodworking.

This does not mean that at the end of the process there will be half as
many carpenters as plumbers, however. In the marketplace, when the
relative price of carpentry falls against all other goods and services, the
individuals in the market—with their limitless demands for goods and
services—now find they can afford more woodworking, and they trade
more of their labor for woodworking relative to all other goods and
services. But this doesn't mean that other vendors lose business.
Remember Jones, who has already acquired the carpentry services on
his shopping list, has eighty dollars left over. He uses a little of it to
work less himself, but he uses most of it to buy up other goods.

Neither do Smith's competitors lose in any absolute sense. This is
because, at the lower price of woodworking relative to all other goods,
the general demand for it is booming. Smith's competitors are doing
better even though they are losing relative ground to Smith.

If new carpenters continued to pile into the marketplace, Smith and his competitors would all lose out because of the new efficiency. But this does not happen. As soon as the new efficiency becomes known, prospective new entrants hesitate to get into the craft. Sure, the demand for carpentry seems to be rising, but neither Smith nor his competitors are increasing their demands for carpenters. At the same time, there is a slower rise in the demand for other goods and services, but all the producers for these seem to be increasing their demands for labor. Jones, for one, is now experiencing more demand for his work than he is willing to supply, and if he cannot become efficient, he will either have a new competitor, or his existing competitors will expand. He does this by adding a helper. He pays the helper five dollars an hour and discovers that by having the helper do all the work that is really only worth five dollars an hour—lugging tools, cleaning up, holding wrenches, etc.—what used to take three days of work now takes two. He can charge fifteen dollars an hour instead of ten dollars an hour, but the customer is only interested in the total charge, which remains the same for two days work at fifteen dollars as three days at ten dollars. Jones has the same amount of money at the end of the week as he did previously, but he feels much better, his back doesn't hurt from lugging around tools, he is learning how to hire and train helpers, and his mind is free a bit to think about further expansion. Meanwhile, his helper, who was unemployed, demanding goods but unable to find a demand for his supply of labor, is now running around the marketplace buying goods and services with his five dollars an hour. Smith, on his end of town, soon feels the prosperity of Jones' helper, who is buying a suit of clothes from Adams who can now afford some carpentry work. Even if Jones does not immediately gain efficiencies after hiring his helper sufficient to offset the five dollars an hour, so that at the end of the week Jones has less money than if he had worked alone, he not only adds into the balance his improved state of body and mind, but also reckons that with time the helper will learn more and the efficiency of the team will improve, and at some point the helper will be adding nominal vaiue to the teamwork in excess of his hourly wage. The helper, who keeps accounts balanced in his own head, knows he is being paid more than he is worth at the outset, and is happy to continue working at five dollars an hour after he knows he is technically worth more, at least until he judges that the accounts have been balanced.

We have in this simple economic system of Smith and Jones all the elements of "comparative advantage" and "division of labor" in the global system. There is no argument among competing political ideologies that economic growth derives from the efficiencies born of these elements. Adam Smith opens *The Wealth of Nations* with the sentence; "The greatest improvement in the productive powers of labor, and the greater part of the skill, dexterity, and judgment with which it is anywhere directed, or applied, seem to have been the effects of the division of labour." Smith's example of the pin-making trade cannot be improved upon:

One man draws out the wire, another straights it, a third cuts it, a fourth points it, a fifth grinds it at the top for receiving the head; to make the head requires two or three distinct operations; to put it on is a peculiar business, to whiten the pins is another; it is even a trade by itself to put them into the paper; and the important business of making a pin is, in this manner, divided into about eighteen distinct operations, which, in some manufactories, are all performed by distinct hands, though in others the same man will sometimes perform two or three of them. I have seen a small manufactory of this kind where ten men only were employed, and where some of them consequently performed two or three distinct operations. But though they were very poor, and therefore but indifferently accommodated with the necessary machinery, they could, when they exerted themselves, make among them about twelve pounds of pins in a day. There are in a pound upwards of four thousand pins of a middling size. Those ten persons, therefore, could make among them upwards of forty-eight thousand pins in a day. Each person, therefore, making a tenth part of forty-eight thousand pins, might be considered as making four thousand eight hundred pins in a day. But if they had all wrought separately and independently, and without any of them having been educated to this peculiar business, they certainly could not each of them made twenty, perhaps not one pin in a day. . . .[1]

In the simple example, when Jones takes on a helper the two are supplying labor to the market as a team. They trade as a team, receiving claims on goods and services supplied by others. They can divide these claims among themselves however they wish. So too with Adam Smith's pinmakers, who pool their comparative advantages into a team; it is the team that supplies capital (pins) for exchange in the market-place. The international division of labor is merely teamwork grossed up to national economies. Japan can be thought of as Jones, the plumber. The United States can be Smith, the carpenter. They can trade their labor with each other in the barter economy, outside the purview of government (smuggling). Or they can trade in the money economy, upon reckoning that the efficiencies to be gained in this broader market outweigh the costs of trade regulation and tariffs by national governments. A technological advance by the United States increases the prosperity of Japan, which can then get the same quantity of goods from the United States with less labor on its part, and thus has more labor to offer for other goods in the United States and other markets.

There is then an increase in the supply of labor in the United States and elsewhere to trade with Japan. And Japan is now in a position to add a helper—Taiwan, Singapore, Hong Kong, Korea, etc.—doing more of what it does best and apprenticing its previously unemployed neighbors.

Up until now, we have seen very little of government in this process, except to observe that at critical points individuals who are pondering whether or not to work and where they will work—in the barter or the money economy—take into account the policies of government.

Back at the point where Smith and Jones were trying to decide whether or not to get into the money economy, they each had to consider the amount of red tape this would involve, the number of trips to City Hall to meet entry requirements, fees, etc. They also had to weigh the continuing costs of government once they made initial investments, each reckoning that on each $160 transaction, the government tax would be $20. Suppose the government then increases the amount of paper work by one form and increases the tax on each $160 transaction to $30. Because Smith and Jones were *at the point* of deciding whether or not to get into the public economy (which is another way of saying they were at the margin), the increased cost of entry or increase in the transaction tax will decide them against entry. There is only one way the government can increase the tax to $30 and still have Smith and Jones decide to enter the public economy. Because $10 represents one hour's work to each of them, they must be persuaded that the government will spend that $10 in a way that will save them more than one hour in each $160 transaction in the public economy. This means that the government cannot spend the $10 in a way that benefits those in the barter economy as well as those in the money economy. The government must spend the $10 in a way that benefits the public economy relative to the barter economy.

Say the government proposes to build a bridge between two segments of the economy that are separated by a river. Jones lives on one side and Smith on the other. Without the bridge, it takes one hour of their labor, either in time or in ferry charges, to cross the river to transact business. If the government finances the bridge by levying a $10 tax on every transaction, Smith and Jones are thus encouraged to remain in the barter economy where they can escape the tax because their transactions are not visible to the government. But if the government finances the bridge by charging a $2.50 toll (collecting $10 on four crossings in two days during the $160 transaction), Smith and Jones see that they will have to pay the $10 whether or not they enter the money economy. And once the bridge is up, it is more advantageous to be in the money economy than in the private economy because there is more business requiring use of the bridge in the broader public economy.

The government will often *seem* to recognize this distinction when it raises taxes by ten dollars and announces that the funds will be used to hire more tax collectors and enforcement officials to police the barter economy. The idea is that if Smith and Jones are afraid of continuing business in the barter economy, they will have no choice but to enter the money economy and pay taxes. But the *only* reason Smith and Jones were not in the money economy already is that regulation and taxes took so high a proportion of their marginal product that they could not compete as a carpenter and a plumber. If taxes are now raised in the public economy, they surely cannot compete, and in fact discover that one carpenter and one plumber who had been working in the public economy have now dropped into bartering in competition with them.

Now it is more difficult than ever to barter. The risks of being caught have risen and Smith and Jones each have one more competitor in their trade. They can no longer make a living in their trade, so they enter the public economy at a lower level of skill, perhaps as handymen or gardeners. The carpenter and plumber who just dropped into the barter economy take their places, using up their superior efficiency as craftsmen to offset the extra care and attention they must take to avoid the tax collectors and police. Unemployment does not necessarily result from the ten dollar increase in taxes, however. There are one less carpenter and plumber in the public economy where unemployment is recorded, and perhaps the increase of one handyman and one gardener has resulted in the loss of one of these marginal workers to the barter economy, but there is also the addition of a tax collector and various enforcement officials to the employment rolls.

It is important to note in this process that you cannot tell from an increase in taxes whether economic efficiency will improve or suffer. To answer that question, you must examine where the taxes are spent. Unemployment does not necessarily result from an increase in taxes, but also depends on how the revenues are spent. Unemployment surely increases when a ten dollar increase in taxes is used to finance payments to individuals on the condition that they *do not work* in the public economy. The government, after all, cannot pay individuals for not working in the barter economy because the government cannot observe the barter economy. This usually means that individuals will have a dual incentive for remaining in the barter economy. First, their work is taxed in the public economy; second, they can receive unemployment, welfare, or other subsistence payments even as they continue working in the barter economy. Government programs to "create jobs" usually fail because the designers of the programs ignore the incentives of the barter economy. Such programs frequently assume that because Jones is getting $80 a week in various subsistence payments while unemployed, the government can induce him into the public economy by offering a job at $100 a week or more, perhaps even $200. Such offers are frequently spurned by those the government has targeted, for they would not only have to give up their transfer (welfare, etc.) payments, but also their tax-free work or leisure in the barter economy. The new government jobs will instead attract individuals who are already employed in the public economy, but at lower rates of pay than the new positions being devised by government.

As a general rule of the economic model, the only way government can increase production is by making work more attractive than non-work.* There are only two options consistent with this statement. Government can make work more attractive, or it can make non-work less attractive. It can make work and productivity in the money economy more attractive than either work or leisure in the barter economy by lessening the burdens of regulation, taxation, or tariffs. It can make non-work less attractive, first by reducing non-work subsidies (welfare benefits) if they exist, then by increasing non-work penalties (harassment of bartering by tax authorities threatening physical punishment, imprisonment, slavery, etc.)

This is what Arthur Laffer calls the "wedge model," with the "wedge" being government intervention in private transactions. If Smith and Jones each want to trade sixteen hours of their skills with each other, but in order to complete the transaction must each give the government two hours of their skills, the two must do thirty-six hours work to transact thirty-two. The four hours "tax" is the wedge between them. If the government increases its tax from $20 to $30 on a $160 transaction, Smith and Jones must work thirty-eight hours to transact

---

*The statement may seem childishly simple, but economists frequently argue that when individuals are taxed more they will work harder in order to attain a target level of income or wealth. These arguments can be supported by anecdotes, but cannot be true on the margin. If the person taxed more works harder, then it follows that the person who receives the tax receipts works less, and there are thus neutral effects on income. All economists agree, though, that in addition to an "income" effect there is a "substitution" effect, and that clearly a worker substitutes leisure for work when his tax rate is raised.

thirty-two. If the government then requires that each fill out a form that takes fifteen minutes of their time for each $160 transaction, the wedge widens to six and a half hours. If the form is so complex that each must hire a lawyer and accountant, each paying the lawyer and accountant $5 for every $160 transaction, the wedge widens to seven hours.

The "wedge," then, is not only the financial tax or slice out of the transaction pie, but also all other government burdens on the transaction that require labor. Because the government does not realize revenues from a regulatory order—red tape and paper work—it does not think of such orders as "taxes." But to Smith and Jones, there is no difference between financial taxes and regulatory burdens; each requires precise amounts of labor.*

Here is Laffer describing the wedge model in a November, 1974 memorandum to U.S. Treasury Secretary William Simon.

In order to increase real output growth, it is necessary to focus on why people, machines, land, and other factors of production choose to be employed. Secondly, it is necessary to focus on why firms choose to employ these productive factors.

It is taken here as a simple truth that in part productive factors' choice to work is based upon their ability to earn after-tax income. It is likewise taken as a virtually obvious proposition that the more an employer has to pay his factors of production the less he will want.

Marginal taxes of all sorts stand as a wedge between what an employer pays his factors of production and what they ultimately receive in after-tax income. In the case of payroll taxes, for example, if an employer pays an employee $100 he must also pay his share of the social security contribution of about $5.50. Thus the use of the employee's services costs the employer $105.50. The employee on the other hand has $5.50 deducted from his payroll for his share of the contribution and therefore receives $94.50. The $11 wedge is only the social security taxes. In addition to these taxes, there are also income taxes, sales taxes, property taxes, state and local taxes of all sorts, etc. At our current levels these tax wedge effects are very significant.

In order to increase total output, policy measures must have the effect of both increasing firms' demands for productive factors and increasing the productive factors' desire to be employed. Taxes of all sorts must be reduced. These reductions will be most effective where they lower marginal tax rates the most. Any reduction in marginal rates means that the employer will pay

---

*The wedge is not merely the time in minutes or hours that transactors must work because of government taxation. In the above example, when Smith and Jones were confronted with a complex form, it might have taken them each several hours to fathom it and fill it out. They could each work half an hour at their own skills, though, and pay the receipts (five dollars) to lawyers and accountants, who, on a continuing basis, complete this paper work in a matter of minutes. In this sense, lawyers and accountants operate to reduce the wedge effects of government, keeping Smith and Jones from dropping out of the money economy.

less and yet employees will receive more. Both from the employer and employee point of view more employment will be desired and more output will be forthcoming.[2]

In the modern industrial economy the wedge can be wider than in the pre-industrial era without destroying the money economy, because of the efficiencies of the industrial era. Consider Adam Smith's pin factory of two hundred years ago. Each of ten pin makers, on his own, can make perhaps 20 pins a day. If the government wedge consists of 50 percent taxation, each pin maker is left with 10 pins, and the advantages of making and trading the entire production in the barter economy are considerable. When the ten come together into an enterprise, each making the equivalent of 4,800 pins a day, they are left with 2,400 each after government taxes of 50 percent. There is no incentive to leave the money economy for the barter economy in this case. The efficiencies of collective modern enterprise are so great that it does not pay to fracture it in order to evade the government wedge. The government, though, is not unlimited in its ability to expand the wedge. International trade and competition puts a check on it, for one. Say the U.S. wedge imposed on American Pin is 50 percent, which means that out of a day's production of 48,000 pins, the government gets 24,000 and the enterprise is left with the same amount to trade for the goods and services the ten pin makers desire. Say Japan also imposes a 50 percent wedge on Nippon Pin Co., which also has 24,000 pins left after taxes. If the U.S. government increases the wedge to 28,000 pins, American Pin has 20,000 left for trade. Clearly, in the central market Japanese pin makers will be able to trade their day's production for more than the day's production of American workers. Japanese workers will be more willing to work for Nippon Pin than will American workers for American Pin. Nippon will attract superior personnel, and the productivity of these workers will exceed the productivity of American workers. American Pin cannot simply increase the price of its pins, so that after-tax its workers can trade for the same goods and services as can Nippon's. If it did, other workers in the central market trading the fruits of their labors would buy Nippon's goods and shun American's, until Nippon had to build a second plant, now producing a total of 96,000 pins daily while American Pin went out of business altogether.

American Pin has another alternative. After the government has increased its wedge to 28,000 pins, thereby making American Pin uncompetitive with Nippon Pin, American Pin can ask for relief, pleading with the U.S. government to impose a distinct wedge that is the equivalent of 400 pins against Nippon Pin. The U.S. government

can then impose an "import quota" on Japanese pins, announcing that
henceforth the United States will only permit the importation of the
same amount of pins that were purchased in the previous trading
period. Or, the government could increase its tariff or duty on imported pins, enough so that when the Nippon pins reach the U.S. marketplace, they will not be able to trade for any more goods than the now
higher-priced American pins.

This U.S. barrier to international trade seems to restore the status
quo, but it does not. American workers now receive 20,000 pins daily
after-tax. Japanese workers will still get 24,000. There is now no chance
that American Pin can sell its goods to a third country, for the Japanese
are more competitive, and insofar as American Pin had been exporting
to third countries, it now loses those markets. As Nippon expands, it
attracts superior workers and managers. As American contracts, it loses
superior workers and managers. American Pin, remember, is not only
competing with the Japanese work force, it is also competing with the
rest of the American labor supply. If, at the time the U.S. government
increased the wedge to 28,000 pins daily from 24,000 it also increased
the wedge on all other U.S. transactions by a proportional amount, pin
workers will remain competitive with all other workers in the money
economy. But the money economy will lose marginal competitiveness
with the barter economy. Jones, for example, who may have been
thinking about giving up his bartering as a plumber and taking a job
with American Pin, drops the idea as soon as the wedge on pin workers
rises.

In a free economy, when the government increases the wedge on pin
workers from 24,000 to 28,000, it soon observes these effects. If it is
sufficiently enlightened to see that an increase in tariffs or quotas
against Nippon Pin will damage the U.S. economy more than the
Japanese economy, it still may believe it has freedom to act in other
ways to keep American Pin competitive. An "incomes policy" is the
most usual vehicle. The idea is to either persuade the pin workers that
it is in their interests to accept 20,000 pins after taxes even though their
Japanese counterparts are getting 24,000, or make the policy mandatory
through legislation, prohibiting workers from demanding increases in
wages that will keep them on equal footing with workers abroad. Such
policies may appear to work for a period, as prices and wages stabilize,
but they do not work even momentarily. Just as members of a family or
clan keep account books in their heads, adjusting them with precision,
so too do workers and investors adjust their efforts to precisely
coincide with receipts. Productivity of American Pin declines as existing personnel marginally slough off, as prospective pin makers choose

the barter economy or uncontrolled segments of the public economy, and as investors immediately defer replacement of pin-making plants and equipment, instead wiring financial capital to Tokyo for investment in Nippon Pin.

Let us return now to the wedge condition that prevailed at the outset between American Pin and Nippon Pin, when each was producing 48,000 daily and delivering 24,000 to the government. When the wedge is raised to 28,000 pins, there are two other normal policy pressures applied to the government.

The first is the minimum wage. The ten workers of the pin company are divided into three groups: skilled, semi-skilled, and unskilled. The unskilled are entry-level workers who are just learning the trade. When, suddenly, the workers as a whole see their after-tax income decline because of the increase in the government's wedge, they attempt to increase their after-tax income by pushing up the before-tax wage. They can only do so if the shareholders of American Pin are willing to absorb all the wage increases by accepting a lower return on investment or less reinvestment of earnings to replace worn out plants and equipment. But if American Pin is the marginal U.S. pin manufacturer, and there is no profit to divide in higher wages, only a price increase is possible. And a price increase means a loss of sales to the other manufacturers. Even if the foreign pin makers are closed off with a tariff or quota, there remains the problem of new entries into the domestic market.

American has been paying its skilled workers $5 an hour, its semi-skilled $3.50 and its unskilled $2. With the wage and price adjustment forced by the government tax increase, the wages are now $5.50, $4.00 and $2.50. The price of American pins has had to be raised, and sales fall off to its domestic competitors. But here is Acme Screw Company, which sees this opening in the pin market. It hires the skilled laid-off workers of American for $5.50 an hour, buys the latest easy-to-operate pin-making equipment, hires a dozen housewives at $2 an hour, and with all the inefficiencies can still price the pins at less than American's, thereby driving it out of business.

The minimum wage is an attempt to solve this problem, but it merely creates a new one. Organized labor, which is always the principle force behind minimum-wage legislation, believes that if workers were prohibited from working for less than $2.50 an hour (in this example), American Pin could push up its prices, pay the higher wages to compensate for the increased government wedge, and not face new competition from Acme Screw Company. But if American Pin was indeed the marginal firm, there is no way it could escape the effect of the government wedge expansion, which is to destroy the bottom of the U.S. pin industry. With the increase in the wedge, American Pin has to go out of business, losing out to either foreign or domestic competitors that were already in business, or to a new entry that brought with it marginal efficiencies. The $2.50 minimum wage is, in itself, an infinite wedge between workers whose labor is worth less than $2.50 an hour and the rest of the economy. Not only must Acme Screw pay it, but all of American's healthier competitors, except those abroad must do so. In the Keynesian economic model, it is justified as a means of increasing aggregate demand. But because it stands as a flat prohibition against the entire supply of labor that exists beneath a market value of $2.50 an hour, it is a direct subtraction from both supply and demand. Every increase in the minimum wage induces a decline in real output and a decline in employment. In the limiting case, if, say, no worker were permitted to work at less than $1,000 an hour, there would be no employment and no output in the money economy. Everyone would be forced to barter.

The second policy pressure that emerges when the government wedge expands comes at wages from the opposite direction.

The "solution" is a maximum wage. Here are the ten employees of American Pin left with 20,000 pins after the wedge has increased to 28,000 from 24,000. Previously, the unskilled had been dividing 2,000 among themselves, the semi-skilled 3,000, and the skilled 4,000, a total of 9,000. The cost of materials, overhead, marketing, etc., came to 6,000 pins daily. Bank loans cost 2,000 pins. And the shareholders who put up the money to build the pin factory also got 2,000. The entrepreneur, Williams, who assembled the finances, workers, plans and materials into the enterprise, and who supervises production and marketing of the pins, kept 5,000 pins daily. This totals 24,000 pins. When the wedge increases, 4,000 pins have to come in some way from these factors. Bank loans and fixed costs can't be trimmed, so of the 24,000 previously divided only 16,000 are left to bear the increased tax. If they divide it up proportionately, each will pay an increased tax of 25 percent (even though the increase to 28,000 from 24,000 is only 16 percent). The unskilled workers give up 500 pins, the semi-skilled 750, the skilled 1,000, the shareholders 500, and Williams 1,250.

The argument is then made that the factors who are getting more of the pins should bear more than a proportional share of the wedge, because they can better afford to do so. The wedge should be made progressive. First, the unskilled workers should pay no increase at all because they are the poorest. Thus, there are only 14,000 pins left to bear the burden. Next, it is argued that the semi-skilled should only pay 10 percent or 300 pins, which leaves 11,000 pins to bear the burden of 3,700 pins.

The skilled, it is argued, can't pay 20 percent because that would leave them with only 3,200 pins, only 500 more than the semi-skilled, which is hardly worth the effort of becoming skilled. So it is agreed they pay 15 percent, or 600 pins. This leaves 7,000 pins to bear the burden of 3,100 pins. Only Williams and the shareholders are left to cover this. It is decided that Williams at least is working, so he should pay only 40 percent, or 2,000 pins. The shareholders have to give up 55 percent, or 1,100 out of their 2,000 pins, but it is asserted that they didn't do anything so their income is "unearned" anyway. Thus, the wedge has increased by 16 percent, but the wedge for investors has increased by 55 percent. Williams, who had been making 55 percent as much as his work force, is now making 37 percent as much. Where he had been working, eating, and sleeping pin making to get the enterprise off the ground and keep it in the black, he is now getting less return on his intellectual capital than are his skilled workers, who simply punch the clock and forget pin making beyond the forty-hour week.

What are the results? All along the scale of pin making, there is now less reward for advancing from one step to the next. The unskilled worker gets less reward for becoming semi-skilled, the semi-skilled less reward for becoming skilled, and the skilled worker less reward for becoming an entrepreneur. The entrepreneur, who had been planning expansion, now plans contraction. He had been planning to leave the plant to his son, but his son will not work the same long hours to be rewarded by barely more than the skilled workers, nor will anyone else's son, which means he cannot sell the business except to recoup what equity remains in the plant and equipment. He leaves earlier, does not work weekends, does not replace equipment, so that when his bank loan is paid up he has 2,000 more pins to himself. If he does not die or retire first, he may sell his equity to a competitor and go to work for him in a salaried position. Inevitably, the marginal segment of the pin-making industry is wiped out, and prospective pin makers are either unemployed or working in the barter economy. As the wedge increases again and again and again, to 32,000 pins, to 36,000, to 40,000, American pin-making firms expire one at a time until there is only one left. The government brands this a "monopoly," even though there are dozens of foreign pin-making firms, including Nippon Pin, dominating the world pin trade.

During the process by which the expanding government wedge crushes the American pin industry, the workers become attracted to socialistic political ideology. Indeed, why should ten pin workers be cast onto the unemployment rolls because Williams, who used to be a good employer, is now bleeding his business, frolicking on weekends instead of bringing in orders, and refusing to give his workers their accustomed annual increases in wages?

To see this process clearly, again consider the limiting case. Imagine the government announces that all owners of professional football teams are taxed at 100 percent of their earnings. The Treasury announces that the earnings of the twenty-six teams come to $13 million, and that previously the wedge had been 50 percent, or $6,500,000. The tax will now bring in $13 million.

If owners could earn nothing by assembling such complex enterprises, there would immediately cease to be professional football. Total revenues of the football league, perhaps $150 million, would be extinguished. Treasury would of course not gain $6,500,000, but would lose that amount and much, much more. The football players and other personnel, on total wages of $100 million were paying $40 million to the Treasury and in state and local taxes. The stars were earning several million more in endorsements, and paying high marginal rates on this income.

Sales of football magazines would fall off. Newspaper sales would marginally decline. Football writers would have to find other work. Sales of television sets would decline.

And this is only one side of the supply-demand equation. Professional football is one of the goods and services that workers "demand" with their own labor "supply." They are trading their skills as plumbers, carpenters, nurses, bankers, etc., for the enjoyment of football as entertainment. If football is removed from the marketplace, individuals will of course still trade for other goods and services that remain, but on the margin there will be individuals who choose leisure rather than trade for goods and services other than football. The government will lose the revenues from their now diminished income.

This is a crucial point. People only work to improve their welfare. If they must work to buy football magazines, newspapers, television sets, and tickets to games, many people who enjoy football sufficiently will make that choice. If they no longer have that choice, if football has suddenly disappeared from the marketplace, there is now one less reason to work and one more reason for leisure. The point is important because government does not have to increase the tax wedge to discourage output. It can merely prohibit goods and services from the marketplace. In the limiting case, if the government announced that its tax wedge would drop to zero, but that henceforth nobody could buy anything with the fruits of their labor, all production would cease in the money economy. This would happen as surely as if the government permitted all goods and services to be purchased, but extracted a 100 percent tax wedge on everyone's production.

In this football example, it is obvious that the electorate would not permit the dissolution of football. If the wedge is so high on owners of football teams that the industry is threatened, and the politicians on hand refuse to reduce the wedge in order to reduce the threat, the stage is set for nationalization of professional football. The electorate will accept state ownership and management of the league because it is so vital an element to the national economy. Once the state has removed all the rewards of managing a football enterprise by its 100 percent tax, and acquired the enterprises in collective ownership, it can reintroduce incentives to management. The bureaucrats who are hired for this purpose may not be as devoted and as capable as the private entrepreneurs squeezed out by the government wedge, but at least there will be football and the economy will not be shocked by its sudden extinction.

It is the government wedge that produces the socialistic impulse in the electorate. As the wedge expands, crushing small, weak firms and leaving only the larger and stronger, political pressures emerge to break up the larger firms into smaller ones again. This further increases the government wedge and hastens the contraction of the industry as a whole. There would also be a redistribution of risk; with twenty small firms instead of three—a large, medium, and small—there is at least a chance the small will survive the new competition. The process can end only in extinction of the industry or collective ownership of it.

In the case of Hollywood, the process ended in extinction of the motion-picture industry. A motion-picture studio can be considered the equivalent of Adam Smith's pin factory. Individually, the unskilled, semi-skilled, and skilled people who composed a studio under a manager of talent and finance could not produce a film of sufficient quality to be economic. Drawn together on one lot, their individual talents can be pooled into films of high quality. The difference between pin making and motion-picture production is crucial, however. A motion picture is almost pure intellectual capital. The intellectual capital that goes into pin making is at its zenith at the creation of the enterprise, but thereafter the intellectual capital required to keep it in motion drops to a lower level. The expanding government wedge might crush incentives pushing the pin-making entrepreneur to expand, but the factory can go on functioning for a long time on the initial burst of intellectual creativity. In motion-picture production, each picture requires its own burst of creativity, and is more sensitive to the effects of the government wedge on labor supply.

In the golden age of Hollywood, from 1930 to 1950, the government wedge expanded relentlessly. The high personal income-tax rates imposed by Presidents Hoover and Roosevelt to push the financial burdens of the Depression and World War II onto the higher income classes, at first barely nicked the movie industry. Only a handful of "stars" were making enough to get into the top tax bracket of 91 percent, encountered at $100,000 a year. For each of these stars, there were thousands of employees, each talented in his or her own right. The nation's best writers were doing scripts for $300 a week in the 1930s, and costumers, designers, cameramen, and supporting players were drawing lesser salaries that were also considered princely. Not only were they not giving up a great deal of their labor supply to the government (being in low brackets), but they were trading their labor for goods and services that were almost entirely escaping the government income-tax wedge. The inflation following World War II changed that. The entire industry was pushed up against the higher brackets, and with each push greater tensions were created within the enterprise to distribute the remaining "pins" left by the expanding government wedge. Prices could not rise because attendance would fall off, so studio entrepreneurs could only diminish rewards within the enterprise, watch the quality and productivity of their employees fall, complaining along the way of "socialist" and "communist" impulses within the ranks of the industry unions and guilds.

Had the industry been able to get a tariff or quota system imposed against foreign-produced films, it might have been able to extend its life in Hollywood for a year or two. The public had domestic substitutes for entertainment, however, and as the cost of motion pictures climbed and their quality* fell, it pushed the development of television in the marketplace. The new technology gave entertainment a broader market, as if a new way had been found to double the production of pins to 96,000 from 48,000 with the same number of people, thus temporarily increasing the number of pins left to distribute after the government wedge was approaching 48,000 pins under

---

*When financial rewards diminish as a result of the expanding wedge, it is not the most talented personnel who rise to the top, but the most ambitious, who are willing to put up with almost anything and do almost anything to advance as entertainers. Those with greater talents but lesser stomach are the first to drop away from the competition when financial rewards diminish. Potential Gables, Sinatras, Crosbys, and Hopes drift into other occupations before their talents can blossom. They are replaced by obscene comics, shrieking singers, and copulating actors.

the old method. After an initial burst of creativity in the new medium, the temporary gains of efficiency were already being chewed up by the continually expanding wedge, and the quality of television programing has continued its relentless decline. As the intellectual capital forged in the Hollywood of the thirties and forties dies out, and the talent developed on television during the fifties fades too, pressures for state ownership of entertainment, public television, and taxpayer grants to the "arts" gather momentum.

As the movie studios, followed by television, followed by the pin factories, are crushed by the expanding government wedge, the barter economy expands. And it is not only Jones the plumber and Smith the carpenter trading their labor out of sight of the tax collector. Bartering to avoid tax payment is only the mildest form of immorality resorted to in order to escape the debilitating effects of the government wedge.

Here is Smith in New York City with $30 to spend. He can't make up his mind whether to spend it on two tickets to the Metropolitan Opera, or on one performance by a prostitute. He is on the margin, trying to decide on which of these goods and services he wishes to trade his after-tax income as a carpenter. Let us say that on one visit he trades for the opera tickets, and on the next visit he trades for the prostitute. Now the government introduces its wedge. The $30 that goes to the Metropolitan Opera is divided up among all the employees; musicians, divas, baritones, etc., and they pay taxes on it to federal, state, and local governments. When they are finished, there is only $20 left, enabling the opera troup to trade for only two hours of Smith's labor, or the equivalent in other goods and services, whereas he earned it in three. The prostitute keeps the entire $30 and is able to trade for three hours of Smith's carpentry, or the equivalent in other goods and services. Into this small economy comes Mary S., with every intention of trying to get a job at the Metropolitan Opera, perhaps in the chorus, and to work her way to stardom. If she can't make it in this endeavor, she will become a prostitute. Upon arriving, she learns that the government has just introduced a wedge of 33 percent at the Metropolitan Opera, and it is now relatively more profitable to be a prostitute. Equilibrium is restored on the supply side of this process when so many women become prostitutes that each has to put in 33 percent more time in pursuit of business. It is clear that an increase in the government wedge decreases the quality of opera and increases the supply of prostitutes.*

*In the larger economy, it is of course unlikely that Mary S., the potential opera star, is directly shifted into an underworld occupation. Rather she shifts into a lesser occupation, becoming "underemployed" in the money economy, and the wedge concurrently shifts

All underworld activity of a commercial nature is similarly encouraged by the expanding government wedge. Gambling, the numbers racket, loansharking, narcotics, robbery, and burglary are all fed by expansion of the government wedge. It is extremely difficult to offset these effects by another government activity—police repression. If the government wedge is one third of transactions in the money economy, police have to *perpetually* harass all prostitutes so that as a group they have to spend 33 percent more time doing the same business. The cost to the community in police expenditures is so high as a result that the wedge itself expands, and more repressive measures must follow.

There is far less underworld activity in socialist and communist countries than in market economies, not because there is more police repression of these activities, but because of the way the government disposes of the receipts of its wedge.

In socialist countries, instead of having individuals trade their labor in a central marketplace, central authorities assess the value of individuals and attempt to trade for them, much in the manner that baseball owners trade players among each other or plantation owners traded slaves. Jones the plumber and Smith the carpenter are unknown to each other, although each needs the services of the other. The socialist bureaucracy has them identified, and arranges the trade of their labors, extracting the wedge in the process of transaction. The receipts are spent to provide life necessities to Jones and Smith: housing, medical services, education, and pensions. The government is the only provider of these services, pensions, etc., they must trade their labor when and where the central authorities determine. It does no good for them to have receipts from illicit services, except insofar as these can obtain luxury goods on the black market. Mary S. cannot come to Moscow to try out for the Bolshoi Ballet, but even if she could, and out of failure offered to trade her charms on a streetcorner for thirty rubles tax-free, it would do her no good in finding lodgings.

In the market economies, governments increasingly spend the receipts of the expanding wedge on payments to individuals on the condition that they do not trade their labor in the central marketplace. Americans get welfare benefits, food stamps, unemployment insurance, government housing, and to a greater degree, retirement benefits, explicitly on the condition that they be unemployed. Jones the plumber needs carpentry work and Smith the carpenter needs plumbing work. Having testified to the authorities that they are unemployed,

---

all other employees downward into underemployment classes, where at the margin an aspiring shopperson is the one who actually goes over the edge into bartering via prostitution.

they each receive checks from the government entitling them to buy the services they need from other plumbers and carpenters who are still operating in the money economy.

The socialist system is grossly inefficient because the task of having bureaucrats assess and trade labor supplies of hundreds of millions of people is incredibly difficult. The market system, too, becomes grossly inefficient, perhaps even more than the socialist system when the expanding government wedge crushes out incentives and underemploys an entire economy. There is no reason why it should do so, as we will now see.

CHAPTER 6

Money and Tax Rates

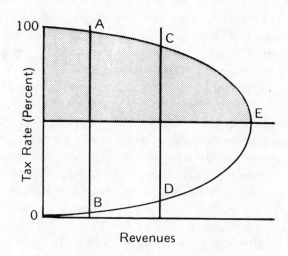

The Laffer Curve

"There are always two tax rates that yield the same revenues," observes Arthur Laffer. When, in the winter of 1974, an aide to President Gerald Ford asked him to explain his statement, Laffer drew the curve shown above to illustrate his point. When the tax rate is at 100 percent, all production ceases in the money economy. People will not work in the money economy if all the fruits of their labor are confiscated by the government. An individual will not work for $1,000 a day if, after taxes, his paycheck comes to zero. Because production ceases, there is nothing for the government's 100 percent rate to confiscate, and revenues to the state are also zero.

On the other hand, if the tax rate is zero, people can keep 100 percent of what they produce in the money economy. There is no government wedge, and thus no governmental barrier to production, so production is maximized. Output of the money economy is limited only by the desire of workers for leisure; but because the tax rate is zero, government revenues are also zero. As was earlier noted, without revenues there can be no government; at zero percent tax rate the economy is in an anarchic condition, and at 100 percent tax rate the economy is functioning entirely through barter.

Thus the Laffer Curve. If the government reduces its rate to something less than 100 percent, say to point A, some segment of the barter economy will be able to gain so many efficiencies by being in the money economy that, even with near-confiscatory tax rates, after-tax production will still exceed that of the barter economy. Production will start up and revenues will flow into the government treasury. By a lowering of the tax rates, we find an increase in revenues. On the bottom end of the Curve, the same thing is happening. With a small tax rate, some segment of the economy finds the marginal loss of income exceeding the efficiencies gained in the money economy and is either shifted into barter or into leisure. But with a tax rate, revenues flow into the government treasury. This is point B. Point A represents a very high tax rate and very low production. Point B represents a very low tax rate and very high production. Yet they each yield the same revenue to the government.

The same condition applies at points C and D. The government finds that by a further lowering of the rate, from A to C, revenues increase with the further expansion of output. By raising the tax rate from B to D, revenues also increase by the same amount.

Revenues plus production are maximized at point E. If, at point E, the government lowers the tax rate again, output will increase, but revenues will fall. If the tax rate is raised, both output and revenue will decline. The shaded area shows the prohibitive range for government, where rates are unnecessarily high and can be reduced with gains in both output and revenue.

The next important point to observe about the Laffer Curve is that, except for the zero and 100 percent rates, there are no other numbers on the Curve. Point E is not 50 percent, although it can be, but is rather a variable number. *It is the point at which the electorate desires to be taxed.* At points B and D, the electorate desires more government goods and services and wishes to pay the higher rates producing the revenues consistent with E. At points A and C, the electorate desires more private goods and services in the money economy, and wishes to pay the lower rates consistent with revenues at E. It is the task of the political leader to determine point E and to follow it through its variations as closely as is possible. This is true whether the political leader heads a family unit or a nation.

The father who disciplines his son at point A, imposing harsh penalties for violation of rules major and minor, only invites sullen rebellion, stealth and lying (tax evasion). The permissive father who disciplines lightly at point B invites open, reckless rebellion, the son's independence and relatively undisciplined growth coming at the expense of the rest of the family. The superior parent seeks point E, which will likely be at a different level of discipline for his son than his daughter, or be different from one son to another.

For the political leader of the nation, point E can be represented by a very low or a very high number. When the nation is at war, point E can approach 100 percent.

At the siege of Leningrad in World War II, for example, the people of the city produced for 900 days at tax rates approaching 100 percent. Russian soldiers and civilians worked to their physical limits, receiving as pay the barest of rations. Had the citizens of Leningrad not wished to be taxed at that high rate in order to hold off the Nazi army, the city would have fallen, with many citizens paying the ultimate tax rate.

The number represented by point E will change abruptly from one day to the next when one day the nation is at war and at peace the next. The electorate's demand for government military goods and services falls sharply and it therefore desires to be taxed at a lower rate. If rates are not lowered consistent with this new lower level of demand for government goods and services, output will fall to some level consistent with a point on the shaded, prohibitive side of the Laffer Curve. After World War I, for example, the rates imposed during wartime were left in place and greatly contributed to the recession of 1919-1920. Warren G. Harding ran for President in 1920 on a slogan promising a "return to normalcy" on tax rates and was elected in a landslide; the subsequent rolling back of the rates ushered in the economic expansion of the "Roaring Twenties." After World War II, wartime tax rates were quickly reduced following V-J Day, and the economy enjoyed a smooth transition to peacetime. In Japan and West Germany, there was no adjustment of tax rates immediately after the war and as a result recovery of their economies was delayed. Germany's recovery began in 1948 as personal income-tax rates were reduced under Finance Minister Ludwig Erhard along with an end to much of the government's regulation of commerce. Japan's recovery did not begin until 1950 when wartime tax rates were finally adjusted.

In each of these examples regarding economic conversions from wartime to peacetime, reduction of *rates* produced increased *revenues* for the government. The distinction between tax rates and tax revenues is one the political leader must fully appreciate if he is to be successful in discerning the desires of the electorate.

The easiest way for a political leader to determine whether an increase in rates will produce increased rather than falling revenues, is by putting the proposition to the electorate. It is not enough for the politician to propose an increase from point B to point D on the Curve. He must also specify how the anticipated revenues will be spent. When voters approve a bond issue to increase construction of schools, highways, or bridges, they are explicitly telling the politicians that they are willing and desirous of paying the higher tax rates that will be required to finance the bonds. In rejecting a bond issue of this kind the electorate is not necessarily telling the politician that it is being taxed sufficiently already and is at point E or beyond. The message is simply that the price in tax rates is too high in terms of the goods and services offered by the government.

Only a tiny fraction of all government expenditures are determined in this fashion, however. Most judgments of tax rates and expenditures by government are made by individual politicians, and it has been the exception rather than the rule throughout history that politicians, by accident or design, have sought to increase revenues by lowering rates. Andrew Mellon, who designed the Harding-Coolidge tax rate reductions of the 1920s, became a national hero as a result and was called the greatest Treasury Secretary since Alexander Hamilton. Ludwig Erhard achieved heroic stature in Germany after his financial policies produced the German "economic miracle," as it was commonly described. The Mellon/Erhard "miracles" were simply confirmation of their opinions that tax rates were in the prohibitive range and could be reduced with beneficial effects on both output and revenue.

The idea behind the Laffer Curve is no doubt as old as civilization, but politicians have always had trouble grasping it. In his essay *Of Taxes*, written in 1756, David Hume pondered this problem:

Exorbitant taxes, like extreme necessity, destroy industry by producing despair; and even before they reach this pitch, they raise the wages of the labourer and manufacturer, and heighten the price of all commodities. An attentive disinterested legislature will observe the point when the emolument ceases, and the prejudice begins. But as the contrary character is much more common, 'tis to be feared that taxes all over Europe are multiplying to such a degree as will entirely crush all art and industry; tho' perhaps, their first increase, together with other circumstances, might have contributed to the growth of these advantages.[1]

The chief reason politicians and economists throughout history have failed to grasp the idea behind the Laffer Curve is their confusion of work and productivity. The politician understands, both through introspection and by observation, that when tax rates are raised, there is a tendency to work harder and longer to maintain after-tax income. What he does not see, because it requires analysis on the margin, is that as taxes are raised individuals in the system may indeed work harder, but their productivity will decline. Hume himself had trouble with this point:

> There is a prevailing maxim, among some reasoners, that every new tax creates a new ability in the subject to bear it, and that each increase of public burdens increases proportionably the industry of the people. This maxim is of such a nature as is most likely to be abused; and is so much the more dangerous as its truth cannot be altogether denied: but it must be owned, when kept within certain bounds, to have some foundation in reason and experience.[2]

Adam Smith, writing his *Wealth of Nations* twenty years later had no such problem because he saw, in his pin factory, that what is important to a nation is not the work of individuals but the productivity of individuals working together. When the tax rates on the pin factory are raised, the workers themselves may work harder, expending more effort to maintain income by offering their free hours to other labor. If the pin-making entrepreneur is the marginal manufacturer, the increased tax rate will cause him to shift into leisure or a lower level of economic activity, and the *system* will lose *all* the production of the pin factory. The politician who stands in the midst of this scene may rightly conclude that the increase in tax rates has people working harder. It is not easy to see that they are now less efficient in their work and are producing less.

To see this in another way, consider that there are three men who are skilled at building houses. If they work together, one works on the foundation, one on the frame, and the third on the roof. Together they can build three houses in three months. If they work separately, each building his own home, it takes them six months to produce the three houses. If the tax rate on home-building is 49 percent, they will work together because the government leaves them a small gain due to their division of labor. If the tax goes to 51 percent, they suffer a net loss because of their teamwork and so work separately in the barter economy and pay no taxes. When they were working together, the government was getting revenues equivalent to the value of three almost fully completed homes. At a 51-percent tax rate, the government loses all the revenue and the economy loses the production of the three extra homes that could have been built by their joint effort in the money economy.

The worst mistakes in history are made by political leaders who, instead of realizing that rates could be lowered as a means of gaining revenues, become alarmed at the fall in revenues as citizens seek to escape high rates by bartering and do-it-yourself work. Their impulse is to impose taxes that cannot be escaped, the most onerous of which is a poll tax or head tax, which must be paid annually for the mere privilege of living. Hume had no trouble on this point:

> Historians inform us that one of the chief causes of the destruction of the Roman state was the alteration which Constantine introduced into the finances, by substituting a universal poll-tax in lieu of almost all the tithes, customs, and excises which formerly composed the revenue of the empire. The people, in all the provinces, were so grinded and oppressed by the publicans (tax-collectors) that they were glad to take refuge under the conquering arms of the barbarians, whose dominion, as they had fewer necessities and less art, was found preferable to the refined tyranny of the Romans.[3]

The trouble with a poll tax, as Hume observed, is that it *can* be escaped. One method of escape is not to defend your country against an aggressor who promises, once installed, to remove the tax. Charles Louis Secondat, Baron de Montesquieu, made a similar observation in Book XIII of his *The Spirit of the Laws:*

> Because a moderate government has been productive of admirable effects, this moderation has been laid aside; because great taxes have been raised they wanted to carry them to excess; and ungrateful to the hand of liberty, of whom they received this present, they addressed themselves to slavery, who never grants the least favor.
>
> Liberty produces excessive taxes; the effect of excessive taxes is slavery; and slavery produces a dimunition of tribute . . .
>
> It was this excess of taxes that occasioned the prodigious facility with which the Mohammedans carried on their conquests. Instead of a continual series of extortions devised by the subtle avarice of the Greek emperors, the people were subjected to a simple tribute which was paid and collected with ease. Thus they were far happier in obeying a barbarous nation than a corrupt government, in which they suffered every inconvenience of lost liberty, with all the horror of present slavery.[4]

Modern governments have at least abandoned the notion of using a poll tax to reach into the barter economy for revenues. It is now easier for citizens to escape such a tax than when it was exacted throughout the Roman Empire. First, the world economy fragmented into many, rather than few states, which means that it is easier for citizens to migrate in order to escape oppressive taxation. Secondly, transportation has shortened distances which also facilitates migration from high tax areas to low tax areas. Thirdly, the global electorate has become more homogenous, and migrating citizens can find pockets of émigrés in most foreign lands with similar national backgrounds and cultures, so it is no longer necessary to live exclusively among "barbarians" in order to escape the crush of taxation by a levy for simply living.

Instead, modern governments go directly to the barter economy in search of revenues. Activities previously not admitted to the money economy and public marketplace because of public disapproval, such as gambling and pornography, are welcomed because of the promise of revenues. This tends to lower the quality of the marketplace itself, hastening the exodus or discouraging the entry of enterprises that have earned public approbation.

Another timeless remedy of governments that find revenues falling in the face of rising tax rates is to increase the number and powers of their tax collectors. This method invariably further reduces the flow of revenues to the treasury. Yet with thousands of years of government experimentation and failure in "cracking down" on tax evasion, the policy remains a favorite of modern governments. Here, at length, is Adam Smith on why such policies are doomed from the start:

> Every tax ought to be so contrived as both to take out and to keep out of the pockets of the people as little as possible, over and above what it brings into the public treasury of the state. A tax may either take out or keep out of the pockets of the people a great deal more than it brings into the public treasury, in the four following ways.
>
> First, the levying of it may require a great number of officers, whose salaries may eat up the greater part of the produce of the tax, and whose perquisites may impose another additional tax upon the people.
>
> Secondly, it may obstruct the industry of the people, and discourage them from applying to certain branches of business which might give maintenance and employment to great multitudes. While it obliges the people to pay, it may thus diminish, or perhaps destroy, some of the funds which might enable them to do so.
>
> Thirdly, by the forfeitures and other penalties which these unfortunate individuals incur who attempt unsuccessfully to evade the tax, it may frequently ruin them, and thereby put an end to the benefit which the community might have received from the employment of their capitals. An injudicious tax offers a great temptation to smuggling. But the penalties of smuggling must rise in proportion to the temptation. The law, contrary to all the ordinary principles of justice, first creates the temptation, and then punishes those who yield to it; and it commonly enhances the punishment too in proportion to the very circumstances which ought certainly to alleviate it, the temptation to commit the crime.
>
> Fourthly, by subjecting the people to the frequent visits and the odious

examination of the tax-gatherers, it may expose them to much unnecessary trouble, vexation, and oppression; and though vexation is not, strictly speaking, expense, it is certainly equivalent to the expense at which every man would be willing to redeem himself from it.[5]

Adam Smith's point on smuggling may now seem obscure, but following are excerpts from a recent editorial by the *Wall Street Journal*, in which the newspaper invites New York State and New York City to cut their combined cigarette tax to ten cents a pack from twenty-six cents:

Through our browsings in the United States Tobacco Journal we have learned of estimates that half the cigarets smoked in New York City are smuggled in from North Carolina, where the tax is two cents a pack. State Sen. Roy Goodman, a Manhattan Republican, says the state and city are losing $93 million a year in this fashion. The smugglers load 40-ft. trailers with 60,000 cartons purchased legally at $2.40 each and peddle them in the city via the organized-crime network for $3.75, which is $1.25 or more below legitimate retail.

Mr. Goodman recommends a one-year suspension of the city's eight-cent-a-pack tax in order to break up the smuggling, plus an increase in the state enforcement field staff to 250 from the current 50, plus five years in jail for anyone caught smuggling 20,000 cartons or more. Last year only nine smugglers were jailed, each for a few months, with the common penalty $10 or $15.

If Mr. Goodman's solution were adopted, at the end of the year the smugglers would be back, and the state would have a bigger bureaucracy. More smugglers would be caught, more judges and bailiffs and clerks would have to be hired, more jails would have to be built and more jailers hired. The wives and children of the jailed smugglers would go on welfare.

Cutting the tax to 10 cents avoids all that. It immediately becomes uneconomic to smuggle. The enforcement staff of 50 can be assigned to more useful work, the state saving $1 million on that count alone. The courts would be less clogged with agents and smugglers, and the taxpayers would save court costs, as well as the costs of confining convicted smugglers and caring for their families.

The state and city would *appear* to face a loss of $50 million or $60 million in revenues, but of course smokers would now buy their cigarets through legitimate channels and the 10 cents a pack would yield about as much in revenues as 26 cents a pack yields now. But that's not all. Legitimate wholesalers would double their cigaret sales, earning higher business profits and personal income that the city and state then taxes.

And don't forget the impact on the millions of cigaret smokers who would save 16 cents a pack. At a pack a day, that's $58.40 per year. At average marginal tax rates, a smoker has to earn more than $80 before federal, state and city taxes are deducted to get that amount. He can thus maintain his or her standard of living on $80 less in gross wage demands per year, which means it becomes economic for the marginal employer to do business in New York, increasing the number of jobs of all varieties and reducing cost and tax pressure on social services.

Among other benefits, the industrious smugglers would have to find legitimate employment. It might be argued that they would be thrown on the welfare roles. But if we know New York City, they are already on the welfare roles, and would be forced to get off once they have visible jobs.[6]

The Finance Office of New York City simply rejected the idea that a lowering of rates would produce expanded revenue, unwilling to take the advice of either Adam Smith or the *Wall Street Journal*. But then, Adam Smith's advice was not taken in England at the time he tendered it. It was not until 1827 that an Act of Parliament tested the theory, and then only by accident. Oddly enough, the accident involved tobacco smuggling. In the five years prior to 1826, the population had increased by 17 percent, but revenues from tobacco duty had fallen 8 percent against the years 1810-14 . . . .

. . . the consumption of tobacco had failed to increase in proportion to the increase in the population. A curious circumstance had happened as regards the duty on tobacco. In effecting the statutory re-arrangement of the duties in the previous year, the draughtsman of the Bill, in error, allowed one-fourth of the duty to lapse in July. Unconsciously he had accomplished a master stroke; for his reduction in the duty was followed by a decrease in smuggling so considerable as to induce Robinson to allow his surplus, estimated at about 700,000 pounds, to go to continue the reduction thus unconsciously effected.[7]

The Politburo of the Soviet Union has the same problem as the Finance Office of New York City; rejecting the idea behind the Laffer Curve. The greatest burden to Soviet economic development is Soviet agriculture. Of 250 million people in the Soviet Union, roughly 34.3 million are engaged in producing the nation's food, of which there is never enough. The United States, with 220 million, employs only 4.3 million in food production, and these produce a surplus for export that is equivalent to a fourth of all Soviet production. The drain on the Soviet economy is not limited to the low productivity of its farm sector, however. Because there are always shortages, and because the state does not use the price system to allocate what is available, but puts farm goods on the market at regulated prices, Soviet citizens spend billions of hours annually waiting on lines. If plentiful food were produced, the Soviets could still allocate via regulated prices in conformance with their ideology, but most of the lines would disappear and the talents and energies of the urban work force would not be drained in queuing. The source of the problem is the high marginal tax rates exacted on the state's collective farms.

The state will provide land, capital, and housing, on a collective. It will also permit the workers to keep 10 percent of the value of their production. The marginal tax rate is thus 90 percent. In producing food from the land, a small expenditure of effort will produce, say, 100 units of production. It may take twice the effort to yield 150 units of production. And a redoubled effort again to produce 200 units. The workers thus face a progressive tax schedule so withering in its steepness that all incentive to put forth any but the minimum effort is lost. By putting in the minimum work, the worker gets land, capital, housing, medical care, and ten units of the output. By quadrupling his effort (not necessarily physical effort, but merely increasing attentiveness to detail), he will get the same services as before and only ten more units of output.

Meanwhile, the peasants on the collectives are permitted private plots, the entire output of which they are permitted to keep. The tax rate on the private plots is 0 percent, with this result:

... 27 percent of the total value of Soviet farm output—about $32.5 billion worth a year—comes from private plots that occupy less than one percent of the nation's agricultural lands (about 26 million acres). At that rate, private plots are roughly 40 times as efficient as land worked collectively .... peasants farm their own plots much more intensively than they do collective land.

Ultimately, the Communist ideal is to have this last embarrassing—but necessary vestige of private enterprise—wither away as industrialized state farming grows in scale and output. Nikita Khrushchev, in spite of rural roots, pursued that end vigorously and earned the enmity of the peasantry. He cut the size of private plots to a maximum of half an acre and made life difficult for the farm market trade. I was told by Russian friends that Ukrainian peasants became so irate that they stopped selling eggs as food and made paint out of them.

Under Brezhnev things have improved. The maximum plot went back up to an acre and measures were taken to improve farm market operations. Soviet figures show the private farm output grew nearly 15 percent from 1966 to 1973.[8]

In terms of the Laffer Curve, what Khrushchev did in reducing the size of the private plots to one-half acre from one acre was to increase the marginal tax rate of the *system* from point C to point A. It was undoubtedly a major cause of his political downfall. Brezhnev, on the other hand, moved the marginal tax rate for the system back to point C, increasing output and revenues back to where they had been; an "economic miracle" of minor dimensions, but one that has undoubtedly contributed heavily to Brezhnev's durability as a political leader. Unhappily, the Soviet Politburo does not seem to be aware that the marginal tax rate for the system as a whole could be further reduced, either by lowering the rate on the collectives by reversing the progressive schedule (90 percent on the first 100 units, 50 percent on the second 50 units, 30 percent thereafter, for example), or by increasing the size of the private plots to one and a half or two acres.*

The secret of Communist China's durability lies in the regressivity of its agricultural income taxation. Only 18 percent of a base-year production is taxed, the first 5 percent at a 100-percent rate, the next 13 percent at a 30-percent rate. All grain produced over the base amount is tax free. With these incentives, communal teams need no private plots to feed the nation's more than 900 million people. No similar incentive system exists in China's industrial sector, although the new leadership in Peking is moving in that direction.

ii

Modern governments have found another way to reach beyond the money economy into the barter or leisure economy for tax revenues. The practice of debasing the currency, or "coin-clipping," is an ancient one. In this century for the first time the practice of currency debasement has been combined with progressive tax schedules, providing at least an illusion that tax rates can be increased in the prohibitive range of the Laffer Curve with beneficial effects on tax revenues.

To get the meaning of this statement, we must first clearly understand the idea of money and inflation. Up until this point the author has been purposefully negligent in discussing money so that the reader would become used to thinking of the economy in real terms, that is, the exchange of one individual's labour for another's. It is only as children when we have not yet learned the concept of money, that we view the political economy in purely real terms. Once we come to understand the concept of money we automatically introduce a confusion into our understanding of the economy, forgetting that we only work in order to trade our labour supply for the supply of other workers. Instead, we come to think that we work for "money," and that money is the object of work.

---

*Not only would farm productivity expand, but so too would urban industrial productivity. The peasants, with their higher after-tax incomes, would consume more of the goods produced in the cities; the urban workers, freed from waiting in lines for meager goods and finding a richer variety of farm goods in the marketplace, would increase their productivity in order to acquire them. Such gains could be realized without tampering with collectivist ideology. Indeed, if marginal tax rates on collective output were to decline to zero after, say, the third 100 units of production, the peasants would tend to lose interest in their private plots and discipline themselves to work the collectives, where the division of labour enhances efficiency.

"Money is not, properly speaking, one of the subjects of commerce," wrote David Hume in 1758, "but only the instrument which men have agreed upon to facilitate the exchange of one commodity for another. It is none of the wheels of trade: It is the oil which renders the motion of the wheels more smooth and easy.[9]

Individuals will readily agree, once reminded, that money is neither the object nor subject of commerce, but merely the medium of exchange. But the confusion is so strong that politicians will insist on keeping thousands of tons of gold locked up in Fort Knox, unable to explain why a medium of exchange should be hoarded, except that their predecessors did so.

It is necessary to understand the concept of money in order to see how misunderstandings of what it is and is not cause political leaders to do things with money that run counter to the interests of the electorate and, unwittingly, to the interests of the political leaders themselves. Once again, we will let Adam Smith put down the foundation for this understanding:

When the division of labour has been once thoroughly established, it is but a very small part of a man's wants which the product of his own labour can supply. He supplies the far greater part of them by exchanging that surplus part of the produce of his own labour, which is over and above his own consumption, for such parts of the produce of other men's labour as he has occasion for. Every man thus lives by exchanging, or becomes in some measure a merchant, and the society grows to be what is properly a commercial society.

But when the division of labour first began to take place, this power of exchanging must frequently have been very much clogged and embarrassed in its operation. One man, we shall suppose, has more of a certain commodity than he himself has occasion for, while another has less. The former consequently would be glad to dispose of, and the latter to purchase, a part of this superfluity. But if this latter should chance to have nothing that the former stands in need of, no exchange can be made between them. The butcher has more meat in his shop than he himself can consume, and the brewer and the baker would each of them be willing to purchase a part of it. But they have nothing to offer in exchange, except the different productions of their respective trades, and the butcher is already provided with all the bread and beer which he has immediate occasion for. No exchange can, in this case, be made between them. He cannot be their merchant, nor they his customers; and they are all of them thus mutually less serviceable to one another. In order to avoid the inconvenience of such situations, every prudent man in every period of society, after the first establishment of the division of labour, must naturally have endeavored to manage his affairs in such a manner, as to have at all times by him, besides the peculiar produce of his own industry, a certain quantity of some one commodity or other, such as he imagined few people would be likely to refuse in exchange for the produce of their industry . . . .

In all countries . . . men seem at last to have been determined by irresistible reasons to give the preference, for this employment, to metals above every other commodity. Metals cannot only be kept with as little loss as any other commodity, scarce any thing be less perishable than they are, but they can likewise, without any loss, be divided into any number of parts, as by fusion those parts can easily be reunited again; a quality which no other equally durable commodities possess, and which more than any other quality renders them fit to be the instruments of commerce and circulation.

The man who wanted to buy salt, for example, and had nothing but cattle to give in exchange for it, must have been obliged to buy salt to the value of a whole ox, or a whole sheep, at a time. He could seldom buy less than this because what he was to give for it could seldom be divided without loss; and if he had a mind to buy more, he must, for the same reasons, have been obliged to buy double or triple the quantity, to wit, of two or three oxen, or of two or three sheep. If, on the contrary, instead of sheep or oxen, he had metals to give in exchange for it, he could easily proportion the quantity of the metal to the precise quantity of the commodity which he had immediate occasion for.[10]

In Smith's simple example, we see butcher, baker, and brewer solving their exchange problems by agreeing on a medium, bits of metal. Where does the metal come from? If it is readily available over the next hill, won't the butcher or baker abandon his trade, scoop up the stuff, and use it to acquire the brewer's beer? Perhaps. But if the brewer accepts the metal for his beer and now attempts to acquire meat and bread with it, but finds none have been produced, he realizes his metal has lost its value as money and thereafter accepts no more of it.

Because there is such need for a money that avoids this kind of pitfall, by trial and error the butcher, baker, and brewer fix on a metal that is not sitting around waiting to be scooped up, a metal so hard to pry from the ground that the butcher, baker, and brewer are not tempted to leave their trades. A fourth trade emerges, the miner, who develops the skills to pry it from the ground and does it so well that he can't be tempted to abandon his trade to become a butcher, brewer, or baker. The metal he pries from the earth has usefulness not only as money but as a commodity, which can be shaped into articles of value. The common metals become cookware, construction materials, etc. The rare metals are shaped into objects of ornamentation, dinnerplate, and jewelry.

In the ancient markets, shoppers carried bars of metal with them to exchange for goods. This inconvenience gave way to the coinage of metal by the government as part of its charge by the electorate to maintain the marketplace. The miner carries his bullion to the open market, some of it being sold to individuals for its use as a commodity, some being sold to the government for conversion into coin. When he sells bullion to the government, the miner is satisfied to give up ten units of bullion and receive coins containing, say, nine units of the same metal. The one unit difference covers the government's cost of coinage and its profit for having undertaken this public enterprise. The difference is the government's seigniorage. The miner is satisfied to give up the seigniorage because he is saved the trouble of persuading merchants of the purity of his bullion and of dividing it into precise amounts in exchange for the goods he desires. The government—the sovereign—perhaps expends a half unit in the minting of the bullion and has a half unit to finance the costs of general government.

This happy condition becomes disrupted when the sovereign attempts to increase his seigniorage. He obtains ten units of bullion from the miner in exchange for nine units of coin, and with this new bullion mints coins that contain only eight units. His cost of minting is still a half unit, and he now has one and a half units that he can use to obtain goods and services in the marketplace. The volume of goods and services in the market has not increased, but the quantity of money has. In terms of this new eight-unit coin, all prices must rise in order to bring the market back to equilibrium: If there are ten apples in the economy and $10.00, each will trade for $1.00; if there are ten apples and $11.00, each apple must sell for $1.10 or someone in the economy will have $1.00 that will buy nothing.

The result of the sovereign's action is price inflation, or a fall in the monetary standard. The effect is almost the same as if the sovereign were still minting nine-unit coins and either strolled into the marketplace and confiscated one unit of goods, or levied a tax of one unit on the market. A confiscation or tax is not as harmful, however, because it only affects the relationship between the sovereign and the market. A decline in the monetary standard has disruptive effects on the relationship of traders in the market.

By debasing the currency, says Adam Smith, the princes and sovereign states that did so . . .

> . . . were enabled, in appearance, to pay their debts and fulfill their engagements with a smaller quantity of silver than would otherwise have been requisite. It was indeed in appearance only; for their creditors were really defrauded of part of what was due to them. All other debtors in the state were allowed the same privilege, and might pay with the same nominal sum of the new and debased coin whatever they had borrowed in the old. Such operations have always proved favorable to the debtor, and ruinous to the creditor, and have sometimes produced a greater and more universal revolution in the fortunes of private persons, than could have been occasioned by a very great public calamity."[11]

In other words, private transactors in the marketplace who had come to trust in the coin of the realm would discover that they could no longer merely concentrate on trading goods. They would now have to expend intellectual effort in studying the coins themselves in over-the-counter transactions. They would have to protect themselves in drawing contracts for future delivery of goods, so that items sold for nine-unit coins could not be paid for in eight-unit coins. Where creditors suffer and debtors benefit by an unanticipated switch in coin by the government, there naturally follows a weakening of the relationship between reward and effort. Some individuals experience windfall gains, some windfall losses. All of this can only have the effect of discouraging trade and production. The more effort traders must put into a transaction, the less energy they have to produce goods to exchange.

The net result is a weakening of the economy, just as if direct taxation had pushed the economy into the prohibitive range of the Laffer Curve. The sovereign experiences an illusion that his debasement of the currency has benefitted the treasury, not realizing that revenues from direct taxation are falling as a result of the economy's decline in output, although he does quickly see that his tax gatherers are only collecting eight-unit coins. In accordance with Gresham's Law (bad money drives out good), citizens who have been stuck with eight-unit coins use them to pay taxes, retaining their nine-unit coins for private transactions where eight-unit coins are not accepted. The sovereign then discovers that miners bringing bullion to market will only give nine units of bullion for the eight-unit coins, which means that the minting of eight-unit coins no longer yields one and a half units of profit, but once again only a half unit. Like a dog chasing his tail, the sovereign then orders the minting of seven-unit coins.

Economists can view inflation from several different time and space perspectives. It is seldom, however, that contemporary observers fully understand its causes, or know how to correct it, at least efficiently. Contemporary understanding of the inflation issue is hardly better than it was several centuries ago, despite the sophistication of very large economic models involving great mathematical and statistical sophistication but very primitive economic understanding.

Plato, for example, witnessed the monetary inflations of the Hellenic world and believed strongly in exchange control, with a soft national money distinct from hard international money. He had seen the seigniorage advantages of replacing hard international money (the Greek drachma) with overvalued domestic money on his first visit to Syracuse (387 B.C.); but it was not until twenty years later that he saw the inflationary consequences of a good idea carried too far. His pupil, Aristotle, however, saw the evils of inflation and advocated a convertible hard money, inside as well as out.[12]

When Mundell talks of "hard" and "soft" money he is not referring to metal and paper. Paper money can be as hard as metal, gold or silver, if the government guarantees that the paper money it issues can be converted on demand into a precise measure of gold or silver. Rather, "hard" refers to a monetary standard that is not permitted to fall, and "soft" refers to a standard that is permitted to fall. Sovereigns who are under the illusion that there are benefits to a soft domestic money are quick to see that only hard money will do for international transactions, because foreign sellers of goods will not accept anything less. Domestic sellers may have no choice, except to respond by putting up prices and paying taxes in soft money.

As Mundell observes, modern understanding of the inflation issue is hardly better than primitive. Modern governments, supported by modern economists, continue to experiment with monetary expansion in the hope of increasing output and revenues. Many of the less-developed countries simply print paper money to pay the costs of government, finding this form of taxation more efficient than direct levies that can be evaded.

Most developed nations, like the United States, do not pay their bills simply by printing money. The first step normally is to issue debt in the form of a government bond or note that bears interest. There are ten apples and ten dollars. The government wants an apple and does not want to tax the dollar from the economy to buy the apple. It issues a one-dollar bond, which is an interest-bearing debt, and one of the ten citizens holding a dollar will presumably be more attracted by the prospect of holding a one-dollar bond than buying an apple. There is no price inflation because there are still ten apples and ten dollars. The government has one of the apples and one of the citizens has a bond. The bond is the government's promise to the citizen holding it to tax one apple out of the future economy and deliver it to the citizen.

In the broad economy, the greatest portion of this public debt is held by banks. Banks hold government bonds or treasury bills because they need reserves, or are required to hold certain reserves by government edict, with which to pay depositors who come to the bank demanding payment. Banks, of course, prefer to hold as reserves interest-bearing debt rather than non-interest-bearing cash, and government bonds can easily be converted into cash.

Like the sovereign who debases his coins by issuing eight-unit money out of ten-unit bullion, modern governments increase the money supply by buying from banks the bonds they had previously issued, thereby substituting non-interest-bearing debt for interest-bearing debt. If there were no public debt, of course, the government could not increase the money supply in this fashion. There would be no debt to monetize.

The effect is exactly the same as if the government did not issue the bonds in the first place, but simply paid its suppliers with printing press money. Where there were ten apples, ten dollars, and one bond, there are now ten apples, eleven dollars, and no bond, with the result that there is a general rise in the price level. Each dollar is worth less in terms of real goods (apples) and debtors thus benefit at the expense of creditors, paying off loans calibrated in the old, more valuable dollars with the new, less valuable dollars. Taxpayers, too, pay their taxes with these new, less valuable dollars, and just as in the old coin-clipping days, for the government to come out ahead revenues must increase by more than the amount of the inflation.

In special circumstances, the government can actually benefit the economy by inflating the money supply. But when this occurs, it is invariably by accident rather than by design. The government, remember, has two instruments by which it influences the national economy. By monetary policy, it can increase, decrease, or hold constant the money supply. By fiscal policy, it can increase or decrease the tax wedge on commercial transactions—making it easier or more difficult for Smith and Jones to trade their labor in the money economy. What effect does a change in the monetary instrument have on fiscal policy? The answer depends on what kinds of taxes the government has levied.

Suppose first that the economy has output of $100 and the government has tax revenues of $20, and that all of the taxes that yield this amount are *specific*, i.e., related to weight, volume, or specific activity. Consumers pay 10 cents a pound for coffee, tea, and butter, 20 cents a quart for beer and wine, $1 for a dog license, $2 for a business license, etc.

The government now doubles the money supply. In the first instance, output remains the same, but the nominal value of output doubles to $200 as all individual prices in the economy more or less double, the general price level in fact doubling. (The price of beer may more than double, the price of wine may less than double.) Where coffee was taxed at 10¢ a pound and it cost $1 a pound, the government took 10 percent of each transaction. There was a 10 percent wedge between buyer and seller, but now the price of coffee is $2, yet the tax remains 10¢ a pound, which is now 5 percent of each transaction. So too with the other specific taxes. The general inflation has reduced the bite of all specific tax wedges, and if the economy had been at point C on the upper end of the Laffer Curve, it has now moved toward point E, or perhaps point D on the lower end of the curve. All transactors in the economy suddenly feel a lightening of the tax wedge after the initial turbulence of the monetary expansion has punished creditors to the gain of debtors. Until the government adjusts its specific taxes, doubling the rates on purchases and fees, the economy enjoys a genuine expansion.

Suppose, however, that our original economy with output of $100 raises $20 in tax revenues through *ad valorem* taxes—taxes in proportion to value. The consumer pays a 5 percent sales tax on the value of goods and services purchased. The businessman pays 40 percent of the value of business profits. The worker pays 20 percent of his income. The landowner pays $5 tax for each $100 of assessed land value.

When the government doubles the money supply and the nominal value of output goes to $200, there is again a general turbulence because of windfall gains and losses among creditors and debtors, but the tax wedge remains precisely the same as before. Where the consumer paid 5 percent of $1 on the purchase of a pound of coffee, or 5 cents, he now pays 5 percent on $2, or 10 cents. So too with all other *ad valorem* taxes, with the wedge remaining the same proportion of all transactions.

Now suppose, in a third instance, that of the original economy's $100 output, the $20 in tax revenues is collected via *progressive ad valorem* taxes, i.e., as the value of the taxed object rises, the rate of taxation rises progressively. The first $50,000 of an estate is tax free at death and the remainder is taxed at 20 percent. The first $50,000 of business profits is taxed at 25 percent, the remainder at 50 percent. The first $5,000 of income is taxed at 10 percent, the next $10,000 at 20 percent, the next $10,000 at 30 percent, the next $10,000 at 40 percent, the remainder at 50 percent.

Imagine there is one such progressive tax in our $100 economy, such that the first $50 of output is taxed at 10 percent, yielding $5, and the remainder at 30 percent, yielding $15. The wedge is 20 percent of $100, or $20. With a doubling of the money supply and output rising to $200, the first $50 is still taxed at 10 percent or $5, and the remaining $150 is taxed at 30 percent or $45. Of the $200 in nominal output, the total tax is $50, or 25 percent of the total. By simply changing the nominal value of output via inflation, the government increases the wedge from 20 to 25 percent. If the economy was at point D on the lower end of the Laffer Curve, it moves to point E, or perhaps to point C on the upper end.

Thus we see three separate and distinct effects on the real economy as a result of inflation, depending upon the type of tax levied by government. In the first, the inflation expands the economy by narrowing the tax wedge. In the second, there is no effect because of the proportionality of the wedge. In the third, because of the progressivity of the wedge, the inflation contracts the economy.*

The same results occur in the international economy when there is an international inflation (which Mundell defines as "the decline of connected monetary standards"). If the primary taxes bearing on international transactions are of a specific nature, i.e., tariffs levied on weight and volume, an international inflation will reduce the international wedge and invite economic expansion. If the tariffs are *ad valorem*, the inflation will neither increase nor decrease the wedge. If the tariffs are progressive *ad valorem* (duty free up to a dollar amount), then inflation increases the wedge, discouraging international transactions.

The difficulty in anticipating the effects of an inflation on a domestic economy or on the international economy lies in the fact that all countries have varying mixtures of these three types of taxation. Until economists and politicians view the economy in terms of the wedge model, instead of viewing it from other perspectives, they have difficulty explaining why a monetary inflation has different output effects in different countries and in different eras.

*   *   *

When an economist speaks of his "model," he does so in the same way in which an artist speaks of his model. The artist who wishes to capture the essence of "woman" or "youth" on canvas will draw on his broad general knowledge of the subject, but will be guided by a single representation, or model. So too an economist knows that the global economy is a complex thing with as many variables as there are people in it. But for policymaking purposes (and policy is ultimately the only purpose served by engaging economic models and their practitioners), there must be a simple, manageable guide that represents the whole, but with a minimum of variables. The economist simply assumes that all

*At the Claremont Conference in Bologna, Italy, in April 1971, Mundell extemporized in this vein: "In 1968 our problem was to stop the inflation without causing a depression. How should we have done that? Should we have done it through monetary policy or through fiscal policy? The actual policy was a tax surcharge—a move that reduced effective demand and thus was partly responsible for the recession that came about in 1969–70. After the tax increase, the inflation actually accelerated. This should not really surprise anyone, since, with a given rate of monetary expansion, a tax increase should lower output expansion and thus increase prices. And when inflation occurs in a progressive tax system, the budgetary policy becomes even more stringent than intended, because people move into higher tax brackets. By any calculation of budgetary tightness, there was great stringency in 1968, 1969, 1970, up to the present time. I can only conclude that the administration's answer to the question of how to stop inflation without causing a depression was the wrong answer, because the policy adopted caused a depression without stopping inflation. By any calculation, the cost of the recession is between $90 billion and $150 billion. And the inflation certainly isn't over yet."[13]

variables will cancel one another out, except, say, for two, and if we focus on these two—perhaps the money supply and the federal deficit—we can manage the course of the economy. The economist knows that his model is only a rough guide to reality, as does the artist. But it is necessary in order to avoid endless dawdling over questions posed by policymakers, and it is convenient; when the policy prescription fails, the economist can blame an "exogenous variable"—one outside the model—for having intruded and spoiled things.

In this sense, there are as many economic models as there are economists. But fundamentally, they all fit into one or another basic category—demand models or supply models. The models rest on the primary assumption that either the *consumer* or the *producer* is the dominant actor in the economy. Demand-siders build models around the idea that John Smith, consumer, is central, and that policy should be directed at his spending habits. Supply-siders build models on the idea that John Smith, producer, is preeminent, and policy should aim at his willingness to work. At this basic level, political distinctions are impossible. Adam Smith, Alexander Hamilton and Karl Marx were supply-siders, for example, while John Maynard Keynes, Milton Friedman, Presidents Jimmy Carter and Richard Nixon all operated within the framework of demand models. It is possible to say that the supply model is generally superior when the policymaker's objective is economic growth; the demand model is relevant when the policymaker is compelled to consider first the needs of the consuming public. Both basic models are "legitimate" and have been around since the dawn of civilization, but it is not possible to say that one is superior to the other, except at a particular time. Policymakers make the choice when confronting the economy that they must deal with—one that invites expansion or one that seems intractably in decline.

The demand model, broadly speaking, works through the consumer's pocket or pocketbook. When the policymaker confronts the problem of recession or depression, the demand economist counsels government intervention to put money into consumer pockets, money to buy the surplus goods that are the visible signs of recession and unemployment. If the problem is inflation, the demand-sider counsels government intervention to reduce the amount of money in the consumer's pocket, thereby reducing the competition for goods that is seen as driving up prices and wages. The demand model is confounded by the problem of "stagflation," a combination of stagnation and rising prices. There is no way to both increase and decrease the amount of money in the consumer's pocket just as there cannot be a surplus and a shortage of goods simultaneously.

There are several kinds of demand-side schools, but the most important are the fiscalists and the monetarists, the former altering tax policy
to manage the spending of consumers and businessmen, the latter
managing monetary policy for that purpose. The fiscalists have developed dual branches of their school. Liberal fiscalists urge higher taxes on
the rich and lower taxes on the working classes during recession. The
theory is that workers spend more rapidly and are more likely to draw
down the surplus goods that constitute recession. Conservative fiscalists
argue the opposite, an idea that liberals call "trickle-down theory."
Business taxes should be lowered and labor's taxes raised (or social
spending lowered). The idea is that businessmen will more likely spend
more wisely, investing in capital goods, while the worker more likely
consumes or squanders without regard for the future. The policy implication suggests lower taxes on "investment," higher taxes on consumption.

When inflation is the policymaker's concern, the fiscalists recommend
increasing taxes on the poor or the rich (depending on the school) and/or
reducing spending on social programs or the military (depending on the
school). Fiscalists also blend into the regulatory school when inflation is
the target. Liberals argue for price controls, and conservatives argue for
wage controls. The theory is that the consumer is either forced to ask for
higher wages because businessmen are raising prices too fast or businessmen increase prices because labor is initiating the process with
excessive wage demands.

The monetarists have a one-variable model involving the "money
supply." By altering the money supply, increasing it when there is a
surplus of goods, decreasing it when there is a shortage of goods—
which means rising prices—the economy can be managed in balanced
fashion. To a monetarist the *quantity* of money in the economy is all-
important. They recommend a rule, one that might even be fixed by law,
that the monetary authority permit the quantity of money to rise only by
a fixed amount. The amount cited for this quantity rule is usually about 3
percent, the monetarists observing that a mature economy can be
expected to grow by 3 percent annually, and any excess of money over
that amount would tend to be inflationary.

In this demand model, as with the fiscal demand model, it is not
possible to combat inflation and unemployment simultaneously; it is not
possible to have both a surplus of goods and a shortage of goods with a
given quantity of money.

In the supply model, unemployment and inflation are considered as
separate problems that can be solved simultaneously. By considering
John Smith, producer, for policymaking purposes, the supply model

assumes that Smith will produce more goods and exchange those goods with others if government tax and regulatory barriers to production and trade are not discouraging. There is no "consumer," per se, in the supply model, just as there is no producer, per se, in the demand model. The supply model contains only producers and traders, the assumption being that all production is consumed, either by the producer himself, by another producer of goods, who has received goods in trade, or by a third party, who trades for current production with a promise to pay back production in the future.

For example, Smith produces food, and Jones produces clothing, and they consume each other's production following trade. Peters, a student or an entrepreneur just getting started, borrows food from Smith and clothing from Jones and promises to pay them with equivalent amounts, plus interest, in the future out of his future production. In the demand model, this latter process is observed occurring through the consumer, Smith, and through policies that encourage him to spend more on current consumption while saving less, or vice versa.

In the supply model, monetary policy is wholly devoted to serving the needs of Smith, Jones and Peters in their roles as producers and traders of current and future goods. The quantity of money is not the focus of the supply model but its *quality*, its ability to serve as a reliable *unit of account*. Money *is*, in the supply model, a unit of account. Smith and Jones need to set the terms of trade with each other in an accounting unit, say fifty loaves of bread for one pair of shoes. With a dollar as a unit of account, we would say a loaf of bread is $1 and a pair of shoes, $50.

For Peters, the reliability of the accounting unit is all the more important because it must retain its integrity over time. Peters borrows fifty loaves of bread from Smith, and Smith expects to be paid back the equivalent in a year or ten years or thirty years. In a primitive barter economy there is no problem. Contracts are drawn in real goods and Peters actually promises to pay back fifty loaves. In a modern exchange economy, all such transactions occur through the banking system, and the bank that arranges the contract between Smith and Peters (who need never be aware of each other) must have them translate their goods into a common unit of account. If the chosen unit of account is altered during the term of the contract it means that Peters has to pay back more than he has pledged (deflation) or he has to pay back less than he has pledged (inflation). In either case, one party or the other has suffered a windfall loss and the other a windfall gain.

In the supply model, altering the unit of account is about the worst thing that a government can do to its economy. The process poisons the relationship between creditors and debtors. Inflation discourages Smith from producing for future consumption. Deflation discourages Peters from producing over and above what he had pledged, with bankruptcy perhaps the result. In either case, Smith and Peters and the entire economy operate below their potential. Yet in the demand model, remember, the dollar as a unit of account is not the relevant focus. The monetarists explicitly would alter the dollar's value relative to goods or other currencies in order to achieve a desired quantity target.

To the supply-siders, the correct target of monetary policy is the price of money. Indeed, it is the only realistic target. It is not possible for the monetary authority to know what the demand for money is on any given day. There are simply too many Smiths, Jones and Peters doing business in the marketplace. The government can't know their precise demands, a reality that the monetarists recognize by simply positing a 3-percent rule. It is just as difficult, though, to know what the supply of money happens to be at a given time. Once the government has given life to the concept of a "dollar," people around the world can trade goods for goods or goods for financial assets (IOUs) and express these transactions in "dollars," and there is nothing the United States government can do about it.

As a "standard of value," the dollar is the same kind of measuring device as a yardstick. The Bureau of Weights and Measures maintains the precise length of one yardstick at thirty-six inches and is unconcerned about the quantity in use in the world. In the same way, if the monetary authority devoted itself to maintaining the value of one dollar as a standard of value, a unit of account, it could be just as unconcerned about the quantity of them in use. The problem is that it is easier to measure distance than to measure value. The supply-side argument for a gold standard rests on the empirical observation that for 2,500 years the global electorate has identified gold as the most reliable standard of value—which means that gold, a specific amount of gold, is the best possible unit of account, the best proxy for all goods, services and financial assets that are involved in the banking system and exchange economy. An ounce of gold can be taken anywhere in the world and exchanged for goods, bonds or other currencies. It can also be transported in time and exchanged for rough equivalencies in goods and services. The "golden constant," Roy Jastram calls it in his 1977 book of that name. Jastram demonstrates that gold's purchasing power has remained remarkably stable over several centuries and that England and the United States avoided currency inflation when they defined the pound and the dollar in terms of a specified weight of gold.[14]

In England, for example, the wholesale-price index was about 100 in 1717, when Sir Isaac Newton, as Master of the Mint, established the pound sterling in terms of gold. It was still 100 in 1930, giving England more than two centuries of price stability, although there were minor inflations and deflations throughout the long period. During the Napoleonic wars and during World War I, the government guarantee of paper conversion into gold was suspended, and inflation ensued. But in the postwar periods, when convertibility was reestablished at the prewar ratios, prices also fell until the prewar price levels were reached. In the United States, the dollar–gold ratio was established in 1792, and except for the Civil War period and briefly during World War I, the dollar remained convertible into gold. The experience with prices was the same as in England. The wholesale-price index was the same in 1930 as it was in 1800. Inflation followed Roosevelt's devaluation of the dollar in 1934, from $20.67 to the ounce to $35; but, as we will see in Chapter 11, the chronic inflation did not begin until the dollar–gold link was finally severed in the seventies.

When the link was formally ended in the spring of 1973 by then Treasury Secretary George Shultz, who scrapped plans to restore the dollar's convertibility into gold, it was the first time in thousands of years that the world was without a single currency defined in terms of gold or silver. The paper dollar, floating free of real values, was now the unit of account for the United States and to other countries who fixed their currencies to the dollar. All currencies floated against one another with no single constant standard.

In the demand model, a paper standard can be theoretically maintained if the monetary authority could systematically match the demand for money with precisely the required supply. If this could be achieved, there would never be a dollar surplus or a dollar shortage. The economy would be in equilibrium, with no inflation or deflation. (Some prices would rise and some would fall, but the general price level would remain constant.) But as we have observed, the monetary authority cannot achieve this kind of "tight money" because it can't possibly know what the supply of money is or its demand at any given time. Crude attempts can be made to match supply and demand according to monetarist formulae, but there will always be error in the system. As a result, debtors and creditors will each have to pay the banking system an extra amount to insure against the currency risk. The more error and the more the future prospect of error in the management of the paper standard, the higher the rate of interest.

In the supply model, it is *assumed* that the demand for money and the money supply are variables that cannot be known beyond crude guesses. Only the point at which supply and demand intersect—the price of money—can be known with precision. The price of money, after all, is its purchasing power. That is, what does an individual or an enterprise have to offer in order to get a unit of money, a dollar? The baker must give up a loaf of bread. The airline must give up one five-hundredth of a round-trip seat on its New York–Chicago run. The borrower must exchange the promise of a loaf of bread, plus interest.

Because prices can be known on a daily, even instantaneous basis, they are the most appropriate target of monetary policy in the supply model. A *price rule* is superior to a *quantity rule*. But just as a bank requires Smith and Jones to convert their commitments of goods and clothing into a common unit of account, the central bank—the monetary authority—cannot maintain the standard of value against an index of goods and credit, loaves of bread, airline tickets, and promises of goods and interest. The central bank can only target one commodity and maintain the stability of the system for any length of time. The United States was on a bimetallic standard from 1792 until the Civil War, the government guaranteeing the dollar in both gold and silver, first at 15 to 1, then at 16 to 1. But because relative prices are always shifting, just as all stars shift around Polaris in the heavens, a double standard is inherently unstable.

As a proxy for all prices, the gold price can be maintained in terms of paper units indefinitely, as long as the sole purpose of the monetary authority is the maintenance of the unit of account. The authority simply offers to buy and sell gold for dollars at a specified ratio, say $450 an ounce, and by settling accounts every business day—satisfying demands for dollars or gold—there is no error accumulating in the system, no dollar surplus or deficit, no inflation or deflation. The government would, in fact, offer to buy at somewhat less than the official price, say $448, and sell at somewhat more, $452, and the private gold market would continue to operate within those "gold points," as they are called.

When the system is operating perfectly, nobody ever buys or sells gold through the government. The government's monetary instruments are deployed to discourage the gold price from hitting the "points." They would simply expand money to stop a persistent gold inflow, or slow the growth of money to stop a persistent gold outflow. If the price falls toward $448, this signals a surplus of gold relative to dollars in the market, and the government must buy bonds with cash, injecting dollars into the market to alter the dollar–gold ratio. As the price approaches $452, it signals a surplus of dollars relative to gold, and the government must issue bonds for cash to adjust the ratio. The central bank and the Treasury can also use other instruments to influence the dollar–gold ratio in the desired direction, buying or selling foreign exchange, thus increasing or decreasing the dollar supply relative to demand. The Federal Reserve can also increase or decrease the discount rate, the interest that member banks are charged, thus increasing or decreasing the willingness of the market to hold dollar assets relative to gold. Or the Federal Reserve can alter its reserve requirement, increasing the amount of reserves member banks must hold as the gold price approaches $452, lowering requirements as the price approached $448. Of course, all four instruments must be used sympathetically or they would be working at cross purposes.

This is the manner in which the Bank of England maintained the gold standard for centuries, with a relatively trivial amount of gold in its inventory. If after decades, generations, centuries, the monetary authority never shows the slightest interest in altering the value of its unit of account, the market's confidence in the standard of value increases and the currency-risk component of the interest rate diminishes to the vanishing point. Confidence in the Bank of England grew to such heights in the mid-nineteenth century that it could issue perpetual bonds, "Consols," bonds that never matured. In the United States, confidence in the integrity of the dollar reached similar heights in the nineteenth century. Railroads could issue 100-year bonds, and corporate debt generally averaged 40-year maturities at the turn of the century.[15]

The United States did suspend convertibility of the dollar during the Civil War, giving rise to greenback inflation. In 1903, Wesley Clair Mitchell of the University of Chicago reviewed the experience and concluded that suspension of convertibility was a costly error to the government. The issuance of greenbacks added more to debt service and military outlays (due to the inflation) than it saved by not issuing the equivalent in bonds. "The resort to a legal-tender paper currency," he wrote, "is a confession of acute financial distress and as such must depress the market for bonds. Therefore, to the financial loss caused by the increase of expenditures should be added a second loss from the unfavorable terms to which the government had to submit in selling its securities."[16]

The implications of Mitchell's insight are profound. To the degree that it is true, it suggests that there is never any reason to alter the unit of account; the government, as the major debtor, may believe it can improve its position by defaulting through currency devaluation, but the hidden negative effects always seem to swamp the supposed superficial benefits.

During World War II, the United States did not devalue the dollar, and it maintained its definition in terms of gold. The capital markets financed enormous deficits at 2-percent interest rates. The deficit in 1945 alone was 22 percent of Gross National Product, and the total publicly held national debt that year stood at 119 percent of GNP. The market knew that the government intended to return borrowed resources after the war according to the same standard of value. This is the importance of the gold standard, not the volume of gold held in government vaults, but the people's confidence that their government did not intend to cheat them. As Robert Hall of the National Bureau of Economic Research explained in 1981, the substantive effect of the classical gold standard "came from the legal definition of the dollar, not the government's control of the money stock. Essentially the same control of prices could have been achieved just from the definition of legal tender, without any control of the private creation of money. In any case, there was no serious attempt to control the deposits of banks, which were a growing fraction of the money supply."[17]

The argument, then, that there is "too little gold," or that the Soviet Union or South Africa "control the gold supply and thus our monetary system," is irrelevant. Because the system aims solely at maintaining the value of one dollar—to thereby maintain the quality of all dollars—it does not need Russian or South African gold. If the Russians bring great amounts of gold asking for dollars, we would gladly comply by issuing them greenbacks, fully expecting the greenbacks would come back from the private market to our gold window. And if no Russian gold came into the system, if no gold were henceforth discovered, the unit of account would be maintained in a mildly deflationary world that transactors, creditors and debtors would take into account and thus avoid distress.

Under a correctly designed, faithfully honored gold standard, it would be observed that the measured quantity of money would grow at a stable rate on the order of 2 percent or 3 percent. As Lewis Lehrman has noted, over time the global production of gold itself has increased by roughly 2 percent annually.[18] As the modern monetarists have discovered, it is extremely difficult to manage a defined money supply in the absence of a gold standard even for brief periods of time. The public creates new forms of money as rapidly as old ones are seemingly brought under "control."

What can be done in the absence of a gold standard is consistent with the demand model. By devaluing the currency, the monetary authority can "put money into the pockets" of debtors at the expense of creditors. In a contracting economy, this is a policy option that the politician may be forced to consider. But it surely is not an option that would be open to repeated use on a major scale because it does have the unambiguous effect of discouraging lending. While last year's debtors are relieved, this year's debtors are discouraged by the shrinking of credit.

In the classical view, the government cannot increase or decrease the quantity of *money* in any real sense. All it can do through monetary policy is change the value of money and in so doing change the relationship between debtors and creditors. When the government devalues the money, it rewards debtors at the expense of creditors, because now debtors are relieved of paying to their creditors as much in the way of real resources. But creditors henceforth demand higher interest rates, on the expectation that the government will again devalue.

If the government changes the value of money in the other direction, causing it to appreciate, creditors benefit at the expense of debtors for the opposite reason, but now debtors can't pay, and creditors don't get what they had been pledged. Interest rates rise to offset the increased risk of deflation. Thus, the government causes interest rates to rise, whether monetary policy is directed at inflation or at deflation, whether the price of gold in dollars is rising or falling—gold being the proxy for all real goods.

In 1949, Ludwig von Mises described the process precisely, and he described the deflation that followed Britain's return to the gold standard after both the Napoleonic wars and World War I at prewar parities. The description, in his magnum opus, *Human Action*, fits the United States and the dollar area in the 1981–82 period, when the price of gold—which had ballooned to $650 in 1980—was falling to the $300 level. This is a classic deflation:

People labored under the delusion that the evils caused by inflation could be cured by a subsequent deflation. Yet the return to the prewar parity could not indemnify the creditors for the damage they had suffered as far as the debtors had repaid their old debts during the period of monetary depreciation. Moreover, it was a boon to all those who had lent during this period and a blow to all those who had borrowed. But the statesmen who were responsible for the deflationary policy were not aware of the import of their action. They failed to see the consequences which were, even in their eyes, undesirable, and if they had recognized them in time, they would not have known how to avoid them. Their conduct of affairs really favored the creditors at the expense of the debtors, especially the holders of the government bonds at the expense of the taxpayers. In the twenties of the nineteenth century it aggravated seriously the distress of British agriculture and, a hundred years later, the plight of British export trade. Nonetheless, it would be a mistake to call these two British monetary reforms the consummation of an interventionism intentionally aiming at debt aggravation. Debt aggravation was merely the unintentional outcome of a policy aiming at other ends.[19]

In this way, the monetary authorities in the United States seemed unaware that the process they called "disinflation" in 1981–82 was in fact a classic deflation that caused a worldwide wave of bankruptcies. Those individuals, enterprises and nations that had acquired high dollar debts in 1980, when gold was above $600, were crushed under the same dollar debt when gold plunged to $300. Another way to look at it is this: It is nice to be in debt to the banking system during an inflation; if you have borrowed a house, the government says you legally need pay back only part of that house as the meaning of money changes. In a deflation, the government requires you to pay back more than a house, perhaps two houses, simply by changing the meaning of the unit of account.

*   *   *

Demand-side models, as we learned, focus on manipulating the amount of money that people spend. To end recession, demand economists suggest using fiscal or monetary devices to put more money into either the corporate vault or consumers' pockets. To fix inflation, on the other hand, demand-siders recommend rigid limits on the amount of money. Faced with both chronic inflation and stagnation, the demand approach is paralyzed, inherently incapable of dealing with either problem in a way that does not worsen the other.

Newsweek writes that "in supply-side theory, *spending* on plant and equipment should create economic activity and nourish *demand* . . ."[20] This is a typical confusion, attempting to force the supply-side analysis into a demand model. Supply-side models, by definition, are unconcerned with spending or demand. Instead, the emphasis is on the producer, on removing obstacles to production and trade. People produce in order to consume, bringing goods to the market to trade for what others produce. In real terms, demand *is* supply—the production of goods and services offered in exchange.

Money that holds its value over time—a reliable unit of account—is essential to those who would offer future production in exchange for something of value today. When the future value of the dollar is extremely uncertain, interest rates rise to cover that risk, and production shrinks to accommodate only short-term transactions.

Supply-siders are concerned with the quality of money, not its quantity. Nobody, except the market as a whole, could ever know how much of what kind of money is appropriate to finance expansion without inflation. Defining the dollar in terms of gold makes the value of the dollar predictable, facilitating long-term contracts such as bonds and mortgages. Maintaining a stable unit of account is not only the most important function of monetary policy, it is the only positive result that monetary policy can possibly accomplish. A gold standard alone ensures that the dollar is literally "as good as gold," by making the dollar convertible into gold at a fixed price.

"Policy is out of date," wrote Robert Mundell, "when a theory more obsolete than necessary is used, and theory is backward when policymakers have to develop *ad hoc* theories of their own or rely on the luck of intuition."[21] Demand-side models, in both fiscalist and monetarist variations, are unable to guide policymakers toward a simultaneous solution to the trauma of inflation and unemployment.

In subsequent chapters we will see how contemporary policymakers have been confounded by the obsolete demand model in an era of stagflation. First, however, we will examine an earlier part of the twentieth century, when progressive *ad valorem* taxes were not yet dominant, to understand a massive economic contraction unaccompanied by inflation.

CHAPTER 7

The Stock Market
and the Wedge

The stock market, which is the most efficient and accurate gauge of future economic activity, moves on a path traced by the wedge model. It moves up or down, appreciating or depreciating the value of the financial assets it embraces, by interpreting the impact of public policy on commerce between individuals and nations. It moves up when it projects a narrowing of the wedge that inhibits such commerce; down when it projects a widening of the wedge. Viewed from the vantage point of the wedge model, a new interpretation of the economic history of the United States from 1919 to the present emerges.

World War I was a war of political succession, as opposed to a violent resolution of economic conflict. It in fact made the world "safe for democracy," in the sense that at its conclusion the global electorate's long experimentation with monarchy was at last over. There would still be crowned figureheads scattered over the terrain—in Britain, Italy, Japan, etc.—but for the first time in the history of civilization there was in 1918 no serious experiment in political aristocracy still underway. The Hohenzollerns gave way to an economically crippled democracy in Germany. The Russias had seen their last czar as they embarked on a new kind of democratic experiment. Except in the colonies of the European powers, the political systems throughout the world were such that a boy of any economic class could grow up to sit behind a political desk at which the buck would stop. It would take a second great war to bring this same condition to the colonies.

The important economic fact at the conclusion of World War I was the magnitude of international war debts. Until 1914, the United States had been a debtor nation throughout its history, a recipient of cash from eager investors abroad. In other words, in 1914 the rest of the world owned more U.S. assets than the United States owned of the assets of the rest of the world. By the war's end, this condition reversed, as Europe not only sold U.S. assets to Americans to finance the war, but also sold European assets (bonds) to Americans to finance the enormously expensive conflict. Rest-of-the-world debt to the United States in 1918 came to $11.9 billion, roughly a third of national income in the United States. Britain, which ran up $4.7 billion of this amount, in turn was owed $11.1 billion by the rest of Europe, much of it in worthless czarist bonds. France came out a net debtor to the amount of $3.5 billion. The rest of the world, excluding the United States, Britain, and France, was in hock to these nations in the amount of $14.8 billion.

That wasn't all. The victors in the war spent three years calculating the war reparations that Germany would have to pay, and finally arrived at the figure of $33 billion. That amount, about equal to U.S. national income, was arrived at by an intricate process of adding up debt incurred by the allies as a result of the war—including pensions for veterans—and more or less approximated the net domestic and international indebtedness of the allies. The problem after every war is to figure out how to pay off the bonds floated to finance that cost not covered by war taxation. The allies sought to have the vanquished Germans pay it all.

The allies did not think they were being unreasonable. Germany had been left relatively unscarred by the war, which was largely fought on French soil. The way the allies worked it out, principal and interest on the $33 billion would amount to 7 percent of Germany's prewar national output. Not a stupendous amount.

The difficulty, not understood at the time, was that Germany like all other nations engaged in the war, had increased domestic taxation during the war and these high tax rates still remained in effect. Point E on the Laffer Curve, the turning point, had changed as Germany shifted from war to peace, and the tax rates thereby shifted into the prohibitive range. A further increase in tax rates to slice 7 percent of prewar output from the economy would only further contract output and revenues. Even if there had been no reparations, the economy could not return to prewar output as long as the tax rates remained in the prohibitive range. Germany actually made a payment of $250 million in the summer of 1921, not by raising taxes, but merely by printing reichsmarks (RMs) and using these to buy up foreign currencies equivalent to $250 million. This naturally flooded the market with reichsmarks without increasing the volume of goods and services they could buy and the price of goods in terms of RMs rose sharply. This burst of inflation caused internal convulsions in Germany. As the medium of exchange lost value as a lubricant to commerce, the economy became less efficient, output fell further, and revenues to the government fell too. The government then printed more currency to pay its domestic bills, repeating the process and inducing the hyper-inflation of 1922-23.

The effect of this hyper-inflation was to wipe out all domestic debt denominated in reichsmarks. This included the bonds Germany floated internally to finance World War I, and also all mortgages and contracts made in RMs. Before the currency was stabilized, the reichsmark supply came to more than 4 quintillion—RM 4,000,000,000,000,000,000. The currency stabilization was possible because government tax revenues did not have to cover internal debt finance, there no longer being internal debt. The savings and financial assets of the German people were wiped out, but so of course were their debts, and their human capital—intelligence, skills, and resourcefulness—remained. The international debt—denominated in gold reichsmarks—and including reparations, remained. It could not be inflated away.

The allies showed little sympathy for Germany even as it observed the hyper-inflation, seeing instead that because Germany had now wiped out its internal public debt, it should be all the easier for it to pay reparations. If it would only raise tax rates! As a result, the allies kept Germany bound to the upper range of the Laffer Curve, from which it would not escape until the 1950s.

The stubbornness of the allies grew out of the fact that they, too, had been pushed into the prohibitive range of the Laffer Curve during the war. With the exception of the United States, they all had to finance not only internal but international debt. Great Britain was in a net creditor position internationally, but how could she pay the $4.7 billion she owed the United States if she were not concurrently being paid the money owed her by the other allies? And how could the other allies pay Great Britain if Germany was not paying reparations?

The answer to these seemingly impossible questions is that if Britain, France, and Germany had reduced the tax rates imposed in war to pre-war levels, there would have been a European economic expansion that would have reduced the size of these international debts *relative to their national incomes.* Britain and France did not do so because they were mesmerized by their domestic and international indebtedness, and Germany did not because of the pressure of her creditors for reparation payments.

Only the United States pulled itself down from the upper reaches of the Laffer Curve. The Wilson administration imposed high tax rates in 1917; an excess profits tax on business, a doubling of the normal corporate rate to 12 percent, and sharp increases on personal income-tax rates. The 15 percent rate on $2 million and above gave way to a 77 percent rate on incomes above $1 million. The lowest bracket, 2 percent on $20,000, gave way to a 6 percent marginal rate on $4,000. The domestic public debt grew to $24 billion from $1 billion because of war finance. This figure mesmerized the Democrats in power, and at the conclusion of the war the high tax rates were left in place with the idea that the revenues would go to paying off the $24 billion public debt. Instead, the United States slid into a recession, as peacetime put the tax rates into the prohibitive range.

In the 1920 elections, the Republican candidate called for a "return to normalcy" on tax rates, that is a return to the prewar rates. In his acceptance speech, Warren G. Harding, Ohio senator, told the GOP convention: "I believe the tax burdens imposed for the war emergency must be revised to the needs of peace, and in the interest of equity in the distribution of the burden."*

Harding won by the greatest landslide in the history of presidential elections at the time, bringing in with him 303 Republicans to the House of Representatives. Harding's Treasury Secretary, Andrew Mellon, wanted the personal income-tax rates to come down to 25 percent as well as removal of the excess-profits tax, but Congress worried that the bite would be too deep into revenues and held him to a cut in the top personal bracket to 57 percent and elimination of the excess-profits tax. The economy crept out of the recession nevertheless.

Unhappily, the Republicans of the era had the same difficulty in seeing the symmetry between domestic tax wedges and international tax wedges that Napoleon had a century earlier. At the same time that Republicans argued for a lessening of the tax wedge between domestic transactions, they argued the need for a greater wedge in international transactions, i.e., the protective tariff. As the Harding administration was winning a lowering of the wartime tax rates in 1921, it was also pushing along the Fordney-McCumber Tariff of 1922. The Democrats, conversely, favored an expanded domestic tax wedge (explicitly on the well-to-do) and opposed tariff protection.

As protective tariffs go, the 1922 Act was not especially onerous, the rates going back up to where they were before the Democrats had reduced them in 1913. The tax-cutting more than compensated and the economy pushed ahead, Gross National Product climbing from $69.6 billion in 1921 to $74.1 billion in 1922. Treasury Secretary Mellon inveigled another round of tax cuts from Congress, now sufficiently

*There were other themes in the speech, including civil rights: "I believe the Negro citizens of America should be guaranteed the enjoyment of all their rights, that they have earned the full measure of citizenship bestowed, that their sacrifices in blood on the battlefield of the Republic have entitled them to all of freedom and opportunity, all of sympathy and aid that the American spirit of fairness and justice demands."[1]

impressed with the economic and revenue effects of the first round. The top bracket was cut to 46 percent from 56 percent and the income threshold at which the top bracket was encountered went to $500,000 from $200,000. The lowest bracket, $4,000, had its rate cut as well, to 1.5 percent from twice that. Again, the economy responded and revenues sufficient to produce another budget surplus came into the Treasury. GNP went to $85 billion, with no inflation. Consumer prices even inched downward from the 1920 level.

The really explosive growth of the decade was still to come. We can see its foundations in a speech by Calvin Coolidge, who succeeded Harding as President upon Harding's death in 1923. The speech, delivered on Feb. 12, 1924 before the National Republican Club in New York, may be the most lucid articulation of the wedge model by a politician in modern times. It is quoted at length here:

In time of war, finances, like all else, must yield to national defense and preservation. In time of peace, finances, like all else, should minister to the general welfare. Immediately upon taking office it was determined after conference with Secretary Mellon that the Treasury Department should study the possibility of tax reduction for the purpose of securing relief to all taxpayers of the country and emancipating business from unreasonable and hampering exactions. The result was the proposed bill, which is now pending before the Congress. It is doubtful if any measure ever received more generous testimony of approval. . . .

The proposed bill maintains the fixed policy of rates graduated in proportion to ability to pay. The policy has received almost universal sanction. It is sustained by sound arguments based on economic, social and moral grounds. But in taxation, like everything else, it is necessary to test a theory by practical results. The first object of taxation is to secure revenue. When the taxation of large incomes is approached with that in view, the problem is to find a rate which will produce the largest returns. Experience does not show that the higher rate produces the larger revenue. Experience is all in the other way. When the surtax on incomes of $300,000 and over was but 10 percent, the revenue was about the same as when it was at 65 percent. There is no escaping the fact that when the taxation of large incomes is excessive, they tend to disappear. In 1916 there were 206 incomes of $1,000,000 or more. Then the high rate went into effect. The next year there were only 141, and in 1918, but 67. In 1919, the number declined to 65. In 1920 it fell to 33, and in 1921 it was further reduced to 21. I am not making argument with the man who believes that 55 percent ought to be taken away from the man with $1,000,000 income, or 68% from a $5,000,000 income; but when it is considered that in the effort to get these amounts we are rapidly approaching the point of getting nothing at all, it is necessary to look for a more practical method. That can be done only by a reduction of the high surtaxes when viewed solely as a revenue proposition, to about 25 percent.

I agree perfectly with those who wish to relieve the small taxpayer by getting the largest possible contribution from the people with large incomes. But if the rates on large incomes are so high that they disappear, the small taxpayer will be left to bear the entire burden. If, on the other hand, the rates are placed where they will get the most revenue from large incomes, then the small taxpayer will be relieved. The experience of the Treasury Department and the opinion of the best experts place the rate which will collect most from the people of great wealth, thus giving the largest relief to people of moderate wealth, at not over 25 percent.

A very important social and economic question is also involved in high rates. That is the result taxation has upon national development. Our progress in that direction depends upon two factors—personal ability and surplus income. An expanding prosperity requires that the largest possible amount of surplus income should be invested in productive enterprise under the direction of the best personal ability. This will not be done if the rewards of such action are very largely taken away by taxation. If we had a tax whereby on the first working day the Government took 5 percent of your wages, on the second day 10 percent, on the third day 20 percent, on the fourth day 30 percent, on the fifth day 50 percent, and on the sixth day 60 percent, how many of you would continue to work on the last two days of the week? It is the same with capital. Surplus income will go into tax-exempt securities. It will refuse to take the risk incidental to embarking in business. This will raise the rate which established business will have to pay for new capital, and result in a marked increase in the cost of living. If new capital will not flow into competing enterprise the present concerns tend toward monopoly, increasing again the prices which the people must pay.

The high prices paid and low prices received on the farm are directly due to our unsound method of taxation. I shall illustrate this by a simple example: A farmer ships a steer to Chicago. His tax, the tax on the railroad transporting the animal, and of the yards where the animal is sold, go into the price of the animal to the packer. The packer's tax goes into the price of the hide to the New England shoe manufacturer. The manufacturer's tax goes into the price to the wholesaler, and the wholesaler's tax goes into the price to the retailer, who in turn adds his tax in the price to the purchaser. So it may be said that if the farmer ultimately wears the shoes he pays everybody's taxes from the farm to his feet. It is for these reasons that high taxes mean a high price level, and a high price level in its turn means difficulty in meeting world competition.

Most of all, the farmer suffers from the effect of this high price level. In what he buys he meets domestic costs of high taxes and the high price level. It is essential, therefore, for the good of the people as a whole that we pay not so much attention to the tax paid directly by a certain number of taxpayers, but we must devote our efforts to relieving the tax paid indirectly by the whole people.[2]

As it gradually became clearer through 1924 that the Coolidge bill, not the Democratic alternative, had sufficient support for passage, and that Mellon would realize his aim of a 25 percent top bracket, the great Coolidge bull market got underway. It had taken four years for the *New York Times* index of industrial share prices to move from 90 to 106, floating around 100 for most of the period. Now it began to climb in earnest and by December, 1924 was at 134. At the end of 1925 it reached 181, pausing at that plateau through 1926, moving again in 1927 to 245 at year's end. Before the *Times* industrials peaked on Sept. 19, 1929, the index had more than quadrupled, to 469, in a mere five and a half years. The Dow Jones industrial average followed a similar track, doubling from 191 in early 1928 to 381 in September, 1929.

There is in the current history of that era no mention of the relationship between the Mellon tax cuts and the Coolidge bull market. In his book *The Great Crash 1929*, John Kenneth Galbraith makes no attempt to explain why the boom occurred. Charles Kindleberger, in *The World in Depression, 1929-39*, puzzles about the cause and, without much enthusiasm suggests that "the boom was built around the automobile," without saying what caused that boom. Goronwy Rees writes in *The Great Slump; Capitalism in Crisis, 1929-1933* that the "restoration of political stability from 1925 onwards was accompanied by a spectacular economic recovery." Rees mentions the Mellon tax cuts, but only by way of denigrating them as reactionary. Two monetarist schools have differing views. Murray Rothbard has a broad definition of what constitutes "money," and so reckons the expansion from 1921-1929 as "an inflationary boom," the money supply by his reckoning having increased by 61.8 percent over the eight years. His *America's Great Depression* seems untroubled by the *fall* in the consumer price index over eight years, from 53.6 to 51.3. Because their definition of money is narrow, Milton Friedman and Anna Schwartz are forced to argue that while the stock market boomed, the economy did not. In *The Great Contraction*, they assert that "Federal Reserve policy was not restrictive enough to halt the bull market yet too restrictive to foster vigorous business expansion."

But of course the period was one of phenomenal economic expansion. GNP grew from $69.6 billion to $103.1 billion. And because prices fell, GNP grew even faster in real terms, by 54 percent over the stretch. On a 1947 index equaling 100, output per man hour of U.S. production workers grew from 44.6 to 74.3 in the decade, a percentage increase of 66.5. The Federal Reserve Board index of industrial production leaped from 12 to 23 between 1921 and 1929.

Modern Keynesians are as baffled by the boom as are the monetarists. From their theoretical vantage point, tax cuts will "stimulate" an economy only if they are concentrated in the lower income classes, which, according to this theory, have "a higher propensity to spend" than do rich people. In any case, the economy will contract if the government runs persistent budget surpluses, yet from 1920 to 1930, Mellon managed to cut the national debt to $16.9 billion from $24.3 billion. Lord Keynes himself never troubled to explain the boom, possibly because he resided in Cambridge, England, and in England there was no boom at all in the 1920s. Great Britain, after all, left the steep progressive income taxes it imposed in 1914 in effect during the peace, and to this day has not reduced them.*

One other nation came down from the prohibitive range of the Laffer Curve in the 1920s, and like the United States it enjoyed a boom. In 1922, Benito Mussolini, a socialist newspaper editor who turned conservative after the war, was invited by the King of Italy to take control of the government, in crisis as a result of severe economic contraction. Mussolini brought with him a finance minister, Alberto de Stefani, who had been a professor of classical economics at the Technology Institute of Vicenza. De Stefani slashed both tariffs and Italy's progressive income tax. The Italian economy went into immediate expansion and even during the 1930s suffered much less economic contraction than the other industrial nations. As we will later see, both Franklin D. Roosevelt and Adolf Hitler misinterpreted the source of the Italian boom, with World War II the result.

ii

It is never possible to say with precision why the stock market rises or falls, any more than it is possible for any individual to precisely discern the wishes of the electorate. In a sense, the stock market is an instrument of the electorate, the most accurate and efficient forecaster of the economic component of the political economy. There are dozens of stock markets around the world, and each of them has some value in this regard, but the only one with the breadth and depth to stand as a

---

*France imposed a steeply progressive income tax in 1920 in the name of tax reform— which the French called a "sucker's tax" (impôt des poires) — to be paid only by those who could not escape it. As the government became more adept at enforcing the tax, the French economy contracted amid steady inflation, culminating in the 1924 financial crisis. Total government revenues, measured in prewar francs, were only a bit higher from 1920-25 than in 1913, when there was no income tax. The crisis ended in 1926 when the leftwing Herriot Cabinet fell and the center-right Poincare Cabinet one week later announced a new tax law, on August 3.

The highest rate of the general income tax was cut from 60 percent to 30 percent. The rates of the inheritance and estate taxes were cut, and at the same time made less steeply progressive. The annual transmission tax on securities was lowered by about 40 percent; the *carnet de coupons*, devised to check evasion of the general income tax as concerned revenue from securities, was abolished.

The franc stabilized, the economy revived, and in the first year of the reform, tax revenues jumped dramatically, from 5.4 billion prewar francs to 7 billion. In the six months from July to the end of 1926, the franc soared on the foreign-exchange market, from two cents to four cents on the dollar.[3]

gauge of the global political economy is the New York Stock Exchange. It is massive enough so that no group of individuals can manipulate it. The companies it aggregates do business in almost every corner of the globe, constantly feeding information of a political and economic nature back to this central marketplace. The marketplace itself exists in a free and uncontrolled information center. It is inconceivable that information that bears on profit or loss can be known anywhere in the world without soon being absorbed by this most sensitive intelligence, which is open to all intelligence directly or indirectly. People will speak of the market being "underpriced" or "overpriced," but there is no real sense in which this can be true. The market is composed of all the people who are active in the market and can with a telephone call become inactive, and also all the people who are inactive, and with a telephone call become active, either by buying shares or supplying information to someone who will buy shares. At any moment, the market is fully priced.

Technically, what the market measures in the process of absorbing information and translating it into a valuation of the market shares is the capital stock of the United States. Think of the market as an instrument that has a mind of its own, over and beyond the total of minds participating in it. The market is the most accurately pro- grammed computer on the planet, the closest expression of the mind of the electorate itself. It places a value on each company within it, based on its calculation of that company's *future* income stream. While the planet itself throws off information that is absorbed by the market pertinent to future income streams, planetary information is relatively trivial because planetary changes, when they occur, are glacial. Sum- mer sooner or later follows spring. The most important information coming to the market is political news. War and peace, after all, can turn on the chemistry of a single mind. Political news is volatile, because it can instantly and dramatically alter the market's future income streams.

It is frequently possible to relate market shifts to political develop- ments with a high degree of certainty, but the market's reasoning is still beyond comprehension. On November 22, 1963, when President Kennedy was assassinated, the Dow Jones Industrials fell 22 points. The market fell because of the assassination, but it recovered all the lost ground the following day and gained 11 more points. If we cannot tell the market's reasoning of why it recovered, how can we plumb its calculations of why it saw future income streams threatened by the assassination?

The Coolidge bull market ended in September, 1929; with finality the following month with the Crash. The most common explanation of the Crash to this day is that the market was overpriced because of speculation, as if this great, sensitive brain was somehow fooled into misjudging future flows of income. As if individuals could bid the market up without other individuals being present to assess value soberly and bid it down. The fact is, from the vantage point of the wedge model, the market at its peak was exactly where it should have been, and the Crash came because the chemistry of a few individual political minds turned the system toward stupendous error. The evidence of what went wrong is therefore magnificently encouraging, for it removes the burden of error from masses of people and places it on a tiny few, who can be forgiven because they were merely human.

The stock market Crash of 1929 and the Great Depression ensued because of the passage of the Smoot-Hawley Tariff Act of 1930.

iii

When any economic unit becomes wealthier relative to the rest of the world, whether the unit be a family or a nation, it becomes uneconomic for members of that unit to persist in work consistent with the lower level of wealth. When Jones graduates from medical school, it soon is evident that his wife need no longer work as a typist unless she desires the non-monetary rewards. If Mrs. Jones should sell a successful novel, it is plain her children no longer need work their way through college.

As the United States became wealthier relative to the rest of the world during 1919-1929, the same happy condition applied, but with an unfortunate exception. A husband easily transfers the rewards of wealth to his wife and family, and so does the successful wife. In a nation, if there is no system for such transmittal, wealth brings its own problems. The system itself can advance to higher levels of prosperity even as a class of individuals within the system is being made obsolete.

So it was in the 1920s. The U.S. economy moved to higher levels of wealth. All *segments* of the economy became wealthier, but some became wealthier at a relatively slower pace. Throughout the economy, individuals became obsolete in the jobs they held at the lower level of wealth and had to adjust to new work. For most, this was a happy experience; promotion. What this invariably means is that the individual uses his physical capital less and his intellectual capital more. Instead of hammering out a widget, he makes one with a widget-making machine. The bank teller becomes a cashier. The laborer is recruited to be an apprentice plumber.

For some individuals, though, transition is not a happy experience. The economy as a whole must move to greater emphasis on intellectual capital and less emphasis on physical capital as it rises to a higher level of wealth. On the margin of society, those who would not make the transition voluntarily are forced to do so by the weight of expansion.

The textile mills of New England, for example, give way to machine tools or electronics manufacturing, which are more "capital intensive," and less "labor intensive." New England becomes too wealthy to produce textiles. Similarly, the Southern states face the same transition by moving small farmers who have been pushing plows into now transplanted textile mills, while other farmers turn in their plows and horses to buy tractors.

Those who resist transition, often because they are too old to begin new careers or must move too far from family and friends, are crushed by progress. This was the dynamic of the late 1920s. All segments of the economy were becoming wealthier rapidly, but the labor-intensive farmer was being wiped out by falling farm prices. That is, a non-farm worker could trade his labor for more farm goods than was the case prior to the expansion. On the other side of the coin, the farm worker could trade his labor for fewer non-farm goods and services. To adjust back to equilibrium, more farmers had to become industrial workers. They were indeed doing so, but the expansion required ever faster transition, and the political system felt this as an irritation.

The Republican Party in 1928 looked at this phenomenon as something to be corrected, as if "balanced" growth meant that the higher level of economic wealth should be enjoyed equally by all segments, industrial and agricultural. This problem, of course, is the primordial question of political economy: what do you do with the fisherman who breaks his leg or the marginal farmer who becomes obsolete? In a fragmented world economy, the question has special complications, for if the wealthiest nation becomes too wealthy to perform labor-intensive work, it must then rely on other nations to supply labor-intensive goods, and the supply becomes vulnerable. It is one thing to shift textile mills from Massachusetts to South Carolina; it is another to shift them to Taiwan and South Korea. The same is true of agriculture. As a political economy expands to a higher level of wealth, its impulse for survival drives toward expansion of its borders to take in land and population that can be committed to labor-intensive goods safely secured. Caesar solved Rome's problem in this fashion by conquest and empire. Great Britain built its colonial empire in the nineteenth century for this reason. When Sir Robert Peel, the British prime minister in 1843 faced the same problem that the Republicans and Herbert Hoover faced in 1928, his answer was the repeal of the Corn Laws—the British protective tariffs on agricultural goods. The rest of the world would supply Britain with labor-intensive foodstuffs. Britain would be free to develop its intellectual capital. The supply line would be secured through colonial empire and the commonwealth agreements. The subsidized British farmers were forced to adjust.*

The Republican Party in 1928 went the other way. It sought to adjust the imbalance in wealth positions between farm and city by raising the protective tariff on foreign agricultural products, stating in its party platform:

> The Republican Party believes that the home market, built up under the protective policy, belongs to the American farmer, and it pledges its support of legislation which will give this market to him to the full extent of his ability to supply it. . . . It is inconceivable that American labor will ever consent to the abolition of protection, which would bring the American standard of living down to the level of that in Europe, or that the American farmer could survive if the enormous consuming power of the people in this country were curtailed and its market at home, if not destroyed, at least seriously impaired.

A tariff is of course nothing more than a tax on international transactions. A domestic tax—a sales or income tax—is a wedge between the trading of labor by Jones and Smith. The tariff is a wedge between the trading of labor by Jones, a national, and Schmidt, a foreigner. The effects on commerce are precisely the same. And just as Jones does not benefit when Smith is taxed, or vice versa, neither does Jones benefit when Schmidt is taxed, or vice versa:

> Gain through freeing imports from taxation does not depend on other countries doing the same. For other countries to tax our exports to them is an injury to us and an obstacle to trade. For us to tax their exports to us is not a correction of that injury; it is just a separate additional obstacle to trade. . . . If one country has good harbours while all the rest have bad ones, it will not realize the advantages of good harbours so fully as if all the rest had good ones also. But it will realize some advantages; it will be better off than if it, too, sank rocks all round its coasts.[5]

The United States from its earliest days imposed tariffs as its chief source of revenue. The idea of a protective tariff took root in the Tariff of 1816, when the shoe was on the other foot. At the conclusion of the

---

*Karl Marx put his finger on the problem: "With the setting free of a part of the agricultural population, therefore, their former means of nourishment were also set free. They were now transformed into material elements of variable capital. The peasant, expropriated and cast adrift, must buy their value in the form of wages, from his new master, the industrial capitalist."[4]

Napoleonic wars in 1815, the fear was that cheap manufactures from Europe would wipe out the fledgling U.S. industries. Thomas Jefferson, who had opposed protectionism earlier, now, at seventy-three years of age, decided that conditions warranted a change: "To be independent for the comforts of life we must fabricate them ourselves. We must now place the manufacturer by the side of the agriculturist. . . . Experience has now taught me that manufacturers are now as necessary to our independence as to our comfort."[6]

Jefferson's political rationale in defense of protectionism had small merit, then as now. It was one thing to protect then, when the United States was a small debtor nation and the revenue from the "protective" tariff was the chief source of financing legitimate government services. (Much of the revenues from the 1816 tariffs paid off the public debt, which meant a decrease in future domestic taxes.) It was quite another matter for the United States to protect when it was the most powerful creditor in the world. In 1928, the transition problems of marginal U.S. farmers were trivial. With hindsight, no GOP argument, political or economic, justified higher tariffs.

Hoover did not appreciate that, in addition to the interallied war debt, the rest of the world had borrowed an additional $11.8 billion from private U.S. sources between 1919 and 1929, although it was pointed out to him. On May 5, 1930, 1,028 American economists petitioned Hoover not to sign the tariff bill if and when it was enacted:

> Our export trade, in general, would suffer. Countries cannot permanently buy from us unless they are permitted to sell to us, and the more we restrict the importation of goods from them by means of even higher tariffs, the more we reduce the possibility of our exporting to them. . . .
> Many of our citizens have invested their money in foreign enterprises. The Department of Commerce has estimated that such investments, entirely aside from the war debts, amounted to between $12,555,000,000 and $14,555,000,000 on January 1, 1929. These investors, too, would suffer if restrictive duties were to be increased, since such action would make it still more difficult for their foreign debtors to pay them the interest due them.[7]

Hoover signed the bill on June 16, 1930, but the stock market anticipated the act and crashed in the last days of October, 1929.

The first signs of distress came in December, 1928 as the market was hit a double blow in the space of two days. On December 5, after the market had closed, Coolidge announced that there would be no further tax cut in the budget he would send Congress for the next fiscal year. This was the influence of President-elect Hoover's hand-picked successor to Andrew Mellon at Treasury, Ogden Mills, who would be Undersecretary to Mellon in the new administration. Hoover, aware that Mellon disliked him and had privately worked against his nomination, could not simply bounce Mellon and replace him with Mills. Mellon was a Republican and a national hero by this time. Had Coolidge sought re-election and won, Mellon undoubtedly would have used the surplus in the budget to ask further tax reduction in 1929. As it was, Coolidge urged Congress to economize on spending in his no-tax-cut budget message, which *The New York Times* observed "sounded more like a message to President-elect Hoover than to Congress."

The stock market was disappointed. On December 6, the Dow Jones Industrials (DJI) dropped 11 points to 279. "Stock Prices Break in Day of Selling As Money Hits 12%—Huge Profits Crumble," announced a front-page headline in *The New York Times* of December 7, 1928.

The market fell another eight points the following day as word got out that the House Ways and Means Committee had scheduled hearings of fourteen subcommittees to take up tariff testimony, and that the hearings would cover *all commodities*, not only agriculture. *The New York Times* reported the schedules on December 7 along with the news that the Republican members of Ways and Means were committed to take up all the items in the tariff law. The market fell twenty-two points in two days.

Having swallowed this news, the market nevertheless recovered. The bill was a long way from being written, let alone passed, and there was plenty of opposition to it. Lame-duck Coolidge allowed himself to think out loud, saying he didn't even think the farmers would be helped by tariff revision. And Mellon on November 23 actually cut the tariff on pig iron from Germany, thereby showing where his heart lay. The market climbed to 300 by year's end and continued marching upward to March 23, 1929, when trouble really began. The hearings were underway, Hoover had been inaugurated March 4, and on Sunday, March 24, the world got bad news on page 2 of the *New York Times*. The Senate, it seems, was now a problem:

Watson Predicts Tariff Difficulties
After Conference With Hoover, Senate Leader
Says Industries Seek Wide Revision
He Will Ask Cement Rise
Other Legislators Will Back Own Industries
Longworth Supports President on Limit

Washington. March 23—The administration program to limit tariff revision to a few schedules is going to encounter much opposition in Congress, Senator Watson, Republican Senate leader said today after a conference with President Hoover on the legislative program for the special session.

"It will be the desire of the Republican leaders to cooperate with President Hoover in every way and prevent the revision of the tariff getting beyond control and opening up the schedules to wholesale revision," Senator Watson said. "Of course the making of a tariff law is always a difficult subject and it is going to be extremely hard to lay down a fixed program and hold revision to a few accepted schedules, since many industries are demanding higher duties, which they claim are necessary to meet the improved production situation abroad. . . . "

Senator Watson said that as the time for the special session approached, the demand for a more thorough revision of the tariff became greater. Senators, he said, were being deluged by industries in their district for changes in the schedules affecting them. He intends, he indicated, to ask for the placing of a duty on cement. The cement industry in Indiana and Pennsylvania, he said, is unable to meet the competition of Belgian manufacturers, who, despite ocean transporation costs, are able to lay cement on the Atlantic seaboard cheaper than it can be produced in the Middle West cement belt.

It is the belief of some Republican leaders that President Hoover will face a serious problem if he attempts to limit tariff revisions to a few schedules. They say they cannot with justice close revision to industry in their own districts. They also point out that tariff revision is accomplished by combinations of interests, and forecast that this practice may be found in the special session.

This was ominous news and the stock market reacted the following day, Monday the 25th, as the *Times* reported on its front page of March 26:

STOCK PRICES BREAK
HEAVILY AS MONEY
SOARS TO 14 PER CENT

Tightening of Country's Credit
Causes One of Broadest Drops
in Exchange's History

---

90 Issues at Year's Low

Tightening of the strings on the country's credit supply, a development foreshadowed last week, but not considered seriously by speculators in the stock market, brought about yesterday one of the sharpest declines in securities that has ever taken place on the Exchange. Only twice in the history of the Exchange have there been broader breaks.

As each hour yesterday brought a lower level of prices, the liquidation increased. Millions of dollars in slowly accumulated paper profits were wiped out as frightened speculators dumped their holdings overboard "at the market," or for what they would bring at a forced sale . . .

There were three principal causes for the break in stocks. They were:

Tight money, with the call rate advancing from 9 to 14 per cent, with acceptances up ⅛ and thirty day funds loaning at 8¾.

Fear of a drastic advance in the rediscount rates by the Federal Reserve Board, or the adoption of equally drastic means to divert the country's surplus credit back to its ordinary and normal commercial channels.

The continuance of an overwrought speculative position, with hundreds of thousands of small and easily frightened speculators in the market, prone to do the wrong thing at the right time and the right thing at the wrong time.

The *Times* was wrong about the reason the market sold off. Unable to see that the market had been forced to reassess the international credit structure as a result of the ominous tariff news from Washington, the *Times* and other Wall Street observers groped for an answer and looked to the Federal Reserve, which was also forced to deal with reaction to the tariff news without knowing it. Nobody could "think on the margin" although the market itself, representing everybody, acted on the margin. Foreigners, liquidating assets in the United States as the tariff news made their debt position worse, would of course produce an excess supply of dollars as they sought to convert dollars into their own currencies, and the Federal Reserve would, in line with practice, sell bonds in order to mop up this surplus dollar supply. The financial markets saw the *effects* of the tariff report and interpreted these as the causes of the market break.

In the same Tuesday, March 26, issue of the *Times*, on page 19, there was further bad news on the tariff for the financial community to read on the way to the market that day:

Give Hoover Tariff Data
Davenport and Treadway Tell Him of
Textile Industry's Needs

Washington. March 25—President Hoover today received a report on the question of increases in tariff rates to protect rayon, cotton, and other industries in New York and New England states, submitted by Representatives Davenport of New York and Treadway of Massachusetts, as members of a subcommittee of the Ways and Means committee during a call at the White House. They declined to indicate the tenor of their report, but asserted that the textile tariff schedules should be greatly increased and that there was little opposition to such action in the Ways and Means Committee.

The Wednesday, March 27 *New York Times* front page gives the results:

STOCKS CRASH THEN RALLY
IN 8,246,740-SHARE DAY:
MONEY GOES TO 20 PER CENT
Market Sets New Record
Stocks Dumped As Loan Rate Mounts, Sending Wide List Down
Bankers Aid Recovery
Heavy Buying Orders in Five Pivotal Securities Help
Stem Tide in Last Hour—300 Issues at Year's Low
$13,874,000 Bond Sales Also Biggest for 1929,
With Many Declines.

The references to "money" going to 20 percent referred only to spot loans to individuals who had bought shares on margin, i.e., who had paid only a portion of the full price of stocks and, with the falling market, had to borrow fresh funds to cover their accounts. Long term rates didn't rise.

This, of course, was not the famous Crash of '29, for the market needed more definite news on the tariff from Washington. The Dow Jones Industrials, which had opened the year 1921 at 72, climbed slowly through the Harding years and soared to 300 at the close of 1928, climbed to 311 before the Watson report brought it back to 281 in two days in March, then advanced to 300, where it hovered through the end of May. The market was sure enough that the House of Representatives would put through a broad tariff boost, which it did swiftly in May, but meanwhile opposition to the legislation began forming in the Senate. It began to appear that the upper body would have the numbers to kill the bill or keep the legislation limited to a few agricultural products. There were forty "Old Guard" Republican Senators, including Senator Reed Smoot of Utah, chairman of the Senate Finance Committee, and they favored high protective tariffs on all commodities. The other senators, thirty-nine Democrats and fifteen "progressive" Republicans, formed a coalition against broad tariff revision. The progressives were also in coalition with the Old Guard Republicans to push through a tariff hike on agriculture, which the Democrats opposed. In June, Senator Borah of Idaho presented a resolution to the Senate that would give the "sense of the Senate" as reflecting a desire to keep tariff revision limited to agriculture. His resolution lost thirty-nine to thirty-eight, but was understandably counted a victory for the anti-tariff forces because almost all of the nineteen senators who were absent or not voting on the resolution were members of the Democratic-Progressive GOP coalition. Up went the stock market, to a 347 Dow Jones average on July 31, to 380 on August 30, and to 381 on September 3, when the summer recess ended and Congress came back to Washington from the grass roots. The Dow Jones Industrials would not see the number 381 again for more than a quarter of a century.

The decline over the next several weeks was "orderly and produced no panic,"[8] drifting to 352 on October 10. Pressure on investors who were on margin accounts increased in the following two weeks as call money tightened up in the New York banks, loans declining by $120 million, "largely as a result of withdrawals of funds by foreigners,"[9] who were again liquidating assets in either direct or indirect response to the tariff problem.

On October 21 the high-tariff bill that had been written in the Senate Finance Committee by Senator Smoot and the Old Guard Republicans, was on the Senate floor for its first big test vote. Senator Thomas of Oklahoma offered a motion to recommit the bill to the Finance Committee with orders to bring back a bill limited exclusively to the farm tariff schedules. There was a problem, though, with this motion almost identical to the promising Borah resolution of the previous June. The Democrats had always wanted "consumer representation" on the Tariff Commission, and Smoot and the Old Guarders had put this provision into their bill. And the Progressives, who also liked this provision, now took up the argument that if they permitted only farm schedules in a new bill, they would be unable to reduce industrial rates. Senator LaFollette of Wisconsin took the lead in making this argument, and Senator Thomas warned him:

I will make the prophesy, that if this motion does not carry, you will not reduce the rates of existing law, you will not be able to muster upon this floor sufficient votes even to reducing many of the increases in the pending bill.[10]

The *New York Times* headlines the following day tell what happened:

(column 2, p. 1)	(column 5, p. 1)
Senate Firmly Bars	Stocks Slump Again
Farm Tariff Limit	But Rally at Close
Thomas's Recommital Plan	On Strong Support
Lost 64-to-10 Vote	Continuation of Selling Wave
Borah Motion was 39-38	Depresses Most of List
	In Day of Excited Trading

The DJI lost but 3 points, to 320, although the blue chips do not help the rest of the market. But there is still hope. Maybe LaFollette is right. Maybe Thomas is wrong.

Indeed, the front page of the *Times* of October 23 suggests that LaFollette may be right after all:

(column 4)	(column 5)
Stocks Gain Sharply	Tariff Cuts Forced
But Slip Near Close	In Chemical Rates
Vigorous Recovery Marks	Senate Coalition Wins
Most of Day and Many	Test Vote, 45 to 33, on
Issues Show Net Advances	First Schedules Taken Up

The Dow Jones Industrials gained 6 points, to 326, on this encouraging development, but on October 23, an hour before the market closes, it went into a nosedive and fell 21 points. The October 24 *Times* front page tells the story:

(columns 1-2)	(column 2)
Prices of Stock Crash	Coalition Breaks
In Heavy Liquidation	Over Carbide Rate
Total Drop of Billions	13 Democrats, 3 Republicans
Crash in Final Hour	Desert as Senate Rejects,
	42 to 37, Halving of Cent Duty

The crash occurred in the final hour after the vote in the Senate was known, although not a word appeared in the press making note of this remarkable coincidence. How could it make so much difference to the market whether the rate on carbide was one penny or a half-penny per pound? Moreover, chemicals were only the first of 15 schedules involving more than 20,000 items.

Why should the market care about the next item, casein, a product made from skim milk and used in the manufacture of glue and slick paper? Was it a farm item or an industrial item? Maybe both. The old rate was 2½ cents a pound. The House left it at that. Senate Finance bumped it up a penny, to 3½ cents. What would the full Senate do?

The next day, Thursday, October 24, would be time enough for the full Senate to take up casein.

John Kenneth Galbraith describes that next day on Wall Street:

> The panic did not last all day. It was a phenomenon of the morning hours. The market opening itself was unspectacular, and for a while prices were firm. Volume, however, was very large, and soon prices began to sag. Once again the ticker dropped behind. Prices fell farther and faster, and the ticker lagged more and more. By eleven o'clock the market had degenerated into a wild, mad scramble to sell. In the crowded boardrooms across the country the ticker told of a frightful collapse. But the selected quotations coming in over the bond ticker also showed that current values were far below the ancient history of the tape. The uncertainty led more and more people to try to sell. Others, no longer able to respond to margin calls, were sold out. By eleven-thirty the market had surrendered to blind, relentless fear. This, indeed, was panic.[11]

The panic was over by noon and prices firmed. In the late afternoon there was even something of a recovery. The *Times* market headline the following day even pushed news of the tariff off the front page, to page 25, as the headline went half the page:

WORST STOCK CRASH STEMMED BY BANKS;
12,894,650-SHARE DAY SWAMPS MARKET;
LEADERS CONFER, FIND CONDITIONS SOUND

Losses Recovered in Part
Upward Trend, Start
With 200,000-Share
Order for Steel

What, after all, had happened on the Senate floor that morning? Would the rate be 2½ cents or 3½ cents? Senator Shortridge, a friend of the dairyman, argued that the rate should go to 8 cents a pound, so U.S. purchasers of casein will have to buy the U.S. product, thus using more skim milk, and raising the profitability of dairying. Notwithstanding protests from the senators from paper-making states, the Senate that morning worked out a compromise with Shortridge, raising the casein rate to 5½ cents—by one estimate an 87 percent *ad valorem* rate!! The vote was 52 to 19, with the anti-tariff forces claiming a victory in keeping the rate from going to 8 cents!

By afternoon, the anti-tariff forces had reassembled, pushing through amendments cutting other chemical rates, and putting crude chicle on the free list. Thus Black Thursday ended, with only a 6½ point drop in the DJI when the smoke had cleared, although the broader list of shares was down badly.

On Friday, the Senate coalition was still holding from its Thursday afternoon gains and the market improved:

(page 8)	(page 1, columns 6-8)
More Chemical Rates Cut	STOCKS GAIN AS MARKET IS STEADIED
In Test Vote of Day, Chamber By 48-30 Defeats Rise in Duty on Non-Shatterable Glass	BANKERS PLEDGE CONTINUED SUPPORT
	HOOVER SAYS BUSINESS BASIS IS SOUND

Trading is Near Normal
Officials are Optimistic

The DJI enjoyed a gain of almost 2 points, to 301, and the next day lost only 2½ points, the market experiencing its quietest day all week with not much happening in Washington. On Sunday morning, the *Times* reported on page 14 that some of the Old Guard were worried that if more chemical rates were cut by the coalition, the bill might fail in the special session scheduled to end December 2. Senator Reed of Pennsylvania, who wanted high industrial tariffs for his manufacturing state, predicted the bill would fail in conference with the House because it would find changes being made by the Senate to be unacceptable. On the front page, there was only reassurance:

Debacle Inevitable
Wall St. Now Says

Market Grossly Overbought
Consensus of Economists
Bankers and Brokers

All are Optimistic Again

From his "Watch Tower" column on the financial page, *Times* man Richard V. Oulahan quoted Senator Thurston's remark that "Nobody wants it and everybody is for it." Wrote Oulahan: " 'Everybody,' of course, means the Senate and not the American people, among whom there seems to prevail a decided apathy with regard to what the Senate is doing with the tariff."

On Monday morning, the financial community read in the *Times* that:

Leaders Insist
Bill Will Pass

Smoot and Borah
Contradict Reed,
Who Told Philadelphians
Bill Was Dead

Washington. Oct. 27—While the fate of the tariff bill admittedly is in doubt in the minds of many of the Senators now trying to agree on a measure that can be passed and meet the approval of the President, a statement made by Senator Reed of Pennsylvania in a Philadelphia speech last night that the bill would die in the present session came as a surprise to the Republican and Democratic leaders here.

Senator Smoot, Republican of Utah, chairman of the Senate Finance Committee, took direct issue with Senator Reed and, although agreeing that chances of the bill passing in the special session were dim, predicted that it would be acted on in the regular session opening in December. . . .

Senator Borah also took issue with Senator Reed.

"My opinion is that the tariff bill is not going to die," he said. "I believe it is going to be made into a good bill and that it will be passed. I think those who have the power to write the bill have the power to pass it."

Senator Simmons, leader of the Democratic forces, said that his party intended to see to it that the President's plan to relieve agriculture was carried out. He added that if the bill died, the Republican party would have to kill it.

The coalition guaranteeing a tariff bill now included the Republican leaders of the Old Guard *and* Progressives *and* the leader of the Democratic forces. Tuesday's front page of the *Times* reveals what the market did after absorbing this information:

STOCK PRICES SLUMP $14,000,000,000
IN NATION-WIDE STAMPEDE TO UNLOAD;
BANKERS TO SUPPORT MARKET TODAY

Premier Issues Hard Hit
Unexpected Torrent of Liquidation Again Rocks Markets
Days Sales 9,212,800—Nearly 3,000,000 Shares
Are Traded in Final Hour—The Ticker Lags
167 Minutes—New Rally Soon Broken
Selling By Europeans and "Mob
Psychology" Big Factors in Second
Big Break

The DJI lost a shade over 38 points, closing at 260, and over in the corner of the *Times* front page was a small story about senatorial pleadings with Hoover to tell what he thought about the tariff. Hoover said nothing. There was also a complaint from Senate Republican Leader Watson that the Democratic delays that held up passage of the tariff bill might be charged with responsibility for the crash in stocks. Senator Tydings, Maryland Democrat, responded by saying that the Republicans were causing the delay.

On Tuesday, October 29, all the reports coming out of Washington seemed to be aimed at assuring the stock market that the tariff bill would not be killed, that it would be pushed through somehow, and this new coalition of Republicans and Democrats would see to it.

On October 30, the *Times* found room in column two to make this report (Coalition Fighting Move to Kill Tariff), even though so much of the front page reported on Black Tuesday:

STOCKS COLLAPSE IN 16,410,030-SHARE DAY
BUT RALLY AT CLOSE CHEERS BROKERS
BANKERS OPTIMISTIC, TO CONTINUE AID

The DJI settled at 230, and in the following days rallied weakly before reaching new lows until November 13, when it hit bottom for the year, at 198. On November 13, in a surprise move explicitly aimed at "showing confidence" in the business community and the strength of the nation, the Hoover administration announced a tax cut on personal incomes. True, it was only 1 percent but Andrew Mellon himself made the announcement, an indication that a shaken Hoover was hearing Mellon, not Mills. Congress whipped through the tax cut in less than a month. Before December was out, the Dow Jones Industrials climbed back to 263.

Congress did in fact adjourn its special session without completing work on the bill, but as Senator Watson predicted in October, work resumed with the regular session and through the spring the Senate completed the 15 tariff schedules. The Senate and the House then went into conference to work out differences in their two versions. The compromise that emerged in June reflected a one-third increase in the 1922 rates.

Through much of this period the stock market was heartened. The DJI rose to a high of 294 in April, as chances of defeating the bill improved. For one thing, the rest of the world was horrified at the prospect of passage and was applying vigorous pressure on the White House. Foreign governments filed thirty-four formal protests, and many began slapping on retaliatory rates in advance. The implied promise was that they would be repealed if Congress backed away at the last minute or if Hoover vetoed the bill. There was, for example, the protest from British India:

> Please protest vigorously against states proposition of duty on cashews because 1000% increase unjustified whilst U.S. not producing cashews, otherwise cashew industry in British India will be destroyed.[12]

And from Greece:

> The Minister of Greece avails himself of this opportunity to point out that the export of American products, agricultural as well as industrial, holds the first place in Greece imports, and whatever changes occurring in the tariff would necessarily affect the purchasing power of Greece to the detriment of American goods.[13]

Mussolini's Italy was furious. Congress had sharply increased the tariff on olive oil, not because it competed with a domestic product, for there was no U.S. olive-oil industry. U.S. packagers of raw imported olive oil worried that Italians were beginning to ship packaged oil, and pressed Senator Goldsborough of Maryland to push through a high rate on all but bulk oils of all kinds.

> The Italian reaction took the form of indignant editorials charging that the United States was attempting to corner the gold supply and ruin the entire world, especially Italy. The campaign against American automobilies was especially bitter. Italian drivers were embarrassed and annoyed at having their tires punctured, their windows spat upon or broken, and further harassed by the Royal Automobile Club of Italy which wanted to publicize the names of all Italians buying American automobiles and to demand an official statement of reasons for their choice. The importation of new cars was stopped by unheard-of duties. For example, a duty of $815.50 was imposed on each Ford car; $950 on a Plymouth; $1,385 on a Chrysler 77; and $1,660 on each Chrysler Imperial. American agencies closed up by November 1930, and Ford closed his assembly plant.[14]

The stock market began a slow slide again in April as such protests brought no new word from the White House. Head counts in the Senate showed that the one slim hope of defeating the bill on final passage lay with Senators Reed and Grundy of Pennsylvania. They were the two most fanatical advocates of high industrial rates, who were furious (or pretending to be furious) that the compromise rates were not higher! But this was a slim hope, and on June 13 the Senate voted, as the *Times* reported the following day:

SENATE PASSES TARIFF BILL BY 44 TO 42; FIVE DEMOCRATS HELP 'REGULARS' TO WIN; EUROPE TAKES FIRST MOVE IN REPRISAL

Interests Abroad Combine
Copper Firms of England,
Germany and Belgium
to Stop Buying Here.
Others Expected to Join
American Experts Interpret It
as Definite "Answer" to
Our Tariff Program
Heavy Losses are Feared

House is Set to Act Today
Republican Leaders Say
Hoover Will Sign Bill
Before July 1
Borah Assails Measure
Crowded Galleries Hear
Watson Lead in Defense
of Highest Rates in
History

On this news, the stock market broke 14 points on the DJI, to 230, precisely where it was on the bottom of Black Tuesday, October 29, 1929. The only possibility remaining was that Hoover, who still had not spoken, would veto at the eleventh hour. After the market closed Saturday, Hoover chose Sunday the 15th to make his announcement: "I shall approve the tariff bill."

**HOOVER SAYS HE WILL SIGN TARIFF BILL;
HAILS FLEXIBLE CLAUSE AS GIVING POWER
TO CORRECT FAULTS, END FOREIGN PROTESTS
PERFECT ACT 'IMPOSSIBLE'**

President Sees a Method
of Scientific Adjustment
at Last
Against More Agitation
Uncertainty over Measure Only
Retards Business Recovery,
He Declares
PLATFORM PLEDGES CITED

Hoover, as the headlines indicate, rested much of his argument on the administrative features of the act, which permitted him to raise or lower any rate by 50 percent. In the years that followed almost no use was made of this provision, and when it was, the rate was more often raised than lowered.

On Monday, the stock market reacted to the loss of the last frail hope. The June 17 *Times* front page reported:

**DEMOCRATS TURN TARIFF FIRE ON HOOVER
AS SENATE SENDS BILL TO WHITE HOUSE;
BREAK IN STOCK AND COMMODITY PRICES**

Selling Swamps Exchange
Leading Issues Tumble as
Wall Street Assails the New Tariff
Cotton and Wheat Down
Former Touches the Lowest in
Three Years With Grain Sagging
in Chicago
Many Margins Wiped Out
Much of the Liquidation Due to
Brokers Calling in Vain for
Further Deposits

The National Association of Manufacturers, though, predicted that the new tariff, when it became law, would bring "a breath of relief to all industry and all business." Organized labor also approved. Big business, big labor, and big government were in agreement.

The Great Depression was at hand, however, and as country after country took retaliatory tariff actions against the United States, the stock market sank lower, the Dow Jones Industrials finally hitting rock bottom on July 8, 1932, a few days after Franklin D. Roosevelt won the Democratic presidential nomination on an anti-tariff platform. On that day the DJI hit 41, against its September, 1929 high of 381. There were plenty of other reasons for the market to fall to that low level in the two years following Hoover's signing of Smoot-Hawley, however.

Mellon, for example, had become an embarrassment to Hoover. His magic had failed. The symbolic 1 percent cut in income tax rates had not done much to stem the collapse. In December, 1930, Hoover announced that the budget had gotten out of balance. With the sharp increase in tariff rates, revenues from customs fell sharply and in 1933 hit $250 million from 1929s $600 million at the lower rates. The 1 percent tax cut of the previous year was therefore allowed to lapse. In addition, a freshman senator from Texas, Wright Patman, brought impeachment proceedings against Mellon. The grounds were that the Treasury Secretary, who had been a multi-millionaire when he took office in 1921, became richer during his tenure as his financial assets appreciated. In return for Hoover's removal of Mellon, who was exiled to London to be Ambassador to the Court of St. James, impeachment proceedings were dropped and Ogden Mills stepped up to become Treasury Secretary in name, as he had been in fact since Hoover's election in 1928.

Hoover now had, as a result of the 1930 elections, a Democratic House and a Republican Senate (the electorate would have to wait until 1932 to pitch out Senators Smoot, Watson, and Reed). By the spring of

1931, it seemed that the United States was more or less back in equilibrium, having adjusted to the higher international wedge of the tariff act. Hoover and Mills, though, still worried about the budget. The government had run a deficit of more than $1 billion in the preceding 18 months, and Hoover and Mills believed this was causing a drag on business confidence. Hoover proposed an increase in the income-tax rates to remedy the situation.

Most one-term Presidents only have time for one truly disastrous decision, but Herbert Hoover squeezed in two. Having widened the international wedge, he proceeded to put the domestic tax wedge back where it had been when Harding took office in 1921. He did, though, have help from the Democrats who now controlled the House, 220 to 214, and had control of the tax-writing Ways and Means Committee. The personal income tax was pushed up to a 63 percent bracket at $1 million from 25 percent at $100,000, and to 4 percent at $4,000 instead of 1 percent at that income. A host of business taxes were piled on too. The House passed the bill on April 1, 1932, with 162 Republicans and 164 Democrats approving; 37 Republicans and 27 Democrats in opposition. On June 6, 30 Republican senators and 16 Democrats voted for a bill the Senate not only pushed higher, but also made retroactive to January 1, 1932; 11 Republicans and 14 Democrats opposed. Hoover signed the bill on June 6, 1932. The retroactivity feature of the tax boost was Hoover's last gift to Roosevelt. As the March 15, 1933 deadline approached for payment of 1932 tax liabilities, taxpayers throughout the nation had to withdraw funds from the banks. The bank panic of 1933 was the result. Roosevelt's "bank holiday," announced as soon as he was inaugurated March 4, 1933, merely enabled the Federal Reserve to reflow tax receipts to the banking system.

Roosevelt now only had to carry through on his campaign pledges and the Democratic platform of 1932. The platform had "condemned" the Smoot-Hawley tariff and pledged "reciprocal tariff agreements with other nations, and an international economic conference designed to restore international trade and facilitate exchange."

Roosevelt had gotten the Democratic nomination by expertly wooing the divided wings of the party, the internationalists and the "intranationalists." The former, led by Senator Cordell Hull of Tennessee, who had been ranking Democrat on the Ways and Means Committee of the House in 1929 when the tariff bill was written, believed the nation's economic problems had international roots. Hull himself was single mindedly devoted to repeal of the tariffs, but other members of the international wing were eager to join the League of Nations and recognize the Soviet Union. The *intra*nationalists were identified with newspaper publisher William Randolph Hearst, who argued that the United States should solve its own problems first, and only then look outward. Hearst and these Democratic conservatives were not especially opposed to tariff reductions, but rather focused on opposing the political and diplomatic aspects of internationalism.

In February, 1933, before his inauguration, Roosevelt named Hull Secretary of State. For the rest of the year, Roosevelt was an internationalist of the Hull variety. From April 8 onward, Hull had the spotlight. The April 9 *Times* reported:

ROOSEVELT SCRAPS POLICY
OF ECONOMIC NATIONALISM
TO ASSIST WORLD PARLEY

Old Course Condemned
Hull Lays World Slump to 12
Years of Isolation by the Republicans
11 Nations Invited Here
Trade Revival is Sought
Agreement for Lower Tariffs
Will be Urged to Spur the
Exports of Surpluses

The stock market surged, and continued a steady advance throughout 1933, rising with almost every statement by Hull. The DJI finished the year at 100, from 59 on April 8.

Roosevelt, though, had no intellectual commitment to Hull's program, and was also listening to the intranationalists that he had assembled around him, the Brains Trust. These were three academics, Raymond Moley, Rexford Tugwell and A.A. Berle, plus Treasury Secretary Henry Morgenthau. Morgenthau most directly helped to unwittingly dynamite Hull by attempting to drive up farm prices through devaluation of the U.S. currency.[15] The move was viewed for what it was in fact, a "beggar-thy-neighbor" act, with nationalistic motives of precisely the type that underlay the Smoot-Hawley Act. The Roosevelt-Morgenthau gold manipulations stunned international diplomats assembled in London at the World Economic Conference inspired by Hull, and U.S. efforts aimed at arranging instant truces on tariffs and exchange depreciations broke down in acrimony. Hull still had enough backing to win enactment of the 1934 Reciprocal Trade Act, which enabled him to chip away little by little at Smoot-Hawley rates over the rest of the decade. But by December, 1933, any real interest by Roosevelt in a Hull solution to the crisis had dissipated.[16]

He turned instead to internal remedies, which meant national planning; the New Deal. The idea was to use the central government both to promote economic growth through regulation of business and to assure balanced growth between industrial and agricultural sectors. This meant a re-allocation of resources away from the direction they would normally flow in a free market, either by government direction, government partnership with business and labor (in syndicates, which is why the process is sometimes called syndicalism), or taxation and spending. The Brains Trust was impressed not only by the Soviet experiment in central government direction, but in 1933 there was a general interest in Washington and other world capitals in what Mussolini had accomplished in Italy:

> Although his favorable reaction to Soviet developments in the mid-1920s moved Tugwell in new directions, it needs to be stressed that planning had taken hold almost everywhere in the industrial world outside of the United States. Beginning in the late 19th and early 20th centuries, Great Britain, without reference to Marxism, moved away from laissez-faire toward "planned prices, planned manpower, planned investments, planned allocation of materials—and the redistribution of incomes that has taken place through steeply graduated taxation". . . . Bismarck's backing of national railroads and health insurance in Germany, as well as the growingly dominant role of powerful industrialists also reflected prevailing economic and social trends in Europe.
>
> In Italy, the laissez-faire policies of the years 1922-25 gave way in 1925-26 to the syndicalist state with workers and employers organized into twelve national syndicates. Business and government entered into a formal partnership under Fascism. The relationship that developed, in the opinion of one recent observer, represented an institutionalization of patterns followed by Western democracies in more disguised forms. "The difference was more in form than in substance with the Fascists shouting what the others, perhaps more wisely, preferred to whisper." While probably generally true of Europe, the United States remained an exception (in 1933).[17]

Unfortunately for the global electorate, the virtues of syndicalism were a mirage. The Soviet economic advances of the mid-1920s should not be surprising, for the Soviet revolution had rid the nation of all domestic and international debt, which was simply repudiated. Central planning has its economic costs and inefficiencies, but these negative effects were for a while overwhelmed in Russia by the leap from the very top to the bottom of the Laffer Curve.

Enchantment with Mussolini's syndicalism was also misplaced. The rest of Europe was practising in whispers what Mussolini was shouting in Italy, but Mussolini was not practising what he was shouting. The economic foundations of Mussolini's power were built by his finance minister, De Stefani, in the first weeks and months after he climbed to power in 1922:

> DeStefani's program was coherent. It was inspired by a laissez-faire philos-

ophy which, in principle, was totally acceptable to business. Public enterprise was to give way to private initiative wherever possible. Public controls over production were to be abolished. Restrictions in the scope of governmental action would make it possible for the government to reduce and reform the bureaucracy, thereby gaining greater administrative efficiency and lowering operating costs. The reduction of public expenditures was to be accompanied by fiscal reforms, which was to increase governmental revenue by the paradoxical device of actually lowering tax rates and simplifying tax laws. De Stefani's rationale was that unrealistically high tax rates and complicated tax laws reduced revenue by encouraging widespread cheating and by making it virtually impossible for government officials to verify tax returns.[18]

The economy boomed, revenues flowed into the treasury, the lira appreciated steadily, and in 1924 the Fascists won two thirds of the seats in the national legislature. Mussolini thus won a democratic vote that Hitler never could.

Mussolini adapted the trappings of syndicalism, and these imposed economic costs on Italy, but he was much less the central planner than he seemed to the outside world:

Far from being fully absorbed into the Fascist state as the idea of totalitarianism implies, organized industry managed to retain a degree of autonomy. If the Fascist state turned out to be considerably less totalitarian in practice than it was in theory, the reasons are to be found in Mussolini's political techniques and in the resistance and resourcefulness displayed by outside groups, foremost among them the industrialists.[19]

Italy's real strength in the 1920s and early 1930s was in its tax and hard-currency policies, which remained in place even after De Stefani left the government in 1927. Not until late 1935 did Mussolini seriously begin chipping away at these fundamental benefits, and when he was forced to raise taxes to finance his Ethiopian campaign a year later the Italian economy soured. Mussolini introduced new taxes in October 1937 and his popular support faded with the economy.

Intrigued by Mussolini's seeming success with syndicalism as a basis for economic policy, both Roosevelt and Hitler tried it—Roosevelt with a whisper, Hitler with a scream. But neither noticed the De Stefani tax reforms, and, they gave no thought to cutting the high rates they inherited. They both chipped away at tariffs. Hull's most important reciprocal tariff treaty was finally negotiated with the British Commonwealth in December, 1938. Hitler's finance minister, Hjalmar Schacht, was successful in negotiating duty-free bilateral trade agreements with two dozen raw-material producing nations. But high domestic taxation in the United States kept the depression going.

Roosevelt surely could not have succeeded politically with his New Deal program of "Tax and tax, spend and spend, elect and elect," had the Republicans admitted their tariff errors of 1929-30. But they were still at it, as, for example, in the GOP platform of 1936:

The New Deal administration . . . secretly has made tariff agreements with our foreign competitors, flooding our markets with foreign commodities . . . We will repeal the present reciprocal trade agreement law. It is futile and dangerous.

The GOP was still pushing domestic and international wedge increases, so the voters looked upon Roosevelt as being at least half right, and they could still juggle the Congress to get what it wanted. In 1935, needing revenues for his spending programs and still unhappy about deficit finances, Roosevelt pushed through a major tax increase that lifted income-tax rates to a new high, 79 percent on incomes above $5,000,000. In 1936, he was back again for taxes and revenues, now hitting not only people with high incomes, but also successful business enterprises. Congress gave him what he wanted, the economy slid into the 1937 recession, and the new Congress, elected in the November, 1936 Roosevelt landslide, finally took matters into its own hands in 1938:

Despite the President's objection, the Congress passed in May a Revenue Act which reduced the capital gains tax and the undistributed profits tax and provided for the latter to expire at the end of 1939. The President criticized this action severely but, in a move unprecedented for him, allowed it to become law without his signature. In June, 1938, Congress enacted the appropriations for the spending program.

June was also the bottom of the recession. Thereafter the economy rose gradually but visibly. However, in August, 1939, just before the economic effects of the European War began to be felt, production and employment were still a few percentage points below their mid-1937 peaks.[20]

Hitler had a marvelous opportunity to boom the German economy by riding down the Laffer Curve when he took power in the spring of 1933. In fact, his way to power had been paved by Hoover's 1929-30 error on Smoot-Hawley, compounded in Germany, which had the weakest economy in Europe, and was naturally the country on the margin when Hoover signed the tariff on June 16, 1930. The contraction in Germany was immediate, as financial assets fell and businesses cut back. The German Chancellor, Heinrich Bruning, in the spring had responded to a weakening of the economy by announcing an agricultural assistance program and protectionist measures by emergency decree. Now, in June, revenues fell and Bruning reached for austerity. On July 7, he

. . . introduced further financial proposals demanding heavy sacrifices from all classes. Government expenditure was cut; there were increases in direct and indirect taxation, including supplementary income tax of 5 percent, rising to 10 percent on unmarried persons; a special contribution, the *Reichshilfe*, involving a reduction of 10 percent on all public salaries; an increase in contributions to the unemployment insurance fund, producing a saving of 100 million marks on unemployment relief; and there were increases in municipal taxation.

This savage program of deflation was again passed by emergency decree. The Reichstag, however, which had allowed the first emergency decree to pass without opposition, now made use of the constitutional provision permitting it to nullify the decree. Bruning replied by dissolving the Reichstag.

This has been described as "one of the most fatal events in the history of the Weimar Republic". It brought to an end the last Reichstag in which there was a parliamentary majority for the Republic, and plunged Germany into an acute political crisis which lasted until the appointment of Hitler as Reichschancellor.[21]

When Hitler came to power in 1933, fascinated with Mussolini's syndicalist style, he—like Roosevelt—left the tax rates where he found them. There was no way, then, for the private economy to expand as it had in Italy. There was, however, immediate economic relief from the mere fact that the cloud of war reparations disappeared with Hitler's ascendency. The Lausanne agreement of July 9, 1932, was the last try by the allies to arrange payment of at least a part of the war debts, and Hitler immediately announced that within months the agreement would not be worth three marks.[22]

Although he left the explicit tax rates high, Schacht did chip away at the domestic and international wedges. The economy expanded, but in so distorted a fashion that it compressed the tension between agriculture and industry into an explosive problem that Hitler sought to solve through *Lebensraum*, or conquest.

The reduction of the international wedge came through Schacht's "New Plan" of September, 1934. This was a twisted version of Cordell Hull's reciprocal-trade approach. Schacht arranged twenty-five bilateral trade agreements with nations that produced primary resources. Those nations would send Germany raw materials and receive credits, which they could use to buy finished German goods. The arrangement eliminated the tariff wedge on both ends of the transactions, but tilted the German economy wildly toward industry and away from agriculture. In his autobiography, Schacht recalled:

This policy laid me open to vigorous attacks from abroad. It certainly was in direct contradiction to previous concepts of multilateral trading and to the most-favored-nation treatment. Scientists in every country stigmatized this system as a repudiation of every well-known economic theory. What mattered to me however was not the classical tradition of my economic theory but that the German people should be provided with the necessities of life. Today when the whole world thinks and acts in terms of bilateral treaties the reader will scarcely be able to imagine the turmoil created by Germany's trade policy in the thirties.[23]

The second of Schacht's wedge reductions drove in the same direction, inflating industry at the expense of labor-intensive production, especially agriculture. Corporate dividend income was taxed both as corporate profits and as personal income at the high Bruning rates. Schacht imposed a scheme whereby corporate profits would not be taxed at all if they were reinvested. To encourage "efficiency," small corporations did not get this break, which meant they were swallowed up by bigger firms or disappeared. Industry was thus forced to grow whether it wanted to or not. Shareholders could liquidate their equity if they needed funds to live on, but always at distress sales, for the German stock market remained stagnant through the Hitler years—the country flooded with paper financial assets that the market worried might never be realized. Again, there was no such plowback provision for agriculture, so the effects also were to create a squeeze on the farm sector.

At the same time, Hitler's agriculture minister undertook a farm "reform," of which Schacht approved, that returned German peasantry to a feudal existence. In 1933, the average German farmer was paying 12 percent of his output as interest on his debt. Hitler "solved" the problem of farm bankruptcies merely by prohibiting foreclosure by creditors. Farmland henceforth could only be transferred by inheritance. There was, naturally, immediate farm relief, achieved by stripping creditors of the value of their mortgages. But the act tied the farmer to the land, discouraging the kinds of transfers, combinations, and investments that are necessary to increase productivity. By late 1935, Germany had been advanced 500 million marks worth of foodstuffs and raw materials which had yet to be redeemed in finished goods. Hitler pressed his idea of *Lebensraum,* i.e., that Germany's problem was that it was gifted intellectually and short-changed terrestially. By absorbing land to the east, he would weld together German industry and finance with Polish and Russian mining and food, ending all problems of foreign exchange in the process.

The global electorate had come too far over 2,000 years of advancing democratic systems to countenance another Caesarian experiment in lowering trade barriers by conquest. Hitler got away with *Anschluss,* merging Germany and Austria in 1938, and thereby increasing the economic efficiency of both. Even there, however, he showed himself to be a poor leader. Where Caesar had lowered tax rates in the lands Rome absorbed, Hitler tried to manipulate money as a boon to the

Austrians, against Schacht's correct advice that "an automatic rise in prices is bound immediately to cancel out any artificial overvaluation of money."

But the global electorate would not let him get away with any more than *Anschluss*. Where Caesar's empire lasted 500 years, Hitler's was wiped away in 7. In 1945, the world could again return to peaceful experimentation with political and economic ideas.

CHAPTER 8

The Failure of the
Economic Models

The failure of the Marxist model: Workers will not make an uneconomic trade of their labor unless they are forced to do so. If workers cannot pool their comparative advantages to maximize productivity, they must then trade more labor for a specific good. This increases the marginal attractiveness of leisure, which in turn increases the necessity of the state to force work to attain a desired level of output.

The failure of the Keynesian model: The death of bond illusion. The Keynesian model relies on the willingness of a worker to make an uneconomic trade of his labor for a bond. The government attempts to increase demand by increasing the sale of bonds, spending the proceeds on free goods and transfer payments. Will a worker trade more of his labor, thereby increasing output, if he is given free goods and cash without working?

The failure of the monetarist model: The death of money illusion. The monetarist model relies on the willingness of a worker to make an uneconomic trade of his labor because of an increase in the supply of money by the state. Will workers who refuse to trade their labor in the central marketplace when the money supply is X be willing to trade when the supply is 2X?

"In the field of economic and political philosophy there are not many who are influenced by new theories after they are 25 or 30 years of age, so that the ideas which civil servants and politicians and even agitators apply to current events are not likely to be the newest."[1] This was the observation of John Maynard Keynes in the midst of the Great Depression, by way of advertising his own ideas as the newest while intimating that the conventional wisdom of the era was obsolete.

Keynes was probably right. But to the degree that he was, the observation is as true now as it was in 1936, and civil servants, politicians, and agitators are as burdened now with old ideas—including those made new by Keynes in 1936—as they were during the Great Depression. The current economic models, which have been unable to explain the concurrent inflation and contraction of the late 1960s and 1970s, were also incorrect, however, in writing off as obsolete the classical ideas that dominated the nineteenth century and the early years of the twentieth. Certainly the 1,028 American economists who pleaded with Hoover not to sign the 1930 tariff act were by and large schooled in the classical tradition, yet somehow the failure of politicians to accept such advice has come, with the help of Keynes, to represent the bankruptcy of those old ideas.

None of the prevailing theories could explain the 1929 Crash any better than they could explain the preceding boom. Until this writing, no one has linked the Crash with the breakdown of the anti-tariff coalition of the Senate in the last days of October, 1929. Samuelson, a rigorous Keynesian, suggests a series of "historial accidents" as cause of the Crash. Galbraith, an eclectic Keynesian, sees the Crash as the pricking of a psychological bubble involving speculative greed. Rothbard, who thinks the boom was inflationary, advances easily to the idea that the Crash was the pricking of a monetary bubble. Friedman carefully avoids offering a theory, and to his credit acknowledges that his general theory for some reason does not fit the period:

> The stock of money . . . failed to rise and even fell slightly during most of the expansion—a phenomenon not matched in any prior or subsequent cyclical expansion.[2]

The Marxian model, which sees classical theory as inherently self-destructive, does not feel it has to offer an explanation of the Crash or the ensuing contraction because Marx said it all:

> It is enough to mention the commercial crises that by their periodic return put the existence of the entire bourgeois society on trial, each time more threateningly. In these crises a great part not only of the existing products, but also of the previously created productive forces, are periodically destroyed. In these crises there breaks out an epidemic that, in all earlier epochs, would have seemed an absurdity—the epidemic of over-production. Society suddenly finds itself put back into a state of momentary barbarism; it appears as if a famine, a universal war of devastation had cut off the supply of every means of subsistence; industry and commerce seem to be destroyed. And why? Because there is too much civilization, too much means of subsistence, too much industry, too much commerce.[3]

The Marxian idea does not concern itself with economic growth, but with economic contraction, a perfect counterpoint to Adam Smith's *Wealth of Nations*, which presents a growth, not a contraction model. Beneath the sarcasm and rage of *Capital* and the *Communist Manifesto*, there is an undeniable admiration for the efficiencies of the laissez-faire growth model. Indeed, it is super-efficiency that flaws capitalism in Marx's view. The system is so efficient that it "over produces," which means there must be periodic crashes, contractions, in order to restore equilibrium. The masses take the brunt of the contraction. They ultimately must react politically to defend themselves against this cycle of pleasure and pain. The proletariat takes matters into its own hands, if only to smooth out the cycle and distribute both the pleasure and the pain more equally among all classes.

The Marxian model, as a result, approaches the task of designing a system of political economy with a fixation on contraction. In constructing a framework, the first objective is to minimize the painfulness of contraction. Only as a second order of business does it look at expansion. But in the first order, the Marxian model commits itself to submerging individualism into collectivism, for it is the untrammeled individual who is viewed as driving the capitalist system toward overproduction, boom, and bust. The means of production must therefore be owned not by individuals but by the collection of individuals who compose the state.

The Marxian model does not deny that individuals, operating in their self-interest, bring economic benefits to the whole. It merely argues that a system designed with a fixation on expansion is inherently unstable; constant expansion would require individuals to be constantly driven toward accumulation for its own sake, as a miser piles up wealth, and this competition brings boom and bust.

Fanatically bent on making value expand itself, he ruthlessly forces the human race to produce for production's sake; he thus forces the development of the productive powers of society, and creates those material conditions, which alone can form the real basis of a higher form of society, a society in which the full and free development of every individual forms the ruling principle. Only as personified capital is the capitalist respectable. As such, he shares with the miser the passion for wealth as wealth. But that which in the miser is a mere idiosyncrasy, is, in the capitalist, the effect of the social mechanism, of which he is but one of the wheels. Moreover, the development of capitalist production makes it constantly necessary to keep increasing the amount of the capital laid out in a given industrial undertaking, and competition makes the immanent laws of capitalist production to be felt by each individual capitalist, as external coercive laws. It compels him to keep constantly extending his capital, in order to preserve it, but extend it he cannot, except by progressive accumulation.[4]

What is denied by Marx, and other political economists who advance collective models, is that there is any natural connection between individual self-interest and economic welfare for all. The connection exists only insofar as human institutions, i.e., the state, compel the individual's self-interest into channels that do enhance the common good.

All of the Marxian theory rests on this first assumption, this severing of any natural link between self-interest and the commonweal. If economic self-interest is not necessary to enhance the commonweal, the design of the Marxian system flows automatically toward human institutions that direct all activities to maximize the commonweal. It becomes only a matter of reshaping individuals so they will work for mankind, seeing in this common undertaking the true realization of their self-interests.

Insofar as this Marxian model succeeds, it is as a contraction model. As a system designed to protect members of the political economy against contraction shocks, it unquestionably does so in superior fashion to systems geared solely to growth, heedless of periodic shocks. The Soviet Union, the People's Republic of China, Fidel Castro's Cuba, have demonstrated an ability to minimize the social effects of economic contractions, minimize the swings in the economy itself, and provide sufficient growth to keep the economy from redistributing itself away. In addition, the systems seem able to maintain the general support of their respective electorates, for if they did not we would expect to see more visible signs of internal dissension.

Where the collectivist model falls short of its designer's promise, though, is on income growth. If the collectivists are correct, and there are human institutions capable of having individuals extend themselves for the commonweal first, and their self-interest second, such institutions have not yet been found. In a communal environment, individuals will continue to put effort into the economy only insofar as the economy is capable of completing the transaction. Individuals continue to make precise calculations of what their physical and intellectual capital is worth in trade, and cannot be persuaded to make an uneconomic trade by promises of distant rewards. Linkages of effort and reward have to be as close in a state economy as in a private economy. Workers do not respond to the exhortation that if everyone works harder, each individual will have more, unless they have confidence that more will be forthcoming. The state cannot fool workers into extending themselves, even in the hope that such deception will expand the goods and services available for distribution.

As long as the bosses pretend they are paying us a decent wage, we will pretend that we are working.—Soviet workers' saying, 1970s.[5]

The problem for a state attempting to nurse growth out of the Marxian model is a familiar one. Workers do not, after a point, wish to work harder in order to obtain more, for that necessarily means they must give up leisure. Workers at that point must be able to work less, but more efficiently, to obtain the same level of goods and services in exchange. They are then ready to work more, up to the original point of expended physical and intellectual capital, to expand output in absolute terms for the system. (On average, they will also wish to use some of these efficiency gains to increase their leisure, but there will still be expanded output.)

If there are no such efficiency gains, the worker is merely being invited to give up non-market activity (leisure and bartering) in order to give more time and effort to the communal market. In a real sense, he is being offered less for more, and it should then come as no surprise to anyone that less is produced for the system as a whole. Given its ideological reluctance to employ direct material rewards as incentives to expanded output, the state is led to employ punishments to force workers to make uneconomic trades of their labor. The most severe penalties in the Soviet Union, for example, are reserved for "economic crimes," i.e., bartering, for these drain productive effort away from the official, statistical economy.

No one . . . denies the existence of the counter-economy. The press runs many articles about corruption, thieving and illegal profiteering though, characteristically, it never publishes broad statistics that would portray the overall dimensions of underground operations. But there are always several publicized each year in which economic criminals against the state are sentenced to death for operations that run into hundreds of thousands of rubles and occasionally top a million. (The death penalty for economic crimes was reinstituted in 1961, obviously because the problem was getting more serious.) In 1966 one press report revealed that one-fourth of all crimes in the country involved misappropriations of state property.[6]

Thus, the state not only attempts to persuade or fool workers into making uneconomic trades of their labor, but also explicitly forbids workers from making economic trades of their labor when such trades do not conform to ideology.

Yet by all accounts, economic welfare in the Marxian economies continues to improve, slowly and steadily, often even relatively to the Western free economies. This is because they are often more efficient in penalizing non-work than the Western economies are in rewarding work. In the Soviet Union, for example, the work force is about 125 million out of the population of 260 million. In the United States, the work force is 85 million out of a population of 220 million. And of course, in the Communist nations, there are no subsidies for non-work as exist in the West, no cash payments for unemployment relief, welfare, food stamps, which at least marginally attract workers toward leisure and barter. In this fashion, the Marxian economies can give up the efficiencies of individualism and free trade, and keep pace with the Western economies.

But this seems possible only as long as the Western economies burden themselves by remaining in the prohibitive range of the Laffer Curve. Unnecessarily high tax rates on domestic transactions effectively cripple the free economy just as surely as bureaucratic error, compounded at every production point, cripples the state economy.

It also remains to be said that Marxian experimentation with explicitly forced labor, under Stalin in the 1930s, seems to have been more or less permanently abandoned for the simple reason that it cannot work. A new Communist nation, which has a work force that developed skills in a non-Marxian environment, can perhaps increase output by terrorizing this intellectual capital, but once this stock has passed away through age and death, the next cohort will not be able to produce even at the point of a gun. The future of the Marxian experiments—in Russia, China, the Eastern bloc of Europe, and Cuba—would seem to lie in development of individual incentives that are somehow made compatible with what is, primarily a redistribution model.

ii

British-style socialism emerged as an idea in the last quarter of the nineteenth century, coincident to the slowing of Britain's growth rates of the previous sixty years. The gentle contraction produced a mild form of Marxism, Britain attempting to graft a contraction model to a growth model and balance income growth and income redistribution. Self-interest would still be the primary motive force, but the state would nudge it toward collective welfare.

A fair representation of this idea was summarized in the *Liberal Industrial Report* of 1928, which sought to show "the unreal character of the supposed antithesis between Socialism and Individualism. While there was a place for public concerns to undertake work of great importance which for various reasons did not attract private enterprise on an adequate scale, and where unavoidable conditions of monopoly made private enterprise dangerous, it was the function of the state to establish an environment in which normal competitive conditions could flourish with the greatest efficiency and the least possible waste."[7]

The essence of this idea was more political than economic, offering an approach rather than a system. Somehow, individualism would continue to provide growth; socialism would cushion against contraction. It remained for John Maynard Keynes to systematize this notion into an economic model. For one thing, continued reliance on individ-

ualism as the mainspring for growth meant that the collectivist idea of
state-owned enterprises was relatively unimportant. Basic industries
need only be nationalized if and when private investors did not show
sufficient interest in maintaining them. Ownership of the means of
production was, in any case, unimportant so long as the state held the
means to control production. In the Keynesian model, the instruments
to perform this task were already in the government's hands, if only
the government knew how to use them.

Like the Marxian model, the Keynesian model is primarily a redistribution model. It relies on self-interest, individualism, free trade, and
free markets for economic growth. The state merely provides the safety
net to cushion in periods of contraction. Its failure comes in its use,
both by Keynes but more especially his followers, as a method of
actually spurring income growth through income redistribution!

To understand the Keynesian model, it must be remembered that
Keynes devised it in the midst of the greatest economic contraction of
modern times, his *General Theory of Employment, Interest and Money*
appearing in 1936. In addition, Britain had been in depression
throughout the 1920s as well, with the unemployment rate rarely
dipping below 10 percent and at times touching 20 percent. Keynes
gives little indication in his theory or writings in general that he is
aware of the disincentive effects of high tax rates on commerce. And
neither he nor his legion of followers distinguish between tax rates
and tax revenues, which are always treated as one and the same. It
seems incredible, but at the time Keynes penned his *General Theory* he
was surrounded in Britain by both mass unemployment and the
highest tax rates on personal incomes in the world, yet he made no
connection between the two.

It is no wonder, once this oblivion on his part is taken into account,
that Keynes could open his *General Theory* with so savage an attack on
classical theory. He ridicules the heart of classical theory, Say's Law,
which is that "Supply creates its own demand," by restating it in his
terms and then announcing that the law is "equivalent to the proposition that there is no obstacle to full employment."[8] But how can this be
true if there is so much unemployment?

Jean-Baptiste Say (1767-1832) is thus too easily disposed of by Lord
Keynes, who sees the periodic crises of capitalism as involving "under
consumption," rather than Marx's "overproduction," although both
concepts are precisely the same. Consider the following accurate
summary of Say's position by an unfriendly essayist:

> Say's optimistic productivism was not shaken by the economic crises of the
> early nineteenth century. He held that all overproduction could be only

partial. Either certain products are too abundant in one place only because in another men have not produced enough to purchase them or, if products pile up everywhere, it is because of artificial hindrances to their exchange. An economic crisis is therefore in large part a social and political crisis. Were customs barriers, which obstruct the exchange of products for products, and privileges, which hinder the exchange of products for services, wiped out, subsequent crises would by this one stroke be reduced materially.[9]

Policymakers throughout the industrial nations had done exactly the opposite of what Say's Law implied in arranging the Great Depression. Yet Keynes opens his tract by blaming Say, dismissing classical theory, and wrapping up *The General Theory* without a single mention of tax rates or tariffs.

What Keynes saw around him were unemployed men and women, ready, able, and willing to work, but an investor class unwilling to assemble them into productive enterprises. Instead of "investing," by which Keynes meant the risking of capital in ways that might create new wealth, investors were not investing sufficient amounts of real resources to equal the amount of real resources saved at full employment. In other words, the economy at full employment desired to save, say, 10 percent of its output, but investors were not willing to invest that amount.

The solution, given this view of the problem, is self-evident. The state should invest the difference, giving bonds in return to the private savers, and using the borrowed resources to assemble the unemployed into productive enterprises or even unproductive enterprises. At the time these ideas came to Keynes, he was rejecting the notion that the problem could be solved by monetary expansion. A monetary expansion supposedly lowers interest rates and thereby induces greater willingness of investors to utilize real resources. In the early thirties, though, interest rates were so low that Keynes argued they had hit bottom, and any increase in the money supply would merely create further "stagnant pools of money." By his method, he asserted, the economy would benefit even if workers were paid to dig holes and fill them up, for they could then use their wages to draw down the overproduced, underconsumed stockpile of goods and services.

The central assumption on which this Keynesian system perches is a requirement of illusion in the system—specifically "bond illusion." The Keynesian system considers irrelevant the fact that an increase in government debt must require higher taxes in the future to service that debt. In the Marxian model, remember, it was hoped that workers would work harder on the ideological promise (verbal bond) of being repaid by other workers, who were also working harder based on the same ideological promise. Wealth could be expanded by mere exhortation.

In the Keynesian system, all that is different is that savers who otherwise would not find a counterpart in private investors in the market—because investors cannot receive what they calculate investments are worth—are now given bonds by the state in order to finance government investment. A written promise thus substitutes for the Marxian promise of collectivism.

The Keynesians themselves know that their theory, at least at the outset, involves the deception of savers through bond illusion. The government issuance of a bond is, after all, not only a promise to pay future resources, but also a promise to tax the economy in the amount of the bond in order to make it good. The supposed difference between future taxation and present taxation is the entire incentive to increased demand that underlies the Keynesian model. Insofar as the electorate believes that future taxation is preferable to present taxation, it will expand demand and thereby output, thus *reducing* the overall burden of taxation.

In other words, if output is 100 and savings 10, the state can borrow the 10 and distribute it to consumers who will spend it, and with the multiplier effect, push output to, say, 130. The bond could then be paid back, leaving a net gain to the economy of 20. Even if 10 of that amounts only to holes dug and filled, there still remains 10 extra of real output.

With the magic of bond illusion, the government can in this fashion manage the economy to smooth out the rough spots that led Marx to predict the doom of capitalism. "Demand management" simply involves increasing government spending, via deficit finance, in recession, and increasing government taxation (to reduce the deficits) when the economy "heats up" in a boom.

This is the preferred method of Keynesian demand management, but there are also variations that are technically acceptable in this model. Savings, remember, are anathema to an economy that is faltering. Rich people save more of their income than do poor people. So taxing the income of the rich and distributing the proceeds to the poor, who will spend rather than save it, "may prove positively favorable to the growth of capital."[10]

While we see, then, that increasing future taxation through debt finance of unproductive enterprises is economically beneficial, and that increasing taxes for savers to reward spenders is also likely to favor the growth of capital, a second variation cuts in the other direction. By *lowering* taxes in periods of contraction (by which Keynes means lowering tax receipts) and financing the resulting deficit with future taxation (bond finance), the economy also benefits. The mechanism, once again, is bond illusion. The government borrows money from savers, giving them bonds, to finance tax cuts that leave more money in the hands of consumers to spend. Jones has $100 but will not spend it. The government borrows it from him and gives him a $100 bond, and simultaneously cuts Jones' taxes by $100. Jones thus "feels" wealthier, having $100 in savings, plus $100 that he did not have to remit to the government in taxes. He spends a good portion of this, and the economy revives. Jones must be taxed $100 plus interest in the future to pay off the $100 bond that he holds, but the Keynesians assume that Jones does not realize this, and in being turned from a saver to a spender by this deception, he revives the economy and unwittingly lowers his future taxes.

The amazing thing about this one variation of the Keynesian model is that it works! And it works not for the reasons given by Keynes; neither the electorate nor its instrument, the stock market, can be deceived by bond illusion (or the voters would happily approve bond issues to finance the digging and filling of holes). It works because it is the one variation that happens to coincide with Say's Law and the implications of the Laffer Curve.

To reduce "taxes," after all, means the government must in some way reduce tax rates. If the rates are cut where they are on the prohibitive range of the Laffer Curve, this removes the barriers to commerce that Say inveighed against, expanding tax revenues with the expansion of output and the tax base. Thus it was that the only successful "Keynesian" economic event of the past 40 years was the Kennedy-Johnson tax cuts of 1962–64, coincident with the Kennedy Round tariff reductions of 1964 that reduced rates in the United States, Europe, and Japan through a "round" of negotiations. The Keynesians congratulated themselves for the success of these classical policy steps. The highest rates were slashed from 91 to 70 percent while the lowest rates went from 20 to 14 percent; in addition, a variety of business tax-rate reductions were made.*

Oddly enough, while conservatives for forty years have been decrying the Keynesian model with a vehemence that almost matches their declamations against Marxism, the classical and Marxian models are much closer to each other than either are to Keynes. The Keynesian

*Had Kennedy only cut the lower rates, thus increasing the progressivity of the system, the economic effect almost certainly would have been negative.

"revolution" of the 1930s was hardly unknown to Karl Marx in the 1860s. Marx used his most withering scorn to declaim against debt finance and bond illusion:

> The only part of the so-called national wealth that actually enters into the collective possessions of modern peoples is—their national debt. Hence, as a necessary consequence, the modern doctrine that a nation becomes the richer the more deeply it is in debt. Public credit becomes the *credo* of capital. And with the rise of national debt-making, want of faith in the national debt takes the place of blasphemy against the Holy Ghost, which may not be forgiven.
> The public debt becomes one of the most powerful levers of primitive accumulation. As with the stroke of an enchanter's wand, it endows barren money with the power of breeding and thus turns it into capital, without the necessity of its exposing itself to the troubles and risks inseparable from its employment in industry or even in usury. The state creditors actually give nothing away, for the sum lent is transformed into public bonds, easily negotiable, which go on functioning in their hands just as so much hard cash would. . . .
> As the national debt finds its support in the public revenue, which must cover the yearly payment for interest, &c., the modern system of taxation was the necessary complement of the system of national loans. The loans enable the government to meet extraordinary expenses, without the taxpayers feeling it immediately, but they necessitate, as a consequence, increased taxes. On the other hand, the raising of taxation caused by the accumulation of debts contracted one after another, compels the government always to have recourse to new loans for extraordinary expenses. Modern fiscality, whose pivot is formed by taxes on the most necessary means of subsistence (thereby increasing their price), thus contains within itself the germ of automatic progression. Over-taxation is not an incident, but rather a principle.[11]

Present-day communist systems, which have issued from Marxian theory, do not have the Western variety of public debt. There are no Soviet or Chinese or Cuban "bonds." The public debt is instead "implied" by the collectivist system itself, in the sense that citizens give up current resources on the system's implicit promise that in the future other citizens will also give up current resources to those who did so earlier. Western nations have this variety of public debt as well, in their social-security systems. The official U.S. public debt, for example, is now roughly $900 billion, but this is only the amount represented by palpable bonds. Actuaries can estimate the current value of resources promised to all participants in the Social Security system and calculate that the deficit, over the next 75 years, now amounts to roughly $4 trillion. There are no "bonds" backing this promise of payment, only the word of the government, which is to say, the people. But there is no more illusion in this kind of bond than in official bond finance; as individuals sense the value of the social-security commitment weakening—the nominal claims promised fading with the ability of the economy to yield resources—they compensate with private savings, even strengthening family ties as a form of old-age insurance.

None of this is to suggest that there can be no benefits to debt finance through bond issuance. If workers have a choice between paying present taxes in order to give resources to the government or getting bonds in exchange for their resources, they may prefer the latter, which will mean future workers will have to be taxed more to pay off the bonds. But there is no illusion in this choice. Immediate output can expand through debt finance, but the electorate understands that future output will have to fall by precisely that amount. In war, especially, when the electorate desires to maximize current output, debt finance makes perfectly good sense. In periods of sharp peacetime contraction, caused by foreign or domestic political errors for example, debt finance may also be preferred by the electorate. Why? There are at least two reasons: Income redistribution is most needed during sharp contractions to keep the poorest and weakest elements of society from being crushed, and tax finance of a redistribution only causes a sharpening of the contraction. Secondly, the electorate knows future taxes will have to be raised to pay off the bonds, but there is always the chance that the future will also bring wiser political leaders.

The failure of the Keynesian model is not due to its failure to work, but rather to its failure to work as advertised. If it had merely been presented as a model for increasing output during periods of economic duress at the expense of output during better times, its disciples would not now have to struggle to explain why it has been unable to produce growth, with or without inflation, except when it is coincident with the classical model. Politicians have ceased thinking of the Keynesian model as one of expansion and employ Keynesian economists merely to rationalize their income-redistribution programs. And liberals who at one time viewed the Keynesian magic as an antidote to Marxist impulses are attracted more and more to collectivist notions—central planning, detailed regulation of commerce, wage and price controls. The buoyant optimism of the Keynesians, which peaked with the Kennedy-Johnson tax cuts, has given way in the stagflation of the 1970s to Malthusian notions. If Keynes can no longer produce growth, it must be because the planet has finally rebelled and will no longer permit growth. But this is after all where Keynes began:

Before embarking on his great venture in persuasion, Keynes drew a sketch of the economic and social background of the political events he was about to survey. With but slight alterations of phrasing, this sketch may be summed up like this: Laissez-faire capitalism, that "extraordinary episode", had come to an end in August 1914. The conditions were rapidly passing in which entrepreneural leadership was able to secure success after success, propelled as it had been by rapid growth of populations and by abundant opportunities to invest that were incessantly re-created by technological improvements and by a series of conquests of new sources of food and raw materials. Under these conditions, there had been no difficulty about absorbing the savings of a *bourgeoisie* that kept on baking cakes "in order not to eat them." But now (1920) those impulses were giving out, the spirit of private enterprise was flagging, investment opportunities were vanishing, and bourgeois saving habits had, therefore, lost their social function; their persistence actually made things worse than they need have been. . . .

The *General Theory* is the final result of a long struggle *to make that vision of our age analytically operative.*[12]

This is much too harsh an indictment of Keynes, for it suggests a conscious design on his part to sell the *General Theory* as a growth theory when Keynes knew it was really a stagnation thesis. Nevertheless, the upshot is the same. The Keynesian ideas, rigorously applied, inevitably make the Malthusian condition analytically operative. When the economy is in the upper reaches of the Laffer Curve, an increase in spending financed with bonds only moves the economy further up the Curve. In the absence of a policymaker who understands that tax rates can and should be cut when they are unnecessarily high, the economy no doubt will be in contraction, and some form of state relief will become necessary. The electorate will patiently redistribute during contraction, awaiting the political leader who, by accident or design, provides resumption of growth by traveling down the Laffer Curve.

iii

Keynes was writing about the end of laissez faire, which is to say the obsolescence of classical economic theory, in the Britain of the 1920s. He failed to observe that Britain was being smothered by the unnecessarily high tax rates imposed during World War I and never cut back, a mistake Britain had not made in 1815 following the Napoleonic wars. Thus, classical theory was not obsolete, but forgotten or misunderstood by the political class. But as we saw, the essence of Say's Law was still sensed in the United States, thanks to Andrew Mellon, and it was not until the Crash of 1929 and the Depression that followed, that classical theory was almost universally renounced. The Marxian model took on a new lustre as capitalism stumbled again. State capitalism, in fascist and New Deal forms, emerged as a counterforce for outright collectivism. And the Keynesian model, with its emphasis on state manipulation of monetary and fiscal instruments rather than direct ownership, came to centerstage in the West as the cleanest antidote to Communism.

The submergence of laissez faire and the ascendence of state management of the economy in one form or another brought another casualty to classicism. The role of money. For the 200 years preceding World War I, and in the United States until the 1929 Crash, money was viewed as simply a medium of exchange; in Hume's words, "the oil which renders the motion of the wheels [of commerce] more smooth and easy." Monetary policy was as a result consigned to a simple role, having nothing to do with expansion or contraction of commerce or employment. It would maintain stable prices and it would do so by maintaining the gold standard.

The beauty of the gold standard was that it tied governments to the planet, which changes glacially, and limited the freedom of politicians and bureaucrats who are apt to act precipitously. The government did not need computerized econometric models to tell it when to increase or decrease the supply of money, for the computer that operated under the gold standard was the electorate itself, interacting with the planet.

If individuals came to the Mint with gold, asking money in exchange, the government knew automatically that the electorate in combination with the planet had decided that the supply of money was too low and should be increased. When individuals came to the Treasury with paper money and asked for gold, the government knew that the money supply was too high and should be lowered. Because the prices of all commodities are interconnected in the marketplace, as the price of gold in terms of paper money was held constant—say twenty dollars per ounce—all prices would remain constant. Relative prices would not, of course, remain the same. The price of apples could rise as the demand for them, for some reason, rose, or the supply of them, for some reason, fell. But the rise in the price of apples would cause marginal apple consumers to shift to oranges or bananas (or something else) and cause producers of other things to shift into apple production. Relative prices would adjust. The same thing happens when the government has no standard by which it regulates the money supply; relative prices adjust even if there is a horrendous inflation. But when the government has a standard of some sort, and fixes the price of one commodity in terms of its money, relative prices of all commodities change around that price.

If all individuals in the economy decided suddenly that they would look for gold, because the only price that the government was guaranteeing was that of gold, at twenty dollars an ounce, the economy would be in trouble. The government would soon have enormous stockpiles of gold, and individuals would have huge stockpiles of paper money, but there would be nothing in the marketplace to buy. But this did not happen, nor could it, because the electorate does not view money as a storehouse of value, i.e., a commodity that has worth beyond its usefulness as a medium of exchange. The electorate will exchange its labor for a precise quantity of money, that which it precisely needs to lubricate the wheels of commerce. It will not exchange its labor for money not needed for transactions.

This, though, is the theory of the monetarists. It is not a new idea. The notion that people will work for "money," as a form of wealth, whether or not there is anything that money can buy, is no doubt as old as public, as opposed to private, money. Where Keynes revived the ancient idea that people will work for bonds, under the illusion that they can be exchanged for real goods, and that this illusion causes more real goods to be produced, the modern monetarists rest their arguments on money illusion.

The monetarist school, nominally headed by Milton Friedman of the University of Chicago, has for the past three decades years vigorously opposed the Keynesians. The two major political parties in the United States have tended to align with one school or the other, the Democratic Party with the Keynesians and the Republican Party with the monetarists. Yet the Keynesians and the monetarists are, at heart, as close to each other as they are both distant from the classical and the Marxian schools, neither of which glues its framework together with illusion.

The money-illusion idea is as simple as Keynesian bond illusion: Jones, the plumber, and Smith, the carpenter, will not come into the marketplace to exchange their labor. The monetarists argue that by increasing the supply of money, both Smith and Jones will want more—not as a medium of exchange, but as a storehouse of value, a form of wealth. In coming into the market and trading their labor for this incremental wealth, Smith and Jones increase the economy's output. There is now more money in the system and the monetarists agree that prices will rise, so that Smith and Jones are back to where they began. If they want to do the exchange a second time, the amount of money each receives no longer leaves a bit extra as a further form of wealth, so they do not come into the market. But at least the economy has gotten one transaction out of them, so that all of the increase in money has not gone exclusively into price increases, but has yielded a little output too.

The monetarists, we see, make much more modest claims about what their form of illusion can accomplish. And illusion can only last for a while, so the monetarists are careful to warn the political leaders that the monetary tool only works in the "short-run." (Keynesian bond illusion is also implicitly short-run, with Keynes arguing that in the long run we are all dead anyway.) According to Friedman, monetary policy "cannot peg interest rates for more than very limited periods," and "It cannot peg the rate of unemployment for more than very limited periods.[13]

Friedman's short-run is shorter than Keynes'. The economy will adjust in a year or two. Because of this limitation, he advises active use of the monetary tool only on special occasions, specifically at the end of wars to assist the process of adjustment as the economy converts from war to peace production. In practice, however, the monetarists have been less restrained in their advocacy of monetary policy as a means of reducing unemployment and interest rates.

A critical assertion of the monetarist school is that the Depression of the 1930s was a failure of monetary policy. Here was one instance where the short-run would have made a difference, says Friedman:

> The Great Contraction might not have occurred at all, and if it had, it would have been far less severe, if the monetary authority had avoided mistakes, or if the monetary arrangements had been those of an earlier time when there was no central authority with the power to make the kinds of mistakes that the Federal Reserve System made. The past few years, to come closer to home, would have been steadier and more productive of economic well-being if the Federal Reserve had avoided drastic and erratic changes of direction, first expanding the money supply at an unduly rapid pace, then, in early 1966, stepping on the brakes too hard, then, at the end of 1966, reversing itself and resuming expansion until at least November, 1967, at a more rapid pace than can long be maintained without appreciable inflation.[14]

As the statement suggests, the monetarists have precise views that change from month to month on what the money supply should be, and money alone may have caused the "Great Contraction." While the monetarists are by self-admission unable to explain the boom of the 1920s, and have no specific opinion on the cause of the 1929 crash, they are certain the contraction of the U.S. money supply as they define it was the problem of the 1930s.

The money supply had indeed collapsed, falling by roughly a third between October 1930 and March 1933 as banks collapsed, extinguishing deposits. As Hoover dealt the economy his double-barreled wedge increases—on tariffs and domestic tax rates—real incomes and production fell. This fall in real incomes and output brought with it a reduction in the demand for money at the going level of prices. The electorate simply had need of one third less money. If prices could have risen by one third, there would have been no need for the banking collapse. The monetarists do not see it that way. If the Federal Reserve had only increased the money supply instead of worrying about the gold standard and inflation, the contraction would not have taken place or would not have been as severe, they say.

The fall in the money supply did not occur soon enough to explain the stock market Crash in 1929. Indeed, the godfather of the modern monetarist school—Irving Fisher of Yale—issued almost daily statements between October 24 and 29, 1929, to reassure investors that the economy was sound and the market full of bargains (he lost between $8 million and $10 million of his personal fortune in the crash). We assume his analysis took place within a monetary framework. If the Federal Reserve had countered the fall in the money supply by pumping new reserves into the banks via the printing press, i.e., buying government bonds with currency, it would merely have produced a Great Stagflation. This is what occurred in the 1970s when the political leaders were simultaneously listening to the Keynesians and the monetarists, practicing bond illusion and money illusion at the same time.

In fact, the monetarists bear a portion of the blame for the depths of the Depression in the 1930s, for it was the idea of Irving Fisher that underlay Roosevelt's manipulation of the gold price in the summer of 1933, which blew up Cordell Hull's economic conference and any chance of bringing a quick end to the monetary and trade wars. The Fisher idea was to raise the price of gold in order to raise prices of all commodities as a way of reviving production. Roosevelt did raise the price, to thirty-five dollars from twenty dollars an ounce. This devaluation of the dollar was viewed by U.S. trading partners as a mercantilist move, to gain benefits at home at the expense of foreigners, which it partly was. The net effect was to raise prices, but not production, and Roosevelt gave up on monetary manipulation.

The Friedmanites have never been impressed with this failure of money illusion. Nor are they impressed with the Federal Reserve's expansion of money in 1932. Galbraith recalls:

> The Federal Reserve by 1932 had sufficiently suppressed its fear of inflation so that it was able to go into the market and buy government bonds and thus substitute cash for securities in the vaults of the banks. This policy it continued in ensuing years. The consequences of this action too were deeply disappointing. Before, it had been taught that when banks had reserves in excess of requirements, they would, some minor periods or examples of caution excluded, expand their loans and therewith their deposits and the money supply. The history of the small banks on the frontier suggested that this expansion

would be undertaken not with an excess of caution but in a reckless absence of caution.

Now the banks simply sat on the cash. Either from a shortage of borrowers, an unwillingness to lend or an overriding desire to be liquid—undoubtedly it was some of all three—the banks accumulated reserves in excess of requirements.[15]

The plain fact is that the modern monetarist model has even less to recommend it than does the Keynesian, which at least has a policy overlap with the classical model. That is, where Keynesian "tax" reduction requires faith in bond illusion if you are a Keynesian, you can rely on "tax rate" reduction in the classical system without any belief in bond illusion.

Why is it that economists can build elegant, mathematical edifices atop a foundation of illusion? The simple answer is that they examine the world a piece at a time in trying to fathom how it works when put together. The jargon of the trade terms this "partial equilibrium analysis."

As an example, let us consider a horse race. Suppose we want to find out what the odds on each horse will be at post time, and we can locate, in advance, every horseplayer. Might we not be able to interview the horseplayers, find out what horses they will bet on, the amounts they will bet, and grind all this into a computer to come up with the odds? If we were partial equilibrium analysts we would try, but we would be wrong. The horseplayers would go to the track, and most of them would do exactly what they said they would do in the interview. But many would watch the tote board, and observe that the horses they originally picked now carried shorter odds than had been thought possible, and other horses now carried longer odds. The "general equilibrium" at post time would look far different than any inferences made by partial analysis. Many of the horseplayers would be clouded by illusion, but for this horseplaying electorate—as with all others— the smart money would compensate (in finance, the word is "arbitrage") to the last dollar.

Almost all of modern macro-economics involves illusion. Bond illusion implicitly assumes that future taxes do not change as the result of changes in the amount of bonds issued. Money illusion implicitly assumes that prices do not change as a result of the amount of money issued. In this sense, both bond illusion and money illusion involve partial equilibrium analysis. Both the Keynesians and the Friedmanites can trace their intellectual parentage to Alfred Marshall, whose Marshallian curves drawn before the turn of the century are the essence of partial equilibrium economics. Our model, both political and economic, has its foundation in the works of Leon Walras, whose Walrasian analysis is based on general equilibrium considerations.

If we think back to the horseplaying example, we can understand why partial equilibrium analysis tends to become dominant in political circles. Of what value, after all, is a general equilibrium economist who, when asked what the odds will be at post time, is forced to answer with uncertainty, under no illusion that the morning line will be a constant in the minds of the bettors. The politician, who wants to act on a degree of certainty, looks to economic advisors who are prepared to tell him that if the money supply is increased by 3.768 percent in the following two quarters, everything will be rosy, but if it is increased by only 2.965 percent all hell will break loose. Or if the federal deficit is $11 billion, the economy will be stimulated to full employment, and if it goes to $12 billion, the economy will overheat.

The worst problems caused by the Keynesians and the monetarists during the past decade have not resulted from their specific policy advice, however. It makes little difference to the economy whether the deficit is $11 billion or $20 billion or the money supply increases by 3 percent or 5 percent as the monetarists measure it. But as we will see in the following chapter, the economists grew frustrated when their advice was taken and did not work. The problem, they concluded, was the structure of the world economy. And this they set about to correct with results that could only have been anticipated by a general equilibrium economist.

CHAPTER 9

The Building of Empires

The joining together of political units by conquest, liberation, or colonization permits economic efficiencies that automatically move the combined unit down the Laffer Curve, reducing the wedge by common currency, common language, common laws, and removal of tariff barriers.
Alexander and the Caesars: The building of the Roman Empire.
Napoleon, Peel, and Parliament: The building of the British Empire.
The United States and the end of World War II: Trial and error toward U.S. hegemony.

In chapter 2, in which we observed that the political impulse of civilization is toward a world government that approximates a solution to the succession problem, we used a hypothetical example to illustrate the consolidation of political markets. Having added the economic model, let us now repeat this exercise to illustrate the force that drives toward consolidation of political economies.

Imagine the United States did not exist in its present form. Instead, imagine fifty sovereign nation states, each with its own national government. The people of each state speak different languages or variations of the same tongue. The predominant religions differ, and perhaps in some all but the state religion are banned. Each state has its own system of customs and tariffs. Each, its own tax structure. Each, its own currency and monetary authority, and its own system of laws, criminal and civil.

Given this condition, the standard of living of the citizens of these fifty nations would inevitably be much lower than at present. The people of the fifty nations would still transact business with each other, but with much greater difficulty. A significant portion of each nation's population would have to be pulled away from production of goods and services and channeled into the mere effort of exchange. Specialists in language variations would have to be developed so that business entities in Kansas and New York could understand one another in order to transact. Currency specialists, "money-changers," would be required to assay the value of each nation's money so that businessmen could have confidence in their transactions. As well as each nation having its own domestic tax wedge, each nation would have an international wedge against commerce, with added paperwork and financial costs for every transaction across borders.

Even worse, the mobility of each citizen of the fifty nations would be limited. If a citizen of New York was unhappy with the government of New York, he could only go to those other nations that permitted immigration. And even then, he and his family would have to adjust to a new language. Perhaps their religion would be treated inhospitably or prohibited outright.

Each nation state would have its own national defense system, with all states having standing armies, and the coastal states having navies as well, to protect against other maritime powers across the oceans as well as against the other coastal states.

Clearly, the costs of having fifty nations instead of a federation of states in one nation would be enormous, so much so that we would not recognize the continent if we saw it in such condition, such would be its relative poverty. Indeed, it could hardly survive in a world of other nations as they exist at present.

Such is the condition that Alexander of Macedonia encountered in 336 B.C., upon the assassination of his father Philip. The world he saw was a world of fragments, countless governments, currencies, legal systems, religions, armies, languages, customs. It was as if the twenty-one-year-old heir, who had been schooled in government and philosophy in his formative years by Aristotle, understood the enormous costs to the world of fragmentation and the enormous benefits that would accrue through unification. In the next dozen years, before his death in 323, he conquered "the world," not by enslaving it, but by snapping—one small piece at a time—the barriers to communication and commerce that had lain over Europe, the Mediterranean, and Asia Minor like a spiderweb.

Imagine, in our hypothetical America, that a political and military genius sets out from New York to conquer New Jersey. As he does so, both New Jerseyans and New Yorkers discover the efficiencies of unity. The New Jersey army merges into the New York army, but a segment of both is freed for production, and the costs of maintaining armies through taxation falls in both regions. Not only does spending fall, but tax rates can be lowered too, a double surge down the path of the Laffer Curve. The same occurs with the elimination of border costs of commerce between New York and New Jersey as tariff walls fall, as two monetary authorities merge into one and a common currency replaces dual systems. Mobility of citizens increases and languages and customs merge, as long as the New York political genius does not attempt to *impose* language, religion, or customs on the conquered terrain. If in this first campaign the New York genius has a sense of what he must and must not do to cut through the spiderweb, the citizens of adjoining states—Pennsylvania, Connecticut, etc.—may still resist conquest, but not as vigorously as New Jersey did when it was still unknown what kind of political leader the New Yorker would be.

Alexander the Great was just such a military and political genius, conquering the world with such subtlety that more often than not the city-states in his path simply threw open their gates to him. He not only did not impose a religion where he conquered, but would pay homage to local religions by worshipping at the temples, even ordering reconstruction of those that had been damaged in warfare. (The modern presidential candidate in the United States dons a Stetson hat in Dallas and eats Bar-B-Q, then travels to Brooklyn where he puts on a yarmulke and eats a bagel.) Where Alexander imposed systems, they were welcomed happily, substituting for instance a faithful silver coinage standard for the elaborate bimetallism of Persia or the myriad moneys of Asia Minor.

When he died after a drinking bout in his thirty-third year, during the fever preceding death his generals asked him to whom he left his empire, and he answered, "To the strongest."

Like most great men he had been unable to find a successor worthy of him, and his work fell unfinished from his hands. Even so his achievement was not only immense, but far more permanent than has usually been supposed. Acting as the agent of historical necessity, he put an end to the era of city-states, and, by sacrificing a substantial measure of local freedom, created a larger system of stability and order than Europe had yet known. His conception of government as absolutism using religion to impose peace upon diverse nations dominated Europe until the rise of nationalism and democracy in modern times. He broke down the barriers between Greek and "barbarian," and prepared for the cosmopolitanism of the Hellenistic age; he opened hither Asia to Greek colonization, and established Greek settlements as far east as Bactria; he united the eastern Mediterranean world into one great web of commerce, liberating and stimulating trade. He brought Greek literature, philosophy, and art to Asia, and died before he could realize that he had also made a pathway for the religious victory of the East over the West. His adoption of Oriental dress and ways was the beginning of Asia's revenge.[1]

According to the Encyclopaedia Britannica, "It is not untrue to say that the Roman Empire, the spread of Christianity as a world religion, and the long centuries of Byzantium were all in some degree the fruits of Alexander's achievement."

Alexander had left his indelible imprint on the world, a taste for economic unification, and although his "empire" itself dissolved with his death the memory of unification remained. The global electorate, though, had more work to do on the succession problem, for Alexander had not even left an adopted son to carry on.

While the Greek experiments with democracy terminated in the fratricide of Athens and Sparta, at least the idea was imported by Rome for further trial. The Greeks had demonstrated that a democracy based on automatic rotation of political rule among the entire citizenry was impractical, as impractical as it would be to annually rotate the management committee of General Motors among all the workers. The Roman experiment divided and weighted the voting classes, but did not draft citizens for political leadership. The man at the top would have to get there by climbing the slippery slope in competition with those of his fellow citizens who were interested in trying.

It was 271 years after Alexander's death that the world found his successor in Julius Caesar. The global economy had been fragmented again, but not nearly to the degree it had been prior to Alexander, and there was a crude system of democratic succession to provide for continuity, once Caesar put the world economy together again. In 52 B.C., Caesar conquered Gaul, adding to the Empire a country twice the size of Italy and expanding the economic marketplace by five million people. Once subdued, Caesar treated the conquered tribes with such lenience that even when they could have broken loose in the civil war that followed, Rome being helpless to retaliate, they did not do so. For three centuries Gaul remained a province of Rome, learning the Latin language and transforming it, prospering in the Roman peace, channeling the culture in northern Europe.[2]

When Caesar crossed the Rubicon into Italy three years later, its cities opened their gates to him, welcoming him as a liberator and champion of Italian rights. Instead of confiscating the estates of his opponents to feed his near-empty coffers, he held back, winning at least the neutrality of the middle class. When he entered Rome, he proclaimed a general amnesty and restored order and municipal administration with free use of the state's money. "But with unscrupulous impartiality he deposited in the Treasury the booty from his later campaigns."[3]

Now Caesar was on top. In five years he laid the foundation for a system that would endure for 500 years in the West and for 1,500 years in the East.

(He) distributed lands to his veterans and the poor; this policy, continued by Augustus, for many years pacified the agrarian agitation .... (He) spent 160 million sesterces in Rome on building programs .... Having eased the pressure of poverty, he required a means test for eligibility to the state dole of grain. At once the number of applicants fell from 320,000 to 150,000 .... (He) continued the Gracchan policy of inviting businessmen to support the agrarian and fiscal revolution . . . . Many of the great capitalists, from Crassus to Balbus, helped to finance him, as similar men helped finance the American and French revolutions. Nevertheless, Caesar ended one of the richest sources of financial profiteering—the collection of provincial taxes through corporations and publicans. He scaled down debts, enacted severe laws against excessive interest rates, and relieved extreme cases of insolvency by establishing the law of bankruptcy essentially as it stands today. He restored the stability of the currency by basing it on gold and issuing a golden aureus, equivalent in purchasing power to the British pound sterling in the nineteenth century. The coins of his government were stamped with his own features and were designed with an artistry new to Rome. A novel order and competence entered the administration of the Empire's finances, with the result that when Caesar died the Treasury contained 700 million sesterces, and his private treasury 100 million . . . . As a scientific basis for taxation and administration, he had a census taken of Italy, and planned a like census of the Empire.[4]

Had Caesar not adopted Caius Octavius as his son, the planned census of the Empire would likely never have been taken. After Caesar's assassination in 44 B.C., the Empire plunged into civil war, and it was sixteen years before Octavius returned victorious to Rome to become the new Caesar, Augustus, not only the son Alexander never had, but an extremely competent one at that. At his return:

Rome was full of men who had lost their economic footing and their moral stability: soldiers who had tasted adventure and had learned to kill; citizens who had seen their savings consumed in the taxes and inflation of war and waited vacuously for some returning tide to lift them back to affluence; women dizzy with freedom, multiplying divorces, abortions, and adulteries.[5]

For 44 years, Augustus consolidated the Empire, finally getting to his adoptive father's plans for an Empire-wide tax census in the year of Christ's birth. (In the Gospel of Luke: "in those days there went out a decree of Caesar Augustus that all the world should be taxed.") In fact, it was because of this decree that Joseph and Mary were en route to Bethlehem, Joseph's town, in order that he might be enumerated. Because of this coincidence and the baldness of Luke's wording, Augustus is usually treated harshly in modern depictions of the birth of Christ. But the census was the most important act of Augustus' reign, for in spreading the tax burden over all the Empire, it enabled rates to be lowered on those who had been bearing all the burden, ended the need by the government to confiscate incomes and property of those most visible, and thus encouraged wealth generally to resume its accumulation and spread. The *Pax Romana* was underway, its golden age lasting until 180 A.D. and the death of Aurelius, when his son, Commodus, traveled up the Laffer Curve through profligate incompetence. The Empire splintered slowly but steadily as successive emperors fought contraction by tax and spending policies that moved it further up the Curve. By 301, after 100 years of spending, tax, and monetary manipulation had yielded chronic stagflation, Diocletian decreed universal wage and price controls under penalty of death. Attempts to employ bond illusion or money illusion to expand inevitably seem to lead to wage and price controls, as the electorate counters illusion by raising wages and prices. It was not until the American and French revolutions of 1776 and 1789, both rebellions against the upper reaches of the Laffer Curve, that the global electorate could seriously reestablish the quest for world government that ended with the Pax Romana.

ii

We related in chapter 2, before detailing the economic model, the essential features of Napoleon's role as successor to Alexander and the Caesars in igniting the electorate's push toward a unified political and economic market. Unlike Alexander and Caesar, who began with conquest and brought reforms afterward, Napoleon began with internal reforms made possible by the Revolution, especially the lowering of domestic tax rates, the stabilizing of the currency with a gold Napoleon, and reform of French law with the Napoleonic Code. ("My real glory," he wrote, "is not the forty battles I won—for my defeat at Waterloo will destroy the memory of those victories . . . . What nothing will destroy, what will live forever, is my Civil Code.") The ingredients of the Code took hold in the train of Napoleon's armies, spreading over much of the Continent, thereby providing legal solutions to feudal regimes and ending the virtual enslavement of the peasant to the land.

For the last time we will quote from Durant's monumental historiography:

> . . . Even in his lifetime he [Napoleon] had a Hegel, who, unblinded by frontiers, saw in him a world force—the compulsion of events and circumstances speaking through a man—forging fragments into unity, and chaos into effective significance. Here—first in France, then in Central Europe—was the *Zeitgeist*, or Spirit of the Time: the need and command for order, ending the disruptive excess of individualistic liberty and fragmented rule. In this sense Napoleon was a progressive force, establishing political stability, restoring morality, disciplining character, modernizing, clarifying, codifying law, protecting life and property, ending or mitigating feudalism, reassuring peasants, aiding industry, maintaining a sound currency, cleansing and improving

administration and the judiciary, encouraging science and art (but discouraging literature and chaining the press), building schools, beautifying cities, repairing some of the ravages of war. Helped by his prodding, Europe advanced half a century during the fifteen years of his rule.[6]

Most present-day historians seem to suggest that Great Britain in 1815 had a golden age almost visibly spread before it, that with the defeat of Napoleon it was almost inevitable that the rest of the century would belong to Britain. But the future did not seem that bright to the British citizen of the day. More than twenty years of war had left Britain with a staggering public debt. Forty years earlier, on the eve of the American Revolution, the British debt was £126.8 million. In 1815, it stood at £900.4 million. At mid-century, British historian Thomas Babington Macaulay looked back on the fears of that colossal debt:

> At every stage in the growth of that debt the nation has set up the same cry of anguish and despair. [After the Peace of Utrecht] the nation owed about fifty millions; and that debt was considered, not merely by . . . fox-hunting squires . . . but by profound thinkers, as an incumbrance which would permanently cripple the body politic. Nevertheless . . . the nation became richer and richer.
>
> Then came the war of the Austrian Succession; and the debt rose eight millions. Pamphleteers, historians and orators pronounced that now, at all events, the case was desperate.
>
> Under the prodigal administration of the first William Pitt, the debt rapidly swelled to £140 million . . . Men of theory and men of business almost unanimously pronounced that the fatal day had now really arrived. . . . It was possible to prove by figures that the road to national ruin was through the national debt. It was idle, however, now to talk about the road; we had reached the goal; all was over; all the revenues of the island . . . were mortgaged. Better for us to have been conquered by Prussia. . . . And yet [one] had only to open his eyes to see improvement all around him, cities increasing, marts too small for the crowd of buyers, harbors insufficient to contain the shipping . . . houses better furnished . . . smoother roads.
>
> [After the Napoleonic War] the funded debt amounted to £800 million. It was in truth a . . . fabulous debt; and we can hardly wonder that the cry of despair should have been louder than ever. . . . Yet like Addison's valetudinarian, who contrived to whimper that he was dying of consumption till he became so fat that he was shamed into silence, she went on complaining that she was sunk in poverty till her wealth . . . made her complaints ridiculous. The . . . bankrupt society . . . while meeting these obligations, grew richer and richer so fast that the growth could almost be discerned by the eye.
>
> A sum exceeding [£240 million] was in a few years voluntarily expended by this ruined people on [the construction of railroads]. Meanwhile taxation was . . . becoming lighter; yet still the Exchequer was full . . . . The prophets of evil were under a double delusion. . . . They saw that the debt grew; and they forgot that other things grew as well as the debt.[7]

Not only was Britain's *debt* "fabulous" in 1815. In 1820, the Edinburgh Review observed that taxes were on the same order:

The schoolboy whips his taxed top; the beardless youth manages his taxed horse, with a taxed bridle, on a taxed road; and the dying Englishman, pouring his medicine, which has paid 7%, into a spoon that has paid 15%, flings himself back upon his chintz bed, which has paid 22%, and expires into the arms of an apothecary, who has paid a license of £100 for the privilege of putting him to death. His whole property is then immediately taxed from 2% to 10%. Besides the probate, large fees are demanded for burying him in the chancel. His virtues are handed down to posterity on taxed marble, and he will then be gathered to his fathers to be taxed no more.[8]

What made the Industrial Revolution and the Pax Britannica possible was the audacity of the British Parliament in 1815. Spurred by middle-class agitators such as Henry Brougham, the legislature rejected the stern warnings of the fiscal experts and in one swoop eliminated Pitt's income tax, which had been producing £14.6 million or a fifth of all revenues, and tariffs and domestic taxes that had been producing £4 million more. Had the British left their tax rates high in an attempt to quickly pay down their debts, the sixty-year bull market that followed would not have been possible. As it was, the nation moved down the Laffer Curve in a "return to normalcy" on tax rates. As the economy surged in the following decades, expanding revenues were used both to pay down the debt and reduce other tax rates. By 1855, the £900 million debt had been paid down to £808.5 million, and although the Russian War of 1855-57 added £30 million, by the end of the century the debt was chiseled down to £639 million. Over the same eighty-five-year period, interest rates on government bonds dropped steadily, from almost 6 percent in 1815 to less than 2¾ percent. When Sir Robert Peel brought back the income tax in 1846, the effect was not to push the economy back up the Curve, because Peel's sole intent was to use the income-tax revenues to repeal the Corn Laws, the duties on foreign grains. The reform was enormously beneficial, because the income tax fell across all lines of production, while the Corn Laws subsidized agriculture at the expense of all other producers. The economy became more efficient as a result of the reform.

But it is hardly accurate to suggest that British economic expansion did not get underway until Peel ended the Corn Laws and brought back the income tax. Modern historians who have been taught that the income tax is a "good tax" often seem troubled that it was removed in 1815, as if the economy could not do without it.*

In fact, it was the robust expansion of the British economy in the years to 1846 that forced the issue of agriculture versus industry.

---

*See, for example, Trevelyan, G.M., *British History in the Nineteenth Century and After (1782-1919)*, Longmans, Green and Co., London, 1937, p.180

Between 1816 and 1875 Britain was to become the world's workshop, the world's banker, and the world's trader. . . . By 1860 she was supplying half the world's output of coal and manufactured goods. In 1830 world production of coal was about 30 million tons, of which Britain produced four-fifths; in 1870 it was about 220 million tons, of which Britain produced half. . . . In 1870 the external trade of the United Kingdom was greater than that of France, Germany, and Italy combined and three times that of the United States. The output of pig iron had risen from 700,000 tons a year in 1830 to about 3,800,000 in 1869-71, and to over 6,500,000 in 1871-73. While many industries were dependent on the coal fields, the main growth had been in cotton. Cotton was the one industry into which mechanization had cut deep by 1820. Textile operatives were more than 10 percent of the working population in 1841. . . .

Between 1815 and 1851 occurred the most rapid economic development of domestic resources in the whole of British economic history.[9]

Britain had become too rich relative to the rest of the world to produce the food she consumed. The Corn Laws not only kept out cheaper grains from abroad, but in subsidizing domestic agriculture as it had been arranged in the eighteenth century—sharecroppers working for the landed gentry—the Corn Laws delayed capital intensive farming that eventually did produce more food with fewer people. In a real sense it was the planet that forced repeal of the Corn Laws, for when the Irish potato crop failed in 1846, the starving Irish could not be fed from the inadequate British granaries. The Corn Laws simply had to be ended to permit entry of grains from the United States. Even so, a half million Irish died of starvation in 1846-47.

Because growth was almost continuous in this sixty-year period, laissez faire worked beautifully. But as the Irish famine showed, a nation without a fallback system to meet unexpected economic contraction would suffer staggering social costs. The free-market "solution" to the famine, repeal of the Corn Laws, was really a partial solution to the next hypothetical famine; there simply was no government mechanism to prevent starvation. While economic growth resumed, bigger and better than ever, the electorate began seriously pushing Parliament toward a social-support system. It would take another thirty years, and the disastrous British harvests of 1876-79, before the coin was turned and the forces of income redistribution supplanted the forces of income growth.

Meanwhile, the problem of balancing the budget each year was a delightful one for the Chancellor of the Exchequer. For as each tax reduction invited a new wave of expansion and further increase in the tax base, tax rates had to be reduced again in order to prevent surpluses from developing.

The explosion of British wealth was felt worldwide as Britain became the world's leading creditor nation, sending out surplus goods and receiving financial assets (bonds) in exchange.

It was this vigorous, competitive, hideous and yet dazzling community which was the great exporter of the capital which made it possible to open up the vast but hitherto untapped resources lying in the hinterlands of new continents. All the underdeveloped parts of the world were calling for investments. Nearly a quarter of the £2.4 billion which was added to the capital of the United Kingdom between 1865 and 1875 was placed abroad, while a sixth went into houses and a tenth into railways at home. . . . It has been argued that the effort and the expense which went into the development of the colonial empire were at the cost of improvements which might have been made at home. This is to ignore the indirect gain which came from bringing new areas with new products into a worldwide system of multilateral trade. The small volume of direct trade with many new colonies often contained an element which played a vital part in some more complex interchange of other types.[10]

Instead of each country arranging bilateral trades with other countries, carefully keeping accounts balanced, Britain's position at the center of world trade and her willingness to accept paper financial assets in exchange for goods made possible complex three- and four-way trades. Britain sold finished goods to producers of primary materials, who paid for them both by sales to continental industrial nations and the United States, and by sending bonds to British investors. The industrial nations paid the primary producers and the United States by their sales of semi-finished products to Britain. The United States, a net importer, settled its accounts by its inflow of British investment.

As long as the world pie was expanding, prosperity fed on itself as protectionist pressures in each nation abated, permitting steady worldwide lowering of tariffs. France began peeling away its skyhigh protective rates in the 1840s. In Prussia, seventeen fragmented states joined together in a tariff union (Zollverein) in 1833, providing for free trade between these German states. (The people of Germany gathered with long wagon trains at the various internal boundaries and waited for the stroke of midnight, January 1, 1834, when the tariff union came into being, and then crossed amid cheers.)[11]

Italy and Russia also moderated their rates through the mid-century, and Britain, the leader of the free-trade parade, by 1875 had only twenty revenue items on its dutiable list. The constant expansion of world trade meant a diminishing of internal national complaints about an "export of jobs," and thereby a lessening of external frictions. Except for a few minor skirmishes, as in Crimea, and the Civil War in the United States (which itself had deep roots in the conflict over tariff policy between the industrial North and agrarian South), the world was at peace until the end of the century. In the vital sense of the term, it was a Pax Britannica.

The unwinding of the Pax Britannica occurred because of economic contraction without national or international systems for ameliorating the pain that comes with contraction. France, for example, experienced a terrible harvest in 1875, and responded by putting up tariffs. The German Empire, unified under Bismarck, had built upon the free-trade policies of the Zollverein, and through the early 1870s lowered rates until, by 1877, 95 percent of all imports entered free. But this was the first of three horrendous British harvests and Britain, in order to import more food, pushed out more manufactured goods. German industrialists, irritated by this "dumping" against which they had to compete, applied pressure until tariffs were raised. Russian industrialists, complaining they could not compete against cheap German manufactures, succeeded in pushing up tariffs in 1893. Germany responded by raising its tariffs against Russian goods, and Russia came back by doubling its rates against German goods. A troubled truce was finally negotiated, but commercial irritations persisted up to 1914. At the same time, France's protectionist tariff irritated Switzerland and Italy, which engaged in similar tariff wars, and with protectionists in the saddle, Italy abandoned its low-tariff policy in 1887 for high rates that did not come down until the Mussolini era.

Britain meanwhile held fast to its free-trade policies, but the relative contraction it felt in this period turned its electorate in search of social systems to deal with contraction:

After 1870 the government of Britain became more and more concerned with two main tasks: (1) where there was reason to believe that the free play of individual choice and judgment would be beneficial, the government had to secure that there should be neither force nor fraud nor the obstruction of legal forms to hamper the creative power of individual self-help; (2) where the play of individual choice and judgment did not in fact produce the goods and services which common sense suggested—and experience confirmed—were desirable and possible, the government had to try to provide them. If the mechanism of the market was to produce what it could, that mechanism had to be properly serviced. Things necessary to civilized life that a market could not provide the government should provide if possible.[12]

At the same time, some of Britain's colonial investments began to haunt her (as we will see in a later chapter), applying pressure on the budget. In 1871, unification of Germany aroused Parliament over the state of national defenses; Prime Minister Benjamin Disraeli needed more money. His chancellor, Sir Stafford Northcote, solved the problem of 1876—a prospective deficit of £774,000—by raising the income-tax la : to three pennies on the pound from two. The London *Economist* of April 8, 1876 observed: "The great advantage of our financial system—one which no other country possesses equally—is that we have at command a tax, of which the amount can be raised without affecting trade, and without pressing painfully on anyone except when its amount is very high."

The income tax was surely all of this, and certainly Britain was by now wealthy enough to provide broader public services, such as free primary education and unemployment insurance. Public spending on social services quadrupled between 1900 and 1914, and income-tax rates glided upward to finance these costs. The British economy continued to grow, and while the growth rates were less dramatic than in the boom years of mid-century, the nation seemed to have hit upon a comfortable compromise of the growth and distribution models. The peaceful blending of Adam Smith and Karl Marx was largely the work of the Fabian Society, "revolutionary" socialists who formed in 1883 because of the distress in the political economy.

The political and economic irritations between the crowned heads of Europe intervened to produce the dynastic fratricide of World War I. Once and for all, the global electorate cleared the scene of Hohenzollerns, Habsburgs, Romanovs and Ottomans, making the world "safe for democracy."

The British Crown survived as a showpiece, but unfortunately so did the steeply progressive tax rates Britain had imposed to help finance the war. A hundred years earlier there was a Henry Brougham to agitate for a return to normalcy on British tax rates after Waterloo. Now, in 1918, there was no similar pressure to get the economy off the upper sweep of the Laffer Curve. Until 1914, the British income tax had been very nearly proportional; except for tax-free personal and family allowances on subsistence income, all income classes paid the same rates. After 1914, the system was progressive, and the work of the Royal Commission of 1919 was not to determine whether or not wartime rates could be reduced in order to expand revenues, but to streamline the system of progressivity and make it more "equitable."[13] This began the reversal of Britain's course in the nineteenth century. Instead of tax cut, expansion, revenue increase, tax cut, etc., the trend in Britain has been tax increase, contraction, revenue decline, tax increase. Balancing the budget became the process of increasing the "supertax" on higher incomes.

As a result, Britain dragged through the 1920s, unemployment hovering at 5 percent throughout. British politicians and economists, unaware that the problem was in the tax structure, began doubting free-trade principles and a monetary system tied to the planet through gold. When world depression followed the Wall Street Crash, John Maynard Keynes ended his lifelong advocacy of free trade, and in 1931 (as Britain was again increasing tax rates to balance the budget) Keynes provided intellectual support for a return to protectionism and a break with the gold standard. The return to protective tariffs in Britain was coupled in 1932 with enactment of "Imperial Preference," by which only the British territories could enjoy preferential tariff schedules. It was an economic blessing to Britain through the 1930s that she had a colonial empire within which untrammeled trade could be maintained. And the mildness of Britain's tariff schedules relative to Smoot-Hawley is a prime reason why Britain's depression was not as severe as the United States. But the return to protectionism in and of itself was a further blow to the world economy:

> The decision to enact Imperial Preference, made at the Ottawa Conference in 1932, had a particularly injurious effect on Japanese exports to British colonial territories. It seems permissible to say that this decision played some part in strengthening the pro-war party in Japanese politics; and it may have influenced Germany also.[14]

There would be no opportunity for Britain to repeat this process. At the end of World War II, Winston Churchill and his Conservatives—who favored continuation of colonial empire—were turned out of office by the British electorate. With India's independence in 1947, the last vestige of Pax Britannica was over.

iii

From its earliest days, Americans showed a remarkably sensitive aversion to the upper reaches of the Laffer Curve, which is not surprising. The colonies had been peopled with the exported malcontents of the Continent during the eighteenth century, people fleeing the wars of Europe and the bond finance and taxation that strangled personal initiative. Andrew Mellon, the financial wizard of the 1920s, remembered being lectured at the knee of his grandfather (who left Scotland for Pittsburgh in 1805) on the evils of European public finance—specifically the sale of government bonds followed by a government currency inflation that rendered the bonds worthless.* A

---

*We have an on-the-spot report of mid-eighteenth century Europe from Montesquieu: "A new distemper has spread itself over Europe, infecting our princes, and inducing them to keep up an exorbitant number of troops. It has its redoublings and of necessity

violent antipathy to taxation and spending resided in the brains and bones of the colonists. The American Revolution and Independence thus became inevitable on the day in 1765 when the colonists learned that a Stamp Act had been passed by the British Parliament upon the instigation of the Chancellor of the Exchequer, George Grenville.

Grenville's problem was that the British debt had grown by £52 million during the Seven Years' War of 1756-63 and the taxes imposed in Britain during the war had not been reduced. Yet he needed new revenues. Meanwhile, the colonies had enjoyed unprecedented prosperity during the war, and the colonial assemblies had voluntarily floated bonds to raise funds to help the crown finance its war in Europe. Grenville, impressed with the prosperity in the American colonies, was not similarly impressed with their arguments that they were still paying higher taxes to pay off their bonds.

In an evil hour [Grenville] determined to send the tax gatherer to our colonies in America. His scheme consisted of two parts: a proposition for certain duties at the ports, such as we term customs; and an internal tax, by means of duties similar to those in this country termed stamp duties. The customs part of the scheme ... the colonists were willing to allow as a regulation of commerce and ... made no serious objection.

But the terms of the recital to the taxing Act engaged their serious attention. It ran that—"it was expedient that new provisions and regulations should be established for improving the revenue of the kingdom; that it was just and necessary that a revenue should be raised in his majesty's dominions in America for defraying the expenses of defending, protecting, and securing the same; and that parliament was desirous to make *some* provision in the *present* session of parliament *towards* raising the said revenue in America." And these expressions were considered, by the colonists, to imply an indefinite extension of imperial taxes in America, of which this Act imposing duties on merchandise at the ports was but a first instalment, and accordingly seemed to open out a vista of future taxation without an end.[15]

The colonists reacted furiously and spontaneously in a display of civil disobedience. They would not pay the stamp taxes, duties on the filing or conveyance of documents. This was taxation without representation:

---

becomes contagious. For as soon as one prince augments his forces, the rest, of course, do the same; so that nothing is gained thereby but the public ruin. ... Great princes, not satisfied with hiring or buying troops of petty states, make it their business on all sides to pay subsidies for alliances, that is, generally to throw away their money. The consequence of such a situation is the perpetual augmentation of taxes; and the mischief which prevents all future remedy is, that they reckon no more upon their revenues, but in waging war against their whole capital. It is no unusual thing to see governments mortgage their funds even in times of peace, and to employ what they call extraordinary means to ruin themselves—means so extraordinary, indeed, that such are hardly thought of by the most extravagant young spendthrift.[16]

The peal of remonstrance which sounded across the Atlantic found an echo in this country; for our merchants represented the effects of the Act as equally disastrous to them, inasmuch as the Americans, then indebted to them in about four millions, refused to pay their debts or to renew their orders while the Stamp Act continued in force. Moreover, the course of justice was suspended for want of stamped paper, so that their debts could not be recovered.[17]

In six months, the outcry in the colonies and the echo in Britain was so great that, over Grenville's determined opposition, the Stamp Act for America was repealed.

In the process, the colonists had given Grenville a lesson in the Laffer Curve, as Stephen Dowell, assistant solicitor for England's Inland Revenue, recalled a century later:

The probable yield had been calculated at 60,000 pounds, or, according to some, 100,000 pounds a year. The actual yield for the six months the tax was in force was 4,000 pounds, which, trickling into the English treasury by driblets— 3,000 in 1767, and 1,000 in 1768—proved insufficient to pay the expenses attending the execution of the Act, which amounted to 6,837 pounds. Such was the result of what Burke termed the process of "shearing the wolf."[18]

With independence from foreign tax gatherers, the "wolf" for a century and a half refused to be sheared except at its own convenience. George Washington inveighed against foreign entanglements and struck a responsive chord in the electorate. Foreign entanglements meant expenses and taxes, not to mention the potential for war. The states jealously guarded their rights to tax and the Federal government kept its expenses so low that customs duties were more than sufficient to pay the costs of the central government, and by the 1830s the national debt had been paid off completely.

It was the vast frontier that, more than anything else, kept the politicians of the era from expanding government expenditures and taxation. If a people would cross an ocean to escape the upper bend of the Laffer Curve, surely they would move another 100 miles west, or even across state borders, to escape spendthrift politicians.

Foreign investors learned about this peculiarly American mobility the hard way. In the 1830s, British capital flowed in a mighty stream into the United States as the level of Britain's wealth rose and investors looked globally for higher returns than were available at home. British investors were especially dazzled by the returns of investment in the Baltimore & Ohio Railroad, and were soon eagerly pressing cash on state governments to finance public works, canal building being among the most favored. When recession swept the United States in 1842-43 as a result of the failure of the Bank of the United States (an event wrought by Jacksonians who believed in bond illusion and money illusion), state revenues fell and interest could not be paid on state debt without raising taxes. But the states could not raise taxes:

> The debts incurred had really been far beyond the means of pioneer states. In Louisiana, for instance, a three dollar tax upon every man, woman and child in the state would have been necessary to meet the annual interest, if taxation were to be resorted to. And there were reasons why this was not feasible. Why should the pioneer farmer remain to be taxed? Land was cheap and unlimited beyond the Mississippi. His household had not forgotten how to be self-supporting. A very small tax in one place . . . would cause small owners to sell out for what they could get and leave the burden to fall upon less migratory capitalists.
>
> In the face of the unwillingess of all classes to be taxed to pay interest, there was in most states no recourse. The public works on which the borrowings had been spent were incomplete and therefore unproductive. . . . The reflection that such obligations could not be quite binding derived a gloss of patriotic sanctity from the consideration that much of the debt was owed abroad and to non-Christians.
>
> Under these circumstances nine states stopped payment of interest in the course of 1841-42. Two states, Michigan and Mississippi, repudiated them outright. . . . Thus one hundred million dollars in deflated securities were piled upon the losses from banking, canal and mercantile investments which the British had already suffered in the United States.[19]

It does not seem entirely coincidental that the Sixteenth Amendment to the Constitution, the income-tax amendment, came on the heels of the closing of the western frontier. Arizona achieved statehood in 1912 and the Sixteenth Amendment was adopted in 1913. Once the Federal government got possession of this national tax power, there could be no escape in a nation without frontiers.

The Wilsonian Democrats of the period saw income taxation as an alternative to tariff revenues, which to that time had been the chief source of revenues to the government. Representative Cordell Hull of Tennessee, the fanatical opponent of Smoot-Hawley in 1929-30, was just as fanatical in 1912 as the leading advocate of the Sixteenth Amendment. Conservative ideologues, then and now, rue the event as the birth of the welfare state and the beginning of the end of capitalism, individualism, and laissez faire in the United States. But the modern New Left populists also look back in dismay on the Sixteenth Amendment:

> The major portion of the taxes in America comes from the person who is earning $3,000 to $25,000 a year. Regardless of what the Internal Revenue Service would like the public to believe, it has always been and always will be the small wage earner who bears the heaviest burden of taxation. The passing

of the income tax law, which became the 16th Amendment to the Constitution, squeaked by close to Christmas when few congressmen were there to oppose its passage. . . . The bill's passage certainly was not the mandate of the people, as they would have voted it down.[20]

The tax began modestly enough, as you see in the accompanying table of its history. But it rose rapidly as the United States entered the war in Europe. Indeed, its presence as a "seasoned" tax—one the government had experience in collecting—was an important consideration of the Wilson government's decision to enter the war, for it made finance of the U.S. effort relatively easy. It might thus be argued that—to the degree it assisted U.S. entry and hastened the end of the war in a way that advanced democracy and doomed monarchy—the tax was implicitly mandated by the electorate.

From this perspective, the income tax also enabled the United States to move in the direction of world leadership in the political dimension, which it had foresworn at its birth. The British Empire was on its way to collapse. The Soviet Union was beginning its experiment, explicitly accepting at its birth the challenge of foreign entanglements, evangelizing an international world order under collectivist principles.

As we saw in chapter 7, the period from 1919 to 1939 represented an extremely ragged passing of the baton from Britain to the United States. The United States was the dominant economic power. It had become the world's creditor. In terms of the simple political model, the U.S. electorate was prepared to be taxed at higher rates to fulfill this role, to shift point E on the Laffer Curve. But individual politicians in the United States fumbled in making sense of this new condition. It could expertly move down the Curve by lowering domestic tax rates because this ground was familiar to an America of the pre-1914 era; there was still an Andrew Mellon who had learned at his grandfather's knee.

But the protective tariff, the primary source of government revenues prior to 1924, was still residing in the bones of the nation's political leaders, although not the electorate's, and it stumbled the world into a second international war.

The United States has done much better since 1939 on the road to Pax Americana. (Mundell prefers to describe the period 1815-1914 as "Equilibrium Britannica," and the period since 1945 as "Disequilibrium Americana)." Although individual Americans thus far have not been taught that Smoot-Hawley caused the Crash of 1929 and invited the Depression, everyone has been taught that it was a contributing cause to the Depression. So the name "Smoot-Hawley" and the notion of protectionism remains a fresh deterrent to an American-led relapse

History of Federal Individual Income Tax Exemptions and First and Top Bracket Rates

Dollars unless otherwise specified

| | Personal exemptions[a] | | | Tax rates[b] | | | |
| | | | | First bracket | | Top bracket | |
Income year	Single persons	Married couples	Depen-dents	Rate (percent)	Income up to	Rate (percent)	Income over
1913-15	3,000	4,000	. . .	1	20,000	7	500,000
1916	3,000	4,000	. . .	2	20,000	15	2,000,000
1917	1,000	2,000	200	2	2,000	67	2,000,000
1918	1,000	2,000	200	6	4,000	77	1,000,000
1919-20	1,000	2,000	200	4	4,000	73	1,000,000
1921	1,000	2,500[c]	400	4	4,000	73	1,000,000
1922	1,000	2,500[c]	400	4	4,000	56	200,000
1923	1,000	2,500[c]	400	3	4,000	56	200,000
1924	1,000	2,500	400	1.5[d]	4,000	46	500,000
1925-28	1,500	3,500	400	1⅛[d]	4,000	25	100,000
1929	1,500	3,500	400	⅜[d]	4,000	24	100,000
1930-31	1,500	3,500	400	1⅛[d]	4,000	25	100,000
1932-33	1,000	2,500	400	4	4,000	63	1,000,000
1934-35	1,000	2,500	400	4[e]	4,000	63	1,000,000
1936-39	1,000	2,500	400	4[e]	4,000	79	5,000,000
1940	800	2,000	400	4.4[e]	4,000	81.1	5,000,000
1941	750	1,500	400	10[e]	2,000	81	5,000,000
1942-43[f]	500	1,200	350	19[e]	2,000	88	200,000
1944-45[g]	500	1,000	500	23	2,000	94[h]	200,000
1946-47	500	1,000	500	19	2,000	86.45[h]	200,000
1948-49	600	1,200	600	16.6	2,000	82.13[h]	200,000
1950	600	1,200	600	17.4	2,000	91[h]	200,000
1951	600	1,200	600	20.4	2,000	91[h]	200,000
1952-53	600	1,200	600	22.2	2,000	92[h]	200,000
1954-63	600	1,200	600	20	2,000	91[h]	200,000
1964	600	1,200	600	16	500	77	200,000
1965-67	600	1,200	600	14	500	70	100,000
1968	600	1,200	600	14	500	75.25[i]	100,000
1969	600	1,200	600	14	500	77[i]	100,000
1970	625	1,250	525	14	500	71.75[i,j]	100,000
1971	675	1,350	675	14	500	70[j,k]	100,000
1972	750	1,500	750	14	500	70[j,k]	100,000
1973 and after	750[l]	1,500[l]	750[l]	14	500	70[j,k]	100,000

Sources: Adapted from *The Federal Tax System: Facts and Problems. 1964*, Materials Assembled by the Committee Staff for the Joint Economic Committee. 88:2 (GPO. 1964); and relevant public laws.

a. Since 1948 taxpayers and their spouses who are blind or over sixty-five have been allowed additional exemptions.

b. Beginning in 1922 lower rates applied to long-term capital gains. See text, pp. 106-11.

c. If net income exceeded $5,000, a married person's exemption was $2,000.

d. After earned income credit equal to 25 percent of tax on earned income.

e. Before earned income credit allowed as a deduction equal to 10 percent of earned net income.

f. Exclusive of Victory tax.

g. Exemptions shown were for surtax only. Normal tax exemption was $500 per tax return plus earned income of wife up to $500 on joint returns.

h. Subject to the following maximum effective rate limitations:

Year	Maximum effective rate	Year	Maximum effective rate
1944-45	90.0 percent	1951	87.2 percent
1946-47	85.5	1952-53	88.0
1948-49	77.0	1954-63	87.0
1950	87.0		

i. Includes surcharge of 7.5 percent in 1968, 10 percent in 1969, and 2.5 percent in 1970.

j. Does not include 10 percent tax on tax preference items beginning in 1970.

k. Earned income was subject to maximum marginal rates of 60 percent in 1971 and 50 percent beginning in 1972. Beginning in 1975 earned income credit of 10 percent of earned income up to $4,000 (phased down to zero at $8,000) allowed.

l. In addition to the personal exemptions, a per capita tax credit of $30 was allowed for 1975, and $35 per capita or 2 percent of the first $9,000 of taxable income, whichever is higher, for 1976 and 1977.

Source: Joseph A. Pechman, *Federal Tax Policy*, 3rd ed. (Washington, D.C.: Brookings Institution, 1977), pp. 298-9.

into international trade wars. In fact, much of the prosperity of the last thirty years has derived from America's leadership in moving the industrial world down the Laffer Curve via trade negotiations, the Dillon Round of tariff reductions under Eisenhower, and the Kennedy Round of tariff cuts under Kennedy and Johnson. The one brief foray into trade protectionism occurred under President Nixon in 1971, when he imposed a 10 percent surcharge on imports—an act denounced by both Keynesians and monetarists although, as we will see, it was the counsel of Keynesians and monetarists that led Nixon down that alley.

The most serious and persistent economic problems of the postwar era have occurred because of personal income tax rates, and the failure of politicians and economists to understand how easily and almost unnoticed they can carry an economy into the upper range of the Laffer Curve.

The outbreak of peace in 1945 was more propitious than it had been in 1918, for the world in general and the United States in particular had learned much from the former experience. The United States was now comfortable with the idea that it was the foremost economic and political power and should act accordingly. It initiated a United Nations that would simulate a world parliamentary body, a mock government that would have the important advantage of forcing world opinion on the United States through a forum on U.S. turf (although, in its earliest years, the United States viewed the United Nations as a vehicle for disseminating its views to the rest of the world). Had the global electorate been represented at such a forum in 1929-30, in the world's financial center—New York City—it is conceivable there would have been more success in preventing the currency and trade wars that brought international economic and political collapse.

In fact, this was the primary concern of the Western industrial nations as they prepared for peace in the last years of World War II, establishing forums and mechanisms that would militate against economic nationalism. On August 4, 1945, a week before Hiroshima, Nagasaki, and the end of the war with Japan, President Truman signed three bills designed to promote international economic cooperation: A U.S. commitment of $5.9 billion to the International Monetary Fund that had been designed in 1944 at Bretton Woods, N.H., and to the World Bank's stabilization fund. Plus, an increase of $2.8 billion in the Export-Import Bank's lending authority, providing that amount of credit assistance to Europe in the following twelve months. Another measure took a small step toward lowering the high wartime tax rates, but there were already pleas for serious tax cuts in the wind.

The other crucial difference between 1918s peace and 1945s was the attitude toward the defeated powers. There was now less talk of exacting reparations from Germany and Japan. Such popular sentiments for retribution that existed would have to be satisfied with war-crime tribunals. If the memory of the poor experience with reparations after World War I was not sufficient to inspire charitableness in Washington, the threat of the Soviet Union and communism did the rest. Heartland Republicans were forced out of isolationism to internationalism by the challenge from Moscow, and foreign policy became bipartisan. The last serious talk in a Republican party platform of a protective tariff was in 1944. Thereafter, the focus of GOP power moved from the Midwest to New York, a process completed with its nomination of Eisenhower over Ohio's Taft in 1952.

What of the United States economy? World war had certainly ended the unemployment of the Depression, and according to the government statisticians national income had soared. But it makes no sense to speak of the war economy as constituting "prosperity," although modern Keynesians like Galbraith persist in doing so. The entire populace worked much harder and output measured in dollars boomed, but after subtracting war materials from output, real incomes were lower during the war than they were in the Depression. There was little to buy, and what little there was was rationed. Much of the national income rise was in increased holding of government debt; the workers accepted bonds in lieu of goods.

Yet to the followers of Keynes, the war years seemed palpable proof of the master's teachings on government spending and bond finance. Here is Lekachman in his admiring biography of Keynes:

> Devoted Keynesians were impatient with the New Deal only because its leaders spent too little too seldom. If anything, the Second World War was a still plainer exemplification of the accuracy of the Keynesian analysis and the Keynesian cure. The lavish American and English outlay upon the instruments of modern war created tremendous deficits, rapidly sucked into military uses idle human and non-human resources, and in remarkably short order created economies rejoicing in bouyant demand, factories operating at capacity, and overfull employment. The objective of the exercise was victory. The means to victory were the grim public works of modern armies and navies. The financial techniques were above all borrowing and credit creation. And the consequence was the ready achievement of the objective which for a decade had eluded the grasp of policy-makers—steady, high employment.
> What was to be expected after military spending was turned off? Many if not most Keynesians anticipated a replay of the 1930s: the same deficiencies of aggregate demand, the same sluggishness of investment, the same mass unemployment—indeed, the same evident failure of enterprise capitalism to insure the public happiness.[21]

The smooth conversion to a peacetime economy was almost an embarrassment to the Keynesians; in early 1945 they had been steadily forecasting that there would be at least 5 million if not as many as 11 million unemployed in the spring that followed peace, unless great government spending projects were undertaken. In retrospect, they can only grasp at the argument that there was both a "pent-up demand" for consumer goods, and enormous liquidity—the $250 billion in built-up savings represented by the growth of the public debt.

This argument rests on an almost manic faith in bond illusion: The American people are owed $250 billion by the American people, and as a result the American people are wealthy enough to satisfy their pent-up demand for goods. In Britain, the demand for consumer goods had been "pent-up" longer and deeper, and the savings of British citizens expressed in terms of national debt was even greater per capita, yet Britain slumped. Upon even a minute's reflection, the foolishness of this most durable of economic myths must become evident, for after every war excepting those of plunder there is pent-up demand and bloated "savings" in the form of public debt.

There were, instead, solid reasons the U.S. economy shifted so smoothly to peacetime prosperity, confounding the "Secular Stagnation" theorists. Among the most important, as Herman Kahn has pointed out, was President Truman's decision to settle government contracts with American industry on what amounted to a handshake. Had he followed alternative advice, and made industry prove every dollar claim, conversion to peacetime would have been delayed for several years in the courts.

In the same vein, the New Deal regulators who had been trying to run the U.S. economy from Washington in 1939, and had been immobilized by the one-dollar-a-year businessmen who came to Washington to run the war, were not reactivated after V-J Day. Instead of academic theorists, the Truman Administration was peopled with Main Streeters and Wall Streeters: Forrestal, Draper, Lovett, Hargrave, McCloy, Hoffman, Whitney, Strauss, and Harriman, to name just a few.

When the decisions were made on the post-war economy, the Keynesians lost at every turn. They cannot even take credit for the tax cuts of 1945, which Truman and the Democrats and Republicans of the Seventy-ninth Congress decided upon, for they were too busy insisting upon expanded peacetime public works*

*Herbert Stein's Fiscal Revolution in America details the debates and triumph of the tax-cutters over spenders in this period, pp. 169-196. It should be noted that the "conservatives" no longer use the classical arguments used by Mellon and Coolidge in the 1920s, but are already in the Keynesian framework themselves, a splinter group that Lekachman terms "commercial Keynesians."

The business and financial community knew as well as these things can be known that there would be major tax reduction in 1945. In the August 4 measure that Truman signed, the exemption on excess-profits taxation had been boosted to $25,000 from $10,000, and the Congress was geared to move quickly upon the arrival of peace. By November 12, 1945, we see on the front page of the *New York Times*:

BILL TO CUT TAXES
BY $5,920,000,000
GOES TO PRESIDENT

Senate Almost Unanimously
Votes Measure and Truman's
Acceptance is Indicated

Deep '47 Slice Foreseen

Hope for $5,000,000,000 Drop
for Individuals Voiced—12
Million Off Rolls in '46

The reference in the headline to a "Deep Slice" in 1947 of a $5 billion drop for individuals comes from the Congressional Republicans. Senator Robert Taft of Ohio, ranking Republican on the Senate Finance Committee, was already gearing up to get the GOP back on its pre-Hoover track of personal tax cutting, a challenge to the Democrats and Progressives in his own party who wanted the next round of fiscal policy to go to increased government social spending.

In fact, it proved as good an issue in the 1940s as it was in the 1920s, for in 1946 the Republicans won control of Congress for the first time since their victory in 1928. The Eightieth Congress stormed into Washington in 1947 and by June had a $6 billion tax cut on Truman's desk, slashing rates across the board. Truman vetoed, not so much upon the advice of those Democrats who wanted to begin social spending as upon the advice of the economics profession. Inflation was the fear in 1947, and both liberal and conservative Keynesians advised Truman that another tax cut would be inflationary. Congress failed to override the veto by a handful of votes, and Senator Taft had another run at it, modifying the bill in hopes of picking up a few more Democratic votes. Truman vetoed a second time and again, while the House overrode, the Senate failed by two votes. Taft vowed to try again in 1948.

This time he succeeded, but by now the Keynesians—liberal and "commercial"—had become embedded in Washington. An idea denounced 200 years earlier by David Hume in his essay on taxes showed up in a Treasury circular on November 21, 1947, a contradiction to the

Laffer Curve that remains the prevailing view in Washington to the present day:

Another offsetting consideration is based on the high demand for income by many individuals who desire to maintain relatively fixed or even increasing levels of consumption and saving. If taxes take larger proportions of their incomes, the incentives of these individuals to work tend to be increased rather than decreased. They will try, within the limits of their abilities, energies and opportunities to earn more to attain and maintain the desired incomes after taxes. A tax reduction would tend to reduce these incentives to work and slacken their efforts, since their objectives could be met with smaller incomes after tax.[22]

Taft managed to chip only four points off the highest brackets, getting it to 82 percent from 86 percent. In order to pick up the Democratic votes to override Truman, he was forced to make the bill appear more egalitarian, but in making the percentage cuts deeper at the bottom than at the top, the progressivity of the schedules steepened. What was worse, though, was that Taft's concession implanted the notion in the GOP that henceforth tax-rate cuts could not appear to favor the rich, and 1948 was the last year the Republicans proposed straightforward cuts in the high brackets.

Thereafter, the GOP would only propose indirect relief to high-bracket taxpayers, i.e., loopholes so complex that the voters would presumably be unaware that the rich were being favored. The most important feature of Taft's 1948 tax cut was such an indirect measure, although one that cannot properly be called a loophole. The measure permitted husbands and wives to split their incomes for tax purposes. Thus a man earning $50,000 could impute $25,000 of that to his wife, and the taxes would be figured on the lower rates. In terms of our economic model, the level of U.S. economic expansion since 1948 would have risen significantly less without the income-splitting provision.

In spite of the economic forecasts that led Truman to resist the GOP tax cuts, the 1948 cut was followed by a steady *decline* in the rate of inflation.

The embarrassed economists then and now explain why inflation abated by stating that the economy moved into recession in 1949. Thus, the tax cut was a bit of dumb luck. Why, though, should there have been a short, sharp recession in 1949 after the Taft tax cuts took effect on the first of the year?

The likeliest answer, in this model, is that the economy had been living for two years in the anticipation of sharply reduced personal income-tax rates. While it did get reductions, which would prove

important after 1949, that one year was clouded by Truman's performance after his election in November, 1948. Truman should not have
been elected in 1948, given the low state of his popularity as he
resisted, throughout 1947-48, the expressed desires of the electorate for
lower tax rates—evidenced by the GOP congressional sweep in 1946.
Truman's opponent, Thomas E. Dewey, began the campaign with such
an enormous lead in the polls that he attempted to coast to victory by
speaking only platform platitudes. If the voters wanted "chicken" and
Truman was saying "parrot," Dewey was saying nothing. And in his
belief that he had lost the 1944 campaign to Roosevelt by not being
"liberal" enough, when Dewey did take mild positions, they tended to
shy from support of the 80th Congress in favor of progressive positions. Only 51 percent of eligible voters showed up to vote and Truman
won by a hair.*

Truman, though, took his narrow victory as a mandate for tax
increases! In the budget he prepared after his victory for presentation
to the now Democratic 81st Congress in January, 1949, he demanded a
$4 billion tax increase to fight inflation. Commodity prices broke in
January just as the Taft tax cut of the previous year took effect, and
statisticians could thereafter show a fall in the rate of inflation.
Investors who had been buying commodities as an inflation hedge
could now sell off commodities and get into financial assets, turning
the inflationary boom into a real expansion. The real expansion
awaited news from Capital Hill on Truman's $4 billion tax boost, and as
unemployment figures swelled month by month, the Democratic Congress chilled to the idea of a tax cut. On July 13, Truman finally threw
in the towel, announcing over radio and television that because of the
recession, he would no longer ask for a tax cut. Unemployment peaked
at 6.7 percent in July and that was the end of the 1949 recession.

A year later, Truman could ask for sharp increases in tax rates and get
them swiftly. In June of 1950 the Korean War began, and to help
finance it the government imposed a 77 percent excess-profits tax on
business and increased personal income-tax rates, pushing the top
bracket to 91 percent on $200,000 from 82 percent.

In 1952, the American voters elected a Republican President and
Congress for the first time in twenty-four years, and the Korean War
ended on the heels of Dwight Eisenhower's inauguration. With a
Republican in the White House, the Republicans in Congress were
eager to slash back tax rates. The GOP chairman of the House Ways and
Means Committee, Daniel Reed, introduced the first bill of the session,

*For a wonderfully readable account of the 1948 campaign, see Jules Abels' *Out of the
Jaws of Victory,* (New York: Henry Holt & Co., 1959).

H.R.1, to reduce personal income-tax rates by 30 percent and permit the excess-profits tax to lapse on July 1.

It was at this juncture that Eisenhower made the worst decision of his presidency. He faced two lines of argument, the same two that had confronted Hoover in 1931. The congressional Republicans, Reed and Taft, made the Mellon arguments that the rate cuts would expand the economy, increase revenues, and balance the budget. Eisenhower's economic advisors, especially Treasury Secretary George Humphrey, argued that taxes should not be cut as long as the budget was in deficit. At his press conference on February 17, 1953, Eisenhower revealed his bent on the issue:

In spite of some things that I have seen in the papers over the past 8 or 9 months, I personally have never promised a reduction in taxes. Never. What I have said is, reduction of taxes is a very necessary objective of government. . . . But I believe, and I think this can be demonstrated as fact by economists, both on the basis of history and on their theoretical and abstract reasoning, that until the deficit is eliminated from our budget, there is no hope of keeping our money stable.

In another month, he had made a firm decision, and not only refused to support H.R.1, but made sure it was bottled up in the Rules Committee and could not get to a vote on the House floor. Here is Eisenhower's rationale, articulated at his March 19 press conference when asked if he could support the Reed bill:

I want the revenue. [Laughter] As a matter of fact, ladies and gentlemen, I think we must have it. . . . Now I recognize that this means pretty tough going for a little while. But once we are on that sound basis, when we can believe that prices are stable so far as the value of our money is concerned, we will be far better off, the taxes could come down with a certainty and a confidence that I think will be very necessary.

This wasn't enough. The administration also asked for an extension of the excess-profits tax for six months in order to gain $800 million in revenues. Senator Taft, furious, predicted that the Republicans would deserve to lose the 1954 elections if they did not both cut tax rates and balance the budget.

As soon as the war ended, the economy slid into a recession that continued into 1954. Instead of "gaining" $800 million in excess profits, the recession cost the government roughly $10 billion as general revenues fell and unemployment and welfare costs rose. When the excess-profits tax did end on January 1, 1954, the economy began to grope out of recession, and congressional Republicans pushed through the only tax reductions of the Eisenhower years, a meager cut in excise rates. The congressional Democrats hooted at the Republicans and plumped for their tax program, a bill to increase personal income-tax exemptions. The White House opposed this idea as being fiscally irresponsible, which it was not, and the Democrats won control of Congress in the elections that followed.

Through the rest of the decade, the Republican President and the Democratic Congress were at a standoff on taxes. The administration wanted to cut business taxes in the erroneous belief that only by encouraging savings at the expense of consumption could the economy expand in a non-inflationary manner. But Eisenhower's advisors feared that if the administration made such a proposal, the congressional Democrats would open the tax codes to reduce taxes on personal incomes in the lower brackets, thus (in this view) encouraging consumption at the expense of savings, and inducing inflation. From the moment Eisenhower rejected Daniel Reed's tax bill in the spring of 1953, the Republican Party has been in the grip of this thinking, and as a result has steadily lost power as a party.

iv

In spite of tax rates that kept the U.S. economy in the upper reaches of the Laffer Curve throughout the 1950s, the U.S. economy continued to grow. Unlike Hoover, who had deeply driven both domestic and international tax wedges into the U.S. economy, Eisenhower kept the international peace, politically and economically. The U.S. economy grew by virtue of the genuine economic boom abroad, especially the explosive growth of Germany and Japan. Most of the industrial nations reduced tax rates after World War II, especially those such as excess-profits taxes that are traditional sources of war finance. (In Britain, the excess-profits tax was 100 percent.)

But it was in Germany and Japan that the most systematic attention was given to moving down the Laffer Curve, once they got the idea. For West Germany and Japan, the first postwar years were economically stagnant as little adjustment in the extraordinarily high wartime rates was permitted by the occupation forces. Japan's problems were compounded by the insistence of the United States that the mammoth Japanese trading and industrial corporations be broken into small pieces, in accord with U.S. antitrust theories. (Almost as soon as occupation ended, the fragments began merging back together into mammoth corporations.)

In Germany, it took a financial panic in the spring of 1948 to enable the government to shake free of the uppermost hinges of the Laffer Curve. At that point, German citizens were still paying a 50 percent marginal tax rate at an income of $600 and 95 percent on incomes above $15,000. On June 22, 1948, Finance Minister Ludwig Erhard announced cuts that pushed the 50 percent rate to $2,200 and the 95 percent rate to $63,000. A year later, the rates on the lower and middle brackets were slashed again, pushing the 50 percent rate to $5,000. In 1953, they were cut again, across the board: The 50 percent bracket went to $9,000 and the top bracket came down to 82 percent. In 1954, the top bracket came down again, to 80 percent, and in 1955, it was pulled down sharply, to 63 percent on incomes above $250,000, and the 50 percent bracket went up to $42,000. Yet another tax reform took place in 1958, this time the government exempting the first $400 of income, cutting again in the middle brackets, and bringing the top rate down to 53 percent. In the same period, the rate on dividend income fell from 65 percent to 15 percent.

It was this systematic lowering of unnecessarily high tax rates that produced the German economic miracle, just as the Mellon tax cuts boomed the U.S. economy in the 1920s. As national income rose in Germany throughout the 1950s, so did revenues, providing the government the wherewithal to construct a social support system as well as a powerful national defense system. Because revenues remained at roughly 35 percent of Gross National Product throughout the period from rags to riches, though, liberal Keynesians can argue through their economic model that the tax-rate changes had little or no effect on economic growth in Germany. Here, for example, is Karl Hauser of the University of Frankfurt:

> The present tax system, with its relatively high burden on German taxpayers, goes back to the time of the First World War. No substantial lifting of the wartime tax burden was possible during the 20s; it survived both the Third Reich and the Great Depression. Its aftermath made it impossible to ease the burden. A moderate amount of relief has come only during the last decade.[23]

To the Keynesian, who sees no difference between tax rates and tax revenues, nothing has changed in Germany. The government was getting 35 percent of national income sixty years ago and is still getting 35 percent of national income. The difference, of course, is that with correct rates, Germany's national income has risen tenfold.

Japan went at the Laffer Curve in a slightly different fashion. Instead of concentrating on direct rate reduction, Japan has since 1950 punctured its tax codes with myriad loopholes. After all, the American occupying authorities had in 1947 designed a progressive tax system for the Japanese (as well as a constitution). The 85 percent rate was reached at $14,000, and the Japanese economy as a result was going nowhere, despite the current myth that the Japanese people are somehow genetically industrious. The United States sent a task force of economics professors to Japan in 1949, which recommended an overhaul of the system that would have meant even higher wedges. Perhaps rather than show ingratitude at what their visitors had wrought by peeling away the insanely high rates, the Japanese decided to tatter the system with loopholes, exempting huge slabs of income from taxation.

The combined income-tax rates (central, prefectural, and municipal) thus rise to a top rate of 93 percent on $300,000, but there are so many exemptions from gross income to arrive at taxable income that the high nominal rates rarely bite. Over the years since 1950, most of the allowances have been introduced with the argument that they will encourage savings, when in fact all of the changes have had the actual effect of expanding production. Instead of establishing giant government bureaucracies to dispense social services at great expense, corporations are permitted to count as business expenses the welfare and recreational services they dispense to employees. The first $40,000 of pension payments are tax free. Gift and estate tax rates are steep, rising to 70 percent at $570,000 (50 percent at $110,000), but because the tax is levied on the heirs after an estate has been subdivided, it is rare for an estate to be taxed at high rates. (Wealthy Japanese need only adopt children, often grown sons of friends or relatives or poor, but promising college students, to avoid paying the higher estate-tax rates that apply to non-children.)

The most remarkable facet of Japanese tax policies since 1950 is the consistency of the reductions. In every year since 1950, the government has cut marginal tax rates on personal and/or business income, either directly through rates or indirectly through tax preferences ("loopholes"). Budget surpluses, real or anticipated, are thus given back to the private sector to spend. Economic growth has been spectacular, with GNP rising from $16 billion in 1952 to $300 billion in 1972. And of all the industrial nations, there has therefore been less political pressure on the government to spend. The accompanying table illustrates the zealousness of Japan in staying on the bottom rung of the Laffer Curve.

What the table indicates in each category is not the actual revenue loss to the Japanese Treasury (for each year's tax cuts have resulted in revenue gains). Rather, the table is Treasury's estimate of revenue loss in a static environment, as if the Laffer Curve were a straight line. Another way to express the Japanese policy of annual tax-rate reduc-

Estimated Annual Tax Changes in Japan, by Type of Change, Fiscal Years 1950-74 [a]
Billions of yen

	National taxes										
	Individual income					Corporate income					
Fiscal year	Total	Exemptions	Rates	Special tax measures	Total	Rates	Special tax measures	Other direct taxes	Indirect taxes	Local taxes [b]	Total
1950-53	−386	−272	−86	−28	−25	31	−56	16	−138	−46	−580
1954	−31	−29	0	−2	−3	0	−3	−3	20	−26	−43
1955	−53	−23	−13	−18	−12	−14	2	0	−1	−7	−73
1956	−23	−23	0	0	−14	0	14	0	7	12	11
1957	−110	−40	−85	15	22	−2	24	0	20	12	−81
1958	−6	0	0	−6	−22	−20	−2	−3	−6	−20	−57
1959	−23	−28	−12	17	−4	0	−4	0	20	−8	−16
1960	0	0	0	0	0	0	0	0	70	−12	−5
1961	−56	−38	−23	5	−40	0	−40	0	19	−13	−90
1962	−50	−25	−23	−2	−1	0	−1	−2	−62	−40	−156
1963	−67	−32	0	−35	13	0	13	0	4	−18	−68
1964	−75	−66	0	−8	−59	−5	−54	−5	19	−56	−174
1965	−65	−92	0	26	−57	−28	−28	−1	7	−9	−124
1966	−158	−101	−53	−4	−99	−50	−49	−15	−39	−53	−364
1967	−93	−142	11	38	−30	0	−30	−3	32	−19	−113
1968	−125	−135	−11	*	*	0	*	0	57	−21	−89
1969	−183	−142	−41	*	2	0	2	0	*	−95	−276
1970	−289	−173	−131	15	75	97	−22	0	8	−97	−302
1971	−415	−286	−107	−22	12	0	12	−7	93	−87	−403
1972	−32	0	0	−32	31	0	31	−12	9	−98	−103
1973	−375	−335	0	−40	27	0	27	−40	10	−146	−524
1974	−1,783	−1,467	−260	−56	352	424	−72	0	316	−113	−1,228

Source: Research and Planning Division, Minister's Secretariat, Ministry of Finance, *Quarterly Bulletin of Financial Statistics, 1st and 2nd Quarters, 1973 and 1974 Fiscal Years* (Tokyo, September 1973 and 1974), pp. 68-69. Figures may not add to totals because of rounding.
* Reduction of Y 500 million or less.
a. These estimates of the effect of the tax actions are based on the official economic projections included in the annual national budget. This effect is estimated on the assumption that the tax revision had been enacted at the beginning of the year. The 1971 figures include the effect of tax changes in the budget at the beginning of the fiscal year and of a supplementary tax cut enacted in October 1971.
b. Includes prefectural and municipal governments.

Source: Joseph Pechman and Keimei Kaizuka, *Asia's New Giant: How the Japanese Economy Works* (Washington, D.C.: Brookings Institution, 1976), p. 325. The authors warn that "little of this experience is transferable—or should be transferred—elsewhere; its viability depends on the particular character of the Japanese people and their political system."

tions is as a percentage of revenues. For the twenty-four years represented by the table, Japan cut rates by roughly 11 percent annually, and at the end of the process revenues were $63 billion, or four times the nation's GNP at the start of the process.

The drawback of Japan's method of moving down the Laffer Curve— by loopholes rather than by rates—is that while national income (savings plus consumption) has boomed, the economy has been skewed toward savings. When an individual's income-tax rate is reduced, he has an unbiased option on disposal of the added income; the government does not influence his decision on whether he should save more or consume more. Because the government biases the tax system toward savings, Japan as an economic unit saves more relative to other national economic units. That is, it unnaturally imports bonds (invests abroad) and exports goods. There is no question but that Japan's prosperity has benefitted the entire world economy, but this marginal bias has been an ever-present irritant to other political systems. Japan constantly faces protectionist threats from U.S. and European politicians, which, when acted upon, slow the Japanese economy. This results in fewer Japanese imports from the rest of the world and an even greater trade surplus. The correct solution in our model is for Japan to cut tax rates directly instead of indirectly, permitting growth of national income without the bias toward saving.

In absolute terms, Japan's economic performance since 1950, like Germany's, has been a blessing to the entire world economy. By contrast, Great Britain has performed miserably, a relative drag on the world economy given the potential of its intellectual capital. Again, after World War II, it made the mistake of not pulling tax rates down sufficiently to spur individual initiative. Instead, from the very outset, the postwar Labour Government concentrated on using tax policy for Keynesian objectives, i.e., increasing consumer demand to expand output.

On October 23, 1945, Chancellor of the Exchequer Hugh Dalton did announce tax cuts, but of the following nature: A 40 percent cut in the excess-profits tax (instead of its outright elimination); an elimination of the average 33 percent sales tax on household appliances (a correct move that in itself was sufficient to send the stock market up); a 50 percent cut in personal income-tax rates in the lower brackets; a 10 percent cut in the middle brackets, and an increase in the already high surtax on the upper brackets. Increased surtaxes on larger incomes, said Dalton, are intended "to continue that steady advance toward economic and social equality which we have made during the war and which the Government firmly intends to continue in peace."[24]

Sir John Anderson, Dalton's Tory predecessor, got the opposition off on the wrong foot by praising the Labour budget, offering relatively mild criticism about the higher surtax on the top brackets. He coupled this criticism with a complaint about the continued high rate of government expenditure.

From that day in 1945, there has been no concerted political voice in Britain arguing for a reduction in the high rates. Conservatives have

supported and won tax reductions on business, with stress on investment-tax income credits. But while they have argued for lowering
progressivity from the 83 percent rate that bites at £20,000 (roughly
$35,000 at current exchange rates) of earned income and 98 percent on
"unearned" income on investments, they (as with Eisenhower in 1953)
insist that government first lower spending in order to permit the rate
reductions. While Tories have been in power on and off since 1945, and
could have brought down the confiscatory top rates, Keynesian and
egalitarian arguments have so dominated all political parties in Britain
that the rates remain almost precisely where they were in the postwar
years, and inflation has constantly increased the income thresholds at
which the rates apply.

v

The impasse on tax rates was broken in the United States when John
F. Kennedy succeeded Eisenhower. Kennedy ran against Nixon in 1960
on an economic growth theme. He promised to "get the country
moving again." Nixon was bound by Eisenhower fiscal dogma and
Kennedy won by an eyelash.

At first, Kennedy was not thinking about tax rates as a source of
economic expansion. The Keynesian advisors around him were eager
to try public-works projects to expand the economy, and a $1.5 billion
package was sent to Capitol Hill. But Treasury Secretary Douglas
Dillon, a Wall Street Republican, and House Ways and Means Chairman Wilbur Mills were not keen on deficit spending, and it was clear
the Republican-Southern Democratic coalition in Congress would be
tough on this vehicle. Kennedy's alternative, then, was to work the tax
side of the Keynesian model. The liberals would go along with a one-
year tax cut for lower incomes, to increase consumer demand as a
"pump priming" device. But Dillon, Mills and the Republicans
wouldn't buy that either.

In April, 1961, Kennedy made his first stab at a growth package that
would win conservative and liberal support. It was an 8 percent
investment-tax credit (businesses could deduct 8 percent of the value of
new investment in fixed capital from their tax bill) for the conservatives, and a series of small "tax reforms" for the liberals; tightening up
on businessmen's use of expense accounts, for example. It was immediately clear that Kennedy had misfired. Neither conservatives nor
liberals liked the plan.

Dillon wanted to bring down the high income-tax rates, but he didn't want to chance losing revenues, and promised that "next year" a tax reform package would be sent up that would bring down rates as well as close loopholes in the tax code (tax rates that are lower for certain classes of income recipients). This meant that for every dollar lost there would be a dollar gained, with indeterminate effects on the Laffer Curve. Commerce Secretary Luther Hodges spoke incessantly of lowering rates on personal and corporate incomes, but was not taken seriously by anyone.

The stock market had been at 600 (Dow Jones Industrials) when Kennedy was elected, and it began moving up as soon as the tax-credit proposal was made, reaching a high of 741 on November 15, 1961. Although there had been no movement on expansion policies, at least the noises coming from the White House seemed promising to the market. But as the stalemate continued both in the administration and on Capitol Hill, and the budget for the following fiscal year was announced at a $7-billion deficit with no new ideas presented on what to do, the market drifted downward on a gradual slope and by March, 1962, was at 700.

On April 10, the Kennedy bear market got onto a steeper slope when the President lost his temper with U.S. Steel, publicly excoriating its president, Roger Blough, for increasing the price of steel. Was this the first step toward a regulatory "solution" to the recession? Wage and price controls, central planning, the New Frontier breaking down into the New Deal? By the end of April, the DJI was at 655.

In the week of May 20-25, with a national economic conference in Washington, it surely seemed that things were getting worse. Walter Reuther of the auto workers plumped for government planning of the economy. George Meany of the AFL-CIO announced a national campaign for a thirty-five hour week to produce more jobs. Kennedy spoke glowingly about the growth of the European economies at a press conference, which could have been taken to mean interest in moving toward European-type socialism. The DJI skidded further to 611, losing 22 points in the week, the biggest drop since Hoover signed Smoot-Hawley. Panic was in the air. Was this another Crash?

At his press conference, Kennedy talked about how the stock market had been overpriced. Unnamed administration officials were quoted as saying that "many people were jolted into realizing that inflation was not here to stay when the Administration put pressure on steel labor and the steel industry on wages and prices."[25]

On Monday, May 28, the market plummeted 35 points, to 576, and it appeared to all the world that 1929 might be repeating itelf. Stock markets around the world tumbled too.

In this crisis atmosphere, Kennedy met with his advisors at 10 A.M. on Tuesday, May 29, trying to decide what to do. For the two hours that the meeting lasted, the DJI continued to plunge, falling 23 points.

At noon, Treasury Secretary Dillon and Commerce Secretary Hodges emerged to talk to the press. It was the first time in the administration that such a meeting was followed by a discussion of the proceedings. Even as Dillon was telling newsmen he didn't see need of a quick tax cut just because the market was falling, Hodges began his press conference and it took over the wires, interpreted as a prediction that a tax-cutting package would soon be sent up. The *New York Times* reporter summed it up: "It is virtually certain that the tax proposals the Administration plans to announce later in the year will provide for a net cut in taxes. That is, the proposals will be a combination of increases and reductions, with the reductions greater than the increases." This was precisely the news the market wanted.

From its bottom until the market closed at 3:30 P.M., the DJI soared, gaining 50 points in a few hours and closing at 603.

Kennedy had done well, but he still had problems. When he announced his plan on June 7, "an across-the-board reduction in personal and corporate income tax rates," he made it clear that this was not substituting for the loophole-closing reforms, but would add to it in providing for a "net tax reduction." The Democratic party liberals would not stand for a tax-cutting plan that left out an attack on loopholes and tax havens. And Republican conservatives, forgetting their heritage as tax cutters, viewed the idea of enlarging the $7 billion-plus deficit with horror. In the weeks ahead, as Kennedy began detailing his package of tax cuts and tax reforms, the stock market began its slide again. By the end of June, the DJI was touching 535.

It soon became clear that Kennedy's tax cuts couldn't fly when burdened with the reforms. The tax-cut proposals were superb, cutting the 91 percent top bracket to the 65 percent range and the lower rates to 14 percent from 20 percent; he wanted the corporate rate cut to 47 percent from 52 percent. But those Republicans and Dixiecrats who were prepared to be "fiscally irresponsible" in supporting the tax cuts would not support the "reform" measures. By February 1963, in an address to the American Bankers Forum, Kennedy

... emphasized both his interest in tax reform and the higher priority he attached to tax reduction. To attentive hearers it was evident the President was willing, however reluctantly, to accept from Congress tax reduction by itself, if this was the best he could get. It is possible that he might have secured more for tax reform if he had not revealed his own heart so openly.[26]

By August, 1963, it was clear that the only hope Kennedy had of enacting a bill was to ditch reform entirely and go exclusively for reduction. The liberals were enraged, openly and bitterly criticizing Kennedy, but the AFL-CIO, more interested in jobs than loopholes, stuck with him. And with reform out of the way, businessmen and daring Republicans could now support him.

Still, diehard Republicans and disappointed liberals dragged their heels. It is quite possible that had Kennedy not been killed by an assassin on November 22, 1963, the measure would not have been enacted even through 1964.

The stock market fell 22 points on the news of Kennedy's assassination. The most likely explanation is that the market was uncertain whether this was an isolated event or a broad conspiracy that would threaten the very foundations of the global political economy. On November 26, when the market reopened, it was clear the assassination was an isolated event. It was also clear that President Lyndon Johnson would not only carry forward the Kennedy program, but also would be able to hammer it through in the name of the martyred President.

"No act of ours," Johnson told Congress five days after the assassination, "could more fittingly continue the work of President Kennedy than the early passage of the tax bill for which he fought all this long year. This is a bill designed to increase our national income and Federal revenues, and to provide insurance against recession."

Such sentiments had already been broadcast prior to the market's opening the previous day, and in capitalizing the news, the DJI rose 33 points. After Johnson's address to Congress, it climbed 9 more.

By February, 1964, when Johnson at last could sign the tax bill into law, the DJI had risen another 50 points to 800. The recession ended, unemployment and the inflation rate fell. The outflow of gold from the United States that had so worried Kennedy abated. In the next two years, per capita GNP grew by $320 (in constant, un-inflated dollars), against $112 for the eight Eisenhower years. The stock market continued upward, on February 9, 1966, piercing the 1,000 mark during midday trading before sliding back.

In real terms, adjusted for inflation, the market has been sliding ever since. And so has the economy.

What went wrong?

CHAPTER 10

The Breakdown
of Bretton Woods

The international monetary agreement of 1944 as a condition of Western economic expansion. The U.S. links the dollar to gold; the rest of the world links to the dollar. Keynes and the scarce currency clause.

The failure of the United States to understand the nature of the agreement made in 1944: Domestic monetary expansion in an open economy thought to be closed.

The universal failure to understand the impact of dollar inflation in a dollar sphere of widely different tax systems.

Vietnam and the Great Society end the Kennedy expansion, and the United States turns to monetary expansion to fight contraction, increasing real tax rates domestically and internationally.

The monetary system splinters under pressures of global economic contraction. The Keynesians and monetarists win their objective, closing economies through floating exchange rates. World inflation, stagnation. Swimming against the tide in Canada, Germany, Japan, and with the tide in Britain and Italy.

By 1944, the political leaders of the West knew that somehow trade protectionism and currency warfare had crippled the world economy in the 1930s and helped bring on World War II. Yes, there was Hitler, but there was the gnawing guilt among the allies that the insanely unworkable indemnity provisions of Versailles had incubated the germ that grew into Hitler. These mistakes were to be avoided. Lord Keynes, who in 1919 had quit the British Treasury in protest against Versailles, now in his last years was called upon by his government to help design a structure of international finance that would help avert a third world war.

The Bretton Woods Agreement of 1944 was the design of the American and British treasuries, Keynes for the British, Treasury Undersecretary Harry Dexter White for the United States. (In July, 1948, communist spy Elizabeth Bentley testified before a House committee that White was a member of her ring. White died of a heart attack in the ensuing controversy.) Although not exactly what Keynes wanted, it was a sound agreement as evidenced not only by its durability—it held together for a quarter of a century—but its coincidence with unparalleled global economic expansion.

Keynes had wanted a world bank, the kind of bank that would exist if there were in fact a one-world government. Participating nations would have their own currencies, but they would be fully convertible one to another through this world bank, which Keynes called a Clearing Union. The bank would issue its own currency, the Unitas, and would maintain its value not by tieing it to gold, but by the wisdom of its directors. World traders, world travelers, would transact across international borders with the Unitas, and there would thereby be great efficiencies. Having the world's interest at heart rather than the narrow interests of any single nation, this world bank would be a friendly bank, especially to nations in distress. Keynes remembered the flight of capital from Britain to the United States in 1925, when the Bank of England, not wanting to put interest rates up to draw the capital back, came hat in hand to the Federal Reserve and pleaded with the United States to lower interest rates so that the capital would flow back to England. Keynes envisioned a friendly world banker automatically adjusting for such "hot-money" flows. (To this day, economists ignore the fact that it was the Coolidge tax cuts that drew foreign capital to the United States.)

Such a plan would have real merit only if the world bank of issue tied its currency of issue to gold rather than the wisdom of its directors, and in 1944 the United States possessed most of the world's gold reserves. Instead of an International Monetary Bank, White insisted upon an International Monetary Fund (IMF), which would not be able to issue its own currency, but would be given a pool of gold and currencies by participating nations. It would, in friendly fashion, help out nations like Britain of 1925 by lending from this common pool, thus smoothing out hot-money flows without politicians having to beg hat in hand.

Keynes' victory was on the "scarce currency clause." Above all else, he wanted to avoid a situation where Britain finally had to resort to raising internal interest rates in order to keep sterling from flowing abroad, for to Keynes this meant contracting the British economy and accepting high levels of unemployment. If England ran out of borrowing capacity at this IMF pool, he believed it would have no other alternative but to raise interest rates. Sterling would become scarce at home. If that happened, said the scarce currency clause, Britain could slap on currency controls to prevent its citizens from sending capital abroad.

The fact that the parties could agree to such a clause indicated that there was no understanding of the true nature of the problems of the depression. When a nation moves up the Laffer Curve, and in the distress capital flows out to other countries, the nation cannot improve its economy by imposing currency restraints, which can only add a further wedge to transactions and make the problem worse.

It was a blessing to the world economy that the Keynesian notion of a world central bank that could expand credit without the planetary restraint of gold was rejected. Not that Keynes was an inflationist. Had he not written in the 1920s that: "Lenin was certainly right. There is no subtler, no surer means of overturning the existing basis of Society than to debauch the currency. The process engages all the hidden forces of economic law on the side of destruction, and does it in a manner which not one man in a million is able to diagnose."[1] Rather, he believed that intelligent and honest men could run a world bank without gold and without inflation.

Nevertheless, the argument was still between "soft money" (Keynes) and "hard money" (White). With the United States possessing $24 billion in gold bullion, it did not need theories to keep it away from an idea cut loose entirely from the metal.

The hard-money/soft-money debate is, of course, as old as money and banking. Plato, perhaps trusting the wisdom of his philosopher kings, was, like Keynes, a soft-money man. Aristotle, his student, who saw the debilitating effects of well-meaning Platonic inflation, was like Alexander Hamilton a hard-money advocate.[2]

The Keynes-White debate had exact parallels in the early history of the United States. In Alexander Hamilton's arguments on behalf of a national bank, he was explicitly Aristotelian: "What government ever uniformly consulted its true interests in opposition to the temptations of momentary exigencies? What nation was ever blessed with a constant succession of upright and wise administrators?"[3]

When Hamilton, Madison, and Jay argued in the Federalist papers for the efficiencies of Union, the efficiencies of a common currency were not argued, although the arguments were surely in Hamilton's mind at the time. But Hamilton's common currency would have to be backed by gold, for as he told the House:

The emitting of paper money by the authority of Government is wisely prohibited by the individual States, by the national constitution; and the spirit of that prohibition ought not to be disregarded by the Government of the United States. Though paper emissions, under a general authority, might have some advantages not applicable, and be free from some disadvantages which are applicable to the like emissions by the States, separately, yet they are of a nature so liable to abuse—and it may even be affirmed, so certain of being abused—that the wisdom of the Government will be shown in never trusting itself with the use of so seducing and dangerous an expedient. In times of tranquillity, it might have no ill consequence; it might even be managed in a way to be productive of good; but, in great and trying emergencies, there is almost a moral certainty of its becoming mischievous. The stamping of paper is an operation so much easier than the laying of taxes, that a government, in the practice of paper emissions, would rarely fail, in any such emergency, to indulge itself too far in the employment of that resource, to avoid, as much as possible, one less auspicious to present popularity. If it should not even be carried so far as to be rendered an absolute bubble, it would at least be likely to be extended to a degree which would occasion an inflated and artificial state of things, incompatible with the regular and prosperous course of the political economy.

Among other material differences between a paper currency, issued by the mere authority of Government, and one issued by a bank, payable in coin, is this: That, in the first case, there is no standard to which an appeal can be made, as to the quantity which will only satisfy, or which will surcharge the circulation; in the last, that standard results from the demand. If more should be issued than is necessary, it will return upon the bank.[4]

This is the whole idea of a gold standard. If government issues more currency than is required for transaction purposes, it does not have to rely on a "constant succession of upright and wise administrators" (philosopher kings) to make the discovery. On the margin of the electorate, someone will carry surplus currency to the bank and ask that it be redeemed in gold. This, in itself, tells the administrators that it is time to extinguish rather than create money. And when individuals come with gold, asking currency, the administrators know it is time to cease extinguishing money and to create it. Because the economy is open, with transactions between citizens and foreigners as desirable as transactions between citizens and citizens, the process has the same beneficial effects whether the individual who comes to the bank with paper, asking gold, is a citizen or a foreigner.

Given this background, the great debate over banking in the Jacksonian era is more easily understood. Hamilton got his Bank of the United States, and while its charter expired in 1812, it was renewed in 1816 as the Second Bank of the United States, and this bank operated smoothly under the presidency of Nicholas Biddle of Philadelphia until 1828.

In 1828, Northern politicians ganged up on Southern politicians and enacted the "Tariff of Abominations." Just as, a century later, the northeast manufacturers pushed through Smoot-Hawley, in 1828 New England pushed through this protective tariff. The South, which existed almost solely as a cotton economy that had no competition from abroad, bitterly opposed the tariff, and the struggle did not end until it culminated in the Civil War. But in 1828, economic contraction occurred in the United States just as it did a century later, with trade slowing in anticipation of enactment. Biddle did not know what was happening, any more than the Federal Reserve understood what was happening during the Crash of 1929. All he saw were the symptoms. The state banks were underwriting continued imports from Europe by expanding credit; but foreign banks were not similarly expanding the money supply, so foreigners had slowed their imports of U.S. goods. They were thus in possession of a surplus of U.S. currency and were demanding of the state banks payment in specie (gold or silver). The state banks in turn were taking the paper to Biddle's bank and replenishing their gold base.

In a letter of March 3, 1828, Biddle complained about all this to the cashier of the Baltimore branch:

> For some months past, the importations from France and England have been very extensive, and without great caution, the results may prove highly disastrous. The low price of our exported articles and tardiness with which the crop of Exchange from the South comes into the market this year, have diminished the means of paying for these importations, and resort has been of course to the exportation of coin. The natural correction of this evil—for, beyond a certain limit, it is an evil—is the dimunition of the business of those institutions which are the depositories of the coin, which by rendering bank credits less easy, makes them more valuable. . . . [5]

The "war" between Biddle and Andrew Jackson thus began, as Biddle's Bank refused to play ball with the state banks, the state banks could no longer underwrite imports, and the pain of the contraction was felt throughout the United States. As a result, Jackson was elected president that fall by the very elements of the electorate that had opposed the tariff. Jackson identified Biddle, not the tariff, as the source of the contraction, and vowed to end the Bank's charter. The electorate had attempted to help Jackson by giving him a Congress that opposed the tariff, but favored the Bank. And indeed the tariff was allowed to lapse after the South threatened the Union over its provisions (South Carolina "nullified" the tariff by legislative act and a secession movement sprang up across Dixie). Although Congress renewed the Bank charter in 1832 by wide majorities, with support not only from the South and West, but also from several dozen banks, Jackson vetoed the bill. With the solid support of New York, which desired to end Philadelphia's primacy as the nation's financial center, Congress sustained the veto despite an impassioned prediction by Daniel Webster that the end of the Bank would be disastrous. The closing of the Bank in 1836 would, in itself, surely have caused economic distress with the fragmentation of banking and the resultant loss of efficiencies. But Jackson squeezed in another disastrous decision to make contraction certain. He issued the Specie Circular, which required that payment for Western land sales by the United States be made in gold. Gold was thus sucked out of Western banks causing a collapse of credit, as the gold "floated" between Western banks and the U.S. Treasury, for of course the West needed only time to float back gold from the East. This error, too, was repeated a century later when Hoover signed the 1932 tax increase into law with its provision that liabilities be retroactive to the first of the year. Only then, base money flowed out of banks all over the nation in early 1933 in remittance of these liabilities.

The net result of Jackson's policies, always couched in terms of defending the little man against the rich, was the first major depression in the United States, the financial panic of 1837, and the ensuing economic contraction.

ii

All this was avoided, ironically, when Harry Dexter White—who was at least a communist sympathizer, if not a spy—beat back John Maynard Keynes at Bretton Woods. Not that White envisioned that the U.S. dollar would become the world currency, but he would not buy Keynes' funny money, the Unitas. The dollar emerged as the world currency in the postwar era because it was natural for it to do so. As Mundell puts it, "The gains from using a common international medium are so great that some means of creating one has always been found."[6]

Gold had been the international circulating medium for centuries, but with the coming of the telegraph in the late nineteenth century, its circulation was no longer necessary. The gold could remain stationary and move about by wire, transferred from ledger to ledger as "ink money." This was the pure "gold standard" that ended in 1914. Thereafter, instead of gold circulating internationally as ink on ledgers, the dollar and sterling—convertible into gold—circulated both by hand and as ink as the international medium of exchange. And as Britain shriveled as a military and economic power, while the United States advanced, the dollar became dominant. The Bretton Woods Agreement and U.S. economic might after World War II gave it undisputed dominance.

There are two great advantages to one, rather than more, international circulating medium. The first, universally recognized by economists because it is so obvious, is that it is so much easier to do business without having to pay money-changers at every border. The second, which some economists prefer to ignore, is that when there are dozens of currencies there are dozens of monetary authorities. As each authority tries to figure out how much money is needed in its domestic economy, there is always inescapable daily error.

In the twelve Federal Reserve (Fed) districts of the United States, each regional bank of the Fed attempts to accommodate the money needs of its region on a daily basis. If one region produces too much money, and another too little, private individuals in the latter can borrow from private individuals in the former through banking or other trade channels, and the error is reduced. Over time, the errors by region balance out, and we never hear of a shortage of money in one part of the United States relative to other parts.

This is almost, but not quite, the way the Bretton Woods system operated. Instead of setting up a system that would approximate the fashion in which the 12 Federal Reserve Districts correct balance of payments differences with each other, by expanding or contracting the money supply, the Bretton Woods agreement tried something else.

Imagine, in the above example, that instead of all 50 states balancing payments with one another by expanding or contracting the money supply, one state had a different role. New York, say, would not have to stay in balance with the other states. Theoretically, one state could be excused, because if 49 states have zero balances, the 50th automatically has a balance of zero. New York could then use this extra measure of freedom by making sure that the system *as a whole* had "proper" monetary policy, so that in the system *as a whole*, commerce would not be hindered by a paucity or excess of money growth.[7]

In other words, instead of all nations increasing or decreasing their respective money supplies by watching the ebb and flow of gold at their treasury, and circulating gold as the international medium, each country watched the ebb and flow of U.S. dollars at their treasury. The United States had no such responsibility. If everyone else stayed in balance, the United States would automatically be in balance. The U.S. responsibility was to watch the ebb and flow of gold and to maintain the value of the dollar so that one ounce of gold equalled thirty-five dollars.

Under this system, only the United States could increase the world money supply. It was of no use for, say, the Bank of England to even attempt to increase its domestic money supply. It couldn't do it. If it bought British debt by printing money, the individual who held this fresh money (or some other individual in the system) would appear at another window of the Bank of England and demand dollars. Under the agreement, the Bank would have to give him the dollars. It would extinguish the sterling upon receipt. And it would get the dollars by selling debt to the U.S. Treasury. At the end of the cycle, the British debt position and money supply would be precisely the same as at the outset.*

The system would work perfectly, as long as the Federal Reserve conducted monetary operations the way Nicholas Biddle wanted to run the Second Bank of the United States: Stop printing dollars when people showed up with dollars demanding gold. The world economy would always have precisely the right amount of money.

U.S. politicians and the Fed never viewed its Bretton Woods role in this light. Just as Andrew Jackson blamed Biddle for the recession of 1828, not supplying enough money, U.S. politicians came to view any downturn in the U.S. economy as a sign that there were not enough dollars in the system. If there were more dollars, interest rates would fall, wouldn't they? And with lower interest rates, businessmen would expand output, wouldn't they? The common delusion was that, for all practical purposes, the United States was a closed economy, because, after all, wasn't its trade with the rest of the world only about 5 percent of its Gross National Product? Trifling.

So when Eisenhower in 1953 tried to boost the U.S. economy out of recession, instead of cutting tax rates, he leaned on the Federal Reserve. The Fed printed dollars and, because all currencies were fixed together, the surplus flowed around the world. Say the Fed printed $100. Here's what would happen:

Because the United States is roughly 50 percent of the world economy, the surplus in the United States would be roughly $50. An individual would show up at the Bundesbank with that $50 and demand Deutschemarks. On this day, the Bundesbank takes the $50 and gives the individual the Deutschemark equivalent, 200 DM. It then wires the U.S. Treasury that it wants to buy $50 worth of gold with its newly acquired dollars. The Treasury transfers the $50 worth of gold to Germany's account in exchange for the $50. The world's money supply has increased by $100—$50 of which is in dollars and $50 denominated in Deutschemarks.

Because the world money supply has risen, the world price level will try to follow. But because the United States fixes the price of gold in the free market, gold at a fixed price will become a bargain relative to all other goods, whose prices are tending to rise. The citizens of the world economy will buy gold with their newly acquired money until

*The process is described in detail in Arthur B. Laffer's "The Economic Consequences of Devaluation of a Reserve Currency Country," in *World Monetary Disorder*, ed. by Patrick M. Boarman and David G. Tuerck (New York: Praeger, 1976) pp. 79-89.

the price level is almost exactly back to where it was. In this instance, the United States would have lost $100 worth of its gold reserves and the money supply would have increased only marginally.

By ever increasing the amount of gold held by the private sector, the U.S. government was able to lower the relative price of gold and thereby allow for the prices of all goods to rise, bringing with it an increase in the world money supply. In just this fashion, through the 1950s and 1960s, the dollar penetrated deeper and deeper as world money.

In this arrangement, all the economic incentives drove the United States to create more money than was really needed, and forced the other countries to produce less of their own currencies if they wanted to avoid inflation. People and enterprises all over the world did more and more of their business in dollars, finding the United States always there to supply money when needed, while their own monetary authorities seemed to be cutting back. In exchange for its real good, the banking service, the United States was receiving other real goods—autos, radios, etc.

But it's one thing for New York to drive everyone else's money out of the other 49 states, and quite another for the United States to push out foreign currencies by running constant balance of payments deficits. For the most part, the U.S. deficits were not the fault of the United States, but the natural result of its having been the most efficient supplier of money in the world. The dollar became, says Mundell, "the major intervention currency, a reserve asset for central banks, the standard of contract, the standard of quotation, the invoice currency, the major settlement currency, the major reserve asset for commercial banks, the major traveller's currency, the major external currency for indexing bonds, and the major clearing currency." In so many ways, foreigners were demanding dollars rather than their own national currencies.[8]

The system did break down, though, and Washington must be blamed for this. To run a dollar standard, the United States certainly did not need $24 billion in gold bullion, for the value of monetary gold is not as a medium, which requires tonnage, but merely as an error signal, to alert administrators when too many dollars are being printed. By 1965, the United States had sloughed off $12 billion of its gold tonnage. Had it desired to hold that amount, it was time to take Bretton Woods seriously and keep dollars more attractive than gold by not printing as many or, when demand for dollars declined in recession, by mopping up the surplus with bonds.

President Johnson, like King Canute, instead tried to hold back the tide by the power of decree. In 1965, he slapped voluntary restrictions on U.S. overseas investment, and when that did not halt U.S. balance-of-payments deficits, he made the restrictions mandatory in 1968. The private market flowed right around these restraints by creating the Eurodollar market.

The financial innovation, which has taken on a life of its own, was the private substitute for the imperfectly working official system. The foreign branches of U.S. commercial banks accommodated the thirst for dollar liquidity abroad that the U.S. government was trying to choke off. Because foreign deposits of U.S. dollars are not subject to the reserve requirements imposed against domestic deposits, the banks could and did become efficient *private creators of money.* When the Fed slowed its creation of dollars, the Eurodollar market speeded up its creation, and vice versa. In an important 1974 empirical study, Laffer found this relationship to hold in each of the last 14 years. *The Federal Reserve could now only kid itself into thinking it could slow down the economy by contracting money growth, or stimulating the economy by expanding money supply.* The marketplace had found a substitute for the Fed.[9]

In the spring of 1971, as the Federal Reserve tried desperately to expand the U.S. economy by flooding it with dollars, the rest of the world came demanding gold. On August 15, 1971, Richard Nixon ordered the gold window closed, ending the international currency's link to gold for the first time in 1,500 years. There began the worst inflation of the century.

Mundell was asked the following spring, would it have been possible to have kept the gold convertibility?

It could have been kept, Mr. Mundell replied. Ending convertibility broke the last link within the international monetary system. One of the arguments used by the United States for abandoning gold was that other countries have done it, too. The fact was that it made sense for the United States to remain tied to gold because of its unique position in the world economy. Gold represents, in an allegorical sense, the tieing of the financial system to the world's resources—gold, dug out of the ground, acts as an error signal when we start to inflate the system too much. When the gold runs out, it warns the system to control its inflation. The world economy is expanding past the point at which its resources can tolerate it. Canada and Britain gave up their gold requirements in the late 1930s, but the fact that the United States kept its gold requirement at that time maintained the link between the world financial system and its gold base. People say we can do anything if we have correct management, even if we abandon gold, because we can always duplicate the policies we would have followed with the gold mechanism. That is true, but what do we do? If you look back at 1965-68, the sin of that period was overexpansion of the money supply, which led to inflation. That would not have been possible if the constant warning had existed that gold was disappearing from the system.[10]

Why, did the private market, the instrument of the electorate, take international money creation into its own hands? Why would the private market cause the terrific inflation of the 1970s? The answer is that the alternative would have been worse.

Money, remember, was linked not only to gold, but also to the real economy through the progressive tax systems of the United States and the nations of the world. Throughout the entire period of Bretton Woods, the economists of the world were almost unanimous in ignoring this fact, as well as the even more disturbing fact that every progressive personal income-tax system in the world was different, some rising gently, some rising steeply.

Because the United States was the only nation that could increase the world money supply, it was the United States that determined the rise in the world price level. And every time the United States ignored the danger signal from gold, as it tried to expand the U.S. economy and employment through inflation, the private market of business and labor had to scramble to adjust their terms of trade with each other. While the attempts at inflating the economy did not and could not work, wages and prices inevitably rose in the adjustment scramble. And of course every time this happened, Americans would be pushed into higher tax brackets through the progressivity of the system. The wedge would thus deepen and the U.S. economy would travel up the Laffer Curve into recession, exactly the opposite of what the policy-makers had intended by their monetary ease.

As the U.S. price level rose, forcing the U.S. private sector to adjust, the price level of course rose at the same pace around the world through the fixity of currencies. In each nation linked to the dollar, a similar adjustment had to take place on wages, prices, and investment returns, except that in those countries that had steeper progressions in their income-tax system, the final adjustment up the Laffer Curve had to be greater. For those countries like Germany and Japan, systematically cutting tax rates every year, the economies could grow at full employment despite the U.S.-induced price inflation.

At first, the impact was mild, both because the United States was not attempting to expand through monetary inflation (except for the brief Eisenhower experiment in 1953), and because nations such as Britain and Italy, while refusing to adjust their income-tax brackets on egalitarian grounds, were quietly opening loopholes in business taxation that enabled the private sector to move back down the Laffer Curve, albeit less efficiently.

The Kennedy tax cuts, providing the correct antidote to unemployment and output, gave the world a breather from U.S. monetary expansion. But from February 9, 1966, when the stock market hit 1,000 and began its long decline, the impact of U.S. inflation on income-tax progressivity began biting in earnest, both at home and abroad. Why did the market begin turning down?

The likeliest explanation, in our model, is that the market, observing the deepening commitment to Vietnam—which meant a tax on resources—and Johnson's commitment to Great Society spending—which also meant a tax on resources—was forced to conclude that U.S. movement up the Laffer Curve was becoming not a question of "if" but "how far."

American economists who have participated in manipulating the U.S. economy since 1966 will insist that real incomes have risen. But that is only because of their statistical measures. "Real income" is not a measure of final consumption, because it also includes an individual's purchases of bureaucratic employment, other government purchases, increased private transactions required as a result of government regulation (including the services of lawyers and accountants required by the tax codes), and increased production due to government restrictions, i.e., safety standards, transportation controls, health standards, pollution controls, and food and drug controls.

In the summer of 1977, with the DJI below 900, the stock market had discounted the U.S. capital stock by roughly 60 percent as measured in 1966 dollars. As one rough measure of real income, consider that a newspaper reporter four years out of college in 1964 could buy a three-bedroom, air-conditioned new home on a quarter-acre, for $1,000 down and $125 per month, including principal, interest, taxes, and insurance, the $125 equal to the reporter's weekly salary. The comparable reporter today may earn $300 a week and have difficulty affording rent on a one-room efficiency apartment. Where prices have kept up with after-tax income to a closer degree, as with consumer durables, it has been through more aggressive exploitation of planetary resources and less efficient use of intellectual capital.

In 1967, Britain's distress was so sharp, given the impact of U.S. inflation on her steeply progressive tax system, that she devalued the pound. This first snapping of Bretton Woods' foundation was argued as Britain's need to become competitive, lowering her export prices. But cheapening the value of currency on the exchange market is no different than cheapening it in the domestic market by printing money. There is no money illusion in either case and the terms of trade do not change to make the devaluing country either more or less competitive. The devaluing country experiences more inflation than the rest of the world by the full amount of the devaluation, as an empirical study by Laffer of fourteen devaluing nations has demonstrated.[11]

In the process of inflating, the devaluing nation causes a further scramble of adjustment in the private sector as workers move into higher tax brackets. The devaluing country moves up the Laffer Curve a bit more, stifling initiative and output more, which is the essence of the "British disease," as it has come to be called.

The only effect felt by the devaluing country is through changes in its indebtedness. Holders of British debt, whether public debt or private debt, have to accept payment of these debts in currency that buys less than it did when it was loaned. The debtors are relieved at the expense of the creditors, and the devaluing country has, on average, as many debtors as creditors.

Those who lent money at a fixed rate of interest, or contracted to supply goods or services at a fixed price or who agreed to work for a year or longer at a fixed wage, discover that the addition of these marginal transactions, through excessive monetary expansion, has put prices up, and their wages have lost purchasing power. While those who borrowed or bought enjoy an offsetting benefit, the net effect is weakening of the relationship between reward and effort. Henceforth, if excessive policies continue, they will demand compensation in the form of higher interest rates, higher fixed-price contracts, and higher wages and/or cost of living adjustments.[12]

In 1969, France was similarly distressed and devalued, but DeGaulle wisely accompanied devaluation with a tax reform that more than offset the push of inflation up the Laffer Curve. France would save its worst mistakes for 1975-76, when after the worst of the inflation had hit the French economy, French President Valery Giscard d'Estaing promoted austerity in the form of higher tax rates.

The source of the problem in the 1960s, we must remember, was the United States. In fixing responsibility, it is not enough to charge the economists for failing to understand the nature and responsibilities of Bretton Woods. Going to our political model, it is clear the Republican Party in the United States failed to read the success of the Kennedy tax cuts, which they had opposed, and in the aftermath could not prevent the Democratic Party from engaging in its natural inclination (as a party of income redistribution) to spend. By 1965, as revenues poured into the Treasury from the expanding economy, the GOP remained immobilized. Instead of recommending return of the surpluses via further rate reductions, Republicans watched in dismay as Johnson and the Democrats not only spent revenues in hand, but also committed anticipated future receipts to Great Society spending programs.

Although the liberal Democrats had taken credit for the success of the Kennedy tax cuts, they did not like the idea of tax-cutting as a continuing economic tool. Keynesian doctrine does not differentiate between tax-cutting or spending increases as a method of *producing deficits*—the deficits themselves being the spur to economic expansion.

But as a result of the struggle of 1962-64, the Keynesian school divided in two. Conservatives, who identified with Republicans, were biased toward tax-cutting and were labeled "commercial Keynesians" by liberals, who favored the spending route as a means of achieving both economic expansion and a redistribution of wealth at the same time. By spending future receipts on social programs, the liberal Keynesians in the mid-1960s confounded the commercial Keynesians. Each new federal budget contained a built-in deficit as a result of previous spending commitments. Republicans, committed to a balanced budget as a means of fighting inflation, were thus put in a position of demanding spending cuts and/or tax increases! In the decade 1964-74, not a single Republican advocated tax-rate reductions. Instead, as Great Society and Vietnam spending increased in 1966, the Republican leadership pressured President Johnson into proposing a 10 percent surtax on personal incomes.

Even so, the U.S. economy was in marvelous condition in early 1966. It was in such good shape, in fact, that to the Johnson economists it looked "overheated," and they began to slow it down. They would "fine tune" the economy, and as they began this process the Dow Jones Industrial average began its long slide from 1,000. To the Johnson economists, the fact that the DJI hit 1,000 was in itself evidence that the economy was overheated. Here is how they reviewed their "success" of 1966:

By any standard, then, 1966 was a big year for the economy. Gross National Product (GNP) expanded by a record $58 billion in current prices and reached $740 billion. As in the two preceding years, a major advance in business fixed investment was a key expansionary force. And the rising requirements of Vietnam added $10 billion to defense outlays. State and local spending and inventory investment also rose strongly.

As a result, 1966 was in some respects too big a year, especially in the early months. Spurred by the defense buildup, total demand—public and private—forged ahead at an extraordinarily rapid rate in late 1965 and early 1966. Strains developed in financial markets. Demand outstripped supply in several sectors which were already near full utilization. . . . Many of the new orders simply added to backlogs and put upward pressures on prices. Some of the excess demands were met by imports, reducing the U.S. foreign trade surplus and retarding progress toward equilibrium in the balance of payments. . . .

After years of stimulating demand, policy was called upon to restrain the economy. The need for restraint was recognized at the start of the year. Monetary policy assumed a restrictive stance. In anticipation of large increases in private expenditures and defense outlays, tax policies were applied to curb private demand. In 1964 and 1965, an expansionary tax policy had stimulated the economy; but in March 1966, restrictive tax changes were enacted at the President's request. Excise tax cuts were postponed, and income-tax payments were accelerated. . . .

The initial restraining measures, reinforced by the previously enacted rise in payroll taxes, began to take effect in the spring. By the closing months of 1966, it was clear that the brakes had worked. The economy had shouldered the burden of active hostilities without the need for cumbersome and inefficient controls and without losing its basic health and stability. It was shown that policy could work both ways; it could restrain the economy, much as it had been able to provide stimulus during the preceding five years. In particular, the power of tight money as a tool of restraint—as well as its uneven impact—was demonstrated beyond any reasonable doubt.[13]

This was the last time the presidential economists would boast that they could successfully contract the economy by throwing monkey wrenches into it. The U.S. economy was now headed up the Laffer Curve, with Democrats and Republicans competing with policies to accelerate that movement. In the elections of 1966, the electorate replaced forty-seven House Democrats with Republicans. At least the larger GOP presence slowed the pace of new domestic spending commitments, but military spending for Vietnam continued to expand. And rather than cut back on the absolute level of domestic spending to accommodate Vietnam spending, Johnson pushed through his 10 percent surtax with the cheerful assistance of the Republicans.

The Vietnam quagmire was Johnson's demise, forcing him to announce in March, 1968 that he would not seek re-election that year. But it was probably the 10 percent surtax that gave Richard Nixon his narrow victory over Hubert Humphrey that fall. Vietnam dominated the campaign, with Humphrey tied to Johnson's war policies and Nixon offering unspecified pledges to somehow extricate the nation from the war. As Humphrey moved steadily away from Johnson on the war issue, he gained strength, and by Election Day the postures of the two candidates on the war issue were indistinguishable, albeit vague. On the economic issue however, Nixon had steadfastly pledged to end the Johnson war tax and balance the budget. Humphrey, oblivious to the importance of this issue as he grappled with the campaign's main theme, remained firmly tied to Johnson, who insisted that continuation of the surtax was necessary.

It fell to Nixon, then, to preside over the U.S. economy during the global convulsions of the 1970s. And he began by hedging on his campaign pledge to end the surtax. Soon after the 1968 election, in December, Nixon's economic advisors got word from the Johnson people—who were then preparing the fiscal 1970 budget for presentation in January—that Johnson wanted Nixon's commitment to continue the surtax. If Nixon would not give such a commitment, Johnson would present a budget, without the surtax revenues, that would be artificially balanced. Or at least the Nixon advisors feared it would be balanced with gimmicks that would disappear upon close scrutiny. Nixon would then be left with an impossible problem of balancing it in actuality in order to meet his other campaign commitment. They advised Nixon to give Johnson such assurance, and Nixon did so. The economy drifted into the 1969 recession, which of course meant a loss of federal, state, and local revenues of several times the "gain" in surtax revenues the Nixon advisors were seeking to preserve.

The 1969 Tax Reform Act was an important victory for the liberal Keynesians, who got from Nixon what they could not get under Kennedy. The 10 percent surtax was extended through fiscal 1970. Because a surtax is a tax on progressive tax liabilities, it is doubly progressive, with sharply adverse effects on output.

But at least the surtax would expire. Far worse, Nixon agreed to permanent "reforms" that have similar effects on tax progression. The investment tax credit was repealed on the argument that instead of subsidizing machines, the nation should subsidize people. The "savings" from repeal of the tax credit would go into manpower-training programs, though, not personal tax cuts. Thus, a lower tax rate was replaced by a new spending program, all of which seemed perfectly logical to the conservative Keynesians who advised Nixon.

Probably the worst "reform" that Nixon swallowed was a tightening of the tax treatment of capital gains, which instantly cut in half the potential rewards from high-risk entrepreneurial investments. The Treasury estimated that the reform would add $1.1 billion to revenues in 1970 and by 1975 increase revenues by $3.2 billion annually. Instead, 1969 revenues of $7.1 billion fell to an average of $4 billion in the following four years. This savage chopping at the most efficient of the "loopholes" in the tax codes has since 1969 no doubt cost the Treasury countless tens of billions of dollars of lost revenues and the economy hundreds of billions of dollars of lost output. Even more ominous is the fact that most new technology is developed by small, high-risk enterprises, and these have been shrinking steadily since 1969. The major U.S. corporations, which apparently believe they benefit little from favorable treatment of capital gains, hardly lifted a finger against the 1969 changes. It is the bright young college graduate in engineering or physics, or the energetic young entrepreneur, who is chilled by the forbidding rates of capital gains taxation. In 1977, most discussion of capital gains in Congress is in the direction of tightening treatment even further.

The direct long-term effect of the 1969 Tax Reform Act was bad enough. The indirect effect was far worse. For as the economy struggled through 1970, with the rate of inflation (5 percent) and the rate of unemployment (5.6 percent) appearing in combinations not seen before, the Nixon economic team groped desperately for a new prescription and decided to have a go at money illusion and bond illusion in a major way. A report of November 9, 1970:

> The Nixon Administration is plotting a major shift in economic policies in an effort to halt rising unemployment. Its goal is to achieve full employment by the middle of 1972 which, not coincidentally, is a Presidential election year. The effort is likely to result in two big, successive deficits in the Federal budget of $15 billion a year. . . .
>
> "There may be some temporary alarm on Wall Street, in the money markets, when we come in with a planned budget deficit in January," says Herbert Stein, a member of the President's Council of Economic Advisors. "But people will accept the full-employment concept."
>
> Elements of the drive reportedly will include:
>
> *Holding to current tax rates while "planning" a budget deficit of perhaps $15 billion for the fiscal year that begins next July; a deficit of about $15 billion in the current year already has been predicted by congressional sources.
>
> *Pumping up the economy rapidly through Government spending and credit policies, stirring the growth rate to a peak late in 1971, then permitting it to cool to a "normal" and steady full-employment level by mid-1972.
>
> *Holding the inflation rate to 3 percent through this period by vigorous efforts to increase national productivity and by labor policies designed to resist excessive wage demands.[14]

The idea that was sold to Richard Nixon was the "full-employment budget concept," a Keynesian variation developed in 1947 by Herbert Stein and others. Stein's argument was that tax policy was an inappropriate tool to expand or cool down an economy, because of the political process. If you asked Congress to lower taxes, it would cut them too much and the economy would "overheat." If you asked Congress to raise taxes, it would drag its feet, as it did with Johnson's surtax, and the delay would cause inflation to build itself into the economy. Better, he said, to leave taxes alone and vary spending. How? The government, he said, should spend the dollar amount that it would receive in revenues if the economy were fully employed (with unemployment at no more than 4 percent). The resulting deficit in and of itself would move the economy toward full employment of resources, the government would taper off on spending before inflation was ignited.

This "full-employment budget idea," Nixon told Congress the following January in his budget message, "is in the nature of a self-fulfilling prophecy: By operating as if we were at full employment, we will help to bring about that full employment."

Nixon loved the concept, for it gave him money to spend on his initiatives along with an intellectual justification for deficits. And he needed funds to fuel his "New Federalism." Lyndon Johnson's Great

Society programs not only spent future federal funds before receipt, but also sucked state and local governments into a taxing and spending competition. This was because most of the Johnson programs for housing, health, education, and welfare were "dollar-matching" programs. Typically, the federal government would provide 75 percent of the funds if the state and local governments came up with the rest. Rather than lose their share of this bonanza, most state and local governments drained away their taxing and borrowing capacity in order to participate. By the time Nixon arrived, the chickens of the Great Society were coming home to roost. Mayors and governors pleaded with Washington to send money to fund these social programs so they would not have to ask their electorates for more taxes. The idea took hold in the Nixon White House that because the federal government is the most efficient tax gatherer, and the local governments are the most efficient spenders, Washington should raise tax revenues and share them with the provinces. The Stein full-employment budget concept enabled Nixon to unveil a $4 billion revenue sharing scheme in January, 1971.

The whole exercise proved fatal to the international monetary system and brought on the global stagflation of the 1970s.

The problem was not the $15 billion or so in planned deficit, which would not have made a great deal of difference to the economy. But an adjunct to the economic "Game Plan" as it came to be called was the requirement that the Federal Reserve expand the money supply at a rapid rate to accommodate the self-fulfilling prophecy of full employment. And in December, 1970, Nixon could tell the National Association of Manufacturers in a New York City speech that Arthur Burns, chairman of the Fed, had "assured" him that the Fed will "provide fully" for the nation's money needs as the "economy rises toward full employment" because of the planned deficit.[15]

Why a monetary expansion? Why not just a deficit?

Among all the other fine-tuning calibrations of the Nixon economists was the belief that nominal Gross National Product—the dollar value of the nation's goods and services—had to rise by certain amounts to cut into unemployment by certain amounts. The dollar GNP in 1970 had been $977 billion. To meet the employment targets in 1971, which would produce the tax revenues forecast in this dream, the dollar GNP in 1971 would have to rise to $1.065 trillion, a one-year rise of $88 billion. To get that kind of nominal increase would require a vigorous expansion of the money supply and, as 1971 began, all eyes were on the Fed, wondering if Burns would do his part.

Alexander Hamilton and Nicholas Biddle surely turned in their graves. The Nixon economists had forgotten, if they ever knew, that the United States was part of a world economy, linked not only through trade but also through the international monetary system. The problem Biddle confronted in 1828 repeated itself, but where Biddle called an end to the game, Burns kept it going. In the first two quarters of 1971, he expanded the money supply at an annual rate of 11 percent. And the banks, flush with reserves, underwrote an expansion of imports into the United States. The foreign exporters took their dollars and turned them in at their central banks for their currencies, and the foreign central banks showed up at the Fed demanding interest-bearing Treasury bills with rumblings from some that they would rather have gold. The United States was not increasing the domestic money supply. It was increasing the world money supply, and at the same time having no beneficial effects on U.S. output and employment. The 5.6 percent unemployment of November, 1970 became the 6 percent unemployment of April, 1971, and hardly a soul in Washington could understand the international money flows. The Nixon economists, who viewed the United States as a closed economy, had gotten everything they wanted. Yet by April it was clear the Game Plan was not working.

The strategy faltered at first because Arthur Burns, chairman of the Federal Reserve Board, was slower in expanding money and credit than the White House economists desired. Mr. Burns, worried about inflation, wanted the Administration to exhibit more open concern about the wage-price increases. After Mr. Nixon successfully wrestled over prices with the oil and steel industries, and over wages with the construction industry, Mr. Burns opened the money faucet. For the last two months he has been pumping out money so fast that he has just about satisfied the White House.

With the nation now "awash with credit," in Mr. Burns' words, another problem surfaces. When U.S. interest rates were high a year ago, Europeans holding dollars were rushing them to the United States to get in on the bonanza. Now, with the rates on U.S. Treasury bills having dropped in the last 18 months to about 3½ percent from 8 percent, this "hot money" is flowing back to Europe.

As a result, European central banks hold large quantities of dollars. The U.S. Treasury, to keep the European banks from getting too nervous about this "short term" problem of the dollar, earlier this month borrowed $1.5 billion of these Eurodollars at 5 percent interest, which is 1½ percent higher than the Treasury now has to pay for short-term loans in the U.S. market. Still, the European bankers visited Mr. Burns at the Fed last week, urging him not to loosen credit in the United States much more, for the good of the international monetary system.[16]

The domestic economists, though, did not care about the international monetary system. Indeed, they began to view it as a nuisance. Had the United States not been linked to the rest of the world through fixed exchange rates, they reasoned, the monetary expansion could not have flowed abroad. Instead of U.S. citizens using the expanded money supply to buy "cheap" foreign goods, they would have used the fresh money to buy U.S. goods, and the domestic expansion would have taken place. Wouldn't it? At the very least, Keynesians and monetarists of every stripe argued earnestly, the "overvalued" dollar should be devalued. A devalued dollar, you see, would not be able to buy those cheap foreign goods, and would have to stay home to do its work in fulfilling the self-fulfilling prophecy. At the very most, both Keynesians and monetarists also began arguing earnestly, the fixed-system of Bretton Woods should end and give way to "floating" exchange rates. The United States should not have to worry about international money flows while it was trying to solve its internal unemployment problems. It should treat balance-of-payments deficits with "benign neglect," argued Harvard's Gottfried Haberler, who with Milton Friedman was the most outspoken advocate of floating rates, the shattering of Bretton Woods.

It would be unfair to Haberler and Friedman, though, to identify them with such singularity. For in the spring of 1971, almost every U.S. economist was a closed-economy, partial-equilibrium economist. There were differences between Keynesians and monetarists, but on this point they stood shoulder-to-shoulder, and Nixon and Treasury Secretary John Connally, who were blamed for the results, never had a chance.

Here, for example, is Keynes advising his followers:

Under the influence of this faulty theory (of international payments balance) the City of London (Bank of England) gradually devised the most dangerous technique for the maintenance of equilibrium which can possibly be imagined, namely, the technique of bank rate coupled with a rigid parity of the foreign exchanges. For this meant that the objective of maintaining a domestic rate of interest consistent with full employment was wholly ruled out. Since, in practice, it is impossible to neglect the balance of payments, a means of controlling it was evolved which, instead of protecting the domestic rate of interest, sacrificed it to the operation of blind forces. Recently, practical bankers in London have learnt much, and one can almost hope that in Great Britain the technique of bank rate will never be used again to protect the foreign balance in conditions in which it is likely to cause unemployment at home.[17]

And here is Professor Friedman advising his followers:

For the United States in particular, exchange rates are an undesirable guide (to the proper level of money supply). It might be worth requiring the bulk of the economy to adjust to the tiny percentage consisting of foreign trade if that would guarantee freedom from monetary irresponsibility—as it might under a real gold standard. But it is hardly worth doing so simply to adapt to the average of whatever policies monetary authorities in the rest of the world adopt. Far better to let the market, through floating exchange rates, adjust to world conditions the 5 percent or so of our resources devoted to international trade while reserving monetary policy to promote the effective use of the 95 percent.[18]

The extension of this logic on the part of the Keynesians and monetarists is inescapable: Economic isolationism. Why worry about the 5 percent of our resources devoted to international trade? To promote domestic employment, why not float? Why not another Smoot-Hawley Tariff Act?

Such was the climate of intellectual opinion in the summer of 1971 as the Nixon strategy unraveled, both Washington and Wall Street sensing a national slide into financial panic. On August 2, there was the following report:

If it's always darkest before dawn, surely the sun will soon be shining on the U.S. economy. The series of economic reports that have hit the White House in the past 10 days could not have been much blacker. And unless there is better news just ahead, the number of people in the Capital who still have faith in Mr. Nixon's economic strategy will have dwindled to a handful of stalwarts in the White House.

The dismal economic news seemed unending: The Consumer Price Index rose at an annual rate of 6 percent in June. The budget deficit for the fiscal year that ended in June was $23.2 billion. The Government's index of leading indicators fell 0.5 percent in June, the first drop since October. The foreign-trade deficit ran to $363,000,000 for June, the third successive monthly deficit. There are strikes galore. Unemployment is high. And the stock market is falling.[19]

Nixon announced his new game plan on August 15 and the crisis atmosphere broke.

President Nixon did not have to prepare the American people for his New Economic Policy. They were ripe. In recent weeks, the voices from the heartland had swelled to a roar: "Do something about the economy. Do anything. But do it now."

Richard Nixon did it. In fact he did everything, all at once. Everything his critics said he should do. Everything his supporters said he should do. Everything they were afraid he would do. He piled it on for what seemed an orgy of Presidential action, and added some more for good measure, just to be sure no one would doubt that something indeed had been done.

A 90-day freeze on wages, prices, and rents. A 10 percent tax on imports. A suspension of the convertibility of the dollar into gold. A proposed 10 percent investment tax credit. A proposed repeal of the 7 percent auto excise tax. A proposed speed-up in personal income-tax exemptions. A 10 percent cut in foreign economic aid. A 5 percent cut in Government personnel. A six-month postponement of Government pay raises.

Relief was instantaneous; mass confusion followed. For two days the stock market soared euphorically, breaking all records for volume.[20]

When so much varied news comes to the stock market at once, it is impossible to argue credibly that it "soared euphorically" because of specific pieces of the Nixon package. We can only state as a matter of opinion that, consistent with the model presented here, the market reacted positively to the varied measures to lower tax rates—which is what the economy needed—and that the other measures (controls, surtax, ending of gold convertibility) were extraneous and negative factors.

At the time, after all, the wage and price freeze, the 10 percent surtax on imports, and the closing of the gold window were presented as temporary measures, while the lowering of tax and spending items were both permanent and at the same time palpable evidence of an important change in the White House toward the economy. By coming down the Laffer Curve on tax rates, the demand for dollars would increase, and concurrently the Federal Reserve would stop being whipped by the Administration into trying to boom the economy by printing money.

It can also be pointed out that as the "temporary" aspects of the August 15 package took on added seriousness, the stock market went into another slide. The U.S. trading partners reacted violently against the import surtax, which John Connally would not relax until he could win in exchange a devaluation of the dollar. When the Western nations insisted that part of the devaluation be against gold, and Connally refused, there was turmoil in stock markets around the world. In the first week of December, as the world learned that Connally had relented and there would be a compromise, an attempt to rebuild Bretton Woods around gold at thirty-eight dollars instead of thirty-five dollars, the Dow Jones Industrials gained sixty-one points in six trading sessions.

Later in the month, the new pattern of exchange rates was announced in Washington, after representatives of the ten leading industrial nations negotiated them in the buildings of the Smithsonian Institution. President Nixon termed this "Smithsonian Agreement" the "most significant monetary agreement in the history of the world."

What Nixon's hyperbole seemed to reflect was the belief, imparted to him by both Keynesians and monetarists, that henceforth the international monetary system could be run on wisdom alone. This was the same idea that Keynes proposed in 1944 and White wisely rejected. The United States did not reopen the gold window. And Mundell, at a conference in Geneva in January, 1972, promptly foresaw a dramatic increase in the price of oil and thence all other commodities. Without a planetary signal to guide them, the world's monetary authorities would soon be accumulating error and the planet would rebel via its resources.

The inflation that had become worldwide in 1965-71 entered a new phase after the abandonment of gold by the last major country committed to gold convertibility. Confidence in currencies in general declined and a shift out of money and financial assets commenced. A worldwide "scarcity" of land and land-intensive products, including raw materials, emerged. Within two years the price of metals, foods and minerals more than doubled. Shortages of beef, sugar and grains appeared, but gold and oil led to the most dramatic "crises" and received the most attention from the public.[21]

Between 1966 and the spring of 1974, the price of oil rose 344 percent, to $10 a barrel from $2.90. In the same period, the price of rice climbed 375 percent, to $30 from $8 per cwt.; wheat rose 322 percent, to $5.80 from $1.80 a bushel; lead 233 percent, to $28 from $12 per cwt.

The point to be emphasized here is that the inflation of the 1970s was not caused or "compounded" by the action of the oil-producing nations in raising the price of petroleum. Instead, it was the break-down of Bretton Woods and the cutting of the monetary link to real goods, through gold, that led inevitably to the global rise in prices.

The global inflation would not have had such adverse effects on global output and employment if it had occurred in the nineteenth century. Prior to World War I, progressivity in taxation was the rare exception. In the 1970s, almost every non-communist nation in the world—developed and undeveloped—employed progressivity in its tax structure. Personal income taxes, gift and estate taxes, and to a limited degree business taxes are now almost universally subject to progressions. As a result, every increase in the general price level has a ratchet effect on producers and transactors, pushing them into higher rates of taxation for the same productions and transactions, thereby causing a decline in the willingness to produce and transact.

Because of this problem, the destructiveness of monetary misman-agement is far worse in the modern era than anything envisioned by Alexander Hamilton in 1790 or Nicholas Biddle in 1828. Then, a surplus of money would simply reduce financial debts and financial assets. This would be bad enough. Jones, who has $1 million in bonds, of which each $1 will buy a widget, will still have $1 million in bonds after monetary error has produced a surplus. But it will now take $1.10 to buy a widget, so his portfolio is worth less in terms of widgets.

But at least there is no permanent effect on widget producers. With progression in the tax systems, not only does monetary error reduce the value of financial assets; it also expands the tax wedge on widget production. The government must explicitly correct for this push up the Laffer Curve or the producers and transactors under its dominion will be left with a permanent discouragement to commerce.

Observe what happens, then, with a system of floating exchange rates, when monetary authorities are not sharing their errors and keeping the money supply tied to the planet. Say the U.S. dollar at the beginning of the year is worth four Deutschemarks, and in the first six months of the year, error by the Federal Reserve causes the dollar to be worth only three Deutschemarks. In the second six months of the year, the Bundesbank makes the errors in providing surplus money, so at the end of the year the dollar is again worth four Deutschemarks.

The exchange rates are exactly the same at the end of the year as at the beginning. But both the United States and West Germany have progressive tax systems. In the first six months, U.S. transactors adjust to the rise in the general price level resulting from the devaluation: workers, managers, sellers, suppliers, and creditors demand more income for their output, and all wind up in higher brackets as a result. In the second six months, the process is repeated in West Germany. For both countries, the end of the process means parity on exchange rates at the end of the year, but at a new plateau of the Laffer Curve. Inflation and falling output (increased unemployment) occur simultaneously. With 10, 50, or 100 nations involved in the process simultaneously, global stagflation is the inevitable result.

The following table shows the impact of these phenomenon on real growth of the seven major industrial nations:

Growth of Real GNP: Percentage Changes

	Average 1959–60 to 1972–73	From previous year		1973 to 1975
		1974	1975	
Canada	5.1	2.8	0.2	3.0
United States	4.2	−1.8	−2.0	−3.8
Japan	10.9	−1.3	2.1	0.8
France	5.9	3.9	−2.4	1.5
Germany	4.9	0.4	−3.4	−3.0
Italy	5.6	3.4	−3.7	−0.3
United Kingdom	3.3	0.1	−1.6	−1.0

Source: Table compiled by the author from raw data from Organization for Economic Cooperation and Development (OECD).

No country could possibly have escaped losses of wealth and output resulting from the breakdown of the international monetary system. But as the table shows, Canada experienced the shallowest recession of the major nations. And of the seven nations, Canada was the only one lucky enough or smart enough to have indexed its progressive personal income-tax system on the eve of the great burst of global inflation. In his budget speech of February, 1973, Finance Minister John Turner told the Canadian Parliament of his intention to eliminate "the unfair and unintended increase in taxes which occurs automatically as a consequence of the interaction of inflation and a progressive tax structure."[22]

As a result of the legislation subsequently approved, the personal income-tax brackets were moved upward on January 1 of 1974, 1975, and 1976 to account for the rise in the Consumer Price Index for the 12 months ending in the previous September 30. The adjustment was 6.6 percent in 1974, 10.1 percent in 1975, and 11.3 percent in 1976. So as the global inflation was pushing the Canadian economy up the Laffer Curve, this "indexing" system was making automatic, annual corrections to move the economy back down. Thus, while the Canadian economy suffered to a degree because of the global economic contraction, Turner's indexing was the most correct internal adjustment.

The wedge model was not fully understood or appreciated by the Canadians, however, especially Prime Minister Pierre Trudeau. Even with the Turner indexing, the system was unstable because one province of Canada, Quebec, did not fully participate. In Canada, all citizens but those in Quebec file one personal tax return to Ottawa. Ottawa then redistributes the portion of the tax paid that is due the provincial government. In this method, both the federal and provincial tax rates are indexed. In Quebec, though, the citizens file two personal tax returns, one to Ottawa and one to the provincial capital, Montreal. The Ottawa tax rates are indexed, as in the other provinces. But the Quebec rates which range from 10 percent to 28 percent are not. So with each year of inflation, Quebec alone among the provinces was not brought back down the Laffer Curve to the full extent of the inflation. Each year, the wedge between Quebec and the other provinces deepened, setting up economic and political tensions. The separatist movement among the French-speaking people of Quebec, already in existence, was inflamed by these tensions, and Trudeau made serious errors in trying to combat the problem.

His error lay in trying to combat inflation through non-monetary devices. On October 13, 1975, he imposed a statutory prices and incomes policy, applying enforceable guidelines to prices, profits, wages, professional fees, and dividends. Such a policy merely restrains commerce, acts as a regulatory "tax" that pushes the entire economy up the Laffer Curve, but with most negative effects in those areas where economic and social strains are already the greatest, i.e., Quebec.

Trudeau then compounded this error by pushing through the Parliament a 10 percent surtax on all incomes above $30,000, which took effect on January 1, 1976. So even while the brackets are being automatically adjusted to offset inflation, this separate tax action pushed that income class already in the high reaches of the Laffer Curve into a much higher position. Since prices and incomes had had to do more upward adjusting in Quebec during the previous three years of inflation because Quebec tax brackets were not adjusted, the 10 percent surtax on high incomes fell most heavily on Quebec as well.

Finance Minister Turner resigned because of Trudeau's moves. The economy slid relative to the other OECD countries, with unemployment going to above 10 percent in Quebec. The separatist party won the provincial elections. Trudeau's national popularity dropped to a career low. In a desperate effort to expand the economy, he resorted to monetary expansion in 1977, devaluing the Canadian dollar and inviting further inflation, which of course only made matters worse for Quebec. The correct solution would be to remove the controls and the surtax, and adjust and index the Quebec tax rates.

If this prescription were followed, Canadian personal tax liabilities would equate roughly with California's. Compare, for example, the liabilities of a single person in Ontario in 1975 and 1977 (with the automatic inflation adjustment) and California in 1977:

	10,000	20,000	30,000	40,000	50,000	100,000	120,000
Ontario '75	1,907	5,729	10,197	15,180	20,537	50,273	62,540
Ontario '77	1,620	4,993	9,322	14,183	19,273	48,055	60,320
California '77	1,747	5,390	10,263	15,105	20,655	48,405	59,505

Source: Table compiled by the author from raw data from *Individual Taxes in 80 Countries,* Price Waterhouse information guides, January 1975 and January 1977.

In none of the other major OECD countries was there a tax-rate adjustment process during the inflationary burst of 1973-75 that followed the collapse of Bretton Woods. Japan came closest, but because the adjustment process was not automatic, the legislature could manage in only one year out of three (1974) to enact a correct bracket adjustment. The adjustment corrected for the 11.7 percent rise in consumer prices in 1973 at an implied cost of 2.6 trillion yen ($870 million). Japan at the same time adjusted allowances and exemptions at an implied cost of 14.7 trillion yen ($4.9 billion). But the government did not maintain this heroic effort when consumer prices rose 24.5 percent in 1974, 12 percent in 1975, or 9 percent in 1976. And because the growth forces in the Diet lost their nerve momentarily, the redistributive forces gained marginal control, pushing government spending/public works projects as the antidote to contraction. The budget for fiscal year 1976 was the first since 1949 that did not provide for some form of tax rate reduction. Without them, there is no chance for double-digit real growth in Japan, especially in an inflationary environment.

Of the major OECD countries, though, Japan's response to the inflation was far from the worst. Italy's monetary policy was almost the worst of the group, exceeded only by Great Britain's, as evidenced by the following table showing the advance of consumer prices from 1970 to 1976:

	1970	1971	1972	1973	1974	1975	1976
Italy	100.0	104.8	110.8	122.8	146.3	171.1	199.8
France	100.0	105.5	111.7	119.9	136.7	152.8	166.9
Japan	100.0	106.3	111.5	124.5	152.7	171.2	187.7
Germany	100.0	105.3	111.1	118.8	127.1	134.7	140.8
U.K.	100.0	109.4	117.2	127.9	148.4	184.4	215.0
Canada	100.0	102.8	107.7	115.9	128.5	142.3	153.0
U.S.	100.0	104.3	107.7	114.4	127.0	138.6	146.6

Source: Table compiled by the author from raw data from *International Financial Statistics, International Monetary Fund (IMF)*, March 1977.

Consumer prices are a crude measure of "inflation." The basket of goods measured is arbitrary, with variances within a currency region because of differences in local tax wedges. The wholesale indexes are also crude, but more reliable, especially for international comparisons:

	1970	1971	1972	1973	1974	1975	1976
Italy	100.0	103.4	107.6	125.9	177.2	192.4	236.4
France	100.0	102.1	106.8	122.5	158.2	149.2	
Japan	100.0	99.2	100.0	115.9	152.2	156.8	165.4
Germany	100.0	104.3	107.0	114.1	129.4	135.5	140.8
U.K.	100.0	109.0	114.8	123.2	152.0	188.7	219.6
Canada	100.0	101.2	108.3	131.6	160.7	171.5	
U.S.	100.0	103.3	107.9	122.0	145.0	158.4	165.7

Source: Table compiled by the author from raw data from *International Financial Statistics*, IMF, March 1977.

The most accurate guide to *relative* inflation rates, though, is the relationship between the national monetary standards—the currencies themselves. With each currency able to buy a basket of currencies at 100 in May, 1970, the following table indicates the relative appreciation or depreciation of that currency against the basket:

	1971	1972	1973	1974	1975	1976
Italy	98.8	98.5	89.7	81.0	78.8	63.7
France	98.4	101.7	106.3	99.3	109.3	103.7
Japan	102.4	114.5	123.2	115.4	111.7	115.7
Germany	103.6	107.1	119.3	125.5	127.6	132.3
U.K.	100.0	96.7	87.5	84.8	78.3	66.3
Canada	106.4	106.0	102.3	105.6	101.1	106.3
U.S.	96.8	89.8	82.3	84.2	83.5	87.7

Source: Table compiled by the author from raw data from *International Financial Statistics*, IMF, March 1977.

By this measure, Germany, Japan, Canada, and France had the tightest monetary policies during the period, in that order of stringency. Italy, the United Kingdom, and the United States had the loosest monetary policies, in that order of ease. If at the end of 1976 the seven nations decided to fix the exchange rates as they existed at that moment, by expanding or contracting the domestic currencies around one key currency, we would expect that in subsequent years the consumer price indexes and wholesale price indexes would vary until they caught up with the above precise measure.

Monetary "tightness" or "ease" does not depend solely, or even chiefly, on a central bank *supply* of currency into the economy. It also depends on the central bank's *withdrawal* of money from the economy as the demand for money slackens. The central bank is helpless to do anything about a decline in the demand for its money, except to make it scarcer. In the 1970s, money became very easy, first because of commercial inefficiencies caused by fragmenting Bretton Woods. Then, because central banks failed to *withdraw* this surplus money, the inflation pushed national economies into higher tax brackets, the resultant fall in output causing a secondary decline in the demand for money.

Italy's personal income-tax system is among the least effective in the industrial world because of widespread evasion and avoidance. But the fact that nominal rates are not paid does not mean they do not deter commerce. The people who are worth high incomes by virtue of their ability to add value to enterprises—industrialists, entrepreneurs, entertainers, etc., are so visible to the tax collectors that the high nominal rates are true deterrents to commerce. In other words, even if 95 percent of the population does not bother to file personal tax returns and is not punished, the 5 percent who face the highest rates and know they will be dogged by revenue agents will subtract from their efforts, and the entire economy thereby loses productivity.

In 1970, Italy had very high tax rates, but the income thresholds at which those high rates were encountered were also very high. In fact, Italy's personal income-tax structure was competitive, especially in the higher ranges.

The following table illustrates the dramatic rise in the progressivity of the system as it is impacted by inflation, devaluation of the lira against the dollar, and a 10 percent surtax applied by the Italian government in 1974 and 1975. The lefthand column is the marginal tax bracket. The subsequent columns show the income level, converted into dollars, at which those brackets are encountered.

(all units in U.S. dollars)

Bracket	1970	1973	1974 [a]	1974 [b]	1975 [a]	1975 [b]
25%	11,236	9,549	8,805	6,428	8,750	5,373
40%	48,154	40,927	18,868	13,774	18,750	11,513
50%	160,513	136,425	37,736	27,548	37,500	23,025
60%	401,284	341,064	125,786	91,824	125,000	76,750
72%	820,568	682,128	377,358	275,472	375,000	230,250
82%	—	—	628,930	459,119	625,000	383,750

1974 [a] and 1975 [a] reflect 10 percent surtax and 795 lire per dollar in 1974 and 800 lire per dollar in 1975.

1974 [b] and 1975 [b] are "a" columns converted into 1970 dollars.

Source: Table compiled by the author from raw data from *International Financial Statistics*, IMF, March 1977.

The Italian government conducted exactly the wrong policy in 1974-75, believing "austerity" was the answer to inflation. Its creditors, particularly the International Monetary Fund, helped persuade Italy that this was the solution to its economic ills. Even as demand for money fell, the Bank of Italy expanded the money supply. And as inflation alone pushed tax rates higher, the Italian Parliament added the surtax that accelerated movement up the Laffer Curve. The economists tell us that Italy enjoyed "real growth" anyway, at least in 1974, Gross National Product going to 97 trillion lire in 1974 from 58 trillion in 1970. But after you convert lire to dollars in 1974, and convert 1974 dollars to 1970 dollars, you find Italy's GNP in 1974 at $88.5 billion. In 1970 it was $93.4 billion. The value of financial assets crumbled as the politicians drifted from the correct solution. On a 1970 index of 100, stock-market shares should have gone to at least 220 at the end of 1976 to offset price inflation. Instead, the index went to 49, reflecting a 77 percent loss of value in real terms.

The United Kingdom performed almost, but not quite as poorly as Italy, attempting to expand the economy via monetary ease. But there was no surtax to further hasten movement up the Laffer Curve. One reason was that as the process began, Britain already had the steepest progression of the OECD countries in its personal tax structure. The rates rose to 83 percent at £20,000 of "earned income," and to 98 percent of "unearned" income at that same threshold. £20,000, though, was worth $48,000 in 1970. With sterling devaluation in the "float," by 1976 £20,000 was worth only $34,000. And $34,000 of 1976 dollars was worth only $18,156 in 1970 dollars. Britain offset some of this movement up the Curve by widening loopholes on business taxes, and in 1976 and 1977 adjusting personal tax by small amounts. But the high personal tax rates continue to cripple British initiative unnecessarily. Government revenues in 1975, for example, amounted to $72 billion. The deficit came to $16.9 billion. Total revenues from all personal income taxes above the 50 percent bracket amounted to a trivial $600 million. Knocking out the brackets above 50 percent would result in such vigorous economic expansion that revenues would rise by several times that amount and expenditures would fall by several times that amount.

Even with the collapse of the international monetary system and a price inflation equivalent to the United States', tiny Denmark enjoyed real growth in the period by indexing its tax brackets in 1974. Consumer prices had risen 23.3 percent between 1970 and 1973, so the brackets were adjusted upward by that amount in 1974, with provisions for automatic raises thereafter. Correcting for exchange-rate changes and dollar inflation, Denmark's GNP rose from $15.5 billion to $17.2 billion from 1970 to 1975. Denmark's rates are still so steeply progressive that further downward adjustment could be easily accomplished with bullish impact on the economy.

France moved in both directions on the Laffer Curve in 1974. It adjusted the tax brackets for one year's inflation, but at the same time imposed a surtax on tax liabilities ranging between 5 percent and 15 percent. The 50 percent bracket was encountered at $12,980, the 60 percent bracket at $23,000. With the surcharge dropped, the French personal income-tax structure is now, in all brackets except the very top, lower than that of the United States. Here is France versus the United States, liabilities for a married man, two children (the American paying California personal taxes as well):

	$10,000	$20,000	$30,000	$50,000	$100,000	$120,000
U.S.	1,855	3,324	7,026	16,324	44,024	55,124
France	291	1,751	4,082	9,860	28,358	38,853

Source: Table compiled by the author from raw data from *Individual Taxes in 80 Countries*, Price Waterhouse information guide, January 1977

From 1970 to 1974, France enjoyed a smart economic growth. Even correcting for dollar inflation and exchange rates, GNP grew from $146.4 billion to $177.6 billion. But by imposing a surtax at exactly the wrong time, the economy nosedived in 1975. Revenues rose by $3.3 billion, but the slump, supported by makework and welfare-state expenditures, caused government spending to rise by $14 billion. The error was in trying to use monetary policy to cause expansion and a tax surcharge to fight inflation, a reverse of the correct procedure. In 1976, President Valery Giscard d'Estaing and Finance Minister Raymond Barre again tried austerity to arrest inflation, imposing a capital-gains tax for the first time.

Germany's errors were of a slightly different order. Monetary policy was kept tight enough to give Germany the best record in inflation during the period. But when faced with contraction, it went the Roosevelt route of the 1930s, increasing tax rates and government spending. From 1974 to 1975 outlays jumped from DM 138.2 to DM 164.1—almost $10 billion. At the same time Chancellor Helmut Schmidt jumped all the tax brackets by 3 points, the maximum rate going to 56 percent from 53 percent at DM 130,000 (in 1975, $42,348). As a result, GNP fell by 3.4 percent and the federal deficit ran to $11 billion (DM 34 billion).

The German economy has not been in terrible shape as a result, but it has not been able to get back on a high-growth track. In terms of dollars, the personal-tax structure has done well, because of the DM appreciation. In 1970, the 53 percent bracket was hit at DM 130,000 ($35,636) and in mid-1977 the DM 130,000 level hit 56 percent at $56,521. But $56,521 corrected to 1970 dollars amounts to only $24,770. Had Germany been indexed through the 1970s, the 53 percent bracket would not be encountered until DM 187,000, or $81,300. A significant portion of the global contraction would have been avoided.

The United States was the main culprit, however. Having caused the collapse of the international monetary system by the rapid gunning of monetary expansion in 1971, the United States then stubbornly tried to expand production by currency devaluation. As the dollar fell sharply against the Japanese yen, from 360 in 1970, to 350 in 1971, to 308 in 1972, and to 272 in 1973, monetarists and Keynesians throughout predicted benefits to the U.S. economy. Yet all that happened was a price inflation in the United States that remorselessly pushed the economy up the Laffer Curve. As inflation impacted the progressions of the business-tax schedules, the estate and gift-tax schedules, and state and federal personal income-tax schedules, the growing wedge caused steady contraction.

Counting in inflated dollars, GNP grew from $982.4 billion in 1970 to $1,505.7 billion in 1975. But in 1970 dollars, $1,505.7 billion is only $931.1 billion. And of that there was an enormous amount of future taxes promised as represented by official and unofficial expansion of the federal deficit. By this calculation, which government statisticians and economists will not like, real GNP surely fell in those five years. As the progressive tax bite rose, government statisticians told us that federal revenues rose, from $190 billion in 1970 to $280 billion in 1975. But again, converting to 1970 dollars, federal receipts were only $172 billion in 1975.

The numbers collected by the government also masked another development in the political economy that had not been expected by the economists. The social support system had been designed by the Keynesian school with the argument that it would prevent contraction. Counter-cyclical spending on welfare and unemployment benefits would "automatically" arrest an output decline by increasing aggregate demand. Instead, the system encouraged continued decline as workers on the margin found it increasingly beneficial to be unemployed rather than employed.

American workers, both those employed and those unemployed, know something is drastically wrong with the system, even though their politicians, labor leaders and economists are afraid to admit it. Ray Evanoski, a Pennsylvania laborer quoted on our front page a few days ago, realizes something is wrong when he complains that his employer did *not* lay him off. If laid off, he would have collected $100 a week in tax-free unemployment benefits (and would probably been able to get food stamps). As it is, he's stuck with working and taking home $130. The difference, he says, "pays for your gas to work and your lunch. So you don't make out."

Something similar is happening not only to the incentive for labor, but incentives for capital as well. American industry now faces an effective tax rate of almost 75 percent. Corporate pre-tax profits for 1974 are estimated at $145 billion, but the Commerce Department estimates $40 billion of that results from illusionary inventory profits and $11 billion from underdepreciation of fixed assets. Taxes are $70 billion, then, on real profits of $94 billion, leaving $24 billion of real after-tax profits. Thus, there's enough profit to replenish inventory and replace fixed assets, but after last year's estimated $33 billion in dividends—the interest companies pay to attract equity capital—there is minus $9 billion left in the economy for real growth. Even if the Commerce Department estimates are off somewhat, it's clear the economy at present is living off its savings and that the Keynesian stabilizers are working against recovery.[23]

The Keynesians, you see, count federal deficits "investments." The 1975 federal deficit of $75 billion represents an "investment" by the American people in the public sector. As recently as the 1950s, Keynesians at least had in mind construction of public buildings, waterworks, dams and highways when they talked of public investment. No longer.

Spending is not increasing by leaps and bounds because of military requirements. It is not growing because government is rebuilding cities, constructing dams or financing scientific research and development. It is mushrooming at a steadily accelerating rate because of government commitments to give cash to people who are not producing after extracting it from people who are producing. We are in the midst of an explosion of transfer payments.

As recently as 1965, government transfer payments to individuals came to a modest $37.1 billion. Last month, federal, state and local governments were disbursing cash to individuals at an annual rate of $155.9 billion, for which no services are rendered. These include Social Security pensions, government pensions of all kinds, unemployment benefits, black-lung money, food stamps, welfare payments and health-insurance benefits. While the payments of course are defended on grounds of compassion, they are having a serious effect on the economy, by steadily breaking down the relationship between reward and effort. The following table is revealing:

	Govt. Transfer Payments (in billions)	Wages and Salaries	Transfers as % of Wages and Salaries
1965	$ 37.1	$538.9	6.9
1972	103.2	626.8	16.5
1973	117.8	691.7	17.0
1974	139.8	751.1	18.6
December 74	155.9	765.4	20.4

(December figure is at an annual rate.) [24]

This phenomenal rise in transfer payments is only part of the problem in the system, and surely not the triggering mechanism. The triggering mechanism was the faulty use of monetary and fiscal policies by the United States in an attempt to expand output and employment. Even this error could have been avoided had tax-cutting been continued after Kennedy as a means of disposing of anticipated and real surpluses in the Treasury. In 1978, here is what the personal income tax schedule looks like for a married couple filing a joint return, and what it would look like corrected for inflation since 1970:

1970*				1970 Corrected‡			
Taxable Income	Tax	Plus	Over	Taxable Income	Tax	Plus	Over
$ 0-to 1,000	0	14%	0	$ 0 to 1,600	0	14%	0
1-to 2,000	140	15	1,000	1,600+	224	15	1,600
2-to 3,000	290	16	2,000	3,200+	464	16	3,200
3-to 4,000	450	17	3,000	4,800+	720	17	4,800
4-to 8,000	620	19	4,000	6,400+	992	19	6,400
8-to 12,000	1,380	22	8,000	12,800+	2,208	22	12,800

1970*				1970 Corrected‡			
Taxable Income	Tax	Plus	Over	Taxable Income	Tax	Plus	Over
12-to 16,000	2,260	25	12,000	19,200+	3,616	25	19,200
16-to 20,000	3,260	28	16,000	25,600+	5,216	28	25,600
20-to 24,000	4,380	32	20,000	32,000+	7,008	32	32,000
24-to 28,000	5,660	36	24,000	38,400+	9,056	36	38,400
28-to 32,000	7,100	39	28,000	44,800+	11,360	39	44,800
32-to 36,000	8,660	42	32,000	51,200+	13,856	42	51,200
36-to 40,000	10,340	45	36,000	57,600+	16,544	45	57,600
40-to 44,000	12,140	48	40,000	64,000+	19,424	48	64,000
44-to 52,000	14,060	50	44,000	70,400+	22,496	50	70,000
52-to 64,000	18,060	53	52,000	83,200+	28,896	53	83,200
64-to 76,000	24,420	55	64,000	102,400+	39,072	55	102,400
76-to 88,000	31,020	58	76,000	121,600+	49,632	58	121,600
88-to 100,000	37,980	60	88,000	140,800+	60,768	60	140,800
100-to 120,000	45,180	62	100,000	160,000+	72,288	62	160,000
120-to 140,000	57,580	64	120,000	192,000+	92,128	64	192,000
140-to 160,000	70,380	66	140,000	224,000+	112,608	66	224,000
160-to 180,000	83,580	68	160,000	256,000+	133,728	68	256,000
180-to 200,000	97,180	69	180,000	288,000+	155,488	69	288,000
200,000 plus	110,980	70	200,000	320,000+	177,568	70	320,000

*Data from the Internal Revenue Service.
‡Figures calculated by the author.

The tax liability on 1970 income of $10,000 is $1,820. At the end of 1977, the worker needs $16,000 to have the equivalent of his 1970 income. But at $16,000 the worker is in the 28 percent marginal tax bracket instead of, as in 1970, the 22 percent bracket. His 1978 income must be $16,500 for him to have the purchasing power he had in 1970. With the brackets corrected for inflation, he can make $16,000 and have the same after-tax purchasing power. Under the corrected schedule, his tax liability is $2,912 instead of $3,260, a difference of $348. The following table illustrates what happens at various income levels:

1970 Income	1970 Tax	1970 After-tax	1978 After-tax Equivalent	1978 Gross Equivalent	% Increase in Gross
$ 5,000	$ 810	$ 4,190	$ 6,740	$ 8,110	62
10,000	1,820	8,180	13,088	16,480	64.8
20,000	4,380	15,620	24,992	34,850	74.25
50,000	17,060	32,940	52,740	94,730	89.46
100,000	45,180	54,820	87,712	195,900	95.9

As the table indicates, the progressivity of the tax schedules does most of its damage in the higher brackets. The $5,000 worker needs only a 62 percent increase in gross income to keep pace with a 60 percent increase in prices. The $100,000 worker needs a 95.9 percent increase in gross income to match inflation.

Imagine a firm, Acme Widget, which in 1970 had one $100,000 worker (the entrepreneur), two $50,000 workers (the managers), four $20,000 workers (the sales force), ten $10,000 workers (foreman and skilled workers), and fifty $5,000 workers (assembly workers). The payroll is $630,000. The income-tax liability of this work force is $155,520.

With a rise of 60 percent in the general price level by the end of 1977, the payroll should rise to $1,008,000 to enable all workers to keep up. But because of the impact of progressivity, the entire work force is now in higher brackets and the tax liability has increased by an extra $87,060. But prices cannot go up by 60 percent and costs by 73.8 percent. Something has to give. How will Acme Widget save $87,060? The easiest way is for the entrepreneur not to take a $95,900 increase in gross income, because most of his gross increase goes to the government anyway. He can take an increase of $8,840 and save the entire amount, but then he is making $108,840 and his managers are making $94,730.

The market will not permit this to happen. In 1970, the entrepreneur's after-tax income was worth 1.66 times the amount of a manager's. If he absorbs all the effects of progression, his after-tax income will be only 1.1 times that of a manager's. If the market was correct in 1970 in valuing the entrepreneur's skills at 1.66 times the manager's, the same terms must now apply, or the reward for the entrepreneur will not be commensurate with the effort required to become an entrepreneur.

Yet if the reward/effort ratios are maintained in 1978, the work force as a unit will have to irrationally give up more tax revenues to the government than is required to stay within the rise of the general price level. Faced with two irrational options, the work force does some of both. The effort/reward ratios are compressed throughout the system and the tax yield increased over the required minimum. The work force, after much struggling and tension, will "solve" the problem imposed upon it by progressivity and inflation, but the value of all capital in the system is reduced in the process.

Semi-skilled workers now have less incentive to become skilled workers or foreman, foremen less incentive to become salespeople, salesmen less incentive to become managers, and managers less incentive to become entrepreneurs. The value of Acme Widget, as represented by its share prices on the stock exchange, is immediately lowered. At this lower level of efficiency, widget production falls in volume and/or quality, and the real (as opposed to nominal) value of government revenues declines.

This is the process we have observed most clearly in the past dozen years. Skilled construction workers' seemingly irrational strike for higher hourly wages even though 15 percent of their number are unemployed is an attempt to maintain after-tax effort/reward ratios. High-income entrepreneurs and managers accept Martini lunches and fancy business trips (as incentives) in lieu of very high increases in gross incomes that will be eaten away by taxes. Athletes and entertainers appear to get way ahead of the work force in incomes. But when all tax progressions are worked into the equation—estate and gift taxes—a $250,000 star athlete today does not do as well as the $100,000 star of 1970. Yet all of these ballooned incomes must be accounted for in prices or, on the margin, individuals drop out of the money economy. They must opt for more leisure or lower quality of work at the top, and for moonlighting (without taxes), lower on-the-job productivity, or unemployment benefits at the bottom.

Had the progressions been corrected by indexing at the beginning of the process, at least, say, since 1970, there would not have been the need for nearly as much correction. That is, the wedge would not have been automatically expanded with varying impacts on the effort/reward ratios, and there would thus have been both less unemployment and less inflation. Politicians would not have been as tempted, in trying to solve the employment problems created by inflation, to push on the money supply. There would have been less inflation and the international monetary system would have remained intact.

Nevertheless, what happened had to happen, given the level of understanding of the political economy at the time. The unusual economic convulsions of the 1970s revealed more about the mechanisms of the political economy than we knew before. The world had never before seen an inflation of the world money impacting a near-universality of progressive tax structures. There is now, with this new information, a clearer path to political and economic advance at the global level than existed in 1944 when Bretton Woods was put together.

The reconstruction of an international monetary system is now a high priority. So too is the correction of the U.S. tax structure. But what the economic convulsions of the 1970s taught us more than this was the nature of economic error that the developed world has been transmitting to the underdeveloped world over the last thirty or forty years. For reasons that will become clear in the following chapter, the highest priority of the global electorate is to bring relief from this error to the Third World.

CHAPTER 11

The Third World on
the Laffer Curve

The problem of foreign aid: Britain and India in the nineteenth century. Building "infrastructure" in the developing nations of the twentieth century.
   The problem of foreign theoretical aid: Exporting economic ideas to the Third World. Capital formation through forced "state saving." The United Nations task force on growth.
   A survey of personal income-tax progressions in the Third World. The Ivory Coast and Ghana. The impact of inflation in the 1970s. Adjustment in India. Maladjustment in Latin America: Peru and Mexico. A reform program for the 1980s: Backing down the Laffer Curve.
   Capitalism versus Communism in Southeast Asia. Heterodox observations on the decline and fall of South Vietnam.

Since World War II, the Western industrial nations in general and the United States in particular have more or less wrestled earnestly with the economic problems of the "have not" nations—at various times termed the "less-developed countries" (LDCs), the "developing nations," and most recently "the Third World." President Truman had his "Point Four" program of 1949, which envisioned a continuous program of U.S. aid to lift the LDCs out of poverty. The Eisenhower-Dulles years involved significant contributions of economic and military aid to the poorer countries; the self-interest aim was to keep the fledgling nations of Asia and Africa from "going communist." President Kennedy had his "Alliance for Progress" for Latin America, the "Peace Corps" for LDCs in general, and a U.S.-managed political and economic experiment with a "Third Force" in Asia, i.e., South Vietnam. President Johnson shipped mountains of wheat to India in exchange for an Indian promise to take birth-control seriously. And there were always economic missions, from the State Department and World Bank, to lecture the brave, new Third Worlders on how to get ahead.

To get a clearer perspective on those postwar years, in which the giddy romance between the United States and the poor nations became an increasingly hostile relationship, let us drop back a century and observe British "aid" to India.

Until the 1850s, Britain's century-long relationship with its colony on the subcontinent was one of unquestionable benefit to both empire and colony. The relationship was almost entirely commercial, with citizens of Britain and citizens of India trading human and physical resources without direction by the government of either. Britain indeed repatriated "profits" from India through the East and West India Companies, but it was British entrepreneurial skill, marshaling Indian resources into modern enterprises, that made profits possible. And there was no attempt during the Napoleonic Wars to tax Indian resources to help finance the war, the bitter experience of Grenville's Stamp Act on the American colonies being too fresh in mind.

The curse of India in the last half of the nineteenth century proved to be the British boom of the 1820s and 1830s. The hallmark of this blossoming of wealth was the great burst of railroad building in Britain through the thirties. Britain, the wealthiest nation on the planet, understandably became the first spot on the planet to link its markets by rail, and it was private enterprise and private railroads that did the job. Government essentially stood back and watched the private market choose the routes along which rail would be laid and also choose the contractors who would build the railroads of the highest quality and lowest cost.

Dozens of would-be railroad builders competed for work and profits during this orgy of construction, and only the best survived; the companies that would become the first true multinational corporations—in the sense that they exported industrial skills, not merely financial or trading skills. The General Motors and Ford Motor Company of the day were the firms of Thomas Brassey and Sir Morton Peto, the big winners in the competition of the thirties, with Brassey's firm at one point employing some 80,000 men. Once assembled, these firms of course hungered to work even after Britain was saturated with railroads.

So British financial capital flowed to the United States to build railroads there, with British railroad designers, engineers, and foremen sent to manage the work. When the firms spread into Western Europe, there was even a flood of ordinary workers sent with the managers and engineers, until the locals got the hang of railroad building.

Thus there was a tendency, which reached its full proportions between 1852 and 1866, for the original relations between railway companies and their contractors to be reversed. Instead of people desirous of building a railway employing men to build it, contractors built railways and organized companies to sell what they had made. To his burden of technical responsibility for the railway plant, to the task of assembling the elementary factors of production, the contractor added the hazard of its business success. Thru him bonds were negotiated, bankers' accommodation secured. Upon his prestige depended in no small degree the graciousness with which public authorities conceded the building privilege, the eagerness of the investing public to purchase shares.[1]

But as the Americans and Europeans learned the business of railroad building, the Brasseys and Petos and Wythes and Henfreys were pushed out or, in parts of Europe, barred, so all the work could go to locals. Where could these great engines of railroad building know-how next satisfy their hunger? India!

The arguments were duly made in London and Delhi. The railroads had brought prosperity to England, hadn't they? Why not bring India into the nineteenth century?

It remained . . . for Lord Dalhousie—an empire-builder of the power of Warren Hastings and the prestige in London of Cecil Rhodes—to formulate these considerations with the voice of final authority. "Great tracts are teeming with produce they cannot dispose of," wrote Dalhousie in a minute dated April 20, 1853, which is in a sense the fundamental charter of Indian railways. "England is calling aloud for the cotton which India does already produce in some degree, and would produce sufficient in quantity, if only there were provided the fitting means of conveyance for it." Moreover a few railway lines radiating from the three Presidency capitals, Calcutta, Bombay and Madras, would have "immeasurable political advantages." They would "enable the government to bring the main bulk of its military strength to bear upon any given point, in as many days as would now require months." In consequence it would be possible to reduce materially the number and expense of soldiery in India.[2]

In the next dozen years, 75 million pounds were raised in Britain for railroad construction in India. The 5 percent bonds were "guaranteed," not by the British government, but by the Delhi government.

"All the money came from the English capitalist," testified an Indian Finance Minister, "and so long as he was guaranteed 5 percent on the revenues of India, it was immaterial to him whether the funds that he lent were thrown into the Hooley or converted into brick and mortar." Government engineers supervised every detail of expenditure, at the cost of the railway, with no real power to do anything but obstruct. And the company's agents thought only of doing a thoroughly good engineering job, irrespective of cost or appropriateness. The original estimates, especially upon lines built under contract, were doubled and trebled. It was notorious, testified Lord Lawrence in 1873, that "if the work had to be done over again, it could be done for two-thirds the money." Instead of the £8,000 per mile for which Dalhousie planned to cover India with railways, those in operation by 1868 had averaged £18,000, without reckoning dividends advanced upon the guarantee, which were charges upon the future possible earnings of the roads. Down to 1881, more than twenty-eight million pounds had been paid out by the government under the guarantees in dividends beyond what the railways could earn.[3]

Who was to pay for all this if not the Indian taxpayers? And with the taxpayers now burdened with the costs of paying off railways, none profitable, and all more or less along routes chosen by politicians rather than markets, there was coincidental civil unrest.

In the early sixties a military establishment was developed there which cost more than that of any European monarchy, more than the entire army of the British Empire outside of India. And this despite the fact that the introduction of the railways was expected to enable one regiment to do the work of ten.[4]

And now that India had railways, it was prosperous, wasn't it? Surely the Crown government must have assumed so, for

The burdens that it was found convenient to charge to India seem preposterous. The costs of the Mutiny, the price of the transfer of the Company's rights to the Crown, the expenses of simultaneous wars in China and Abyssinia, every governmental item in London that remotely related to India down to the fees of the charwoman in the India Office and the expenses of ships that sailed but did not participate in hostilities and the cost of India regiments for six months training at home before they sailed—all were charged to the account of the unrepresented ryot (Indian peasant). The sultan of Turkey visited London in 1868 in state, and his official ball was arranged for at the India Office and the bill charged to India. A lunatic asylum in Ealing, gifts to members of a Zanzibar mission, the consular and diplomatic establishments of Great Britain in China and in Persia, part of the permanent expenses of the Mediterranean fleet and the entire cost of a line of telegraph from England to India had been charged before 1870 to the Indian Treasury. It is small wonder that the Indian revenues swelled from £33 millions to £52 millions a year during the first thirteen years of Crown administration, and that deficits accumulated from 1866 to 1870 amounting to £11½ millions.[5]

Small wonder, too, that in the literature of Indian economics into the twentieth century these payments were referred to simply as "the economic drain." The railways of course were there, but beyond any doubt they contributed more to the impoverishment of India than to its advance. Here is one final commentary from Jenks:

... the remittance of capital for railways in India did not take the form of consumers' goods. It did not follow upon a manifested rising standard of living. And it did not call to life in India a vigorous industry to provide structural materials. For the case of the railway in India is that of the machine in all lands where it is imported from without. It destroys occupations in economizing labor. And the compensating demand for workmen to mine coal and to make machines which characterized the coming of industrialism in Great Britain, Germany and the United States, was not manifested. India had coal and she had iron. But enterprise and empire could not wait upon their development. These things had to be provided from England. More than one-third of the capital invested in Indian railways down to the early eighties was spent in England for railway iron and the cost of its transportation to the East. The importation of coal from England and the building and operation of railways with staffs which were English from foremen up and who had to be paid according to English standards, diminished further the benefits which could accrue to Indians from the railways. The remaining two-thirds of the railway capital, as the bulk of the public loans not spent upon Home Charges in London, were remitted to India in bullion, mainly silver. Their effects merged with that of the even larger quantities of specie sent eastward in partial payment for the increasing exports from India. For during the fifteen years 1854-69, more than two hundred million pounds in precious metals were imported into India in excess of her bullion exports. Among the consequences of this remarkable movement there were a fall in the value of money and an increase in prices which was serious enough for an investigation in the Bombay Presidency of 1863. It was ascertained that in the comparatively short time grain prices had trebled, prices in general had doubled, wages had risen fifty percent. There had been a consequent stimulus to industry and commerce in the immediate vicinity of Bombay, at least. And the prosperity of all classes had been increased except those with fixed incomes, persons without produce or labor to dispose of, and petty manufacturers deprived by dearness of material of the means of working. The prosperity was a highly precarious one. It was highly disruptive of traditional arrangements. "All our commerce and our enterprise, our greatworks and improved systems," stated the Commissioners who investigated the Orissa famine of 1865, "create or increase the class of laborers depending on regular wages; and all increase of private wealth, enabling the richer to entertain laborers who are no longer slaves or serfs, adds to this class." But persons depending upon regular wages, and bound to no one but in any other economic relation were exposed as never before to the hazards of extraordinary scarcity. Frequent famine was a painful corollary to the transformation of India by British capital. It is a phenomenon that at the best apologists for British rule must take considerable space to explain away.[6]

It is painfully clear from this account that Britain made horrendous errors in India in the 1860s, making one of the most common mistakes of political leadership. Britain was not prosperous because she had railroads; she had railroads because she was prosperous. A parent can encourage a child to study, practice, and develop. But if the parent pushes the child beyond his capacity of the moment, the child's discouragement subtracts from his eagerness to study, practice, and develop. This is the single worst drawback to imperialism, a flaw vaguely covered by the term "exploitation." There is, of course, the other side of the ledger. The parent may err in pushing the child beyond his capacity for formal learning. But there are almost always offsetting benefits, and it is rare for the child to do violence to his parent or to bolt home. Had the costs of British imperialism at any time outweighed the advantages of the electorate of India, Britain could not have held India any more than it could hold the American colonies. India's independence came in 1947, after she had learned the unifying language of English, after the unifying law of English tradition had become ingrained in the nation of India, after the commercial, financial, and social links to England had become so solid that they would remain intact under Commonwealth.

The preceding account also illustrates why modern electorates have developed such a wariness of "big business." The giant corporation is unquestionably more efficient than the small business, otherwise the force of competition in the private marketplace would cause the giant corporation to fragment. The economic arguments on behalf of anti-trust legislation have always been nonsense. The problem of bigness has always been in the political dimension. As long as Thomas Brassey, General Motors, or Exxon can do business in the private marketplace there is no problem. But when economic contraction occurs, for any reason, they turn to government to get them business by forcing it upon the private market. Seemingly benign rationales will always be found, as with Dalhousie's arguments that India should have railways.

After World War II, it was the turn of the United States to repeat the errors of Britain. The arguments and combinations were precisely the same. The colonial era was over, but the United States did not need the framework of colonies to develop a system of "economic imperialism"—the exploitation of the underdeveloped world by pushing it beyond its capacity to develop, in the process burdening the masses of people in the Third World with indebtedness and taxes that have prevented them from developing.

The United States had, in and after 1945, "infrastructure" because of its great wealth—infrastructure being highways, dams, waterworks, schools, bridges, etc. The great wealth lay in the genius of its intellectual capital. Yet the argument took hold that the wealth of a nation derives in large part from its infrastructure, and this became the foundation for the U.S. foreign-aid program. The people of the United States would be taxed to pay for some of the costs of providing infrastructure in the LDCs of Asia, Africa, and Latin America. And the people of the LDCs would get bargain rates in building dams, waterworks, highways, and national airlines. The giant multinational firms of the United States found these arguments pleasing. In the late 1940s and early 1950s there was plenty of work in the private market, as the world reconstructed from the war. But the intellectual capital of Western Europe and Japan soon regained its footing, and the U.S. firms found less profitable work in those places and turned their attention to the Third World.

They could make money by exporting infrastructure, especially by getting Congress to write into foreign-aid legislation the requirement that U.S. aid be spent only on U.S. goods. The big New York City banks—Chase Manhattan and First National City Bank—found the idea pleasing too, for they would bank the projects, through the

Export-Import Bank of the United States, through the World Bank and through spillover that could be privately banked.

Just as the Indian ryot, without being asked, had to pay the costs of railways through ever higher taxes, the already impoverished people of the third world had to pay the costs of infrastructure which, built under government supervision, always seemed to be several times the cost of original estimates.

Here, the U.S. corporations and major banks had the help of the bright young academic theoreticians of Washington and New York, Harvard and Yale. The eager young nations would send their brightest children to the London School of Economics, to Harvard and Yale, to learn the theories of Lord Keynes on how growth would magically follow upon the heels of deficit finance. And their brightest political figures would do turns at the United Nations, where they could mingle with American scholars, thinkers, economists, and bankers through the Council on Foreign Relations, and thereby gain the knowledge of how to propel their infant nations to prosperity.

In 1951, the United Nations Technical Assistance Administration commissioned young Walter Heller—who a decade later became President Kennedy's chief economic adviser—to write the gospel on fiscal policy for underdeveloped nations:

In the underdeveloped economies, taxation is increasingly assigned a far more positive role in the process of capital formation and technological change. The reason for this is implicit in the extremely low levels of income and saving which serve as the source of capital formation.... Propensity to consume out of these incomes is understandably high. Little remains for saving after meeting the pressing demands of sheer subsistence in the lower income strata and of traditionally lavish living, reinforced by the "demonstration effect" of American consumption standards, in the higher income strata.... Even worse, a considerable part of the meager savings is diverted into real estate and inventory speculation and the holding of precious metals, currency, and foreign exchange....

These countries are caught in the vicious circle of extreme poverty, a circle proceeding from low incomes to high consumption propensities to low savings to low rates of capital formation to a continuation of low levels of income. To break out of this circle, apart from foreign aid, calls for vigorous taxation and government development programmes; on this point, expert opinion is nearing a consensus. Fiscal policy is assigned the central task of wresting from the pitifully low output of these countries sufficient savings to finance economic development programmes and to set the state for more vigorous private investment activity.[7]

From Cambridge University in England, Professor Nicholas Kaldor throughout the following decade circled the globe dispensing similar advice, making stunning progress in India by persuading New Delhi to impose steeply progressive tax rates on incomes and wealth. Yet in the early 1960s, Kaldor was discouraged. In the January, 1963 issue of *Foreign Affairs*, the organ of the Council on Foreign Relations, he entitled his exasperated essay, "Will Underdeveloped Countries Learn to Tax?"

The importance of public revenue to the underdeveloped countries can hardly be exaggerated if they are to achieve their hopes of accelerated economic progress. Whatever the prevailing ideology or political colour of a particular government, it must steadily expand a whole host of non-revenue-yielding services—education, health, communication systems, and so on—as a prerequisite for the country's economic and cultural development. These services must be financed out of government revenue. Besides meeting these needs, taxes and other compulsory levies provide the most appropriate instruments for increasing savings for capital formation out of domestic sources. By providing a surplus over recurrent expenditure, they make it possible to devote a higher proportion of resources to building up capital assets. . . .

The fact is that in relation to gross national product the tax revenue of the underdeveloped countries is typically much smaller than in the advanced countries. Whereas the "developed" countries collect 25 to 30 percent of their G.N.P. in taxation, the underdeveloped countries typically collect only 8 to 15 percent.[8]

But by 1963, it could not be argued that the LDCs did not have modern progressive tax systems with very high rates on upper incomes. Rather, Kaldor could only complain that the well-to-do were avoiding the taxes they owed and that the governments were letting them get away with it:

The shortfall in revenue is thus largely a reflection of failure to tax the wealthier sectors of the community effectively. Though progressive income taxes and inheritance taxes exist on paper in most of the underdeveloped or semi-developed countries—sometimes imposed at high nominal rates, mounting to 80 percent or more on the highest incomes—there are few cases in which such taxes are effective in practice. . . . It is probably not an exaggeration to say that the typical underdeveloped country collects in direct taxation (excluding the taxation of wages and salaries) no more than one-fifth, possibly only one-tenth, of what is due—or rather what would be due if the tax laws themselves did not accord wide legal loopholes through exemptions and omissions of various kinds.

This broad generalization requires, of course, a great deal of qualification when applied to individual countries or regions. There are some countries which have been conspicuously unsuccessful in imposing taxes on the wealthy classes—chiefly, I think, the countries of Latin America—for whom the above picture may be an understatement. There are others, chiefly the ex-colonies of the British Empire, which have only recently gained independence but inherited relatively high standards of tax administration from their colonial days: for these it may be an exaggeration. Some countries have made notable efforts in recent years to improve both their legislation and their tax administration. In others, the situation is deteriorating, owing to the paralysing effect of corruption, or to the steady erosion of ancient taxes; there the weight of direct taxation may be less now than it was 50 or 100 years ago. . . .

In many areas of the Middle East and of Latin America, revolutionary pressure continues to build up, as a result of blind opposition to overdue social reforms. Ostensibly it is motivated by fear of Communism: in reality it serves to bring Communism nearer. The problem which has to be solved, and to which no one has yet found a satisfactory answer, is how to bring about that balance of power which is needed to avert revolutions without *having* a revolution. Can it be brought about by outside pressure—by making internal social and economic reforms the quid pro quo for external aid, as in the Alliance for Progress? Or can it be brought about by some organized attempt at the political reeducation of backward ruling classes—a kind of Westernized version of Chinese brainwashing? History does provide cases—nineteenth-century England an obvious one—of a ruling class voluntarily relinquishing privileges for the sake of its long-run interests. But when ruling classes evince no signs of such instinct, can they be made to acquire it?[9]

Two centuries earlier, Voltaire wrote of an eminent surgeon who theoretically devised an innovative technique for operating on a previously inoperable malady. Amid much fanfare, the surgeon then proceeded to demonstrate the technique by performing surgery on a patient with the malady, and the patient died. The surgeon then wrote a book on why the operation should have been successful. Voltaire informs us that he did not read the book. Yet it is instructive to read Kaldor, for we can more easily understand why political bodies that were malnourished a quarter century ago are in far worse condition today. Kaldor was easily the most influential exponent of these ideas, because he was most zealously messianic. But it cannot be too heavily emphasized that these ideas have represented the orthodoxy of the economics profession since 1945, and few economists have not lent support to them.

So thoroughly had this orthodoxy embedded itself in the Western intelligentsia that great men were unable to see the flaws in it even when they looked them in the face. The Swedish economist, Gunnar Myrdal, won a Nobel Prize in economics largely in tribute to his ten-year study of poverty on the Indian subcontinent. Myrdal's three-volume work of more than 3,000 pages, *Asian Drama—An Inquiry Into the Poverty of Nations,* contains only a dozen references to taxation in the nations of the subcontinent. Influenced by Kaldor in this area, Myrdal decries tax evasion and argues for vigorous enforcement of tax laws—an idea that fits snugly within the theme of his work, that subcontinent poverty is caused by "soft" as opposed to "hard" government. The liberal community in the United States applauded this thinly veiled plea for authoritarian rule.

The mystery, though, is how Myrdal could have written the following paragraph—one of his few references to taxes—without realizing its implications:

> Modern income taxation had been introduced in South Asia in colonial times, mainly so that citizens of the metropolitan countries doing business in the colonies should not enjoy an unduly favorable position compared with their compatriots at home; other foreign or indigenous businessmen were taxed to prevent them from having an "unfair" competitive advantage. In the independence era, tax rates have been raised considerably, with the result that now marginal rates in the highest brackets tend to be as high as, or higher than, those in the Western countries, although they are not effective. . . .[10]

Here is the essence of the Third-World problem of poverty in two sentences that elude Myrdal even as he writes them. If tax rates are kept high in the colonies, they will be kept uncompetitive in manufactures, for industry must reward the skills of the industrial entrepreneur with high income. The colony is thereby kept in pastoral condition, combining low levels of intellectual capital with high levels of physical, planetary capital. They must remain suppliers of raw materials. Yet upon achieving independence, the young political leaders of the fledgling nations ask the former colonial masters what they must do to prove themselves as capable of self government, and the answer comes back: "You must learn to tax yourselves more heavily, for in taxation lies prosperity."

The depth of the poisonous error exported to the Third World goes further, however. Both Kaldor and Myrdal speak of marginal tax rates being as high or sometimes higher than in the developed nations. But tax rates have two components, the rate itself and the threshold at which it is reached. The Keynesians never mention the threshold, which, in combination with the rate, makes Third-World personal tax rates enormously higher than those of the developed world.

At this writing, it is safe to say that not more than a handful of the leading political figures of the United States have any idea of the rate-threshold structure in the Third World, a structure that keeps the Third World near the very top of the Laffer Curve. The tax-rate/threshold structure has been the main export of American and British ingenuity since World War II, the primary cause by a long shot of the poverty of the world.

Here are the rates/thresholds of the four nations of the Asian subcontinent in 1974, converted to dollars in the exchange rates of the period:

PAKISTAN		INDIA	
Income Threshold	Marginal Rate	Income Threshold	Marginal Rate
$ 200	10 %	$ 625	10 %
400	15	1,250	17
700	20	1,875	23
1,000	25	2,500	30
1,500	30	3,125	40
2,000	35	3,750	50
2,500	40	5,000	60
3,000	45	7,500	70
3,500	50	10,000	75
4,000	55	12,500	80
5,000	60	25,000	85
7,000	65	(Plus 12½% surtax)	
10,000	70		

SRI LANKA		BANGLADESH	
Income Threshold	Marginal Rate	Income Threshold	Marginal Rate
$ 268	10 %	$ 101	5 %
537	12.5	202	10
895	15	404	15
1,253	17.5	656	20
1,612	20	1,010	25
1,970	25	1,515	35
2,507	30	2,525	50
3,224	40	3,535	60
4,298	50	5,050	65
5,373	60	7,070	67.5
6,448	70	10,101	70
7,522	75		

Source: Table compiled by the author from raw data from *Bulletin for International Fiscal Documentation*, January 1977.

These pitifully high tax rates are palpable evidence of the earnest attempts of political leaders on the subcontinent to follow the Kaldor prescription. In these rates lies not only the reason for the poverty of the subcontinent, but also for the wars and tensions on the subcontinent during the past decade. For even while the rates did not change until 1975, as we will see later in this chapter, the effects of inflation in the last decade to 1975 remorselessly pushed the citizens of the four nations into higher and higher brackets. This, after all, is part of the "sterling area," with currencies tied far more to the British pound than to the dollar. And the first splinterings of the Bretton Woods system were manifest in the British devaluations of the 1960s and early 1970s, which coincidentally inflated the entire sterling bloc into higher tax brackets. No matter that only 5 percent of the 600 million citizens of

India file and pay personal taxes. What sparks of entrepreneurial initiative remained in the money economy prior to the devaluation inflations were soon crushed. And out of the ensuing economic contractions flowed the India-Pakistan wars, the revolution in Ceylon (Sri Lanka), and the fragmenting of Pakistan. Still, the countries of the region cling to democracy, eschewing communist forms, patiently awaiting politicians who understand the nature of the Laffer Curve.

The first break down the Laffer Curve for the Third World came in India, by political accident, if such things are possible. The breakdown of Bretton Woods as the world went into a general scheme of floating exchange rates in the spring of 1973 invited the global inflation that pushed India to the brink of civil war or revolution. In the summer of 1975, Prime Minister Indira Gandhi suspended democratic rule and civil liberties in tardy appreciation of Myrdal's call for "hard" government. Political opponents, revolutionaries, student agitators, and labor leaders were thrown into prison, press censorship began, and Mrs. Gandhi began ruling by decree. These moves, in themselves, would have ensured revolution and guerilla warfare. But as an unnoticed and, in the West, unreported strand of the government's new order, the tax rates were reduced. Finance Minister C. Subramaniam used the suspension of parliamentary activity to put through a pet idea. Not only was the 12½ percent surtax removed, but the top rates were cut to 77 percent from 85 percent. The wealth tax, which had been 8 percent annually on assets of about $2 million, was slashed to 2½ percent, and an urban-property wealth tax, which ranged from 5 percent to 7 percent annually, was abolished entirely. Corporate tax rates were cut and progressive taxes on investment and royalty income were replaced with proportional rates.

The tensions of India were instantly replaced by an extraordinary quiescence. The rupee began climbing against sterling on the exchange markets. The rate of price inflation, which had been running at 30 percent dipped to 10 percent, and real growth of 3 percent was recorded in the following six months—a period of contraction elsewhere in the world. And as treasury revenues exceeded projections by 15 percent, in April of 1976 Subramaniam whacked at personal rates again, cutting the top rate to 66 percent and adjusting brackets down along the line. Where the 60 percent bracket had been encountered at $5,000, it was now hit at $10,000. Bumper crops came in from the farms. Real growth ran to 6 percent in the first quarter and moved to 10 percent for 1976. The consumer price index declined in 1976. Foreign reserves began piling up at the rate of $150 million per month, even as imports of oil doubled.

Unfortunately for Mrs. Gandhi, she did not perceive that it was Subramaniam's tax reforms that had done the trick. Instead, she allowed herself to believe that it was a sharp dose of Myrdalian "hardness" that had put India back on track. Her popularity soared with the economy, and when she unexpectedly called for national elections in March, 1977, it seemed certain she would be rewarded at the polls.

Her campaign, though, violated all the rules of our political model. Instead of identifying the tax cuts as the source of the economy's buoyancy, she turned more and more of the government's revenues to spending programs, when yet another tax-rate cut was in order. Worse, she defended her suspension of democracy in 1975 instead of admitting error, and she weakly defended the government's heavy-handed birth-control program. There, too, it was the real growth in the economy following the Subramaniam tax cuts that led some 4 million Indian males to seek vasectomies in the spring and summer of 1976—it suddenly becoming possible to form financial capital instead of human capital.

The patient Indian electorate had not clung to democracy for thirty years, waiting for a politician who would understand the Laffer Curve, only to reward an accident that attended suspension of the democratic system. Mrs. Gandhi and her Congress Party were pitched out, and almost the entire Cabinet went down in defeat in the parliamentary elections as well. Subramaniam, though, was returned to his seat. Through the summer of 1977, the now ruling Janata Party has shown only faint signs of following his lead by continuing tax-rate reductions, but at least it seems pointed in the right direction.

The net effect of Subramaniam's thrust in the summer of 1975 spread throughout the subcontinent, as the governments of Pakistan, Sri Lanka and Bangladesh followed India's lead with tax reforms that took effect in 1976. Here are the current rates at 1976 exchange rates:

PAKISTAN		INDIA	
Income Threshold	Marginal Rate	Income Threshold	Marginal Rate
$ 500	20 %	₹ 784	15 %
1,000	30	1,470	18
2,000	40	1,961	25
3,000	50	2,450	30
7,000	60	2,941	40
		4,902	50
		6,863	55
		9,804	60

SRI LANKA		BANGLADESH	
Income Threshold	Marginal Rate	Income Threshold	Marginal Rate
$ 217	10 %	$ 64	5 %
439	12.5	129	10
878	15	258	15
1,317	20	419	20
1,756	25	645	25
2,195	30	968	35
2,634	35	1,613	50
3,073	40	2,258	55
3,658	45	3,226	60
4,536	50	4,516	62.5
		6,452	65

Source: Table compiled by the author from raw data from *Bulletin for International Fiscal Documentation*, January 1977.

In comparison with the earlier tables, it appears that the governments actually raised many tax rates in the lower brackets. But this occurs because of the devaluations of the local currencies between 1974 and 1976. In local currencies, all nominal rates were reduced, but in converting the preceding tables to U.S. dollars, the tax reforms plainly were not sufficient to keep up with devaluation and inflation in Bangladesh and Pakistan, where the tax cuts were most timid. Sri Lanka's cut, to a 50 percent top, was easily the boldest cut of the group, and through the summer of 1977 the Sri Lanka economy seems the healthiest of the group, with two upward revaluations of the rupee having the effect of increasing the tax thresholds in dollar terms to even more beneficial levels. Each of the four nations could take savage cuts in the progressivity of their personal tax rates, by steadily raising the thresholds and lowering the rates themselves. As foreign reserves build up, as in India, real growth will be further fueled by lowering tariff and trade barriers. But for all this to occur, the politicians and political parties on the subcontinent must offer themselves at the polls on these terms, or the electorate will turn again to those who offer efficient forms of redistribution during periods of economic contraction.

ii

In the spring of 1976, Robert Prinsky, a correspondent in the London Bureau of the *Wall Street Journal,* traveled to Western Africa on an interesting assignment: Ghana and the Ivory Coast are neighbors, so alike they could be twins. Yet one has done well and one has done poorly since independence. What's the explanation? Here is Prinsky's account:

ACCRA, Ghana—What makes one Third World country travel faster than another up the path to economic development? . . . The countries are neighbors, Ghana and the Ivory Coast. On paper they have much in common. Both lie on the bottom of Africa's western bulge. They have much the same climate and topography. Neither has great mineral wealth. They are broadly comparable, in size and population, even sharing some common tribal groups.

The comparison stops there. The Ivory Coast is one of the success stories of modern Africa, a nation that started with little and now is the most economically advanced state in the region, thanks largely to farm-based development. Ghana is a story of failed expectations, of a comparatively well-off nation that slid into financial and political difficulty with an industrialization program that misfired.

What happened? A look at two towns tells much.

Aby, Ivory Coast, lies beside a lagoon, just across the border from Ghana. Ernest Bile-Kassi, the village chief, tells of the progress that has seen his town swell from 100 to 2,000 people. With profits from growing coffee, cocoa and oil palms, the villagers have built themselves "hard houses" from cement blocks and other modern materials to replace their traditional but less durable mud huts. Aby also boasts a maternity clinic, financed by a local tax, and is planning to build a new church. The existing one "isn't pretty," Mr. Bile-Kassi explains.

Ivorians can afford to replace things that aren't pretty because many of them are prosperous. Since independence from France in 1960, the nation of 6.5 million has become a sizable exporter of coffee, coca, hardwoods, palm oil and a variety of other tropical produce. The proceeds of foreign sales filter down to small growers in villages like Aby.

Shum, Ghana, is a town that clearly has seen better days. Located in cocoa growing country 45 miles north of Accra, the capital, Shum boasts colonial style buildings that are bigger and more impressive than anything in Aby. But they are going to seed. Obviously intended for the cocoa trade, Ghana's biggest business, they are now broken up into small shops and family dwellings. Some have doors boarded up.

Swollen-shoot disease killed most cocoa trees in this area in the 1930s and many farmers left for more hospitable regions, a government official explains. A replanting effort in the early 1960s foundered on political wrangling. Lately, with a World Bank loan, a new replanting program has begun. But this one, too, is encountering trouble. Farmers are supposed to repay loans with deductions at the source from official buying cooperatives. However, they prefer to sell to independent buying agents because cooperatives are often slow in giving them cash for their crops, officials say.

Shum's troubles are symptomatic of Ghana's good ideas, poor execution. "Government after government has plans. Implementation has been a major bottleneck," says an Accra economist. Burdened by a heavy foreign debt that financed construction of largely unviable industries, Ghana lacks the foreign exchange to import sufficient food and machinery. Even vital cocoa production, which provides two thirds of the foreign-exchange, has been allowed to slide, partly due to lack of imported pest-killers. Corruption is common among the dispirited people, foreign residents say.

By contrast, the Ivory Coast's administration is relatively honest and its coca production is swelling rapidly. "It's like Britain and Germany," notes a New York banker who visits Africa regularly. One nation's resources are new and productive, the other's old and inefficient, he explains.

Ghana has inherited much that is British from its former colonial power, including indifferent food, newspapers that feature advice on soccer pools and a strong tendency to self-criticism. But most of the colonial administrators have left as a result of Ghanaians' post-independence effort to take control of their country's levers of power. To most developing nations, independence means going it alone whatever the cost. "I'd rather be poor but proud," one senior Accra official declares flatly.

The Ivory Coast takes a different view. It still is very much tied to its former colonial power, France. Abidjan, the capital, boasts restaurants that could hold their own in Paris. Shops are full of luxury goods, albeit at exorbitant prices. There are 50,000 Frenchmen, helping run key sectors of the economy. Ministers have French advisers and civil servants mingled in with the Ivorian majority. Many private businesses are owned by Frenchmen. Major plantations are managed by Europeans.

This helping hand makes the Ivory Coast much more efficient than it would be if left to the largely inexperienced hands of the country's native citizens, many observers believe. However, it is a reliance that has many critics among the proud peoples of other African states. . . .

Ghana began going it alone in 1957 when Kwame Nkrumah led the former Gold Coast to independence and became his country's first leader. A strong believer in "Africanism," by which he meant replacing Europeans with Africans in jobs, Mr. Nkrumah embarked on a costly industrialization program to develop the economy. Agriculture was clearly in second place, though cocoa was and is by far the country's biggest source of foreign-exchange income.

The Nkrumah administration borrowed heavily abroad to finance its factories. It neglected the development of local raw materials to feed the young industries. Bauxite had to be imported to supply a showpiece aluminum smelter, even though Ghana has untapped reserves of the raw material. Tainted by grandiose ideas and corruption, the country's first government led the country into external bankruptcy. Ghana still is paying off its debts and can't borrow from commercial banks for more than short periods.

Mr. Nkrumah was deposed by a military coup while in Peking in 1966. Since then the military has ceded power to a civilian administration, then seized it back again, but scarcities still abound for both consumer and industrial goods, due to lack of foreign exchange to buy imports with.

The Ivory Coast reached independence in 1960, under the leadership of Felix Houphouet-Boigny, who is still president of the republic. Mr. Houphouet-Boigny was well integrated into the French establishment, having served as a minister in Paris during colonial times. At independence, he was a wealthy landowner with large plantation holdings.

Basically conservative, he wasn't in a hurry to replace French administrators with Ivorian ones. As a planter himself, he didn't regard farming as demeaning. Rather, he based the Ivory Coast's economy on agriculture and growth took off. Starting as one of the most neglected French colonies, due to an inhospitable coast, the Ivory Coast is now the most economically advanced state in West Africa.

When you ask an Ivorian why his country has succeeded where others like Ghana (which could certainly grow anything the Ivory Coast has) haven't done as well, he invariably cites the personality of the president. Most newly educated young Africans seek white collar jobs, which are plentiful in industrialized countries. But Houphouet-Boigny wasn't afraid to push agriculture and he has persuaded people to stay on the job by his own example, Ivorians note. A rich man, too, he set the pace for an honest administration. One Ivorian was recently sentenced to 10 years imprisonment for doing no more than stealing a radio from a friend. Abidjan's slickly produced daily newspaper, *Fraternité Matin*, made a big example of him.

Personally entrenched in power, Mr. Houphouet-Boigny is able to Africanize his administration slowly, with clear benefits to efficiency. "Most African leaders are afraid to move this gradually," says an expert of African affairs in Abidjan.

The country has been helped considerably by the commodity price boom of recent years, a bandwagon that other nations are seeking to climb on. The current Ghanaian administration, led by Col. Ignatius Kutu Acheampong, stresses farming like none of his predecessors ever has. An "Operation Feed Yourself" is aimed at cutting down imports of rice and other items that could be grown at home without a foreign exchange outlay. An "Operation Feed Your Industry" stresses growing crops like cotton that can be used in local textile mills.

But it takes more than deciding options to achieve success. In Ghana, years of apparent government ineptitude and struggling with shortages have lowered morale. Government-controlled newspapers bemoan lack of cooperation for official programs. In the Ivory Coast, though, people are responders. "All you have to do is talk about a new crop like corn and everybody starts growing it," one government official declares.

Here is perhaps what sets the pragmatic Ivorians apart from their neighbors. Africans love to talk and debate politics, notes a senior official in Abidjan. "Here we talk a lot but we also act a lot too."

Action and words. It is a philosophy with wide application in both developing and developed parts of the world.[11]

Prinsky has provided us with a vivid picture of the two Third World nations, twins in every way except that one grows and the other doesn't. But he could not quite find out why, except that Ghanaians are dispirited and Ivorians respond. As we should by now expect, the answer lies in the Laffer Curve.

Here, in the personal income-tax schedules of the two nations, is the single most important variable that sets them apart:

GHANA		IVORY COAST	
Taxable Income	Marginal Rate	Taxable Income	Marginal Rate
$ 261	nil		
469	5 %	$ 813	.09%
887	7.5	1,423	13.04
1,304	10	2,439	16.67
2,139	12.5	3,659	20
3,130	15	6,098	25.93
3,809	25	10,164	31.03
4,552	35	20,329	37.5
6,939	45		
9,026	60		
12,522	75		

Source: Table compiled by the author from raw data from Price Waterhouse.

It is, of course, not in all cases sufficient to merely examine the personal income-tax schedules to get the country's fix on the Laffer Curve. A nation that has low or no personal income tax but exorbitant enterprise tax rates (Soviet agriculture) will be on the upper end of the curve, just as a nation that has effectively eliminated enterprise tax rates via loopholes, but has confiscatory personal tax rates (British industry), must stagnate. The Ivory Coast, though, is prospering because its tax structure is among the *least discouraging* in the world. Even the above tables look worse for Ghana when allowances and exemptions are considered. Ghana exempts the first $563 of household income, but exempting the poorest income classes from tax rates in this fashion is meaningless if the poor have no incomes at all. The Ivory Coast has similar exemptions, but they mean much more because individuals have incomes. In addition, the Ivory Coast exempts interest on government bonds, pension incomes, insurance premiums, and certain capital gains. And other interest payments plus all direct taxes are deductible from gross income to arrive at taxable income.

In 1965, Ghana's GNP on paper still put the Ivory Coast in the shade, $281 per capita to $251. But Ghana's statistics were ballooned with deficit finance for all that infrastructure, and the Ivory Coast's were not. A decade later, Ghana's per capita GNP had slipped to $200, and the Ivory Coast's had climbed to $655.

What about the rest of Africa? In the following table, the top marginal tax rate on personal income tax is given for 1970 and for 1976. In most cases the change merely reflects exchange-rate changes, with a lowering of the rate reflecting an appreciation of the national currency against the U.S. dollar, and an increase in the rate reflecting a devaluation against the dollar. Per capita GNP is given for the latest available year. Ethiopia's tax rates were deceptively low in 1970, it then being one of the few nations in the world with a system that counted gross income as taxable income. This naturally is a formidable deterrent to commerce. A tax reform taking effect in 1976 increased marginal rates dramatically, and still gross income is the same as taxable income, i.e., no allowances for individual circumstances and no deductible expenses in arriving at personal taxable income.

	Top Marginal Rate in 1970/1976		Per Capita Income
Algeria	75	% @ $14,198	$450 ('73)
	75	% @ $16,826	
Cameroon	45	% @ $10,802	$303 ('74)
	45	% @ $12,553	
Congo, PR	65	% @ $21,605	
	65	% @ $25,106	
Dahomy	60	% @ $19,804	
	60	% @ $23,014	
Ethiopia	50	% @ $60,000	$104 ('74)
	70	% @ $15,865	
Gabon	85	% @ $14,403	$320 ('74)
	85	% @ $16,737	
Gambia	75	% @ $24,000	$186 ('75)
	75	% @ $22,580	
Ghana	75	% @ $14,693	$22 ('75)
	75	% @ $12,522	
Guinea	60	% @ $18,004	
	60	% @ $20,922	
Ivory Coast	37½%	@ $18,004	$655 ('75)
	37½%	@ $20,922	
Kenya	70	% @ $ 2,801	$206 ('74)
	70	% @ $ 1,076	
Niger	60	% @ $18,004	
	60	% @ $20,922	
Migeria	75	% @ $ 7,142	$232 ('73)
Senegal	60	% @ $18,004	$317 ('74)
	60	% @ $20,922	
Sierra Leone	50	% @ $16,000	$216 ('75)
	50	% @ $21,260	
Tanzania	95	% @ $ 2,801	$148 ('74)
	95	% @ $ 2,386	

	Top Marginal Rate in 1970/1976	Per Capita Income
Tunisia	52 % @ $15,619 52 % @ $19,123	$708 ('75)
Zaire	60 % @ $19,000 60 % @ $10,957	$145 ('74)
Zambia	70 % @ $ 8,571 70 % @ $ 9,624	$455 ('75)

Source: Table compiled by the author from raw data from Price Waterhouse.

In different tabular form, here is the impact of progressivity on personal incomes in Latin America (on several total remunerations with average exemptions and deductions):

	Total Remuneration in $U.S.						
	10,000	20,000	30,000	40,000	50,000	100,000	120,000
	Income Tax						
Argentina	2,264	5,274	8,284	11,294	14,304	29,354	35,374
Bahamas	No Income Tax						
Barbados	2,961	9,145	15,645	22,145	28,645	61,145	74,145
Bermuda	No Income Tax						
Bolivia	1,248	4,354	8,354	11,666	14,583	29,167	35,000
Brazil	751	3,527	7,520	12,040	16,840	41,596	51,596
Chile	2,504	7,388	12,996	19,296	25,596	57,096	69,696
Colombia	2,174	5,834	9,857	14,146	18,455	40,002	48,620
Costa Rica	847	3,005	5,938	9,703	13,870	36,787	45,953
Dominican R.	809	2,623	5,564	9,392	13,736	35,866	45,666
Ecuador	1,335	4,970	9,360	14,000	18,660	43,480	53,950
El Salvador	643	2,360	4,768	7,798	11,323	34,148	45,198
Guatemala	403	1,704	3,497	5,812	8,437	24,594	32,052
Honduras	560	1,730	3,010	4,410	5,810	16,240	21,580
Jamaica	2,639	8,886	15,336	21,786	28,236	60,486	73,386
Mexico [a]	1,967	6,029	11,306	16,735	22,164	47,750	57,750
Nicaragua	343	1,514	3,684	6,736	10,293	29,664	37,664
Panama	737	2,523	4,708	7,284	10,260	30,552	40,928
Peru	2,031	6,692	12,231	17,892	23,646	54,585	67,461
Puerto Rico	1,669	5,288	10,334	16,156	22,617	59,669	75,521
Trinidad & Tobago	3,535	9,764	15,947	21,447	26,947	54,447	64,947
U.S. (New York)	1,891	5,640	10,219	15,931	22,099	52,936	65,271
U.S. [b]	1,482	4,119	7,973	12,715	17,715	42,715	52,715
Uruguay [c]	No Income Tax						
Venezuela	242	675	1,426	3,053	6,023	15,029	18,941

[a] Mexico has additional state income taxes. [b] U.S. income tax for those states without personal income taxes. [c] Uruguay abandoned its income tax in 1975.

Source: Table compiled by the author from raw data from Price Waterhouse.

The preceding tables, in themselves, do not permit us to draw any definite conclusions about why one Third World country will advance while another stagnates. As previously mentioned, the tax-rates structure of a country has to be considered in total before its position on the Laffer Curve can even be guessed at. And it must be emphasized once more that the revenue side of the ledger cannot be viewed in isolation. Taxes, after all, are the price of government services. A government that spends tax revenues efficiently on goods and services desired by the electorate can have high growth rates with relatively high tax rates. But if revenues elicited from relatively low tax rates are squandered on uneconomic projects, the nominal tax rate must be viewed as exorbitant. That is, a government toll bridge that connects two economies can charge five dollars a trip to finance its construction if the gains to commerce in the two economies are such that sufficient traffic will be generated. But if a bridge provides so little expansion of commerce that traffic is slow even at a toll of twenty-five cents a trip, revenues will not be sufficient to finance its construction, and the government will have to draw revenues from other sources to pay its costs; the economy as a whole is pushed up the Laffer Curve.

We believe it should be obvious, though, that with very few exceptions the Third World suffers from unnecessarily high tax rates on personal incomes. In Africa, even the Ivory Coast's top rate of 37 percent could probably be cut to below 30 percent with beneficial results, and the Ivory Coast now has the most correct tax structure of developing Africa. In Latin America, Venezuela's top rate of 25 percent is probably the smartest on the continent, and Venezuela's per capita income of $2,414 in 1975 led the region. Uruguay's recent experiment in getting along without a personal income tax is a fascinating one. The government wisely concluded that its progressive system was costing more to administer than it was yielding in revenues. Pitching the tax out should move the economy down the Laffer Curve and produce steady internal development. Unfortunately, the Uruguay government balanced its elimination of income tax with steep increases in protective tariff rates and energy taxes (a gallon of gasoline costs roughly $3). Still, the net effect on the economy has been positive and real incomes have been rising since the tax reforms.

Throughout the Third World, the experience with the personal income tax has been the same as Uruguay's. Revenue yield has been so low, and the financial costs and intellectual energies burned up in administering and evading the high rates have been so high, that the Uruguay experiment could be repeated with great benefits to the economy. But reforms need not be this bold. A system of relatively low rates at high thresholds—such as Venezuela's—would yield much higher revenues to Third World countries. This would permit tax-rate reductions in other areas—tariffs, turnover taxes, land, gift and estate taxes, and tax abatement for regional development.

People will pay taxes, in most cases voluntarily, if they are not so outrageously high that they themselves stand as barriers to commerce. Widespread tax evasion is a certain sign that the government involved is trying to enforce or impose rates that are *unnecessarily high.* Latin Americans or Italians or Asians are no more predisposed to evade taxes than are New Yorkers or Germans.

The idea that the people of some countries have a greater propensity than those of others to evade taxes is one of the myths still generally accepted. Taxpayers of countries such as the U.S. or Germany are assumed to have less predisposition to evade taxes than those of some other countries. But as one tax expert has put it "Many years of experience in the Internal Revenue Service, the Board of Tax Appeals, and the Department of Justice have convinced me that the North American is not motivated in his compliant behavior by any love of taxes but, on the contrary, that he has a well-developed capacity for tax resistance." Similarly, a German survey found tax morality to be rather low in that country. Another study on tax psychology indicates that 47% of French farmers, 59% of industrialists and businessmen, and 61% of people in liberal professions think that tax evaders are justified. Some data on the behavior of Italian taxpayers give a hint of the extent of tax evasion in the country: in 1962 the number of voluntary declarations was 1,057,000. The tax authorities "discovered" a number of additional taxpayers which was more than the number declared so that the final number of taxpayers became 2.4 millions. This discovery together with the correction of the incomes reported changed the taxable income from 2 to 3 thousand billion lire.[12]

The survey by Vito Tanzi of personal income taxation in Latin America suggests that if the governments of the region abandoned their attempts to tax the incomes of most of the population, and instead zeroed in on the top 5 percent of income earners, they would generate higher revenues than at present if this high income class paid only an average of 20 percent of income in personal taxes.

Assuming that the government could impose a 20% average tax on the income of this 5% or progressive rates which would average to 20% for the whole group, it can be easily calculated that the revenues from the personal income tax as a share of total personal income could easily be in the range of 5 to 8 percent, which in relative terms would make the personal income tax in those countries more productive than that of Japan, France and Italy, and just about as productive as that of Germany, and slightly less productive than that of the U.S. and the U.K. . . . If 5% of the taxpayers pay most of the tax, why waste time in preventing evasion by the remaining 95%? Taxation is not directed as a mere exercise in civil discipline, but is directed to maintaining governmental solvency by providing sufficient funds to permit the government to carry out all the functions which are demanded of it. This, then, is the main point of the article: in order to have a productive personal income tax in

Latin America it is not at all necessary to tax 90% or even 40% of the population but it will be sufficient to focus on about 5% of it. The rest of the population will be reached anyway through the remaining sales taxes as well as through the social security charges which can be made to yield a surplus.[13]

iii

A faithful duplication of the Venezuelan personal income-tax sched-ules by the nations of the developing world would instantly free them from the bondage of the Laffer Curve's upper limits. A top rate of more than 25 percent is self-defeating. Such a reform would bring enor-mous benefits even to those nations that have partially broken from the top of the Curve and experienced high growth rates. Brazil is a prime example.

Brazil's economic growth in the past decade has been mildly spectac-ular, roughly a 100 percent increase in real per capita income to about $850 in 1976. But we would not call this an "economic miracle," any more than growth in Germany and Japan after World War II was miraculous. Moreover, the source of Brazilian growth has never been understood by the Brazilian government, a military regime that cannot find the path back to democratic rule precisely because it does not understand the nature of its successes.

As with Indira Gandhi's suspension of democratic rule in India in 1975, Brazil's expansion followed the overthrow of the civilian govern-ment of João Goulart in 1964. Goulart's error had been his attempt to maintain the exchange rate of the cruzeiro through fiscal rather than monetary policy. That is, to prevent the cruzeiro from falling *vis-à-vis* the U.S. dollar, high tariff walls were erected around Brazil so that Brazilians would be discouraged from exchanging cruzeiros for dollars in order to buy dollar imports. The autarchic rationale was that in so doing the internal economy would benefit by enabling infant indus-tries to develop behind the protective wall. The economy stagnated instead, and the cruzeiro tumbled anyway.

The military officers and technocrats who took over in 1964 ex-changed Goulart's serious errors for less serious ones and brought relief to the economy. They brought down the tariff walls to "force competition" on Brazilian industry and make it more efficient. This was the correct move for the wrong reason. The tariff cuts simply had the effect of bringing the economy down the Curve, as Brazilian workers and entrepreneurs could use their hard-earned cruzeiros to purchase desirable consumer goods from abroad and thus have added incentive to produce. Brazilian firms did not begin "competing" because a challenge was presented, but because rewards for production were presented.

This error of reasoning on the part of the government led to an error in policy. Thinking a lowering of tariffs would simply have the effect of bringing in imports to force competition, the policymakers decided there must also be a policy to promote exports. Not only were tax subsidies arranged for export items, but a green light was given to expansive monetary policies that would provide a steadily devaluing cruzeiro to make Brazilian exports more "competitive." This money illusion argument has ever since deluded the policymakers.

All the steady monetary expansion has accomplished is pure price inflation. Granted, the inflation of the Goulart era (76 percent in 1963, 82 percent in 1964) has been brought down to the 20-30 percent range in recent years. But had Brazil used its monetary instrument to peg the exchange rate, it could easily have avoided this useless inflation.

The inflation would have crippled the economy by pushing it up the Laffer Curve through the progressive tax system. Here again, the government offset one error with a partial correction. It indexed the tax rates, which prevented inflation from increasing the tax wedge. As the Latin America table indicates, the Brazilian personal income-tax schedules are relatively reasonable, with a 50 percent top bracket that bites above $50,000. But the government went too far, indexing wages, bonds, and contracts in the private sector that should have been left to the private sector to adjust. Nevertheless, on balance the indexing move was a positive one, and as the world went into general inflation with the breakdown of Bretton Woods, Brazil was shielded against its worst impact. As the rest of the industrial world contracted, Brazil's expansion proceeded into 1974 and 1975.

The logic of our economic model, remember, is that when one segment of the total economy is expanding and the rest is contracting, that part in contraction will import bonds from the expanding segment and export goods and services to it. This was exactly Brazil's experience in 1974-75. Its trade deficit mushroomed and its external debt grew apace. Believing this combination to be a sign of serious trouble instead of a reflection of economic growth, the government did what governments know they can do best: It threw a monkeywrench into the economy to slow it down. Its restrictions on capital flows inside the Brazilian economy were already tight—another major error of the technocrats in trying to direct the development of the economy. Now, in January, 1976, external capital controls were tightened. In addition, the trade walls that had brought the military regime to power in 1964 were erected once more. But instead of imposing tariffs, the government simply put down an import screen, with the argument that only essential imports would be allowed into the country. The net effect, predictably, was to snarl the economy in so much red tape that the expansion would end. The rest of the world would no longer be interested in exchanging financial capital for bonds, and Brazil would show an "improvement" in its trade and balance-of-payments accounts.

This scenario would not have been followed as readily if the $22 billion in external debt that frightened Brazil's technocrats in 1975 was private. But roughly 40 percent of it was public debt, arranged to finance government industry. Brazil since 1964, and even before, had gotten deeper and deeper into the ownership of industrial enterprise. Instead of allowing obsolete firms to expire, the government bought them, and as these became a drain on the resources of government, the government steadily became more ardent in its control and direction of capital flows. Today, almost all internally generated capital (savings) flows through the government. Private banking is trivial compared to the banking of government. As long as the Brazilian economy was growing, the misallocation of resources caused by this method of capital allocation could be blinked away. But in contraction, it not only piles up rapidly, but sticks out in red ink, and Brazil had to add $2.5 billion to its external *public* debt in 1976. This was the most visible installment of the price it will pay for the economic errors of January, 1976. How much Brazil was encouraged in this direction by its creditors, the private banks of New York and the public banks of the IMF, is beyond knowing. But there was at the time no critical comment of Brazil's moves from these quarters. It is not unreasonable to suspect that Brazil's private creditors were urging "austerity" on the government so that its bonds could be paid. This cannot be done so easily when the debt that private creditors hold in any economy is private debt, for there is a multitude of potential private borrowers as well as a multitude of private creditors.

Brazil's growth would resume if restraints on external trade and capital flows were removed. But that is only part of the solution.

From the beginning of its direct intervention in 1964, the military has struggled with the problem of finding acceptable civilian politicians who could win elections, and the freer the elections, the greater the difficulty. None of the authoritarian governments since 1964 has been able to win a viable majority in a truly open election. In 1970 President Medici, for example, whom many foreign and domestic observers regarded as very popular, presided over the most blatantly manipulated elections of the last decade. The overwhelming victories for ARENA (Alianca Renovadora Nacional) that year evidently convinced government strategists that they were at last beginning to find their long-sought civilian political base.

Subsequent elections, under freer conditions, shattered those illusions. The MDB's sweep (Movimento Democratico Brasileiro) in the November 1974 polling for the Congress startled even that party's most ebullient optimists. The prospects for the opposition seem equally bright over the next few years, even though the freedom of maneuver may not equal that of 1974, which included free access to television for the campaign. Then in 1978 will come the election of state governors, which is to be by direct popular vote, according to the constitution.[14]

The regime will not find the path to winning popular mandates until it is able to sort out what it has been doing under authoritarian rule, separating the errors from the correct actions. Unless, of course, the opposition has even less understanding of what the electorate desires. Capital controls, external and internal, must be removed. The government must avoid grandiose spending projects, like the Transamazon Highway, which should come only when private markets can support them. And this can happen much sooner than even the generals imagine, if the private capital market is permitted to flourish in an environment of lower personal income tax rates. The intellectual capital that now crowds around Rio and São Paulo would fan out into the vastness of the nation, developing the market of the impoverished northeast where 30 million Brazilians live as poorly as almost any people on earth. The minimum wage for labor, which does minimal damage in the metropoles, is probably the greatest single deterrent to development in the northeast; the party that champions an end to the national minimum wage for the northeast—or for Brazil, for that matter—will win its votes, we believe.

iv

If the breakdown of Bretton Woods caused one kind of problem for Brazil—a *relative* expansion that produced frightening trade and capital deficits—it produced far worse problems for Mexico. Mexico's tax structure was not indexed as it went through the dollar inflation of the 1970s. Mexico had, since the early 1950s, kept the peso rigidly fixed to the U.S. dollar at 12½ to the dollar. As dollar inflation proceeded and accelerated in the 1970s, pushing incomes into higher tax brackets and thereby increasing real tax rates, Mexico was dragged along. But Mexico's progressive tax structure, too steep to begin with for a nation realistically in development stage, did not get even the minor inflation corrections arranged in the United States in 1975 and 1976. As the table of Latin America tax liabilities indicates, Mexico's wedge is worse than the combined federal-state-city income tax bite on New York residents, even without taking into account the state income-tax rates in Mexico. These rise to as high as 30 percent in the state of Sonora. As economic distress followed inflation in the early 1970s, Mexico added to its problems by trying to manipulate trade and capital flows, both externally and internally.

Despite the considerable difficulties resulting from the demands of a developing economy, the officials of the present and preceding administrations have established as a principal economic goal the maintenance of a stable exchange rate, and have used a broad range of legal and administrative procedures in this effort, including . . . import controls, incentives for exporters and to new industries, substantial investments of public funds in the infrastructure of the country and other areas, as well as extensive price controls in an effort to limit internal inflationary tendencies.[15]

As the economy contracted in earnest in 1975 and 1976, the government hastened the process by borrowing faster and spending more to attempt stimulation of aggregate demand, raising the minimum wage by 22 percent, and increasing duties on about 3,000 tariff items. As of January 1, 1976, some 1,320 items were classed as "luxury" items subject to duties of 50 to 100 percent compared to 652 items previously. The 1 percent general additional tax on imports was increased to 2 percent.

The combined effect of these measures was to cause further contraction in Mexico and a fall in the demand for pesos that was not offset by government absorption of pesos. This forced, in September, 1976, the first peso devaluation in twenty-two years. In two stages, the value of the peso was cut by nearly 50 percent, to the rate of twenty to the dollar. The Mexican government debt that was denominated in pesos was thus effectively halved (at the expense of its creditors) and so was all private debt denominated in pesos. Debtors got windfall profits, creditors got windfall losses, this being the only real effect of devaluation, as all prices in pesos rose to adjust to the new monetary standard—a "nickel peso."

The price inflation, of course, pushed the Mexican work force up the Laffer Curve by forcing everyone into higher tax brackets. Had Mexico adjusted its tax rates drastically to offset the price inflation, it could have kept output from falling. But the Mexican politicians, who were encouraged in the devaluation by U.S. bankers and economists (including the U.S. Treasury), were not urged to adjust tax rates. Foreign creditors never urge a debtor nation to lower tax rates, but rather push them to boost rates. The effect of these errors was to shear away a sizable segment of the Mexican economy in order to restore general economic equilibrium.

Under the circumstances, Mexico's blessing was its border with the United States. The segment of the economy destroyed poured across the border: Entrepreneurial talent and financial capital exited by airplane and telegraph; peons slipped across the border as illegal aliens in search of employment. Had Mexico been an island, with no avenue of escape for these victims of economic error, surely there would have been civil rebellions before equilibrium was restored.

V

The Mexico scenario described here has been a feature of life in all of Latin America, except that in the rest of Latin America there is no border with the United States, and economic error with no escape valve leads to a breakdown of civil authority and military takeover to restore order.

There is very little room for economic error in most Third World countries. This is because whenever a slight contraction occurs, and the debt of the nation contracting begins to look shaky, its foreign bankers swarm in to the capital, nervous about the condition of their loans. If the Third World nation needs an extension of credit, the bankers demand a show of "austerity," which means an imposition of new taxes. What began as a small contraction thus becomes a major one. Peru is currently a classic example. Its crushingly progressive personal income-tax structure has steepened dramatically in the past four years, through devaluations and inflation. By now, the reader should be able to fully appreciate the following dispatch from Lima by Everett G. Martin of *The Wall Street Journal* on Sept. 1, 1977:

LIMA, Peru — "If you want to see what a worried international banker looks like, come to Lima," a local economist says. "They are either here now or they'll be here next week."

Teams from Bank of America, Citibank, Chase Manhattan and Morgan Guaranty have slipped in and out of the city. German bankers have been seen breakfasting at the Hotel Bolivar. Japanese from the Mitsui Bank are due early this month, and several other Japanese bank teams have already come and gone.

Once here, they all follow the same pattern. They make the rounds of local bankers, then knock on the door of whoever happens to be Peru's finance minister. They don't seem particularly happy or confident when they leave. One New York banker was heard to comment to a colleague, "But they haven't even got a plan, not even a plan."

Why are the bankers so concerned? In the past four years they have lent a lot of money to finance development projects of Peru's military leaders—probably in the neighborhood of $2.5 billion. Now Peru's economy is on the rocks, and they wonder whether they will have to pour in more loans to keep the country afloat so that it can continue to pay its debts.

A Key Condition

"We won't do that unless Peru comes to an agreement with the International Monetary Fund on a program to re-establish economic stability," declares a representative of a major U.S. bank. The IMF does lend money to countries having hard times, but first it insists on harsh recovery measures. Once the IMF approves a recovery program, bankers feel assured that additional loans won't go merely to perpetuate a messy situation.

There is no doubt that the situation is messy. Half the work force is underemployed. Prices rose 34% last year and may rise more than 50% this year. The country's international payments balance showed a deficit last year of about $500 million.

Despite the apparent need for help, the Peruvians have twice rebuffed an IMF negotiating team. . . . Peruvian President Francisco Morales Bermudez states emphatically that Peru has never defaulted on a debt and that it won't start now. Bankers who will comment accept him at his word, but they fear that Peru's unwillingness so far to accept a sound economic program could have repercussions throughout the debt-ridden underdeveloped countries of the so-called Third World.

Pattern of Resistance?

"The implications are scary," says one banker who worries that Peru's defiance of the IMF could even become a rallying point for the demands by some Third World countries that all debts of the poorest countries be canceled to inaugurate a new international economic order.

Commercial bank lending to the poorer countries has soared in recent years, reaching levels that have already generated fears about these nations' ability to repay their debts on schedule. In fact, the bankers have already had to refinance the debts of countries as diverse as Zaire and Argentina. And no quick end to such financial strains is in sight . . . .

The biggest problem for U.S. bankers, however, is here in Peru, a country that went on a borrowing binge in 1974-76 and now faces a severe test of its ability to meet debt payments.

How did such a mess get started?

Four years ago commercial banks were eagerly lending Peru money for just about any project the military could dream up. Peru looked like a no-lose situation because its Amazon jungle region was supposed to be practically one vast pool of oil just waiting to be tapped. "We expect Peru to be exporting a billion dollars worth of oil by 1980," a U.S. banker told a friend here then. Besides, new copper mines were about to start producing.

A Green Light

Experts from the IMF, the World Bank and the industrial countries told the Peruvians that between 1975 and 1977 they could easily handle $2.8 billion in new debt to spur economic development. Recalling the scene in Lima at the time, a local banker says: "Foreign bankers wanted to give us money before we asked for it. The Italians had lira for a dam. The French had francs for our steel mill."

The military obliged the project-hungry lenders by turning loose all 18 government departments to devise as many development plans as they could. Observers say they have never seen the lethargic Peruvian bureaucrats so efficient. They came up with 84 projects that they figured could absorb some $6 billion in loans, and they succeeded in getting enough loans—$3 billion worth—to finance 65 of those projects. The projects include hydroelectric dams, irrigation networks, tourist hotels, a copper refinery and plans to make paper out of sugar-cane waste.

Peru took on some 400 foreign creditors and its international debt expanded fivefold, to more than $5 billion, at least half of it owed to private banks. U.S. bankers alone lent a billion dollars to the junta. The Japanese lent half a billion.

Then Peru's luck ran out.

The jungle oil flow turned out to be only a trickle; oil exports will be small at best. And the world's recession knocked down the prices of Peru's other commodities, such as copper, sugar, cotton, lead, zinc and silver. Even the anchovies failed; the fish that made Peru the world's main exporter of fish meal for animal feed have largely disappeared from coastal waters....

But the prize for misapplied funds goes to the $750 million oil pipeline that reaches from the Amazon swamps to the Pacific by way of the Andes Mountains. "We never should have built it," an economist says. "We could have sold the oil to Brazil and earned foreign exchange instead of putting ourselves so deeply into debt." As a matter of pride, however, Peru wanted to use its own oil instead of trading it to Brazil and using income to get oil somewhere else....

What the IMF Wants

The IMF team, which is headed by American economist Linda Koenig, wants Peru to do two things before it will approve a standby credit of about $100 million, a credit that would be less important for its size than for its constituting an IMF seal of approval in the eyes of other bankers. First, the team wants the 1977 budget deficit held down, as an anti-inflationary measure. Second, it wants the value of Peru's currency, the sol, to be continually adjusted against the dollar by a series of mini-devaluations. That policy, which Peru did follow from June 1976 until lately, would tend to spur exports by lowering their price and discourage imports by raising theirs, while avoiding sudden sharp changes....[16]

As usual, we find the IMF economists prescribing slow poison for the Peruvian economy, unable to see that the current "mess" has been largely created by the steady devaluations of the sol interacting with both the personal and corporate tax systems.

In 1976, the sol was held at forty-five to the dollar. In January, 1977, it was sixty-five to the dollar. In September, 1977, it was eighty to the dollar. Here is what these changes did to the progressivity of corporate and personal tax rates:

On corporate taxes, the 30 percent bracket was reached at $2,222 in 1976, at $1,538 in January, 1977, and at $1,250 in September. The 55 percent bracket slid from $22 million to $15 million to $12 million. There is an additional 2 percent surtax on all corporate earnings.

On personal taxes, the 21 percent bracket was reached at $2,222 in 1976, at $1,538 in January, 1977, and at $1,250 in September. The 55 percent bracket slid from $111,000 to $76,923 to $62,500. The 52 percent bracket went from $22,000 to $15,000 to $12,000. The Latin America table on page 257 shows the liabilities for January, 1977, and as high as they are, they were considerably higher by the time Everett Martin wrote his dispatch from Lima in September.

It is hardly any wonder that the political leaders of Peru now resist the advice of the IMF. Peru's debt service now amounts to $700 million a year, which is 44 percent of the country's export earnings. They will of course take any IMF loans they can get in order to pay off the private banks. And the IMF has become a creature of the multinational banks, with IMF Director Johannes Witteveen advocating a multibillion dollar "facility" to "help" the Third World with its debt. The United States would pay $1.5 billion into this facility. The money would be loaned to the Peruvians, conditioned upon austerity, and Peru would hand the cash over to the private banks. The U.S. Congress could just as easily appropriate U.S. tax money and hand it directly over to Chase, Citibank, and the Bank of America.

vi

To the people of the Third World, this whipsawing of "infrastructure" loans, foreign debt, currency devaluations and taxation is more or less what lies behind the phrase "economic imperialism." The demand for debt moratoriums and a new international economic order—a clean slate—is a direct answer (which the creditor nations and banks will of course resist). The indirect answer is internal change in tax structures and development policies that can free intellectual resources and enable foreign debt to be repaid out of expanded output. For this to happen, the quality of economic advice being exported by the West to the Third World must sharply improve.

There are no doubt thousands of discrete theories on why the United States "lost" South Vietnam, and we would not dispute any of them. But events in Vietnam at least do not cut against the ideas expressed in this chapter, and in many ways fit the political and economic model in ways that have not heretofore been expressed.

The rupture of French colonial rule in Indochina, in July, 1954, was distinctly a function of economic exploitation by France finally outweighing French contributions to Indochina in language, commerce, law, education, and medicine. Time and again in the 1930s the Vietnamese peasants had rebelled against the French taxes levied both to finance projects the French thought good for Indochina and to redeem French loans to the region. After World War II, as Britain and the Netherlands made explicit plans to dismantle their colonial empires, France sought to reassert its hold on Indochina and encountered resistance in war by the Vietnamese nationalists, the Viet Minh. In nine years, the French spent 1.6 trillion francs in military and economic support of the war—twice the amount it received in Marshall Plan aid from the United States. The forces of history doomed France in any case, but the first distinct signal in our model that the end was in sight came on May 11, 1953, when France unilaterally devalued the piaster from seventeen to ten francs, thereby withdrawing its chief source of support to the domestic economy of Vietnam.

It was a psychological shock, because it seemed to imply that France was no longer either able or willing to carry the heavy costs of the Indochine War. Furthermore, since the devaluation of the piaster "took place after French financial and commercial interests had completed the transfer of their capital and activities to other parts of the world," Vietnamese nationalists concluded that the French in Indochinese business, and in particular the Bank of Indochina, no longer believed in a military solution of the conflict.[17]

There is no illusion in the electorate. With the devaluation of the piaster and the 50 percent rise in domestic prices that occurred literally in a matter of weeks, the Vietnamese had to immediately calculate upon the departure of France.

From 1954, when the Geneva Agreements divided Vietnam in two at the 17th parallel, communism and capitalism had this social laboratory for a test of strength. It was Ho Chi Minh and communism in the north and Ngo Dinh Diem and capitalism in the south. From 1954 through 1961, Diem was clearly in the lead. In 1955-56, indeed, there were times when it appeared Ho would lose the support of the people who had worshipped him in 1954.

Ho rushed to industrialize, and the Soviet Union and communist China aided this effort not only with material but with technicians to run the factories and train the North Vietnamese. At the same time he rushed to implement a land-reform program, in the process liquidating between 10,000 and 15,000 "rich" peasants—those who held claim to two or four acres of land instead of the prescribed one acre; between 50,000 and 100,000 were imprisoned or deported. Open rebellion took place in November, 1956 in reaction to these cruelties, and while the communists crushed the rebellion, killing perhaps a thousand peasants and imprisoning several thousand more, Ho was smart enough to know he had pushed too hard and was losing popular support. He publicly apologized for the "errors" of the land-reform program and halted the blood-letting in his own ranks.

Oddly enough, the conventional theory of why Diem began losing popular support after 1957 is that he was not bold enough in pressing land reform in the south. That is, he should have been more aggressive in expropriating the holdings of the landlords and distributing land free to the peasantry. But this is a static argument, which rests on the assumption that the contest between north and south was over which could be more egalitarian. U.S. critics of Diem, then and now, equate democracy with income redistribution, and assert that Diem could have won the minds and hearts of the people by taxing the haves in favor of the have-nots.*

Diem gave in to American pressure on land reform. Landlords were given 10 percent cash and 90 percent twelve-year bonds (which proved worthless) for holdings that were distributed at low cost to tenants. But as this solution did not seem to win Diem much affection, the Americans argued that Diem was not expropriating fast enough. In January, 1962, *The New York Times*—the loudest voice for "social reform" of South Vietnam in the United States—editorialized:

Large land holdings have been divided and redistributed to small proprietors. Rural standards of living have been substantially increased and are much higher than in Communist North Vietnam.

Curiously, however, these considerable accomplishments have not greatly enhanced esteem for the identification with the Government among the peasantry. The new farmer proprietors no longer remember that they got their land at a knocked-down price under Government auspices. They only recall that they now have to pay annual installments on its cost to the Government, even though these installments are low. Peasant attitudes are attributable, in part, to effective Communist propaganda and the perversities of human nature. But they are also due to governmental inefficiencies, in some cases to unpopular local officials, to poor Government propaganda and information programs, and to the general aloofness of the regime and its failure to establish sufficient rapport with the people.[18]

---

* Buttinger, whose *Vietnam: A Dragon Embattled* has become one of the most authoritative and comprehensive accounts of the period, makes this static argument in exhaustive detail. pp. 917-1,010. Land reform as a "solution" preoccupied American advisers to Vietnam up to the end of the war in 1974.

Diem's problem with the communists was in the countryside, but the solution was in the cities, the central marketplaces. For the peasants, who trade their crops for the goods and services of the cities, land rents loom as a greater burden when the price of city goods and services rises. They diminish as a burden when the price of city goods and services falls. The price of city goods and services thus had to fall to solve the countryside problem, and this of course required economic growth and commercial expansion in the metropoles.

Unhappily, Diem had left in place the nominally high tax rates imposed by the French during the colonial days. The tax code was festooned with steeply progressive personal income taxes—rising to 70 percent at $20,000, with an additional 24 percent surcharge on dividend income—plus business and consumption taxes of all manner and variety. These yielded very low revenues, but because the government did insist upon collecting them when they became visible, they stood as a barrier to commerce. Their worst aspect was that they invited corruption. Government workers had to pay the taxes, being the most visible to the government. The best positioned government officials were then able to recompense themselves and their aides by extorting bribes from businessmen and entrepreneurs, who had to avoid confiscatory tax rates in order to remain in business.

When hostilities ended in 1954, the economy of South Vietnam expanded fairly rapidly despite the tax system. This was because major efficiencies were possible simply because hostilities had ended. Minor road or bridge repairs alone could bring increases in productivity. Crops came to market instead of being burned by war. But after these one-time efficiencies were absorbed by the economy, it became clear there was something wrong with the structure of the economy. It was not growing fast enough. In 1960, a team of economists from Michigan State University went to Saigon to survey the economy, with the perfectly correct starting assumption that "for the long-run, accelerated economic growth may be the crucial factor contributing to a solution of the security problem."[19]

The economists found that a significant portion of the profits being generated by the South Vietnamese economy were not being reinvested in the economy, but were instead being placed in foreign accounts simply to earn interest. The U.S. economists, though, did not see that it was the high tax rates that were discouraging commerce and investment in the metropoles:

The prime requisite for a satisfactory rate of growth in Vietnam is an increase in the share of investment in the national output. The first step in this direction is to limit consumption so that resources may be released from the production of consumer goods and devoted to capital formation. I believe it is possible to do so. Current living standards in Viet Nam, while not generous, compare favorably to those of other economically underdeveloped countries of Asia. There appears to be some room to reduce consumption. The only effective way to limit consumption, short of complete direct controls, is by vigorously enforcing an effective tax system. This is not the place for a comprehensive analysis of Viet Nam's tax system. But it is apparent that Viet Nam's tax system, which relies heavily on import duties, cannot effectively control domestic consumption. Moreover, taxation as an instrument of control, is inhibited by ineffective and capricious enforcement procedures. It is imperative that the tax system and the tax administration be reorganized. There is no other way, in a free society, to control consumption in a reasonable and equitable fashion.[20]

The Michigan group for the most part wanted expanded tax reveilues to go into industrial expansion. But there were also U.S. advisers who wanted tax revenues to expand so that Diem could go directly after the minds and hearts of the people by giving them good things—like land, schools, hospitals, and social services. The upshot was new taxes for both objectives, as reported in *The New York Times* of January 5, 1962:

U.S. GIVING SAIGON NEW ECONOMIC AID IN FIGHT ON REDS
11- Point Plan Seeks to Raise Living Levels
Vietnam to Alter Tax System

BY MAX FRANKEL

Washington, Jan. 4 — The United States and South Vietnam announced today a "broad economic and social program" to raise living standards in South Vietnam.

The eleven-point plan, covering expanded efforts in public health, education and agriculture and industrial development, was the subject of a joint communiqué issued here and in Saigon.

The program was explained by State Department officials here as an effort to demonstrate Washington's faith in the future of a free South Vietnam, to complement substantial increases in military aid, and to enhance the popularity of President Ngo Dinh Diem.

United States sources said they could not yet estimate the cost of the development program, but they expressed confidence that non-military aid to South Vietnam would rise "appreciably" above last year's total of $136,000,000. The cost of military assistance is secret.

The development efforts are to be financed by the Vietnamese government with the help of new funds being raised through an austerity import duty and tax system . . . .

By agreement between the two governments, priority is to be given to imports "required to meet the needs of the people" and to develop Vietnam's infant industries. Luxury goods will be the most severely taxed . . . .

As a condition of pouring more military equipment and manpower into South Vietnam, Washington has been demanding that President Ngo Dinh Diem adopt forthright measures that would persuade his peasant people that he, more than the Communists, could offer not only security but also substantial material benefits.

In addition, the United States has wanted the President to adopt administrative reforms permitting younger officials a greater voice in Vietnamese affairs and giving local army commanders a freer hand in the conduct of war against guerillas . . . .

The development program is an outgrowth of a study made last summer by a joint committee under the leadership of Prof. Vu Quoc Thuc of South Vietnam and Dr. Eugene A. Staley, a Stanford Research Institute economist.

The Staley mission did not envision specific projects as much as it sought ways of helping South Vietnam develop a financial plan to make them possible.

After further consultations through the fall, financial changes were finally worked out and announced in Saigon last weekend. Their purpose is to adjust the flow of imports toward the most needed goods and to raise additional revenues for development and national defense.

The official exchange rate will be held to thirty-five piasters to the dollar.

The Saigon Government announced a new basic import levy, to be called the "economic development and national defense surtax" at roughly twenty-five piasters to a dollar of value. A further import duty is to be placed against all goods except those defined as necessities and still another duty, called an austerity tax, will be imposed on goods defined as luxuries. The South Vietnam government also will establish a special budget for economic development and it has raised the ceiling on government borrowing from 25 to 40 percent of budget receipts, which now run at about 15,000,000,000 piasters.

The new revenues thus raised from taxes, increased United States aid, and Government borrowing will be channeled into the eleven areas specified in today's communique.[21]

Up to this point, Diem had been holding his own. The economy had not been booming, but it had not been contracting either. Now, it went into contraction. The 71 percent tax on "luxury" goods, which covered most consumer goods, and the tax on foreign-exchange—an indirect tariff on literally all imports, sent prices up in the cities, which meant a decline in the purchasing power of country goods. The military situation began eroding almost immediately.

One of the conditions of U.S. aid to Saigon was that all funds be spent on American goods. This diminished the value of the aid to Saigon, which was thus forced to buy the most expensive goods and pay the longest shipping charges. As the economy contracted in the spring of 1962, Diem pleaded for relief from the "Buy American" rule. A small story on page 6 of *The New York Times* of June 20, 1962 speaks volumes:

SAIGON, Vietnam, June 19—South Vietnam's plea for relief from the "Buy American" policy was caused by Government concern over business stagnation and the first budget deficit in the regime's history.

South Vietnam complains that some United States goods are too expensive, notably industrial machinery and fertilizer, and that shipping costs are excessive.

Saigon wants to buy industrial machines and fertilizer from Japan and other goods from Hong Kong. But both Japan and Hong Kong are among the nineteen countries barred as sources of imports to countries using United States aid dollars.

Vietnamese economists expect the deficit to approach 4,900,000,000 piasters ($68,000,000). American observers regard this estimate as too high but concede that a deficit of 2,000,000,000 or 3,000,000,000 piasters is likely at the end of the calendar year. American observers say the economic stagnation is due not only to the high prices of imports but also to a deteriorating military situation, which prevents the flow of goods to rural consumers, and to a new Government tax on foreign exchange transactions.[22]

On August 19, 1962, the last nail was driven into the domestic economy of South Vietnam:

SAIGON, Vietnam. Aug. 19 — South Vietnam is ready to embark on a large-scale program of deficit financing to help pay for the increasingly costly struggle against Communist insurgency.

This was disclosed today by high United States officials here. They hailed the development as a heartening policy change that would shift the economy of the Southeast Asian country from peacetime to wartime footing.

The new policy is expected to inflate prices . . . .

It was explained that the Government of South Vietnam for its part had undertaken new measures to increase its tax revenues to support its budget. But United States sources said that deficit financing would be necessary for at least two years.

Americans here observed that economists generally agreed that a certain degree of inflation, if kept under control, was desirable for an underdeveloped country. It was termed a stimulant to business.[23]

The sharp economic contraction of 1962 led Diem to increase his authoritarian attempts to regain control, seeing no other solution and by now understandably wary of the advice of his American counselors. But the accumulating social tensions of an economy in sharp contraction grew to explosive force and could not be contained in authoritarian hands without massive blood-letting, and this was no option at all.

On June 11, 1963, an elderly monk, Thich Quang Duc, protested against Catholic "persecution" of Buddhists by burning himself to death in a public square. The persecution was not really religious, but a reflection of the economic contraction. Racial, religious, and ethnic differences are always magnified during a sharp contraction, when a smaller "pie" must be redistributed. Diem, a Catholic, had given Catholics a marginally superior position to defend themselves against redistribution by having them disproportionately weighted in the bureaucracy. The Buddhist crisis of 1963 brought an end to Diem's political support in the Kennedy Administration—which itself had begun the chain reaction in January, 1962, by threatening to withhold military aid unless Diem accepted its tax spending ideas.

President Kennedy explicitly withdrew support from Diem, which meant to the Saigon military that American aid would be ended unless Diem were removed. The generals paid this price by assassinating Diem on November 1, 1963. On November 22, President Kennedy was assassinated. For another decade, Presidents Johnson and Nixon tried by brute force to salvage Vietnam, and a succession of South Vietnam generals installed as presidents of the country followed their advice by enacting more and more social reforms. But nobody ever suggested pulling the internal tax rates down from the top of the Laffer Curve. Instead, inflation pushed them higher and higher, until by the end of the war the 70 percent bracket was encountered at less than $5,000.

CHAPTER 12

Experiment in Puerto Rico

Tracing the political/economic path of Puerto Rico from 1898 to the present. Not a colony, not a nation, not a state. A puzzle for the electorate.

The economic laboratory: A common monetary policy with the United States; a totally separate fiscal system. A tax "haven" at the top of the Laffer Curve.

This book was written as a direct result of a trip to Puerto Rico in March, 1976. The general theory of global political economy described here had been ripening prior to that date, but its flowering occurred decisively with exposure to the political and economic history of Puerto Rico—the catalyst being the island's uniqueness in both the political and economic realms. It is not a sovereign nation, not a state of a federation, not a colony of a nation, but a "Commonwealth" in free association with the United States. Its people are citizens of the United States but as long as they reside on the island do not vote for the President of the United States and have no voting representation in the U.S. Congress. Since 1898, when its colonial status under Spain ended as an outcome of the Spanish-American War, its electorate has been patiently, glacially sorting out political leaders in an apparent historic drive toward statehood. Commonwealth has been one of several way stations in this long drive, a pilgrimage that illuminated and thereby helped crystallize the political model for us.

This political movement has been glacial because of the enormous economic complexities that have cropped up by accident or plan during the eighty years of evolution. Surely the electorate sees the path to statehood, but its task has been to find political leaders on both the island and mainland discerning enough to extract this blueprint, even a piece at a time. These economic complexities, which stand as barriers to statehood, provide startling illumination of our economic model. Since 1900, the island has been inside the U.S. tariff wall, and so there has been no international wedge between island and mainland to stand as a confusing variable in the separate economies. And Puerto Rico has no central bank of its own, no separate monetary authority. Its money is the money of the United States and the monetary policy of the United States serves as the monetary policy of Puerto Rico. Thus, another potentially confusing variable is removed from our examination of the Puerto Rican economy in relation to that of the States. The most important distinction, though, is that throughout this eighty-year relationship, the people of Puerto Rico have been absolved of all Federal taxes. The reason is that taxation without representation is tyranny. Puerto Rico thus has its own domestic fiscal system, enabling us to trace its economic path along that one variable.

This fiscal system, in fact, has been the puzzle and obstacle for the electorate in the drive toward statehood. Because it is explicitly absolved of Federal taxes, but enjoys the benefits of customs' union with the United States, it is never clear that a change to "taxation with representation" would be a bargain. Imagine the son of a wealthy man who is told that if he lives at home he will get all the benefits and allowances of the household, but must observe several strict rules laid down by the father. If the son leaves, he is cut off entirely.

The terms seem fair enough, but they are ultimately demoralizing to the son, who is betwixt and between, not taxed but not represented, knowing independence will mean relative impoverishment, staying on in the household through his thirtieth, fortieth, eightieth year anticipating that something will happen to himself, to his father, or to both that will bring resolution. Either independence or cemented union.

It was clear enough in the earliest years that it was a relief to Puerto Rico to be rescued from the impoverishment of Spanish dominion and adopted by the nearby, wealthy Uncle Sam. Not that the United States showered wealth on the island, but life under Spanish rule—manageable during the mid-nineteenth century—had become miserable as the century ended.

Before the end of the Spanish regime . . . important changes in the economic organization of the Island were occurring. The area devoted to food crops was apparently declining before 1898 and Puerto Rico imported a considerable fraction of the food stuffs it consumed. . . . Over 70 percent of the customs duties collected by the government were levied on imported foods, and in addition there were heavy excise taxes on provisions.

Undernourishment among the common people was apparently chronic, and anemia, the result primarily of hookworm, was so common as almost to justify the claim that it was universal. The diet of the *jíbaro*, or mountaineer, was criticized by Spanish and Island writers as both inadequate and unbalanced. Writing in 1887 a distinguished local physician declared that the nourishment which the great majority of the country people received was so scanty that it scarcely sufficed to replace organized waste, and not infrequently provisions were of such bad quality that their use should have been prohibited.[1]

Being brought inside the U.S. tariff wall was of immediate benefit to the island, but far more important was the first, beneficial fruit of the newly paternalistic United States. As harsh a critic of U.S. "imperialism" in Puerto Rico as Gordon Lewis could write of the early years,

The American people have rarely ignored an open appeal to their generosity and they have given of it willingly, even to the point of wasteful prodigality. The Puerto Rican plight, as it was brought to their attention by journalists and publicists after 1898, did not fail of response on their part. The work of voluntary associations during the thirty years after 1900 was of real and lasting value. The San Juan Presbyterian Hospital became a byword in the Puerto Rican household, and its professional standards were rewarded with the honor of being the first hospital in the West Indies to win accreditation from the American College of Surgeons. The Board of Presbyterian Missions introduced, in the form of the San German Polytechnic Institute, the characteristically American phenomenon of the privately endowed college. The major activity of the American Red Cross inaugurated, and especially through its Public Health Nursing Program, the use of the trained nurse in insular medical organization. The Rockefeller Foundation spent a small fortune in combating such diseases as hookworm and malaria. And Columbia University undertook in collaboration with the University of Puerto Rico, the planned rehabilitation of the island's educational system . . . the reduction in the rate of illiteracy by roughly one half of its appalling 1900 level within one generation, to take one example only, was evidence of the new concepts of public health and public administration propagated by the new regime.[2]

Paternalism, though, went beyond charity relief, college endowments, education, health, and mission services. Until 1917, the island's political status was purely colonial. "Citizens of Puerto Rico" could elect only the lower house of the legislature. The governor was appointed by the President, as was the upper house of the legislature. And unlike Hawaii, there was no provision in the law that the appointed governor had to be a citizen of the island. The President of the United States, too, could veto any Puerto Rican legislation, even that which might pass by a two-thirds majority over his appointed governor's veto.

Chafing under these restraints, the lower house could only attempt to force its will by refusing to pass appropriation bills unless the governor granted political concessions. Because of these frictions, Congress in 1917 gave way by at least conferring U.S. citizenship on the islanders, and a new organic law was passed, delineating Puerto Rican rights and obligations. In this law was the first serious economic setback to the island, the so-called 500-Acre Law. This prohibited corporate ownership of more than 500 acres of agricultural land.

Here was the same kind of well-intentioned paternalism that afflicted U.S. policy toward Vietnam. That is, the notion of small farms being the foundation of democratic capitalism leading to an authoritarian decision to fracture large farms, along with their economies of scale. By acting as a tax wedge against land ownership, it inadvertently diminished the value of land and increased the relative burden of explicit land taxes. It also discouraged the development of proficient entrepreneurs capable of assembling large farms (just as, in Vietnam, land reform dispossessed the shrewdest businessmen in every farm region, who would then migrate to the cities, leaving the countryside bereft of the cream of its leadership). The 500-Acre Law temporarily arrested the development of the island, less so as in time it was enforced less and less.

An even worse and enduring blow to the island came in 1920 with passage by the U.S. Congress of the Merchant Marine Act, a law that burdens Puerto Rico to this day. This coastwise shipping act prohibits goods from being shipped by water in foreign-owned or built vessels between points on the coast of the United States.

The act was of course not purposely aimed at Puerto Rico, but was meant rather as protection for the U.S. merchant fleet. But more than anything else done by Congress it has arrested the economic development of Puerto Rico. At the time of its enactment, it almost canceled out the advantage Puerto Rico felt by being inside the U.S. tariff wall. The rates charged by American ships were then higher than rates charged by foreign ships, and over the years the differential has grown. Even in 1930, Cuba could import rice from Asia in foreign bottoms at the same price it could be brought from Louisiana in American bottoms. And Cuba, which faced a tariff of 1.75 cents per pound of sugar at the U.S. border could, by shipping in foreign freighters, compete against Puerto Rican sugar, which did not face the tariff.

Over the years economists would add up by simple arithmetic the added dollar cost to Puerto Rican commerce as a result of this shipping differential. In 1976 the direct cost was about $60 million. But this was the smallest cost. If foreign ships coming to the island with goods could pick up Puerto Rican goods for shipment to the mainland, far more traffic would have been generated in Puerto Rico, with island agricultural and industrial entrepreneurs looking to global markets rather than being dominated entirely by the United States. Cumulatively, the legislation has no doubt cost the island billions of dollars of national income, and at the same time forced Puerto Ricans to leave the island for work on the mainland to escape this barrier to commerce.

That is, if a widget plant could be set up in Puerto Rico for sales to the mainland and the world, without this burden of transportation costs, Puerto Ricans would not have to move to the mainland to man it.

The twenties were boom years in the United States, as Mellon and Coolidge worked the economy down the Laffer Curve. But Puerto Rico could not get going. In a report of 1930 by the Brookings Institution, the decade is summed up admirably:

Ever since 1921 Puerto Rico's financial history has been marked by rising public expenditures, increased taxes, and a mounting public debt. During recent years, indeed, Puerto Rico's debt has included borrowing to cover a deficit in current funds, and, on a few occasions, the government has been unable to meet payrolls and other urgent bills when due.

Two conditions help to explain the readiness of the Island to strain its credit and revenue resources. The first was the psychological effect of the sudden unprecedented rise of sugar and tobacco prices after the war. For a few seasons, plantation corporations made great profits, and wages rose to two and three times their former level. . . . The authorities hastened to make hay while the sun shone, hopefully prognosticating a long spell of sunny weather, and to capture for local use as large a share as possible of the corporation profits that were speeding out of the Island. In this mood they started programs of public improvement and a campaign of public expenditure all along the line that, though desirable in their purpose, called for appropriations much larger than any in the previous experience of the Island. The second condition was the obvious need for numerous additional public improvements and services, such as roads, hospitals and schools. Continental leaders and Island leaders were equally ambitious to place Puerto Rico as nearly on a par as possible in these respects with the rest of the country.

The ambitions of the government resulted in a conflict with corporation and other taxpayers which precipitated a crisis in government finances. This followed the collapse of business prosperity in 1921 and was the natural result of the continuation of the policy of increasing the tax burden during a period of depression. The corporation taxpayers had little interest in the expansion program of the government and at this time became actively antagonistic. They initiated legal proceedings which were temporarily successful in enjoining tax collections to an aggregate amount of several million dollars. A new Governor, unfamiliar with conditions and evidently unassisted by competent financial advisers, approved a budget which produced a deficit of five million. Subsequent budgets were balanced and gradually the floating debt due to the deficit was being extinguished when conditions were again thrown into some confusion by the hurricane of 1928.[3]

The Puerto Rican progressive tax on personal income was introduced in 1913, on the heels of its enactment on the mainland. During the war, though, as the mainland pushed rates up skyhigh to assist in war finance, the island rates remained nominal. But in 1921, then again in 1924, the island administration became more aggressive in use of the income tax to gain revenues for their ambitious spending projects, just as on the mainland, Coolidge was going in the opposite direction. On the eve of the Stock Market Crash of 1929, here is a comparison of the tax systems. Observe that in every case the burden is higher, if only a bit, in Puerto Rico:

Kind of Tax	P.R.Law	Federal Law
Personal Income		
Normal Tax:		
Exemptions— Single	$1,000	$1,500
Married	2,500	3,500
Per dependent	400	400
Nonresidents	None	1,500
Rates— Residents:		
First $4,000	2%	1½% above exemptions
Second $4,000	4	3 above exemptions
Above $8,000	6	5 above exemptions
Nonresidents	6	5 above exemptions
Surtax:		
On net above $10,000, at varying rates beginning with		
1% of the first $4,000 up to	25%	20% above $100,000
Deduction for earned income		
¼ of the tax on incomes up		
to a maximum of	$10,000	$30,000
Corporate Income		
Exemption of $3,000 only if net income is under (other-		
wise no exemption)	$10,000	$25,000
Rate	12½%	12½%
Partnership Income	Same as corp. tax	Taxed to partners as individuals
Distribution of		
partnership profits	Subject to surtax	No tax

Source: Victor S. Clark et al., *Porto Rico and its Problems* (Washington, D.C.: Brookings Institution, 1930), p. 201.

With rates uniformly higher than the mainland, receipts as a percentage of income were lower. The economy could be maintained on agricultural exports, being inside the U.S. tariff wall. But the tariff advantage meant nothing to agricultural development for domestic consumption. Given the combination of personal, corporate, and partnership tax rates, it was then and now unprofitable for entrepreneurs to assemble enterprises that could collect, transport, and market locally grown foodstuffs in competition with imports. It was never clear to politicians in Puerto Rico that the problem lay in unnecessarily high tax rates. Occasionally, though, the relationship between tax rates and revenues would be so direct and immediate that the effects of the Laffer Curve were obvious:

During the past crop [sic] the South Porto Rico Sugar Company did not import cane from Santa Domingo which represented a decrease in revenue from Customs receipts of approximately $250,000. No doubt, this attitude of the said sugar corporation was due to the increase in the tariff rate on sugar cane from $1 to $2.50 per ton, which it is alleged is prohibitive.[4]

In the Depression of the 1930s, Puerto Rico suffered with the rest of the world, but its shelter inside the high Smoot-Hawley tariff wall was now an even greater advantage in relative terms. More importantly, in terms of *relative advantage*, was the fact that when Hoover and Roosevelt successively increased tax rates on the mainland during the 1930s—on a large scale making the mistakes Puerto Rico had made in the early 1920s—Puerto Rican tax rates remained stationary. Now, there were relative advantages to doing business in Puerto Rico and these showed themselves in the gradual expansion of the needlework industry. The garment trades had grown throughout the 1920s, the export value rising from $107,000 in 1920 to $15 million in 1929. Expansion continued into the 1930s and by 1938 nearly 60,000 Puerto Ricans were directly employed in the trade, with exports exceeding $20 million. But in 1938 came a severe blow to this industry and Puerto Rico from the New Deal: The Fair Labor Standards Act, establishing a minimum wage of twenty-five cents per hour in manufacturing. At that time in Puerto Rico the skilled wage in the building trades was twenty-five cents per hour, the average needlework wage being half that. The 1940 report of Puerto Rican Tresasurer Manuel H. Domenech tells the story:

Although there seems to be good reason for believing that the enforcement of the Fair Labor Standards Act has been conducive in improving conditions and in increasing the purchasing power of labor groups in certain lines of industrial activity, there is little doubt that as a whole the federal legislation has affected adversely the general economy of the Island on account of its effect on the needlework industry.

Qualified economists maintain that the needlework industry of Puerto Rico is unable to pay the minimum wage stipulated by the law and still operate at a profit. The enforcement of this legislation resulted in mass shutdowns in needlework factories; and qualified estimates point out a figure of 40,000 unemployed needleworkers affecting directly around 80,000 persons on the Island. The amendment of last June, providing for a special committee to recommend the minimum wage to be paid to employees in Puerto Rico is a prospective palliative of the serious problem created by the enforcement of this federal legislation, but it is thought that the amendment will not change the present situation fundamentally.[5]

Enter Luis Muñoz Marín, who was to become the first elected governor of the Territory of Puerto Rico in 1948 and governor under Commonwealth from 1952 to 1965. In 1939, when he was forty-one years old, Muñoz bolted the socialist party and formed the Popular Democratic Party (PDP). As a radical socialist in the 1920s, he yearned for independence for Puerto Rico, and in 1939 his aim was still to lead Puerto Rico to nationhood. But he had in the 1930s become friendly with mainland Democrats and liberals, including the Roosevelts, and his idea of independence had been tempered.

"It was then that my passion for independence became outweighed by my passion for social justice," he recalled. "I became conscious, as I came in closer contact with the *jibaros* (peasants), that although I still believed in independence, the masses of the people of Puerto Rico did not. The masses of people followed me because of my ideas of social justice; if they were doubtful about me, it was because of the independence idea."

"Social justice" for the PDP in 1939-40 was crystallized into an economic program of three points. First, legislation to protect workers in their right to organize for collective bargaining. Second, enforcement of the land law, which prohibited ownership of more than 500 acres; the law had not been enforced for decades. Thirdly, and of immediate importance at the time, a minimum-wage differential for Puerto Rico. . . . The Muñoz plan was to win flexibility on this point from the Democrats in Washington.

This plan, plus eventual independence, was the PDP program he explained to a group of 30 sugar-cane workers in early 1939. "I told them: 'Other politicians have lied to you, and I may be lying to you also. But I want you to take a chance that I am not. And after all, conditions are so bad now that they cannot get worse.' But then," Muñoz went on, "one worker spoke up and said, 'But what about . . .' and drew a finger across his throat. By that I knew he had in mind my idea of independence, that things not only could get worse, but . . ." and Muñoz drew a finger across his throat . . . "if we broke from the United States. From that point on I told the people that I would not consider their votes for independence or for statehood. Political status would not be an issue in 1940, only the program."

In the closing days of the campaign came his master stroke. "We had no money to buy votes, and I argued that even if we did we would not buy votes. But you could not just ask people not to sell their votes. You had to stand for something that was worth more.

"In those days radio advertising did not cost much, only $30 for half hour, and we had $30." At a rally in San Juan, broadcast over the island of 2½ million people, he assembled all the candidates of the PDP, read his program of social justice, and had all the candidates raise their hands to swear an oath that if elected they would vote for it.

The *jibaros* did not sell their votes. And while the PDP did not win a plurality, they won sufficient seats to control the legislature. And the electoral chemistry not only pushed Muñoz away from independence toward commonwealth, but also moved him a step toward capitalism.

"When you are the party in opposition," Muñoz observed, "you can afford to be the party that demands redistribution of wealth. But as we became the party of government, we had to give more room to the idea of growth, so there would be more to distribute. It was in those days that I began to say that if you had to distribute a loaf of bread among many people on the basis of social justice, you will see all the people will starve. You must create a bakery, distribute as much as you can from it."[6]

Muñoz won his minimum-wage differential from Washington, an arrangement that permitted Puerto Ricans to set different minimums for different trades in a way that would cause minimum damage to the economy. This differential was the foundation for Puerto Rico's economic expansion in the decades that followed. Without it, the rest of what came to be called "Operation Bootstrap" could not have gotten off the ground. Officially, though, the centerpiece of Operation Bootstrap—which Muñoz created with the aid of economist Teodoro Moscoso—was a ten year holiday from taxes on corporate profits for new industry that located on the island. A quarter century later, an economist could report:

> The growth rate of total and per capita output in Puerto Rico since 1940 has been one of the highest in the world. Real GNP per capita rose at an average rate of 4.1 percent a year during the forties and 5.2 percent a year during the fifties. In 1954 dollars, per capita GNP rose from $269 in 1940 to $673 in 1961 (to $743 in 1965). . . .
>
> While the industrialization program has attracted widest public attention, economic progress has been general. Food production has risen at a rate which has permitted Puerto Rico to maintain about the same degree of self-sufficiency despite much higher income levels. This degree is quite low, however, only about 40 percent of Puerto Rican food consumption coming from domestic sources. . . . Manufacturing rose from 12 percent of total output in 1940 to 23 percent in 1962, while agriculture dropped from 32 percent to 13 percent. . . .
>
> Manufacturing development has been stimulated by legislation granting manufacturers of products not produced in Puerto Rico in 1947 full exemption from both income and property taxes for periods ranging from ten to seventeen years, depending on the part of the island in which the plant is located; by a wage level which in the late forties was only about one quarter of that in mainland manufacturing plants. . . . Since 1947 about 1,300 EDA-sponsored manufacturing plants have been established in the island, the great majority being branch plants of mainland companies. The failure rate among these new establishments has been about one-third, but 910 of them were still in operation at the end of 1963, with a total employment of about 70,000 workers, or one-tenth of the island's labor force.[7]

Muñoz was by no means flawless, however. He did not run for re-election as governor in 1964, and neither he nor his successors realized that errors he made early in his leadership of the PDP were now catching up with Puerto Rico and would soon smother many of his successes. One of the problems, which Muñoz no doubt foresaw, was that organized labor in the United States—the motive force behind the minimum wage—would apply increasing pressure on Congress to take away the "unfair competition" of "cheap labor" in Puerto Rico by narrowing the differential. In 1964-65, the leeway permitted Puerto Rico was sharply reduced (and in 1974 tightened almost to the vanishing point).

The unforeseen problem lay in the progressive income tax. In 1941, in the interests of promoting "social justice," the PDP had increased the progressivity of the income tax. The normal tax was put up to 7 percent and the highest marginal surtax to 40 percent on $94,000. This partially negated the beneficial aspects of the minimum-wage differential, but the rates were still far below the mainland's. In 1942, with Puerto Rico joining in the war effort, there was excuse to increase the progressivity again, needlessly, to 72 percent at $200,000 along with an additional 5 percent "Victory Tax" that is still being collected in 1977.

In the mid-1960s, the economy began to lose momentum, and the political leadership of Puerto Rico was oblivious to the shift in tax rates that had begun to cut against the island. As the Kennedy tax-rate cuts on personal and corporate incomes were phased in on the mainland, tax-rates there dropped below the Puerto Rican rates. For example, the 70 percent bracket was now encountered at $100,000 in the United States, at $60,000 in Puerto Rico. A second adjustment on personal rates in 1969 in the United States cut against Puerto Rico again. Now, the top marginal rate on "earned" income—wage and salary income as opposed to investment income—would be 50 percent in the United States. Prospective enterprises that had looked to Puerto Rico for lower minimum wages for workers and higher after-tax earnings for managers and technicians could see both advantages melting away.

Another problem in the personal tax structure cropped up. In the United States, since 1949, husbands and working wives could file joint returns or separate returns, after calculating which method offered the lower tax liability. Puerto Rico never made the change, which meant that married couples were required to file a joint return. A manager earning $32,000 would be in the 58 percent bracket and have a liability of $11,844. If he married a teacher earning $12,000 whose liability was $2,604, their joint income would subject them to a liability of $19,152. This is $4,704 higher than the liability for the same incomes at separate returns. The way the couple would have to look at this situation is that the wife's $12,000 income carried a tax liability of $7,308, a discouragement to her working and a discouragement to their remaining in Puerto Rico, given the mobility offered by mainland citizenship.

Another element of the island tax structure that is worth mentioning at this point is the nature of estate and gift taxes. The rates were and are steeply progressive after the first $60,000 is exempted, rising to 70 percent at $6 million. But that is not the worst part. In Puerto Rico, unlike the United States, an individual cannot deduct charitable contributions from gross income. This naturally discourages giving and private solutions to social distress, forcing public solutions with taxpayer funds. It also removes an incentive to wealth accumulation, for if an income earner cannot dispose of part of his wealth to recipients of his own choosing, except by giving after-tax dollars, he is merely accumulating an estate for the state to confiscate. It is one less reason to work, or to work and live in Puerto Rico if you are an individual with the energy and talent to accumulate wealth.

Another difference that works against growth in Puerto Rico is in gifting to members of your family. In the United States, an individual with wealth can pass some of his capital to his children by giving them the best education that money can buy. The total cost of increasing their intellectual capital is naturally subtracted from the dollar amount of his estate and is not taxed. In Puerto Rico, a parent can only gift each child $500 per year including tuition in private school; costs above $500 are subject to progressive gift tax. The conscious design is to prevent the wealthy from evading estate taxes by using financial capital to expand their childrens' intellectual capital. The actual effect is to deny Puerto Rico the use of existing intellectual capital as well as the development of future intellectual capital. The strictures encourage the most talented and energetic Puerto Ricans, on the margin, to migrate elsewhere and at the same time the provisions represent a heavy toll on the bridge from the mainland, discouraging talented and energetic continentals from moving to Puerto Rico to participate in the operation of enterprises.

Statistically, Puerto Rico continued to show "real growth" after 1967 to 1972. But even the slower statistical advance was misleadingly optimistic, and it is highly unlikely that there has been anything but contraction of the real economy. The political successors to Muñoz, sensing the contraction, the souring of the economy in the mid-1960s—and unable to see that it was due to the collapse of the tax advantages—frantically pursued a Keynesian course of bond illusion. In the following decade, the government floated roughly $6 billion in bonds to expand public investments, largely throwing money away by expanding infrastructure and bureaucracy. "Real" per capita income, as measured by the government economists, was thus ballooned. And while the bond finance was expanding current output, the expanding debt burden loomed as a foreshadowing of a future output decline.

And all the while dollar inflation was intensifying the problem for Puerto Rico. For while inflation was pushing the U.S. economy into higher real rates of taxation, it was pushing Puerto Rico faster into higher tax rates. This is because U.S. progressive schedules became less steep as a result of the Kennedy tax cuts of 1964. When the international monetary system blew apart in 1971-73, even continued massive deficit finance by Puerto Rico could not prop up an illusion of real growth. The unemployment rate, which had always been roughly twice as high in Puerto Rico as on the mainland—10 percent when the U.S. rate was 5 percent, 12 percent when the U.S. rate was 6 percent— followed the same path when the U.S. unemployment rate hit almost 10 percent in 1975. The Puerto Rican unemployment rate went to 19.9 percent in August of 1975. Even this number understated the problem:

It should be clearly understood that these rates are calculated by the standard method and therefore, in the case of Puerto Rico, grossly understate our true employment deficiency. The standard method counts as unemployed only those who are actively looking for work, not "discouraged workers" or others who would enter the labor force under more favorable economic conditions.

In Puerto Rico, because of economic conditions, only 42% of the population 14 years and over participates in the labor force, by working or looking for work, compared to 60% in the U.S. If our participation rates were as high as yours on the mainland, our unemployment rate would be around 45% ! ![8]

This astonishing number—only 42 percent of the population 14 years and over participates in the labor force—is of course a measure of the relative unimportance of the money economy in Puerto Rico compared to the United States. The wedge that discourages husbands and wives from working in the money economy by requiring a joint return no doubt accounts for a good part of the difference. But the tax rates themselves do most of the work of promoting barter economics. Even the officially working economy "works" less than it does in the United States. Vacation periods are longer as workers see little sense in bargaining for higher wages, most of which would go to the government in taxes. And the electorate as a whole promotes more and more religious and national holidays.

Not all of this extra "leisure" goes strictly into leisure. The myth of that "lazy Latin" is largely a function of the tax wedge and not the tropical heat. Workers simply use vacations in the money economy to moonlight in the barter economy, trading a lower level of their skills in the market because they can keep more of their less efficient production. In Jamaica, where the tax wedge is among the greatest in the hemisphere, political leaders are forever carping against the laziness and lack of productivity of Jamaican citizens. But Venezuelans and Bermudans, who have the narrowest tax wedges in the hemisphere and the same tropical sun, have no such complaints about their energetic and acquisitive citizens. There is scarcely a sign of poverty in Bermuda, which is—next to Hong Kong—the most densely populated place on earth. With no personal income tax at all in Bermuda, many citizens work two jobs *in the money economy.*

In Puerto Rico, the souring economy went into a tailspin along with that of the United States in the autumn of 1974. But one ingredient of the U.S. political system saved it from the even worse contraction experienced in Puerto Rico. In the fall of 1974, the same American economists who were advising President Gerald R. Ford to increase taxes to fight inflation were advising Governor Rafael Hernandez Colon of Puerto Rico to do the same—that is, the same economic school of thought. President Ford proposed a 5 percent surtax on personal incomes as a result of the advice he received at his Economic Summit Meeting in September, 1974 (even as the stock market was plumeting below 600 DJI). Governor Hernandez Colon also proposed a 5 percent surtax on Puerto Rican incomes, which the islanders immediately dubbed *"La Vampirita,"* or "Little Vampire."

In the United States, there are national elections every two years, and in November, 1974 the Republicans, carrying the burden of Ford's *"Vampirita"* lost three dozen seats in the House of Representatives. In the days immediately following the GOP debacle, White House Chief of Staff Donald Rumsfeld was persuaded by Laffer that the correct policy was tax reduction, not tax increase. It was for Rumsfeld's assistant, Richard Cheney, that Laffer drew his Curve for the first time on the back of a paper napkin in the Two Continents Restaurant a block from the White House. The stock market stopped its decline and began a serious advance in December, 1974 with the first hints that Ford was turning on tax policy. And while the "tax cuts" announced by Ford in February were inefficiently designed by the administration's conservative Keynesians, it made a great deal of difference to the economy that there would be some movement down the Laffer Curve instead of a leap upwards.

In Puerto Rico, there are national elections every four years, and there was no way for the electorate to advise Hernandez Colon that his 5 percent *Vampirita* was precisely the wrong prescription. The legislature, controlled by his party—the Popular Democrats, pushed the tax through and the electorate had to wait until November, 1976 to expel this political party that had controlled the legislature since 1940. In the meantime, the market for Puerto Rican bonds collapsed, the unemployment rate went above 20 percent and stayed there even as the U.S. unemployment rate inched back to the 7 percent level. In asking special relief from the U.S. Congress, Hernandez Colon had no clue that his problem lay in the "responsible" advice he had assiduously followed:

Present market conditions indicate that it will be very difficult to sell over $200 million in bonds yearly for the next several years, instead of $600 million or more which we borrowed in former years. This in turn will mean a reduction of government undertakings such as public buildings, schools, roads, and other facilities needed for development, and will further curtail our already severely depressed construction industry.

This reduction in borrowing capacity has taken place despite the fact that the Puerto Rican government, by increasing ta es 20% and reducing expenditures 18% last year, has achieved a balancec budget. Moreover, financial leaders in both the United States and Puerto Rico have praised the responsible and energetic management of Puerto Rico's fiscal affairs.[9]

The relief Hernandez Colon was asking of Congress was a new organic compact with the United States, one that would permit Puerto Rico to escape minimum-wage requirements and the disadvantages of the coastwise shipping act. But the compact he proposed would also move Puerto Rico toward independence and away from statehood by freeing the island from these and other aspects of U.S. law. The statehood party, the New Progressive Party, vigorously opposed this compact.

The degree of legislative freedom enjoyed by Puerto Rico had, during the contraction of the 1970s, worked against the economy. The Popular Democratic Party that had been created by Muñoz turned to early New Deal ideas of central planning as it wrested with decline. Wage and price controls were instituted, the sugar, telephone, and shipping industries were nationalized, and in 1976 and 1977 sugar subsidies alone drained the taxpayers of $400 million in present and future taxes. The government tried to turn the Government Development Bank into a central bank that could allocate virtually all credit.

None of these things were done in the name of "socialism" and the people immediately surrounding Hernandez Colon could hardly be termed "leftists." They were, rather, technocrats who believed that the disarray they saw around them was the private maketplace breaking down, and that their duty was to substitute state capitalism. One could hardly blame them for not trying to do their best. Had not Hernandez Colon appointed the Committee to study Puerto Rico's Finances in 1974? Were these radicals: James Tobin, Sterling Professor of Economics, Yale University; William Donaldson, dean, School of Organization and Management, Yale University; Kermit Gordon, president, The Brookings Institution; Wilfred Lewis, executive director, National Planning Association; Sidney Robbins, professor of finance, Columbia

University Graduate School of Business; William Treiber, consultant, Federal Reserve Board of New York? Does their report of December 11, 1975 not sound conservative and prudent?

> Capital expenditures by the government and by public enterprises have been financed by debt issues, and now that the volume of debt issues is limited it is inevitable that marginal investment projects will be cancelled or post-poned. The line of least resistance will be to absorb the whole burden of austerity in reduced investment. We urge you not to follow so short-sighted a policy. Public and private consumption should give way, not investment for Puerto Rico's future. Economic progress in Puerto Rico and the promise of a better life for the people require investment in both public and private sectors. Puerto Rico must generate internal saving to finance this investment, especial-ly now that external finance is limited.[10]

Behind these sober sounding words is the same old message. Puerto Rico needs infrastructure, public investment, and now that nobody will lend Puerto Rico more money for such projects, Puerto Rico must generate more internal savings. *La Vampirita* was born and raised at Yale and its damage was done in Puerto Rico. Here is more of Professor Tobin's advice to Governor Hernandez Colon:

> Our fiscal projections . . . assume that tax revenues will grow as economic recovery proceeds and that the tax increase of 1974-75 will remain in force. The fiscal outlook for the next few years is a compelling reason for accomplishing some further much needed improvements in the tax system.
>
> First, land and real property should be taxed on realistic market appraisals, with the substantial exemptions of residences eliminated. This reform would make the tax system more equitable as well as more productive of revenue. We recognize, of course, that so far-reaching a reform must be phased in gradually, but now is an opportune time to adopt the necessary legislation and schedule.
>
> Second, the yield of the income tax can and should be further increased by tighter enforcement and collection. We recognize the progress the Treasury has already made and urge that its efforts be continued and strengthened. Here too equity, as well as revenue, is at stake.
>
> Third, the government should consider further taxes on consumer durables, especially luxuries. For automobiles, graduated registration fees could supple-ment excises in curbing the importation of large cars, with poor gasoline mileage, which seem particularly inappropriate for Puerto Rico today.[11]

This is bad enough, but the report itself goes much further, repeating again and again the observation that for some reason the people of Puerto Rico tend to consume more and save less of what they produce than other people, and that this tendency must be counteracted by state enforcement of saving, i.e., enforcement of existing tax law and passage of new taxes to discourage consumption.

> . . . the special income tax deduction currently permitted for interest paid on taxpayers' personal indebtedness is hard to justify on any grounds. It subsi-

dizes dissaving, it reduces public revenue, and it is quite possibly regressive since richer people pay higher marginal tax rates and are also more sophisticated in filling out tax returns. This deduction, probably never justifiable, is less so now than ever. It should be removed.[12]

By embracing this poisonous set of ideas, concocted by mainland wise men, the Popular Democratic Party in 1976 lost its mandate. Instead of looking to the people for wisdom and guidance, as their founder had, the party of Muñoz Marín looked to an elite for answers which they could impose on the people. A Taoist sage put it neatly twenty-five hundred years ago: "The difficulty in governing the people arises from their having too much knowledge. He who tries to govern a state by his wisdom is a scourge to it, while he who does not do so is a blessing.[13]

In the 1976 elections, as a Democrat replaced a Republican in the White House by a narrow margin, the old Republican Party in Puerto Rico—its name changed to the New Progressive Party (NPP) years ago—not only captured the governor's office, but also both houses of the legislature. The party had returned to power after thirty-six years. It could not have done so without a political leader able to read the electorate's wishes better than Hernandez Colon. It had such a leader in Carlos Romero Barcelo, the mayor of San Juan.

As Muñoz Marín's passion for independence led him to a winning political path in 1940, Romero Barcelo's passion for Puerto Rican statehood was the driving force behind his quest for political power. And just as Muñoz Marín put the independence issue aside in 1940, sensing the masses were not with him on that point, Romero Barcelo in 1976 explicitly put aside the statehood issue, announcing that he would not count a NPP victory at the polls as a mandate for statehood, but rather a mandate for his program.

His program? A return of the nationalized industries to private ownership. An end to price controls. An end to *La Vampirita*, the 5 percent surtax on personal incomes. An end to the requirement that husbands and wives file joint tax returns. The PDP and Hernandez Colon were plastered as the party of high taxes. Documents indicating the government was planning to follow through on the Tobin Report were leaked to Romero Barcelo and advertised—the most damaging document being the tentative plan to end the income-tax deduction for interest on a taxpayer's personal indebtedness. Romero Barcelo offered his party as a tax-cutting party.

In losing, the technocrats of the PDP privately blamed the absence of moral fiber in the people of the island; their refusal to stand still for the austerity plan that the wise men and bankers in New York said was necessary. Had not, they argued, Puerto Rican bonds strengthened in the financial markets in 1977? Was this not a delayed payoff to the austerity plan of the previous years?

No. The strengthening of Puerto Rico's credit in the financial markets tracked with Romero Barcelo's strength in the political market. *La Vampirita* ended in January, 1977.

Tax reform that would not only set Puerto Rico on a path to sustained growth but also on a path to statehood was, through the summer of 1977, debated inside the Romero Barcelo administration. But according to the economic model, the reforms suggest themselves.

In 1975 the total revenue of the government of Puerto Rico was $1,501,819,000. Of that total, $12,256,000—less than 1 percent—was collected in estate and gift taxes. Considering the fact that the taxpayers are propping up the sugar industry with $300 million a year in present and future taxes, outright elimination of all estate and gift taxes would be no great burden to the treasury. But it would hardly be necessary to go that far. An exemption of estates up to $150,000 and a flat 15 percent tax above that amount would produce revenues immediately, and over time produce far more revenues from this source than the present rates would. In other words, the revenue track would be raised far into the future as individuals would now have an incentive to build estates in Puerto Rico. The rationale of the government in adopting this reform should not be to attract the wealthy retired to the island, although that too will occur. The rationale should be based on an internal dynamic, one that gives the citizens of Puerto Rico incentive to accumulate wealth on the island, removing the present incentive for emigration of Puerto Rican human and financial capital. It never seems to have occurred to the authors of the Tobin Report that the reason Puerto Ricans seem to save less of their incomes than other people has nothing to do with racial or genetic inferiority. Puerto Ricans simply smuggle their capital to Florida to escape confiscation by gift and estate taxes. There is thus a statistical illusion: Floridians seem to save more than other Americans; Puerto Ricans seem to save less.

Even if a lowering of the gift and estate tax rates to a flat 15 percent produced lower revenues immediately, the bond market would gladly finance this, realizing the revenue path has tilted upward into the future. This is one of the mistakes made by Uruguay, when it flatly removed personal income and gift and estate taxes entirely. The revenue path for the economy as a whole may have tilted upward, as economic expansion brought expanded revenues from business, excise, and tariff sources, but it is not clear that this is so. Low rates of 10 or 15 percent would have made the future revenue sources clearer.

So, too, with Puerto Rico's personal income tax system. In 1975, the system yielded $323,929,000, almost 22 percent of the total. The rates ranged from 15.75 percent at $2,000 to 40.95 percent at $16,000 to 68.25 percent at $60,000 to 82.95 percent at $200,000. Had the government in that year cut the top rates so that the highest bracket was 48 percent, the treasury would have expected a loss of less than $12 million. Again, this is less than 1 percent of revenues. In this case, it was immediately obvious to Romero Barcelo's secretary of the treasury, Julio Cesar Perez, in a conversation with the author, that the treasury would not lose $12 million, but would gain several times that amount. Tax evasion, after all, is rampant in these brackets. It does no good to crack down on evasion, as the Tobin Report urges, for the more successful the crackdown in the 60 to 70 percent brackets, the faster these remaining people of talent and energy will leave Puerto Rico. By lowering the top rate to 48 percent on the first go-round, evaders who are paying no tax on much of their income will choose to pay 48 percent on some of it. Of course this is not the only beneficial effect on revenues.

In addition to the people in Puerto Rico who are now working and evading taxes on their income, literally the entire island is not producing some level of output because of the high rates. A lowering of the high rates on personal incomes would galvanize *local* entrepreneurial talent, as opposed to the Muñoz idea of tax havens to attract foreign capital. A lowering of the top bracket to, say, 48 percent on all income, and an adjustment of all brackets by 20 or 30 percent on the first go-round would easily produce as much revenue from personal income tax and all other sources as the present rates. But even if they did not, it is clear the revenue path would be tilted upward far into the future, which means if there is a shortfall in first-year revenues, the bond market, either internal or external, would finance the shortfall.

The legacy of Keynes is so powerful, though, that politicians who would not hesitate to spend $500 million in borrowed funds to build "infrastructure," when then they are so advised by Yale, Harvard, and the International Monetary Fund, balk at the notion of cutting $12 million from revenues as a means of expanding the economy and revenues. A good deal of this occurs because political leaders are surrounded by bureaucrats who are in the business of expanding public enterprise. Bureaucrats lose relative power and influence (and rewards) when economic policy promotes private sector expansion. The international banks also tend to discourage solutions that seem to mean an immediate decline in government revenue, for the bankers are first and foremost eager to expand revenues in countries like Puerto Rico in order to have their debt serviced.

A restructuring of Puerto Rican tax rates along the lines mentioned here would bring the economy down the Curve. It would make it easier for the economy to pay off public debt, and raise the value of all financial assets in Puerto Rico. For this reason, government sale of public enterprises back to the private sector—the sugar, shipping, and telephone interests—should follow, not precede, tax restructuring.

The three greatest economic barriers to Puerto Rican statehood have been the structural devices created by Muñoz in the early 1940s to solve the economic problems of the time: the minimum-wage differential, the ten-year tax exemption for corporate enterprise, and the progressive tax structure. It is not entirely coincidental that such measures were created by a political mind attuned to independence. For Romero Barcelo, who is attuned to statehood, the structural devices arranged by Muñoz have to be removed at the same time new structures are created, structures compatible with statehood. He sees, of course, that as a state Puerto Rico could not retain any semblance of minimum-wage differentials or tax-haven status. Nor would it be possible to have a Puerto Rican state with a "local" personal income-tax structure rising to almost 83 percent in the highest bracket, when the highest combination of local personal income taxes in the fifty states is in New York City at 20 percent.

His point of attack, though, must be at the only one of the three Muñoz devices that acted to move the island economy to the top of the Laffer Curve. In the economic expansion that would follow, the minimum-wage differential and tax-haven benefits could be stripped away with little adverse impact on the economy. Along this path, statehood would be possible within a decade.

The question of statehood, though, is of secondary importance. Puerto Rico's problem of stunted growth is, at bottom, the problem of the entire underdeveloped world. It is only easier to see in Puerto Rico because of the island's unique relationship to the United States—its common currency, common market, and separate tax structure. Jamaica's problem is precisely Puerto Rico's, but more desperate because of political failure. Jamaica is a democracy, but there has been no Carlos Romero Barcelo to offer an alternative to the redistributive rule of Prime Minister Michael Manley, and Jamaica drifts closer and closer to the ideas of Fidel Castro on Cuba. Castro, in turn, was the only relief to the Cuban electorate, which had been kept smothered in taxes to service the bank debts accumulated by dictator Fulgencio Battista. Panama is on this same track too, its citizens ground by taxes to pay off infrastructure loans peddled by Nelson and David Rockefeller on the well-meaning advice of the Council on Foreign Relations. The motives, after all, cannot be doubted. The Rockefellers and the forces they represented correctly saw that the antidote to communism was economic growth. Their error lay in seeing foreign aid, which meant loans and taxes, as the instrument of growth. Here, too, it's clear they could easily have been fooled by the effects of the Marshall Plan for Western Europe after World War II, seeing the Plan, not Ludwig Erhard's tax reforms, as the source of European expansion.

Karl Marx observed this process more than a century ago, correctly seeing the debilitating effects of capital's quest for a "vent for surplus" as Britain's capitalists sold railroads to the poor countries. Marx's alternative was collectivism. In Puerto Rico, at least, Romero Barcelo promises to try another.

The alternative was expressed two hundred years ago by Marx's Gemini twin, Adam Smith, in the closing pages of *The Wealth of Nations:*

The territorial acquisitions of the East India company, the undoubted right of the crown, that is, of the state and people of Great Britain, might be rendered another source of revenue more abundant, perhaps, than all those already mentioned. Those countries are represented as more fertile, more extensive; and, in proportion to their extent, much richer and more populous than Great Britain. In order to draw a great revenue from them, it would not probably be necessary, to introduce any new system of taxation into countries which are already sufficiently and more than sufficiently taxed. It might, perhaps, be more proper to lighten, than to aggravate, the burden of those unfortunate countries, and to endeavor to draw a revenue from them, not by imposing new taxes, but by preventing the embezzlement and misapplication of the greater part of those which they already pay.[14]

CHAPTER 13

Energy in Abundance

The earth's crust is layered with hydrocarbons—petroleum, coal and natural gas—and for all practical purposes the supply into the distant future is inexhaustible. Throughout history, energy "shortages" were perceived by political leaders who simply did not know how to find the energy trapped beneath their feet. Frederick Barbarossa created a political environment that encouraged exploration for natural resources, but his legacy afflicts most of the world with an obsolete framework. Thomas Jefferson's superior framework was responsible for making the United States a land of energy "plenty." The energy crisis of the 1970s resulted from a breakdown of the international monetary system. In the generations ahead, energy abundance will follow Third World abandonment of the Barbarossa model and adoption of the Jeffersonian method. Synfuels are unneeded.

There has never been a shortage of energy on earth. Certainly the planet is not energy "scarce" now, nor will it be at the end of the century—or at the end of the next thousand centuries. The planet itself is a ball of energy that rides in a sea of energy. Earth has been absorbing energy from the sun for the billions of years of its existence. The sun's energy has nurtured plant life, which thus captured and preserved energy in the form of coal and gas. The plant life also nurtured animal life, thus preserving energy that now exists in the form of petroleum and gas. In this sense, the human species now warms itself with sunbeams that were cast millions, if not billions of years ago, and have been locked in the earth's crust for eons, waiting to be found and tapped. The earth's crust is layered with solar energy—petroleum, coal and natural gas—only the tiniest fraction of which has been discovered by man. The notion that these deposits of organic hydrocarbons are "exhaustible" is correct only in the sense that they may be depleted some millions of years from now. Indeed, it can be argued that at present, there are more organic hydrocarbons being formed than are being consumed by the entire world population. That is, the plants and animals that inhabit the oceans, lakes and swamps are dying, decaying, and being absorbed as methane into these waters and the icecaps at a faster rate than mankind is now burning coal, oil and gas. Of course, we do not at the moment have the technology to tap this hydrosphere methane economically. But hundreds or thousands of years from now, when the more easily exploited hydrocarbons have been diminished, our descendants will have the technology to extract ocean methane economically, if it is necessary to do so.

It may not be necessary, though. Recently, scientists have been postulating that there is an abundance of inorganic natural gas on earth.[1] One theory is that gas is produced during routine mountain building as the earth's crust shifts and is reshaped; the thesis is that oxygen-poor igneous rocks reduce, under pressure and high temperatures, into methane. Another theory that has been gaining ground among geophysicists is that gas was trapped in the earth's interior as the planet was first being formed, the source being the great amount of methane of the solar system. The implication is that, for all practical purposes, the supply of inorganic gas is inexhaustible, that as gas pockets are depleted, they will be refilled by the vast "bubble" of methane beneath the earth's crust.

The world now consumes about 22 billion barrels of oil a year and roughly 50 trillion cubic feet of natural gas, which is the equivalent of about 8.5 billion barrels of oil. That sounds like a lot, and it is easy to imagine that we are sucking the planet dry, irresponsibly. But it is relatively a tiny amount.

Liquid petroleum that comes from a man-made hole in the ground under its own pressure constitutes only one percent of all the oil in the earth's crust. The rest is "heavy," the shales and tar sands that are more difficult, thus more costly, to extract. If we were to take all the liquid petroleum produced from all the wells on earth since the first, at Titusville, Pennsylvania, in 1859, and poured it into a lake the size of Chicago, roughly 227 square miles, the 330 billion barrels yielded by the earth through 1978 would fill the lake to a depth of only 300 feet.[2] At the time, the estimated worldwide sources of petroleum that could be recovered at current prices and technology would fill the lake to a depth of 2,300 feet. At a United Nations conference in Austria in 1976, the Moscow Academy of Sciences was represented by scientists Nesterov and Salmanov, who estimated the crude-oil resource base at about 12 trillion barrels; at current rates of consumption this would last several centuries. By counting the hydrosphere gases—the natural gas dissolved in the oceans, icecaps, rivers, lakes and swamps—they estimate that the planet contains something like 350 billion trillion cubic feet of natural gas, enough to last 20 million years.[3]

While we can say that there is literally no shortage of energy and that the planet is soaked with it, there does appear throughout human history a lapse in the ability of mankind to find and exploit this enormous energy pool. To use an exaggerated metaphor, we can imagine thousands of Eskimos, over the millennia, freezing to death within the 400-square-mile area of the Alaska North Slope. They surely thought there was an energy shortage while a few feet below them sat the biggest oilfield ever discovered in the United States. In the same way, there was an "energy shortage" in the world of the 1970s, a temporary lapse in the ability of mankind to tap into the energy pool that lay beneath its feet. A world-renowned oilman and geologist, Michael T. Halbouty, put it this way: "There is no shortage of energy anywhere on earth that has not been caused by government." This puts it in a negative cast. Halbouty could say as well that there is no shortage of energy anywhere on earth that could not be solved by government.

Again, throughout the history of civilization the human species has struggled to find political forms, *governments,* that increase the chances of survival through efficient exploitation of the planet's physical re- sources. After the invention of fire, energy was always less of a political problem than food, because the forests could be tapped for firewood, and almost everywhere the populations were small enough to allow reforestation to occur naturally. Trees sprouted and grew faster than they were being cut for firewood. Where population growth overtook photo- synthesis, the failure of the political order resulted in energy shortages. There were no doubt energy-forced migrations and wars thousands of years ago over Middle Eastern deserts.

The two political figures who have had more to do with energy exploitation than anyone else over the last thousand years, with a legacy that extends into the current period, are Frederick Barbarossa, Holy Roman Emperor in the twelfth century, and Thomas Jefferson.

Until Barbarossa's reign, the exploitation of minerals in feudal Europe was confounded by a confusion in law.

When feudal tenure was strong the lord claimed all mineral rights in his land, and mined the deposits with his serfs. Ecclesiastical properties made similar claims, and used serfs or hired miners to exhume valuable deposits from their land. Frederick Barbarossa decreed that the sovereign was sole proprietor of all minerals in the soil, and that these could be worked only by firms under state control. This reassumption of the "regalian right" usual under the Roman emperors became the law of medieval Germany. In England the crown claimed all silver and gold deposits; baser metals could be mined by the landowner on payment of a "royal-ty" to the king.[4]

The decision was, in its time, enormously successful. It ended the insecurity of the patent, but more importantly put mineral properties under the protection of the Crown. It was thus an important step out of the Dark Ages. But what was a good thing for the twelfth century is clearly obsolete in the twentieth century, yet it clings to Europe and most of the world that Europe once colonized as a barrier to energy development. Thomas Jefferson had an idea that bettered Barbarossa's.

Ever since the birth of the republic there had been two main attitudes toward the Western lands. Hamilton and his friends, eager for the rapid growth of manufacturers and for a society of the conventional European type, wished to retard the settlement of the West until the East was fully populated and its potential wealth fully exploited. They thought the federal lands should be sold sparingly, in large units, and at a high price. Democrats like Jefferson and Gallatin, on the other hand, felt that the health and liberty of the country depended on creating a maximum of agricultural freeholders; they thought the federal lands should be made available to any genuine settler, at a price which would not discourage the pioneer. Each group attracted selfish interests: some manufacturers, fearing that wages must rise if the discontented had a place to refuge, wanted the lands withheld; some speculators, confident of their own ability to get the better of farmers and pioneers, wanted the lands offered cheaply and in large quantities. In spite of such camp followers, however, this division on policy was simply another form of the honest and deep division, symbolized by Hamilton and Jefferson, throughout American life.[5]

On this issue, though, the Jefferson idea dominated, at least up until the Civil War. The United States government did not hoard land in the name of the collective interest, but sold the majority of western lands at $1.25 an acre, to encourage settlement. And instead of the "sovereign" retaining mineral rights, the settlers were given patent to these as well. The territories that became states after the Civil War were more heavily influenced by the Hamiltonian idea, with a result that a high percentage of the far-western lands has been hoarded by the collective interest, with mineral rights held by the sovereign in the Barbarossa pattern. The United States government, for example, owns almost 90 percent of Nevada's 110,000 square miles.

The remarkable effect of Jefferson's populist vision was the rapid development of the American oil industry after 1859 and the dominance of American oil-drilling technology down to the present day.

"Oil is found in abundance only if a great many people are looking for it at once in all sorts of unlikely places," Ruth Sheldon Knowles wrote twenty years ago in her history of the American oil industry, *The Greatest Gamblers*.[6] That insight is vital to understanding why there are energy problems in the world today. It is not just that insufficient numbers of people are looking for oil and gas in the United States. It is that too few people are looking for oil and gas all over the world, because most foreign governments discourage exploration in unlikely places. For the most part they do so unwittingly, still trapped in the framework designed by Frederick Barbarossa almost a thousand years ago.

In the United States, because of Jefferson, landowners have possessed the mineral rights to oil discovered on their property. The indigenous exploration industry could develop here, because individual explorers could lease the mineral rights from private landowners and drill, with the sure knowledge that the explorer and the landowner would possess any oil discovered, and that the high risk might yield high reward.

In 122 years, about 3.3 million oil wells have been drilled into the planet's crust. Of this number, 2.5 million were drilled in the forty-eight continental states of the United States, and most of these in the "oil patch," as oilmen refer to the oil-producing Southern states. The rest of the world has been relatively unexplored, especially former colonial nations of Africa and Asia. The United States was the only former colony that, upon achieving independence, abandoned the Barbarossa model. In all other former colonies of Britain, France, Germany, Spain, Italy, Portugal and Holland, the new independent nations carried on as before, retaining the mineral rights instead of selling them or deeding them to the citizenry.

Of the 645,500 exploratory wells drilled on earth by the end of 1975, 616,000, or 95.4 percent, were drilled in the industrial countries.[7] Africa, Latin America, South and Southeast Asia, and China have been barely touched. The United States accounts for 482,000 of the exploration wells, 74.7 percent of the total, and 34.9 percent of the oil in that imaginary Chicago lake of oil. The reason is not simply that the United States has had the skilled manpower, technology, capital, and market, but that it has had policies conducive to exploration and a stable government that has protected the property rights of its private landowners.

C. John Miller, a modern American wildcatter, president of the Independent Petroleum Association of America, captures the essence of the industry's development against this background:

In the cumulative effort of tens of thousands of explorers, successes ranged from abject failure to extraordinary success. The unusually successful became today's multinational oil companies such as Exxon, Texaco, Gulf, Mobil and Standard of California. Each began as a very small enterprise. Each established its first production on privately owned lands, where the petroleum beneath was owned privately, rather than by government. It is unlikely that these companies would ever have started had it been necessary to negotiate with the government for acreage on which to drill.

Under this policy of private ownership, what was the greatest stimulus for the growth of the U.S. oil industry to its present colossal size, consisting of thousands of competitive business entities, small, medium and large? Undoubtedly, the motivating force was people left free not only to own, but to explore and produce, to risk making a profit or suffering a loss. Typical of such people was a man named Patillo Higgins, a town character in the sleepy Texas village of

Beaumont at the turn of the century. Higgins, who had but one arm, became obsessed with drilling for oil on a big mound outside Beaumont. He became a laughing stock, because no less an authority than the United States Geological Survey had declared no oil would ever be found in that part of Texas. But Higgins persevered, and in 1901 two men from Pittsburgh drilled a well on Higgins' big mound, now known to be a giant salt dome. The well at world-famous Spindeltop flowed 100,000 barrels daily and was the beginning of today's Gulf Oil Corporation.

The experience of Patillo Higgins was repeated thousands of times by other visionaries with dreams they would not abandon. If free men like Higgins were the impetus for building the vast U.S. oil industry, who were the beneficiaries? Untold millions have benefited from the wealth created by the production of oil and gas. Cities and towns came into existence and thrived because of oil. But the largest beneficiaries by far, have been the governments of the United States and of the principal petroleum states who have collected petroleum-related taxes, royalties and other revenues amounting to hundreds of billions of dollars.

Had the U.S. government retained ownership of all mineral resources, it is doubtful that even a small fraction of its petroleum wealth would ever have been produced. Governments are neither inspired nor motivated by impossible dreams as are the Patillo Higginses of the world. Governments are constricted by bureaucracies and inhibited by accountability. Private ownership of energy and mineral resources built the United States into the world's wealthiest and most productive society.

The same forces, given an opportunity, could today produce the same kind of economic revolution in country after country where great sedimentary basins holding unlimited promise for energy production lie neglected, challenging no entrepreneur, offering no reward, no enticement to the curious or the hopeful. Many such countries could become petroleum self-sufficient by reforms which would confer the ownership of energy to private landowners who, reacting to the economic promise of such ownership, would inspire an era of entrepreneurial activity matching, on a global scale, that which made the United States the greatest energy-producing nation on the planet.

The key to energy sufficiency for many Third World countries is as simple as implementing true reform, conferring upon ordinary citizens the rights to own, to buy and to sell land and the mineral rights lying thereunder. Such reforms would give rise to a first generation of entrepreneurs eager to reproduce the experience of Patillo Higgins on a global scale.[8]

What Miller is saying, of course, is that, because the correct political conditions existed in the United States, the manpower, technology, capital and market emerged here. Oil exploration in the rest of the world until very recently was almost exclusively done by Americans, certainly by technology developed by Americans. In 1954, there were roughly twenty thousand independent oil companies in the United States, a number that halved by the 1970s, after two decades of government regulatory intervention that discouraged domestic exploration. The number in 1981 was back to fifteen thousand. By contrast, there are not more than five hundred companies in the rest of the world, with one United Nations estimate of only fifty public and private oil companies in all of Western Europe. The conventional view of Western Europe is that it is the Old World, tired, used up. In reality, it is virgin territory; a mere fifty thousand wells have been drilled in all of Europe. The Soviet Union, ironically, is much more heavily explored, for the simple reason that the sovereign owns all property, on the ground and below the ground. The central government need not negotiate with landowners or drilling contractors, a laborious process that impedes the development of Western Europe. The Kremlin simply orders wells drilled, commits the resources, and buys or acquires the physical technology from American companies. A lot of people look for oil in the Soviet Union, on behalf of the government. And a lot is found. But the waste of manpower and resources is enormous, relative to exploration in the market economies.

In most developing countries, even in those with relatively stable governments, the conditions that fostered oil exploration in the United States are absent. Governments keep title either to most land or to the mineral rights of privately owned land. Income taxes are so confiscatory that, should a native landowner possess mineral rights, he probably could not find native capital and labor willing to explore the land, as the government would capture the rewards through taxation. Governments will lease lands to the major international oil companies to explore, but these companies will look only in places where oil is most likely to be found, where siesmology can at least hint at probable finds. Most oil, however, cannot be tracked by seismology, for, like the East Texas field, it is trapped in complex geology and will yield only to myriad explorers taking long shots. One half-joking rule of thumb among the international oil companies drilling in unstable countries is that you should try to pay all costs and make a small profit with the first tanker of oil that leaves the country, on the assumption that what oil remains will be nationalized or confiscated by taxation.

Madagascar, off the southeast coast of Africa, for example, is almost the size of Texas, and lies in one of the world's largest sedimentary basins, where oil is most likely to be found. Prior to 1975, the French controlled the island, and there was almost no exploration, possibly because the French believed that if oil was discovered they would be pitched out. Since 1975, the government and the international oil companies have been wary of one another, and as a result only eighty-three wells were drilled on the island through 1978. Even in secure, developed parts of the world, the combination of high levels of government land ownership and steep personal taxation deters massive exploration. Most of Australia's 3 million square miles is held in collective ownership, and the mineral rights are retained by the Crown. In 1978, a mere fifty-three exploratory wells were sunk, and that was twice the number drilled in the previous year.

In the Middle East, there is little exploration, the sheiks having no desire to find and produce oil at a rate that would diminish the price they can command for their known reserves. Since 1974, the Saudis have averaged a mere ten exploratory wells a year, Iraq only one a year, and the entire Middle East only ninety-five a year. In 1970, there was no serious thought of an "oil shortage" looming on the horizon. Saudi Arabia that year was producing 10 million barrels a day and was officially estimating that by 1980 it could produce 20 million barrels a day. But by 1981, Saudi production was below 10 million barrels per day, and the entire output of the nations comprising the Organization of Petroleum Exporting Countries—of the Middle East, Asia, Africa and Latin America—had tumbled to 22 mbd from a peak of 36 mbd. The drop represented almost a quarter of total world oil consumption in 1978.

Obviously, indisputably, there has been no "shortage" of oil. It could be argued that in the short run there was a shortage in the consuming nations created by the monopoly powers of the producing nations, the OPEC cartel. But this argument is hollow, as if we were to say there developed a shortage of steak in the Smith household because Jones, the butcher, refused to sell it at less than five dollars a pound, a price Smith refused to pay or could not pay.

It was Robert Mundell who had been the first to see that there would be a dramatic rise in the dollar price of oil in the 1970s, not because the supply of oil would fall, but because the consuming nations would become too poor to pay as much per barrel in real terms. Saudi Arabia was prepared to double production to 20 mbd from 10 mbd in the decade of the 1970s, but only if it got twice the real goods in exchange as it had been getting for the 10 mbd. As Mundell saw the United States devalue its dollar, its unit of account, in December 1971, he surmised that it would be only a matter of time before the oil exporters would find the dollars they received buying fewer goods, and that the dollar financial assets they held—claims on future real goods—would also be worth less. They would ask more dollars per barrel to maintain the terms of trade.

American policymakers and economists came to believe that rising oil and commodity prices had been caused by the wealth of consumers, particularly American consumers, squandering resources on oil imports in a way that enabled the OPEC cartel to dictate monopoly prices. Policy was thus directed at making American consumers poorer, forcing them to conserve energy; taxes were raised not only on consumers of oil, but also on domestic producers of oil, to prevent them from making "windfall" gains by charging the OPEC world price. The American auto industry was viewed as a culprit, manufacturing and marketing "gas guzzlers" that encouraged consumers to buy and drive vehicles that play into the hands of the cartel.

Policy succeeded in reducing the level of wealth of the American economy. But impoverishment of a people merely decreases their ability to tap the energy-soaked planet or to buy the energy they require from those foreign producers who have it to sell. The nominal price of oil can only be driven down temporarily by austerity policies that force intermediaries to sell their inventories at distress prices.

The Keynesian and monetarist "demand-side" economists, who view the consumer as the driving force of the economy, are wholly responsible for pushing global policymakers into the current energy problems.

Because their analytical models ignore the simple truth that people produce in order to consume, it does not occur to these economists that, by making it difficult for people to consume, they discourage production. Saudi Arabia, in other words, produces in order to consume. And nations, like individuals, have appetites for current goods and for future goods. The baker produces ten loaves and wishes to consume nine in the present; he wishes to save one for future consumption, when he may be ill or for his old age. He needs a financial asset to replace the tenth loaf of bread, which, because it would spoil, cannot be saved. In the same way, Saudi Arabia desires to produce oil for current consumption, trading barrels for Western goods and services. It also desires to save for the future, trading barrels of financial assets that can translate into Western goods and services at some future date, perhaps when it runs out of oil or when it faces extraordinary expenses. If the United States then seeks to drive down the price of Saudi oil by driving down the domestic demand for oil—through taxation, tariffs, embargoes, quotas, regulations, et cetera—the effect is to weaken the productive capacity of the economy and thus drive down the value of U.S. financial assets. The demand for Saudi oil shrinks, as planned, but the unexpected side effect is that the Saudi appetite for U.S. financial assets shrinks even faster. Oil in the ground becomes more valuable as a future asset than as an American dollar asset, a share of stock or a bond. This explains in large part why Saudi Arabia in 1981 produced less oil than it did in 1970. It also helps to explain why Japan, which has almost no domestic energy sources, could in the 1970s approach the United States in per capita income; Japan did not attempt to forcefully conserve its way through the seventies, but followed a growth path.

Where United States economists and policymakers spent the decade worrying about the level of oil imports and trying to squeeze it down,

Japan worried about not being able to import more oil, and it concentrated on earning that ability through production. Where Saudi Arabia's appetite for U.S. goods and financial assets declined, its appetite for Japanese goods and financial assets expanded. In other words, Japan bent her will to increasing her productive capacity in the face of oil "shortages," even though it meant importing greater quantities of petroleum from the Middle East. Nor did the government have to make this decision. The private sector was left to determine whether it could transform a $30 barrel of oil into products worth more than $30, and if it could, there could be no reason not to import it. The government only had to decide not to intervene for the purpose of "conservation," a decision it implicitly made. We expect the government to intervene for conservation purposes when a living thing is threatened with extinction. We expect local electorates to choose not to permit oil exploration on resort beaches or strip mining in national parks. But it is quite another matter for a "conservation" cry to be raised for the purpose of closing off imports of oil from another nation. This cry was heard repeatedly in the United States of the 1970s and was raised to the level of policy by President Carter in 1977, when he pledged to arbitrarily limit the number of barrels of oil the United States would import from abroad.

The Malthusian fear of an energy depletion is often genuine and has been expressed throughout history. The following is typical:

We have apparently used up to 40 percent of our oil supply . . . Unwarranted optimism, which seems indigenous in most parts of the United States, has led the oil industry and the public to waste this best of fuels. There is need for a countrywide thrift campaign looking to the saving of this essential resource.

Where will my children, and children's children, get the oil they need in ever-increasing amounts? What is to happen when, following the United States, Mexico must reduce her output with the progressive exhaustion of her oil resources?[9]

This dismal energy outlook was attributed to George Otis Smith, the director of the U.S. Geological Survey, in the year 1920. As Alan Reynolds points out, this was not the first forecast of an imminent energy crisis.

Britain faced a severe shortage of firewood around 1550, which led to the substitution of coal for wood and charcoal. The Newcastle Coal Guild, formed in 1600, evolved into a cartel that lasted from about 1665 to 1844, when canals and railways made it feasible for inland coal to compete with coal carried by sea. The Industrial Revolution then flourished on cheap coal. By 1865, however, a distinguished economist, William Stanley Jevons, wrote that British coal would soon be gone. "There is no reasonable prospect," he said, "of any relief from a future want of the main agent of industry."

Meanwhile, the United States faced a serious shortage of whale oil at about the same time. The price of high-quality whale oil quadrupled from 1823 to 1855, to $2.55 a gallon, making it attractive to develop, as lighting sources, synfuels— synthetic fuels—such as paraffin made from shale and kerosene or gas synthe- sized from coal. By 1879, Edison came up with even better forms of lighting.

In 1914, the U.S. Geological Survey predicted that the United States would soon run out of oil. (They said the same in 1926, 1939, and 1949.) Nevertheless, there was considerable optimism about shale oil. A miniboom in shale oil from about 1917 to 1924 was thwarted by the Bureau of Standards, however, and was then rendered non-competitive by discoveries in east Texas in 1930—just as earlier experiments with shale were rendered uncompetitive by Drake's discov- ery of oil in 1859. In the 1920s and early 1930s, several paper companies used cogeneration to produce electricity from steam. That practice was stopped by the Justice Department as a violation of public-utility regulation.

The year 1933 was not exactly a big one for oil consumption. Still, the data proved that, if consumption remained static, oil would be gone in 15 years. But government geologists were again very optimistic about making synthetic gasoline out of coal. One government expert at that time wrote that, "with an increased demand, when petroleum reserves begin to fail, of 250 million tons to be converted to engine fuel, the coal reserves would be ample for 2,500 years."[10]

The pattern repeats itself and will continue to repeat itself throughout history. The energy is there in the earth's crust, waiting to be found, but the bookkeepers, the geologists, the engineers, the accountants come to believe through their static analysis that mankind has come to the end of the line and has only 15 or 25 or 50 years' worth of petroleum and natural gas left. Nor does it matter that they are always wrong in their forecasts. There are always industrialists or governments ready to employ them and their doomsday scenarios for the purpose of persuading taxpayers to finance synfuels, turning base metals into gold or turning coal or shale into synthetic oil or gas or sunbeams into electricity. The alchemists of yore consumed precious resources and diverted attention away from the solutions that their patrons were fundamentally seeking, a path to prosperity. But perhaps modern science owes something to these wiz- ards, if only that they elevated the idea of science over the pull of superstition.

The modern alchemists are the major petroleum companies, the Exxons, the Unions, the Arcos, the Mobils, whose specialty is not in finding oil and gas, but in marketing oil and gas found by the gamblers, the wildcatters, the entrepreneurs. The majors are "energy bankers," and as such are as static in their view of the world as bookkeepers and accountants. Ruth Sheldon Knowles writes in her illuminating history:

Rockefeller had begun by scoffing at ownership of the sources, sure that his monopoly could be sustained by control of refining, pipelining, and marketing. So much oil had now been found that Rockefeller's Trust could not control it. His type of enterprise could not yoke so many oxen. As a matter of fact, the accelerating oil discoveries had begun to break Standard's monopoly even before the Supreme Court, in 1911, ordered the trust dissolved.

Busting the Trust was an ironical joke that had backfired on rampaging President Theodore Roosevelt. He had forced the Trust to break up into thirty-eight companies, but with what results? They still had the same owners, and as yet they were not competing with one another. For the first time—the result of the action—the public was aware of how valuable Standard's holdings were. All the companies' stocks jumped in price. Rockefeller was a hundred percent richer after the dissolution.*

Standard Oil itself had finally realized, before the government began its prosecution, that the real threat to its monopoly came from not owning its own raw material. Still averse to risking money hunting oil, it had begun buying most of the good discoveries.[11]

The motive force behind the major oil companies is the profit from sales of energy, and their principal concern is market share, satisfying as many customers as possible. When they observe that explorers are discovering oil and gas at a rate insufficient to maintain the level of reserves they need as a cushion for their share of market, they begin pushing for alternative sources of supply. The result is synfuel, modern alchemy. The executives of the major oil companies sound an alarm with the government, with their bankers, with their customers, and soon the taxpayers are asked to finance synthetic-fuel projects that will provide a source of energy for our children and grandchildren.

The taxpayers have to be asked to finance these projects, because private investors will not do so; they know that if historical patterns are repeated, a rise in the relative price of oil and gas will increase the rate of exploration and discovery, rendering uneconomic the costly and elaborate synthetic-fuel complexes. But once government has been induced to finance vast synfuel projects, it becomes easier to persuade government to subsidize the synfuel that they produce. Thus, new discoveries can flood the market with natural oil and gas, lowering its relative price, but government can protect its investment by granting price relief to synthetics. It can levy lower taxes on them, purchase them for government use at higher cost, or grant regulatory relief (fixing a low maximum price on natural gas and permitting syngas to sell at a higher price, for

*The aggregate value of the shares increased for the more likely but counterintuitive reason that there is less risk in a portfolio of 38 companies that are now taking greater risks in the competitive field than in a portfolio of one company that takes a minimum of risk. In this sense the joke did not backfire on Roosevelt, whose intent was to enrich the nation, not impoverish Rockefeller.

example). Nuclear-power plants have been subsidized in just this fashion, but environmentalists can succeed in making these energy alternatives uneconomic by forcing high regulatory costs on them, usually with justification.

Once the forces of big oil, big government and big labor (which will happily construct pyramids at time and a half for overtime) get synfuel projects off the ground, it becomes extremely difficult for them to be brought down. As a nation spends its intellectual and physical resources on such uneconomic boondoggles, those nations that have resisted the temptation to follow, or could not afford to do so if they wished, are able in a relative sense to advance by using the less costly natural resources. But in an absolute sense the world always loses when alchemy is practiced. The technological spinoff that mankind acquires, even in construction of a pyramid or a synfuel plant, does not offset the losses to the global electorate because of this misallocation of resources. The source of this inefficiency, though, is not the greed of the major oil companies or a conspiracy between big business and big government. The source is always a flaw in the political system that enables the idea to germinate at all, let alone flourish. Almost certainly the answer to such flaws is more democracy. It is improbable that the electorate would underwrite the massive synfuel projects in a bond election any more than they would vote to finance the pyramids out of their own future tax payments.

The energy breakthrough that will take the world into the twenty-first century will almost certainly be political, not technological. In some part of the Third World, the political leadership will decide to break the legacy of Barbarossa and will adopt the Jeffersonian idea. Mineral rights possessed by the state will be sold or otherwise dispersed to the populace, and tax law will be changed, so that mineral wealth will not be automatically confiscated. In whatever part of the world, whether geologically "promising" or not, there will be discoveries that will encourage the spread of the Jeffersonian pattern. There will be major oil company executives who will worry about this development, because it will mean a new global round of competition and a declining relative price of petroleum—lowering the value of known reserves. But they will be unable to do anything about it once the process begins, because the Jeffersonian idea favors the single individual. When the masses of people hold individual ownership of mineral rights, it becomes extremely difficult for the government to confiscate newly discovered mineral wealth; if one patent is confiscated, all are worthless, and all citizens would realize this immediately. There is safety in numbers, and individual wildcatters who now shun exploration in foreign lands because it means dealing with a government, would feel greater security in arranging partnerships with individual farmers and landowners. In time, an indigenous industry would develop. This is the next frontier.

The idea is rapidly gaining ground in the Third World, although it has not yet taken root. In September 1981, energy experts and diplomats from seventy developing nations convened in Los Angeles at a "small-energy" conference sponsored by the United Nations Institute for Training and Research. William Kucewicz of *The Wall Street Journal* attended the conference and reported:

The aim was to say that energy development can take place in the Third World quickly and relatively cheaply if a free market approach is allowed to work. . . .

India . . . has substantial energy potential in the form of hydro-electric power and shallow gas reserves in its delta regions. But these resources are not being sufficiently exploited because of restrictions that give the Indian government monopolistic control over energy development.

The example of India points up a distinct difference in the management of energy resources between the U.S. and the Third World (and even Western Europe). "In practically all other countries," Mr. [Joseph] Barnea [UNITAR senior fellow] noted, "underground resources belong to the state. The state explores for underground resources either through big government-owned companies or government departments, or it gives concessions to big international companies . . . [But] none of them is really interested in the exploration and development of small energy resources for local use and on a decentralized basis.

Thus, the snag in small energy development in the Third World is not so much technical or even financial. It is institutional. Socialized economic planning retards energy development by holding down the number of participants in the search for new resources and destroying the risk-reward incentive of a free-enterprise system."[12]

Prospecting for oil is a dynamic art—a series of individual techniques—sometimes overlapping, sometimes separated by a time gap—but techniques which lose their usefulness and which leave us without a guide to our prospecting until we devise some new method. The greatest single element in all prospecting, past, present, and future—is the man willing to take a chance.[13]

This was Everett Lee de Golyer's observation early this century. Wallace Pratt, another of the early great oil geologists put it this way: "It is the genius of a people that determines how much oil shall be reduced to possession; the presence of oil in the earth is not enough. Gold is where you find it, according to an old adage, but judging from the record of our experience, oil must be sought first of all in our minds."[14]

Epilogue

To the global electorate, the most important book of the eighteenth century was Adam Smith's *Wealth of Nations*. The most important book of the nineteenth century was Karl Marx's *Capital*. Their importance lay in their ability to assist political leaders in understanding the workings of the political economy, which in turn assists them in fathoming the desires of the global electorate. Can it be a coincidence that both Smith and Marx closed out their monumental books with an almost identical discussion of the pitfalls of public debt, with Smith almost, but not quite, articulating the essence of the Laffer Curve?

How much further coincidence that the most important book of the twentieth century, in the same vein, has been Keynes's *General Theory*, which does nothing less than argue the benefits and magic of public debt? This is a magic that will work briefly, as Keynes intended, when it relies on useful government expenditure. But more importantly, it is a magic that works beautifully, by accident, in a way Keynes did not foresee, when it operates through policies of tax-rate reduction.

Entering the last quarter of the twentieth century, the global electorate has a multitude of experiments in political economy going at once—each a variation on the seminal ideas of Smith, Marx, or Keynes. Smith and Marx will endure as the foundations of experimentation. But the age of Keynes is ending as it must. It has served the global electorate through its successes and failures, which have illuminated the basic insights of Smith and Marx. The global electorate can only choose among alternative paths drawn by individual minds, and Keynes has helped individual minds grope closer to the path desired by the global electorate. How do we, all of us who belong to the global electorate, solve that primordial problem that confronts society when the fisherman breaks his leg? How do we maximize growth while redistributing, and do so without straining the planet? How do we maximize freedom while promoting equality?

There is some combination of Smith and Marx that will dominate the next century and be further refined in centuries thereafter. The likelihood, as the age of Keynes draws to a close in the West, is of a drift back to an age of Smith and Marx. The global electorate will push the West toward a Pax Americana as the United States emerges from adolescence. It has already made headway in pushing the East in the direction of classical Marx, away from the grotesque forms spawned under pressure by Lenin, Stalin, and Mao. Both Smith and Marx would be pleased with this drift, although Marx would see that his idea will almost certainly have to remain subordinate.

Not second-best, merely subordinate, in the sense that output *must* precede redistribution. By denying itself the productive efficiencies of a free-market economy, the Soviet Union can only match the United States and other market economies of Europe and Japan if the political leaders of the West make gross errors in economic management. The relative advance of the communist nations in the past decade has occurred in just such a fashion.

But not entirely so. The youthful nations of Eastern Europe, rambunctious in young adulthood, can no longer be considered "satellites" of Moscow. It is more appropriate to apply an analogy of family. Sons Hungary and Czechoslovakia fought for freedom in 1956 and 1968 by rebellion against the authoritarian Kremlin father and were slapped down. Daughter Poland, in 1970, threw a tantrum over internal policies, not demanding the right to leave home or join a new church, but simply insisting on a new outfit. And Moscow held still while Polish leader Edward Gierek introduced economic reforms that in every way moved toward a broader market economy, including the reduction of tax rates on personal incomes and the decentralization of economic planning, transferring power to allocate capital from the central bureaucrats in Warsaw to the regional state bankers. In the years since, Poland has been among the fastest growing nations on the planet and is now the tenth leading industrial nation. In addition, the Polish electorate learned how to deal with Daddy. In 1976, having absorbed the reforms of 1970 and again feeling hemmed in, Poland threw another tantrum over food prices and Gierek put through a new set of internal reforms while Moscow watched, again cutting personal tax rates and permitting free enterprises of twenty-five employees or less. Adam Smith would give Poland higher marks today than he would his native Britain, at least in economics.

While Moscow has acted apprehensively, it does not seem accurate any longer to say it is being dragged unwillingly by Eastern Europe. While Daddy is still slow to change his ways, he is discovering the comforts of productive sons and daughters. And as similar economic reforms spread through the rest of Eastern Europe, quietly, in the wake of Poland's tantrums, the Soviets are drawing courage to test ideas along similar lines. If Brezhnev would ever realize that his stature as a *passable* leader was secured by his restoration of one-acre private plots to the peasantry, he would aim for heroic stature by permitting two-acre plots—or in some other way moving Soviet agriculture off the top of the Laffer Curve. He should realize, too, that the nationalism of the Baltic states would not intensify, but abate, if they were permitted internal experimentation along Polish lines without having to throw tantrums. Nationalism is not a natural instinct of the electorate, but a form of voting, of rebellion.

Another shade of Marxist experimentation, closer to the original classical version that envisioned democratic evolution through the experience of the working class, is Eurocommunism. The Italian communists, then the French, Spanish, and Japanese, have shaken themselves free of the Leninist dictum that the party must have monopoly power. Instead, they are prepared to contest for power through democratic means. Their strength, especially in Italy and France, has grown dramatically in the past several years as the "free-enterprise" democrats consistently failed to understand the source of the problem: That the global inflation had caused their already too-high tax rates to be pushed even higher. Both Italy and France submitted themselves to "austerity" plans (upon the advice of the International Monetary Fund) that made matters worse. Still, the Eurocommunists find that electoral victory always barely eludes them. They have opposed austerity, which is the source of their strength, but the public does not desire the alternatives they offer, i.e., expansion of the public sector through nationalization.

Eurocommunism would fade today as quickly as it did in the early 1950s if the non-communist parties offered the electorate the kind of tax-cutting policies Ludwig Erhard used in West Germany to expand the economy through the private sector. It is only a matter of time before this happens. At this writing, in the autumn of 1977, Britain's Conservative Party leader Margaret Thatcher is steadfastly pledging to sharply reduce the progressivity of Britain's personal tax rates as soon as her party returns to power. If the Labour government fails to co-opt this issue, it will surely lose the next national elections. Already, the Tories are steadily winning by-elections on this issue, capturing seats in Parliament that have long been considered "safe" for Labour. Once Britain takes this step, the expansion of its economy will have rippling effects through Western Europe, giving courage to conservative coalitions in other capitals to follow her lead. It will then occur to European political leaders in general that the Common Market idea can move ahead only if the internal tax structures of the European nations are made roughly similar, so that a European common currency will not have variable impacts on output and employment through its effects on tax progressions.

In China, the passing of Mao Tse-tung has given that vast electorate of 900 million an opportunity to "vote" in new leadership, through internal consensus-shaping. The result has been a relatively rapid drift in the direction of classical economic forms. Peking has openly embraced the idea of using individual incentives as a means of expanding production, going so far as to twist a Marxist slogan into one more appropriate to Adam Smith: Instead of Marx's idea of communism, "From each according to his abilities, to each according to his needs," Peking proposes, "From each according to his abilities, to each according to his work." If China can find a way to unlock the nation's intellectual capital through incentive systems, for industry as it has for agriculture, rapid growth can follow. Unity with Taiwan is historically inevitable, as is unification of North and South Korea. But it is now not outlandish to consider the possibility that the completed results will mean a China and Korea that more closely resemble Taiwan and South Korea than Marxist models, which has been the conventional assumption by both liberal and conservative intellectuals in the West.

The advantage China has over the Soviet Union in developing a more efficient political economy (which means a freer one both in the market for goods and the market for ideas) is that it did not go through the Great Depression of the 1930s as a communist system. The conventional myth is that Russian authoritarianism has racial connotations built on centuries of despotic rule, as if the Russian people underwent genetic alterations in the process. In opting for their own brand of communism, the Italian and French communists offer this racial argument as a prime reason for variation. But what really happened is that a more pacific form of Marxism became impossible during the global contraction of the 1930s, when Stalin used liquidation of all opposition, real and imagined, and slave labor camps to repress impulses that were primarily economic in origin. Having shaped the system in this grotesque manner, Stalin left this as his institutional legacy. His successors, the Soviet ruling class, have continued to view dissent as ideological rather than economic in origin, unable to "think on the margin." But on a glacially descending line the Kremlin ruling class has been shedding this paranoia, and is beginning to sense that the Laffer Curve exists independent of ideological systems—as with Brezhnev's restoration of the one-acre plots. The next generation of Soviet leadership should progress more rapidly along this line, being even further removed from the conditioning of the 1930s. And they must be, if the Soviet Union is to withstand the competition of a broad economic expansion by both the West and the People's Republic of China.

How surprising it is to Western intellectuals that the Third World has come through the global economic convulsions of the past several years with so few defections to Marxist variations. Since the 1950s, when China and the Soviet Union openly proclaimed their intention to woo the developing nations to their political/economic systems, only Vietnam and Cuba have defected. Yet the largest part of the Third World, in retaining capitalist forms, has been moving toward closer political alignments with Russia and China in international debates. The Third World demand for a "New International Economic Order" is aimed squarely at the West, which is viewed as an exploiter in a way the communist nations are not.

The reason for this, in our model, is that the West is a creditor in a way the communist nations are not. There are no Moscow or Peking banks, private or public, demanding that developing nations squeeze their peasantry and proletariat with higher taxes in order to meet debt schedules. The essence of a New International Economic Order is a plea for debt moratoriums by Western banks, for the Third World sees clearly that as long as its finest intellectual capital is absorbed in the process of meeting debt payments, it is unable to get on with the task of development. Chinese or Soviet aid to the Third World has been of a different order, grants of financial and intellectual capital that can be repaid through political support, which does not require raising the taxes and the squeezing of peasants and proletariat. This was the single most important insight of classical Marx, as he observed close-up the British exploitation of India, and it has remained the greatest advantage over the West of those communist nations that build on Marx. It is an insight the global electorate must preserve, even if it means preserving otherwise unpalatable Marxist systems.

The solution to the Third World development question is in the hands of the United States, the creditor nation. The answer is not debt moratoria, at least in the sense the Third World directly puts the demand. For those who have come this far in this book, it must be self-evident that our model cries out for universal tax reforms, especially on progressive personal rates. The U.S. private banks and the International Monetary Fund they control through Washington cannot remain blind to the Laffer Curve or resist its implications, for their only salvation ultimately lies in its understanding. There will be the predictable arguments that the banks and the U.S. State Department cannot "dictate" tax reforms in the developing nations, but this is nonsense. Having already dictated the terms of development to the Third

World that brought the present tax structures in their train, the United States merely has to announce its political and financial support of the opposite policy to bring a stampede of Third World political leaders anxious to produce greater revenues through lower rates.

Resistance in the United States will come from those single-entry bookkeepers in American business and labor who fear that an expansion of Third World intellectual capital will just mean more competition. Do we really want Peruvians to be manufacturing steel instead of catching anchovies? It is this fear of the Third World that led the U.S. Congress in 1976 to change the tax treatment of U.S. citizens working abroad, increasing the burden on them to such levels that, when it takes full effect, the intellectual capital we had been privately exporting will be forced home. Little Smoot-Hawley bills are passing through Congress, with the Democratic Party now doing the damage.

The Republican Party is now in dismal condition. But if there is to be a Pax Americana during the next century, its foundation will rest on a Republican renaissance.* The solutions to domestic and global economic problems now require primary commitments to income growth, not redistribution, and the GOP will always win a competition with the Democrats over which is more passionate over growth. The decline and fall of the GOP since 1930 resulted not from its lack of passion, but from its failure to understand the nature of the Laffer Curve. Its worst mistake, of course, was to expand the international wedge via Smoot-Hawley in 1930. Then, when it had learned from this mistake and became an internationalist party instead of an isolationist one, it somehow forgot the nature of the domestic wedge. Now only 17 percent of American voters are willing to say they are Republicans. The decline began in earnest when, in 1953, President Eisenhower killed H.R. 1, the GOP bill providing for a 20 percent across-the-board tax cut on personal incomes. The growth prescription of tax-rate cutting was not picked up again by a Republican until 1974, when Representative Jack F. Kemp of Buffalo, New York began promoting the idea. It was only after the Republicans lost the White House that Kemp began enjoying success in selling his plan, which was adopted formally by the Republican National Committee in New Orleans, Louisiana, on September 30, 1977. This was the necessary first step toward a renaissance of the GOP.

The model of the global political economy presented in this book is

---

*The author is a registered Democrat who, as a youth, campaigned for Adlai Stevenson in 1952 and 1956, voted for John Kennedy in 1960 and Lyndon Johnson in 1964, split tickets for Richard Nixon in 1968 and 1972, and almost, but not quite, voted for Jimmy Carter in 1976.

meant only as a framework of ideas for global policymakers. The author does not pretend that it is a "correct" model, but offers it merely as one that he has found more reliable than competing models as a way of looking at the world. And it is meant as an analytical tool rather than a forecasting tool.

Will there be a third world war? The Chinese leadership in Peking say one is inevitable, that it will take war to resolve the competition among systems just as it has before. But the Chinese also say that the world's political leaders must work to at least push this inevitable war into the next century. Our model can't tell us whether or not war will come, but it certainly does not hold that it is inevitable. And surely the Chinese goal of working to push conflict into the future can be realized by adjustment of economic policies as suggested by the model. Most of the political tensions in the world today are the result of the global inflation and contraction of the past decade. A global effort at tax reform, especially in the developing world, would free intellectual resources that have been locked up at least since the Second World War. It may well be that the global electorate *arranged* the inflation as a way of forcing the attention of the developed world to the unnecessary burdens it placed on the Third World, the burdens of grossly incorrect economic theories.

And if these prescriptions are followed and a genuine worldwide expansion follows global tax and monetary reform, what about the planet and its resources? Will wars occur as nations compete for an ever-diminishing supply of natural resources? Our model says no. The planet's bounty is for all practical purposes unlimited, but it yields this bounty stubbornly, at a pace determined by the intellectual resources of mankind. The past decade of inflation and contraction have made it seem that the planet has shriveled in its resources. A reconstruction of a world monetary system tied to the planet through gold or silver or oil or something real, matched by an understanding of the Laffer Curve that did not exist at Bretton Woods, would enable the world to grow without straining the planet. Nor will the world's population continue to expand as rapidly, given these economic conditions, for as individuals can more easily develop their intellectual potential and increase the quality of human capital, they will independently choose to reduce the quantity of human capital they are now forming. The exponential population growth the Malthusians fear will not occur where there is real economic growth.

Conflict is more likely to come as a result of uneven advance. If all members of a family unit save one are developing, the one left behind will cause trouble, drain the resources of those who have been advancing, and create tensions and strife that will block the advance of the unit as a whole. If the West, China, and the Third World manage a major economic advance in the 1980s as the result of simultaneous moves down the Laffer Curve, but the Soviet Union is unable to break through the crusts of ideological dogma that would enable it to advance as well, one would expect an increase in the potential for conflict. A happier outcome would be general global advance, with the fresh economic and political impulses of Eastern Europe spreading into the heartland of Russia.

More important than the Laffer Curve, after all, is the persistence of the global electorate in pushing toward concord. It will not for long permit the smallest part of its membership from being left behind, economically or politically, in this historic trek. For thousands of years the world has been moving toward more, not less, democracy, and it will continue to do so. It will, as it always has, ultimately reject all systems that do not revolve around the individual, for the survival of all ultimately depends on the survival of the least of its members. In this sense, the global electorate is the good shepherd.

Morristown, N.J.
September 30, 1977

NOTES

Chapter 1

1. José Ortega y Gasset, *The Revolt of the Masses*, trans. (New York: W.W. Norton & Co., 1932), p. 138.

2. Will Durant, *The Story of Civilization*, 11 vols. (New York: Simon & Schuster, 1935-1975), 1:671-72.

3. Ibid., 1:662.

Chapter 2

1. Edward Gibbon, *The Decline and Fall of the Roman Empire* (New York: Harcourt, Brace & Co., 1960) p. 1.

2. Will Durant, *The Story of Civilization*, 11 vols. (New York: Simon & Schuster, 1935-1975) 3:644.

3. Ibid., 11:263.

4. Ibid., 11:260.

Chapter 3

1. Sir Isaiah Berlin, *The Hedgehog and The Fox: An Essay on Tolstoi's View of History* (New York: Simon & Schuster, 1953), pp. 69-70.

2. Will Durant, *The Story of Civilization*, 11 vols. (New York; Simon & Schuster, 1935-1975), 1:702.

3. Ibid., 2:291.

Chapter 5

1. Adam Smith, *The Wealth of Nations* (New York: Modern Library, 1937), pp. 2-3.

2. Arthur B. Laffer, memo to U.S. Treasury Secretary William Simon, November, 1974.

Chapter 6

1. David Hume, "Of Taxes," in *Gateway to the Great Books*, vol. 7 (Chicago: Encyclopedia Britannica, 1963), pp. 85-88.

2. Ibid.

3. Ibid.

4. Baron de Montesquieu, *The Spirit of the Laws* (New York: Hafner Publishing Co., 1962), pp. 216-217.

5. Adam Smith, *The Wealth of Nations*, (New York: Modern Library, 1937), pp. 778-79.

6. *Wall Street Journal*, 5 February 1976, p.18.

7. Stephen Dowell, *History of Taxation and Taxes in England*, 4 vols. (London: Longmans, Green & Co., 1884), 2:283.

8. Hedrick Smith, *The Russians* (New York: Quadrangle, 1976), pp. 268-69.

9. David Hume, "Of Money," in *Gateway to the Great Books*, vol. 7 p. 92.

10. Adam Smith, *The Wealth of Nations*, pp. 22–23.

11. Ibid., pp. 27–28.

12. Robert A. Mundell, "Inflation from an International Viewpoint," in *The Phenomenon of Worldwide Inflation*, ed. David Meiselman and Arthur B. Laffer (Washington, D.C.: American Enterprise Institute, 1975), p. 141.

13. Randall Hinshaw, ed., *Inflation as a Global Problem* (Baltimore: Johns Hopkins University Press, 1972), pp. 49–50.

14. Roy W. Jastram, *The Golden Constant, the English and American Experience, 1560–1976* (New York: John Wiley & Sons, 1977).

15. Benjamin Klein, "Our New Monetary Standard: The Measurement and Effects of Price Uncertainty," *Economic Inquiry*, December 1975.

16. W. C. Mitchell, "The Greenbacks and the Cost of the Civil War," in *The Economic Impact of the Civil War*, ed. Ralph Andreano (Cambridge: Schenkman Publishing, 1962), p. 75.

17. Robert Hall, "Explorations in the Gold Standard and Related Policies for Stabilizing the Dollar," NBER Conference, February 1981.

18. Lewis E. Lehrman, "The Case for the Gold Standard," monograph (New York: Morgan Stanley, May 1981), p. 25.

19. Ludwig von Mises, *Human Action* (Chicago: Regnery, 1966), p. 784.

20. *Newsweek*, Jan. 4, 1982.

21. Robert A. Mundell, *Monetary Theory*, (Santa Columba, 1971) p. 77.

Chapter 7

1. *New York Times*, 23 July 1920, p. 4.

2. Andrew Mellon, *Taxation: The People's Business* (New York: Macmillan Co., 1924), app. E, pp. 216–227.

3. Robert Murray Haig, *The Public Finances of Post-War France* (New York: Columbia University Press, 1929), p. 163.

4. Karl Marx, *Capital* (New York: Modern Library, 1906), p. 817.

5. Sir William Beveridge et al., *Tariffs: The Case Examined* (London: Longmans, Green & Co., 1932), pp. 109–10.

6. Asher Isaacs, *International Trade: Tariff and Commercial Policies* (Chicago: Richard D. Irwin, 1948), p. 178.

7. Ibid., p. 233.

8. Milton Friedman and Anna Schwartz, *A Monetary History of the United States, 1867–1960* (Princeton: Princeton University Press, 1963), p. 305.

9. Ibid., pp. 307–8.

10. *Congressional Record*, 21 October 1929, p. 4728.

11. John Kenneth Galbraith, *The Great Crash—1929* (Boston: Houghton Mifflin Co., 1954), p. 104.

12. Isaacs, *International Trade*, p. 231.

13. Ibid.

14. Ibid., p. 236.

15. Charles Kindleberger, *The World in Depression, 1929–1939* (Los Angeles: University of California Press, 1973), pp. 109–231.

16. Elliot A. Rosen, *Hoover, Roosevelt and the Brains Trust* (New York: Columbia University Press, 1977), p. 380.

17. Ibid., p. 166.

18. Roland Sarti, *Fascism and the Industrial Leadership in Italy, 1919–1940* (Berkeley: University of California Press, 1971), pp. 45–46.

19. Ibid., p. 69.

20. Herbert Stein, *The Fiscal Revolution in America* (Chicago: University of Chicago Press, 1969), p. 114.

21. Goronwy Rees, *The Great Slump: Capitalism in Crisis 1929–33* (New York: Harper & Row, 1970), pp. 99–100.

22. Kenyon Poole, *German Financial Policies 1932–39* (Cambridge: Harvard University Press, 1939), pp. 17–18.

23. Hjalmar Schacht, *Confessions of "The Old Wizard"* (Boston: Houghton Mifflin Co., 1956), p. 303.

Chapter 8

1. John Maynard Keynes, *The General Theory of Employment, Interest, and Money* (New York: Harcourt Brace Jovanovich, 1965), pp. 383-84.

2. Milton Friedman and Anna Schwartz, *A Monetary History of the United States, 1867-1960* (Princeton: Princeton University Press, 1963), p. 298.

3. Karl Marx and Friedrich Engels, "Class Struggles" in *Anthology of World Prose* (New York: Halcyon House, 1935), p. 821.

4. Karl Marx, *Capital* (New York: Modern Library, 1906), p. 649.

5. Hedrick Smith, *The Russians* (New York: Quadrangle, 1976), p. 285.

6. Ibid., p. 114.

7. K. B. Smellie, *Great Britain Since 1688* (Ann Arbor: University of Michigan Press, 1962), p. 323.

8. Keynes, *General Theory*, p. 26.

9. Ernest Teilhac, "Jean-Baptiste Say," in *Encyclopedia of the Social Sciences*, vol. 13 (New York: Macmillan, 1934), p. 559.

10. Keynes, *General Theory*, p. 373.

11. Marx, *Capital*, pp. 827-29.

12. Joseph A. Schumpeter, *Ten Great Economists—From Marx to Keynes* (New York: Oxford University Press, 1951), p. 268.

13. Milton Friedman, "The Role of Monetary Policy," *American Economic Review* 58, no. 1. (March 1968): 5.

14. Friedman, *Monetary Policy*, p. 12.

15. John Kenneth Galbraith, *Money: Whence It Came, Where It Went* (Boston: Houghton Mifflin, 1975), p. 213.

Chapter 9

1. Will Durant, *The Story of Civilization*, 11 vols. (New York: Simon & Schuster, 1935-1975), 2:552.

2. Ibid., 3:177.

3. Ibid., 3:182-183.

4. Ibid., 3:192-193.

5. Ibid., 3:211.

6. Ibid., 11:776.

7. Thomas B. Macauley, *History of England*, vol. 3 (Boston: Houghton Mifflin Co., 1901), p. 432.

8. *Economist* (London), 10 April 1976, p. 74.

9. K. B. Smellie, *Great Britain Since 1688* (Ann Arbor: University of Michigan Press, 1962), pp. 139-40.

10. Ibid., p. 212.

11. Asher Isaacs, *International Trade: Tariff and Commercial Policies* (Chicago: Richard D. Irwin, 1948), p. 338.

12. Smellie, *Great Britain Since 1688*, p. 220.

13. F. Shehab, *Progressive Taxation* (Oxford: Oxford University Press, Clarendon Press, 1953), pp. 260-75.

14. Colin Clark, "A Memoir of the 'Golden' Age of the Great Economists," *Encounter*, June 1977, p. 83.

15. Stephen Dowell, *History of Taxation and Taxes in England*, 4 vols. (London: Longmans, Green & Co., 1884), 3:149.

16. Baron de Montesquieu, *The Spirit of the Laws* (New York: Hafner Publishing Co., 1962), pp. 217-18.

17. Ibid., 3:152.

18. Ibid., 3:153-54.

19. Leland Hamilton Jenks, *The Migration of British Capital to 1875* (New York: Alfred A. Knopf, 1927), pp. 102-4. This fascinating book is indispensible to an understanding of the global political economy of the nineteenth century.

20. Irving Wallace and David Wallechinsky, *The People's Almanac* (New York: Doubleday & Co., 1975), p. 356.

21. Robert Lekachman *The Age of Keynes* (New York: Random House, 1966), p. 189.

22. U.S. Treasury Department, Press Service No. S-530, 21 November 1947.

23. *Foreign Tax Policies and Economic Growth* (Washington, D.C.: Brookings Institution, 1966), p. 103.

24. *New York Times*, 24 October 1945, pp. 1, 11.

25. *New York Times*, 29 May 1962, p. 45.

26. Lekachman, *The Age of Keynes*, p. 281.

Chapter 10

1. John Maynard Keynes, *Essays in Persuasion* (London: Macmillan & Co., 1931), p. 78.

2. Robert A. Mundell, "Inflation from an International Viewpoint," in *The Phenomenon of Worldwide Inflation*, ed. David Meiselman and Arthur B. Laffer (Washington, D.C.: American Enterprise Institute, 1975), p. 141.

3. Alexander Hamilton's report to the House of Representatives, 13 December 1790, in *American State Papers, Finance*, 1st Congress, 3rd session, no. 18, I, 67-76.

4. Ibid.

5. Nicholas Biddle to John White, 3 March 1828, "President's Letter Book, Private No. 2," Nicholas Biddle Papers, Library of Congress, p. 353.

6. Robert A. Mundell, *The International Monetary Reform and Development Finance*, University of Waterloo Economic Series, no. 67 (Waterloo [Ontario], 1972), p. 5.

7. Jude Wanniski, "The Mundell-Laffer Hypothesis—A New View of the World Economy," *Public Interest Quarterly*, Spring 1975, p. 41.

8. Ibid., pp. 43-44.

9. Ibid., p. 46.

10. "Minutes of the World Economy Study Group," sixth session, the Adlai Stevenson Institute, Chicago, 10 April 1972, p. 6.

11. Arthur B. Laffer, "Exchange Rates, the Terms of Trade, and the Trade Balance," in *Effects of Exchange Rate Changes*, ed. Peter Clark, Dennis Logue, and Richard Sweeney (Washington, D.C.: Department of the Treasury, 1976), pp. 32-44.

12. Wanniski, "Mundell-Laffer Hypothesis," p. 42 ff.

13. *1967 Economic Report of the President* (Washington, D.C.: U.S. Government Printing Office, 1967), pp. 37-38.

14. "Big Changes Coming in Economic Policy," *National Observer*, 9 November 1970, p. 1.

15. *National Observer*, 7 November 1970, p. 1.

16. *National Observer*, 12 April 1971, p. 2.

17. John Maynard Keynes, *The General Theory of Employment, Interest, and Money* (New York: Harcourt Brace Jovanovich, 1965), p. 339.

18. Milton Friedman, "The Role of Monetary Policy," *American Economic Review* 58, no. 1 (March 1968) : 15.

19. "This Week in Washington," *National Observer*, 2 August 1971, p. 2.

20. *National Observer*, 23 August 1971, p. 1.

21. Mundell, "Inflation from an International Viewpoint," p. 144.

22. *The Adjustment of Personal Income-Tax Systems for Inflation* (Paris: Organization for Economic Cooperation and Development, 1976), p. 42.

23. "Breaking the Tax Barrier," *Wall Street Journal*, 8 January 1975.

24. "The Transfer Payment Explosion," *Wall Street Journal*, 24 January 1975.

Chapter 11

1. Leland Hamilton Jenks, *The Migration of British Capital to 1875* (New York: Alfred A. Knopf, 1927), pp. 137-38

2. Ibid.

3. Ibid., p. 222.

4. Ibid., p. 223.

5. Ibid., p. 224.

6. Ibid., pp. 228-29.

7. Walter W. Heller, "Fiscal Policies for Underdeveloped Countries," in *Readings on Taxation in Developing Countries*, 3rd ed., ed. Richard M. Bird and Oliver Oldman (Baltimore: Johns Hopkins University Press, 1975), pp. 6-7.

8. Nicholas Kaldor, "Will Underdeveloped Countries Learn to Tax," in Bird and Oldman, *Readings*, p. 29.

9. Ibid., pp. 31-37.

10. Gunnar Myrdal, *Asian Drama: An Inquiry into the Poverty of Nations*, 3 vols. (New York: Random House, 1968), 3:2097-98.

11. "A Tale of Two Nations," *Wall Street Journal*, 10 May 1976.

12. Vito Tanzi,"Personal Income Taxation in Latin America," in Bird and Oldman, *Readings*, p. 235.

13. Ibid., pp. 238-39.

14. Thomas E. Skidmore, "Brazil's Changing Role in the International System: Implications for U.S. Policy," in *Brazil in the Seventies*, ed. Riordan Roett (Washington, D.C.: American Enterprise Institute, 1976), pp. 18-19.

15. *Doing Business in Mexico*, Price Waterhouse information guide, March 1975, p. 14.

16. *Wall Street Journal*, 1 September 1977.

17. Joseph Buttinger, *Vietnam: A Dragon Embattled*, vol. 2 (New York: Praeger, 1967), p. 780.

18. *New York Times*, 15 January 1962, p. 26.

19. Frank C. Child, "Economic Growth, Capital Formation, and Public Policy," lecture given at the National Institute for Administration, Saigon, 24 February 1961, mimeographed.

20. Ibid., p. 7.

21. *New York Times*, 5 January 1962, p. 1.

22. *New York Times*, 20 June 1962, p. 6.

23. *New York Times*, 20 August 1962, p. 9.

Chapter 12

1. Victor S. Clark et al., *Porto Rico and Its Problems* (Washington, D.C.: Brookings Institution, 1930), p. xviii.

2. Gordon K. Lewis, *Puerto Rico: Freedom and Power in the Caribbean* (New York: MR Press, 1963), pp. 97–98.

3. Clark, *Porto Rico*, pp. 288–89.

4. "Report of the Treasurer of Puerto Rico, Fiscal 1930–31" (San Juan: Government Printing Office, 1931), pp. 3–4.

5. "Report of the Treasurer of Puerto Rico, Fiscal 1939–40" (San Juan: Government Printing Office, 1940), p. 3.

6. Jude Wanniski, "A Conversation with Muñoz Marín," *The Wall Street Journal*, 24 August 1977.

7. Lloyd G. Reynolds, "Wages and Employment in a Labor-Surplus Economy," *American Economic Review* 55, no. 1 (March 1965).

8. Teodoro Moscoso, testimony before the Subcommittee on Territorial and Insular Affairs of the House Committee on Interior and Insular Affairs, 19 January 1976.

9. Rafael Hernandez Colon, testimony before the Subcommittee on Territorial and Insular Affairs of the House Committee on Interior and Insular Affairs, 9 February 1976.

10. James Tobin, cover letter to Governor Hernandez Colon, "Report to the Governor," the Committee to Study Puerto Rico's Finances, 11 December 1975.

11. Ibid.

12. Tobin, "Report to the Governor," p. 28.

13. Will Durant, *The Story of Civilization*, 11 vols. (New York: Simon & Schuster, 1935–1975), 1:653.

14. Adam Smith, *The Wealth of Nations* (New York: Modern Library, 1937), p. 898.

Chapter 13

1. "Is There Gas Everywhere?" *The Economist*, April 19, 1980, p. 93.

2. Jude Wanniski, "Oil in Abundance," *Harper's*, October 1979, pp. 26–32.

3. I. I. Nesterov and F. K. Salmanov, "The Future Supply of Petroleum and Gas

Technical Reports," UNITAR Conference, Austria, 1976 (Elmsford, N.Y.: Pergamon Press, 1976), Section II, 10:185.

4. Will Durant, "The Story of Civilization," 11 vols. (New York: Simon & Schuster, 1935–1975), 4:622–23.

5. Herbert Agar, *The Price of Union* (Boston: Houghton Mifflin, 1966), p. 190.

6. Ruth Sheldon Knowles, *The Greatest Gamblers* (Norman, Oklahoma: University of Oklahoma Press, 1959), p. 81.

7. Bernardo Grossling, "The Future Supply of Petroleum and Gas Technical Reports," UNITAR Conference, Austria, 1976 (Elmsford, N.Y.: Pergamon Press, 1976), Section I, 2:57.

8. C. John Miller, "Oil Optimism," *Leaders,* Spring 1981, p. 84.

9. Charles A. Anderson, *The State of Energy: 1979* (Palo Alto: SRI International, 1979), p. 11.

10. Alan Reynolds, "A Free Market in Energy," in Robert Poole, Jr., ed., *Instead of Regulation,* (Lexington, 1981), pp. 67–68.

11. Ruth Sheldon Knowles, op. cit., p. 108.

12. William Kucewicz, "Third World Can Exploit Its Energy Resources," *The Wall Street Journal,* October 13, 1981, p. 32.

13. Knowles, op. cit., p. 285.

14. Knowles, op. cit., p. 139.

INDEX

About the Author

Jude Wanniski was born in Pottsville, Pennsylvania in 1936 and was raised in Brooklyn, New York. He is founder and president of Polyconomics, Inc., which is located in Morristown, New Jersey, and which, since its inception in 1978, has been advising both corporate and financial clients on political, economic and communications strategies.

After earning a B.A. in political science and an M.S. in journalism at UCLA, Mr. Wanniski worked for newspapers in Alaska, Nevada and California until 1965, when he joined Dow Jones & Company as the Washington columnist of *The National Observer*. Later, he was an editorial writer for *The Wall Street Journal*, of which he became Associate Editor in 1976. Concentrating on domestic and global political economics and energy, Mr. Wanniski received the 1976 Milburn Petty Award for his energy editorials in the *Journal*.

Mr. Wanniski was also a fellow of the American Enterprise Institute in Washington, D.C., where he researched and wrote *The Way the World Works*. A leading advocate of supply-side economics, he popularized this concept most notably in his essay "Taxes, Revenues, and the Laffer Curve," which appeared in *The Public Interest* in 1978. He drafted the monetary plank in the 1980 Republican Party platform, was an adviser to Ronald Reagan during the presidential election campaign, and later assisted in the formulation of the Kemp-Roth tax reduction bill that was enacted in 1981 as a centerpiece of the Reagan economic program.

Mr. Wanniski and his wife Christine have three children and live in Morris Township, New Jersey.